Praise for Sloan's
Green Guide to Antiquing in New England

"… a wonderful compilation. … I am really impressed with this superb guide to New England antique shops."

> Wendell Garrett, Senior Vice President,
> American Decorative Arts, Sotheby's

"… the best of the guidebooks."

> The *Maine Antique Digest*

"… the ultimate source for those with a passion for vintage."

> *Amazon.com* Travel Editor's
> Recommended Book

"Everything you need to know for a New England treasure hunt."

> The Boston *Globe*

"When antiques are the mission."

> The New York *Times*

GREEN GUIDE TO ANTIQUING IN THE MIDWEST

EDITED BY LISA FREEMAN AND JOHN FISKE

OLD SAYBROOK, CONNECTICUT

Produced by AntiqueSource, Inc., P.O. Box 270, Belmont, VT 05730 USA; (802) 259-3614. Visit us on the World Wide Web at www.antiquesource.com.

Cover photograph of Ohio glass reprinted by permission of the Ohio Historical Society.

ISBN: 0-7627-0383-0

ISSN: 1520-9644

Library of Congress Cataloging-in-Publication data is available.

Manufactured in the United States of America
First edition / First printing

Contents

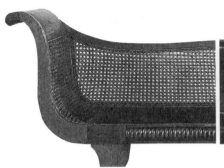

Maps

From the Editors

It is with great pleasure and excitement that we present to you the first edition of the AntiqueSource *Green Guide to Antiquing in the Midwest*. It contains over 2,000 listings for antiques dealers and services throughout the Midwestern states of Illinois, Indiana, Ohio, Michigan, Minnesota, and Wisconsin.

As Minnesota-based dealers with a passion for New England furniture, we depended upon *Sloan's Green Guide to Antiquing in New England* (originally published by The Antique Press under the able editorship of Susan Sloan) as the single best place to find new sources of antiques for both our business and our personal collection. After relocating to Vermont and updating the New England Guide (which we now publish), a similar Guide to the Midwest seemed natural. We have found some wonderful antiques in the Midwest and hope that you will too.

Starting a new Guide from scratch was an enormous endeavor. Various friends and dealers in the Midwest made things much easier, especially those who kindly invited us into their homes during long road trips and those who generously shared their rolodexes and phonebooks. Special thanks go to Tim and Barb Martien, Phil and Judee Harbaugh, Fred and Barbara Aberlin, Marjorie Staufer, Liz Kile, Chuck Muller and Julie Cecutti of *Antique Review*, Gary Ludlow, Randy Hopkins, and Dede Moore.

Back in Vermont, we were very fortunate to have the assistance of Raye Lin Collins, whose good humor and persistence through the data entry and verification processes made the task much more pleasant (and the Guide much more accurate). If collecting antiques is a way to preserve our past, children are the key to our future. Accordingly we dedicate this book to Raye Lin's daughter Morgan, born July 8, 1998. We thank her for not choosing to arrive any earlier!

Mike Ahearn and the staff at Imagesetters of Rutland, Vermont, again did a terrific job with ad creation, typesetting, and design. Joy Hall of The Globe Pequot Press kept the final stages of production moving ahead without a hitch. MaryAnn Dube did a wonderful job compiling and creating the state maps. And Terry Brown Pittaro kept the orders for the New England Guide flowing at a time when our minds were elsewhere. We could not have done this without them.

The dealer listings contained in the Green Guides are available free of charge on the World Wide Web at www.antiquesource.com thanks to Michael Jensen.

From the Editors

Keep an eye on our site for new services and links of interest to antiquers in the coming months. For advertising rates or information about inclusion in future editions, or to order a copy of either the Midwest or New England Green Guides, please contact us at: AntiqueSource Inc., PO Box 270, Belmont, Vermont, 05730; toll-free (888)875-5999; info@antiquesource.com.

Please remember to tell the dealers you visit that you "found them in the Green Guide." Happy antiquing!

Lisa Freeman & John Fiske
Editors
June 1998

How to Use this Guide

The Green Guide is a comprehensive guide to antiquing in the Midwest. It has been compiled with collectors, dealers, and passionate antiquers in mind and is designed to enable you to easily identify antiques shops, publications, services, and antiques-related institutions that meet your individual needs. The Guide is divided into three basic parts.

Following a general introduction to Antiquing in the Midwest, Part I consists of six individual state-by-state sections listing dealers in Illinois, Indiana, Ohio, Michigan, Minnesota, and Wisconsin. Each of these sections begins with a map of the state to assist you in your travel planning. Each state section is organized alphabetically by town name, and within each town, alphabetically by business name.

Each individual dealer entry begins with the business name, address, and phone number, as well as fax and toll-free numbers, email address, and Internet URL if available. This basic information is follow by a brief description of the inventory, often in the dealer's own words. The description is followed by information concerning the price range of the dealer's inventory (**Pr**), the year in which the business was established (**Est**), the days and hours of business (**Hrs**), the size of the retail space (**Sz**), associations to which the dealer belongs (**Assn**), charge cards accepted (**CC**), directions to the shop (**Dir**), and the shop owner's name (**Own**). Group shops are noted by the designation "G" followed by the number of dealers in brackets immediately after the business name. A full listing of association acronyms appears on p. xv.

Finally, each entry includes both QuickCodes and Service QuickCodes to indicate categories of antiques or services that the business sells or provides (**QC**). The letter "S" in front of a QuickCode indicates that this is a Service QuickCode (for example, **S2** is Appraisal, whereas **2** is Antiquities). A list of the QuickCodes and Service QuickCodes appears on p. xiii and on the bookmark that comes with the Guide.

Part II of the Guide begins with a section listing Service Providers. Included here are entries for appraisers, auctioneers, and clock repair specialists, as well specialists in the repair, restoration, and conservation of furniture, porcelain, glass, art, and metalware. We have also included a brief listing of businesses specializing in the reproduction and replication of antiques and parts for antiques. Part II also provides background information on several related aspects of antiques collecting, including periodicals that cover the Midwestern and national antiques trade. A listing of historic homes and museums in the Midwest follows, as well as a listing of the major antiques show promoters in the region.

Part III of the Guide includes three indexes. Index I is arranged alphabetically by business name (*Alphabetical Index to Dealers*). The QuickCodes and Service QuickCodes provide the basis for Indexes II and III (QuickCode Index to Specialties and QuickCode Index to Services). Dealers and service providers are listed under their appropriate QuickCodes by state. To use this index, first determine the QuickCode for the type of antique or service in which you are interested (say Furniture, Period American, which is 52) by looking at the list of QuickCodes on p. xiii or on the QuickCode bookmark. Turn to that heading in the *QuickCode Index to Specialties* and note that dealers who carry Period American Furniture are listed alphabetically by state and town under this heading. Conversely, if you note that a dealer lists QuickCodes 9, 33, and 60 in her entry, you can quickly determine that she carries Art (Marine/Nautical), Coins/Medals, and Garden Antiques by looking up the QuickCodes on p. xiii or on the handy bookmark. The Service QuickCodes work in a similar manner.

Abbreviations Used in Dealer Entries

By appt only	By appointment only (always call ahead)
By chance/appt	By chance or appointment (call recommended)
C	Century
Daily	Seven days a week
Int	Intersection
Jct	Junction
L	Left
Mi	Mile(s)
Min	Minutes
R	Right
Spr	Spring
Sum	Summer
Tpke	Turnpike
Win	Winter
Wknd	Weekends

Shop Sizes:

S = Small	Under 500 square feet
M = Medium	501-2,000 square feet
L = Large	2,001-10,000 square feet
H = Huge	Over 10,000 square feet

QuickCodes

Specialties

1 Americana
2 Antiquities
3 Architectural Antiques
4 Arms/Military
5 Art Deco/Art Noveau
6 Arts & Crafts
7 Art (General)
8 Art (Landscapes)
9 Art (Marine/Nautical)
10 Art (Miniatures)
11 Art (Objets d'Art)
12 Art (Portraits/Figures)
13 Art (Religious)
14 Art (Sporting)
15 Art (Still Life)
16 Baseball Cards
17 Baskets
18 Books/Manuscripts
19 Books about Antiques
20 Brass/Copper
21 Buttons/Badges
22 Ceramics (American)
23 Ceramics (English/Continental)
24 Ceramics (Oriental)
25 Ceramics (Chinese Export)
26 Ceramics (Creamware/Pearlware)
27 Ceramics (Delft/Faience)
28 Ceramics (Imari)
29 Ceramics (Redware/Yellowware)
30 Ceramics (Staffordshire)
31 Ceramics (Stoneware)
32 Collectibles
33 Coins/Medals
34 Country Antiques
35 Clocks/Watches
36 Decorative Accessories
37 Decoys
38 Dolls
39 Ephemera
40 Fireplace Accessories
41 Folk Art (General)
42 Folk Art (Native American)
43 Folk Art (Theorems/Frakturs)
44 Folk Art (Trade Signs)
45 Folk Art (Weathervanes)
46 Folk Art (Wood Carvings)
47 French Antiques
48 Furniture (General)
49 Furniture (Arts & Crafts/Mission)
50 Furniture (Oak)
51 Furniture (Paint)
52 Furniture (Period - American)
53 Furniture (Period - Continental)
54 Furniture (Period - English)
55 Furniture (Pine)
56 Furniture (Reproduction)
57 Furniture (Shaker)
58 Furniture (Victorian)
59 Furniture (Other 20th Century)
60 Garden Antiques
61 Glass/Bottles
62 Iron
63 Jewelry (Costume)
64 Jewelry (Estate)
65 Lighting
66 Maps/Globes
67 Memorabilia
68 Mirrors
69 Musical Instruments
70 Nautical/Marine Antiques
71 Oriental Antiques/Export Trade
72 Pewter
73 Photography
74 Prints
75 Rugs (Hooked/Braided)
76 Rugs (Oriental)
77 Scientific/Medical Instruments
78 Silver
79 Sporting Antiques
80 Textiles (General)
81 Textiles (Lace/Linen)
82 Textiles (Needlework/Samplers)
83 Textiles (Vintage Clothing)
84 Textiles (Quilts)
85 Tin/Toleware
86 Tools
87 Toys
88 Treen
89 Victoriana
90 Vintage Cars/Carriages
91 Wicker

Services

S1 Appraisal
S2 Auction
S3 Bookbinding/Restoration
S4 Building Materials
S5 Cabinetmaking
S6 Chair Caning
S7 Clock Repair
S8 Consignment
S9 Consultation/Research
S10 Display Stands/Glass
S11 Doll Hospital
S12 Estate Purchases
S13 Framing
S14 Insurance
S15 Interior Design
S16 Repair/Restoration/Conservation
S17 Reproduction/Replication
S18 Services to Period Homes
S19 Shipping/Packing/Storage
S20 Upholstery

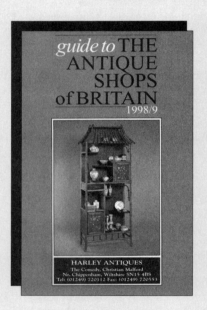

Association Acronyms

AAA	Appraisers Association of America
AARC	America's Authorized Restoration Center
ABAA	Antiquarian Booksellers Association of America
AH	Antiquarian Horologists
AIC	American Institute for Conservation of Historic & Artistic Works
ANA	American Numismatic Association
AWI	American Watchmakers' Institute
ASA	American Society of Appraisers
BHI	British Horological Institute
CAGA	Certified Appraisers Guild of America
CBADA	Crete-Beecher (IL) Antique Dealers Assn Ltd
CSADA	Chicago Suburban Antique Dealers Association
FWADA	Ft Wayne (IN) Antique Dealers Association
GADA	Galesburg (IL) Antique Dealers Association
IABA	Indiana Antique Booksellers Association
ISA	International Society of Appraisers
LCADA	LaPorte County (IN) Antique Dealers' Association
MADA	Minnesota Antique Dealers Association
NAA	National Auctioneers Association
NAWCC	National Association of Watch and Clock Collectors
NIADA	Northern Illinois Antique Dealers Association
NAACD	National Association of Antiques & Collectibles Dealers Inc
NADA	National Association of Dealers in Antiques Inc
NHADA	New Hampshire Antiques Dealers Association
NOADA	Northeastern Ohio Antique Dealers Association
PJG	Professional Jewelers Guild
PN	Professional Numismatists
PSMA	Professional Show Managers Association
RNADA	River North Antiques Dealers Association (IL)
SMADA	Southeastern Michigan Antique Dealers Association
SVAS	Saginaw (MI) Valley Antique Society
TAADA	Toledo Area Antique Dealers Association
WADA	Wisconsin Antique Dealers Association
WCWADA	West Central Wisconsin Antique Dealers Association

AntiqueSpeak

Throughout the book you will find informative short articles on antiques and antiquing. Below is complete directory of these articles for your reference convenience.

Antiquing in the Midwest

The settlement of the Midwest coincided with the expansion and industrialization of the American economy in the first half of the nineteenth century. The identity and prosperity of the newly independent nation was cultivated in the prairies and forged in the mushrooming industries of Ohio and the states around the Great Lakes. As always, the character of the people, of their work and their domestic lives is imprinted in the products that they made and used. And this character is clearly present in the antiques of the Midwest.

Industrial Antiques

While the antiques of the Colonial period were produced largely for the wealthy and the privileged, the early industrialists of the Midwest democratized antiques by producing a wide range of household goods that the average American family could readily afford. Many of these earliest industrial antiques, particularly glass, ceramics, and furniture, are now highly valued both for historical and aesthetic reasons. And the Midwest is the best place in the country to find them.

Though supplies of fuel and raw materials are the key to any industrial development (and both were plentiful in the Midwest), it was communications that really made the difference. The Great Lakes and the region's large navigable rivers, quickly supplemented by canals, enabled early manufacturers to distribute their goods widely and cheaply. Roads and railroads soon followed — the National Road had reached Columbus by 1832 — and by the middle of the century, the Midwest was at the hub of a huge communication and transport system.

Besides being well linked to the rest of the nation, the Midwest was itself a major market. The population, and its prosperity, grew by leaps and bounds throughout the nineteenth century, and this new middle class wanted good homes that were well furnished and equipped with all the latest styles at affordable prices. In meeting this demand, the artisans of the Midwest also developed new styles and forms that now, a century or more later, are rightly classified as "antique."

The Midwest quickly established itself as the main center of glass production, not only of the nation, but also of the world. Pressed glass, the first innovation in glass making for over 2,000 years, was developed here, and by 1840, glass making had become one of the main industries of Ohio. And as the Arts and Crafts movement grew in reaction to mass manufacturing, Ohio glass (and pottery) makers were again at the forefront, producing hand-blown "art glass" and pottery of the highest quality. (For dealers who specialize in glass and American Art pottery, see QuickCodes 61 and 22.)

Furniture making also flourished in the nineteenth century, and by the mid-1800s, Cincinnati had become the largest furniture producer in the nation (it produced far more "Hitchcock" chairs than Hitchcockville ever did). Midwestern furniture makers were also leaders in the Arts and Crafts movement. The popular "Mission" style of furniture, introduced by the Stickley Brothers and widely copied, is distinctly Midwestern, for it was strongly influenced by the design principles of the Prairie School of architecture founded by Frank Lloyd Wright. (See QuickCodes 6 for Arts & Crafts, and 49 for Mission Furniture, and the Museums and Historic Homes section of this book for Frank Lloyd Wright houses open to the public.)

Country Antiques

Although the Midwest was the powerhouse of industrial America, it was also the nation's breadbasket. Its woodlands and prairies were turned into rich agricultural land, and hundreds of small farming communities dotted the region. The large industrial cities needed good transport systems to distribute their products, so they grew close to the great rivers and lakes. But agricultural towns developed around rich land rather than good communications, so many were comparatively isolated and thus had to be self-sufficient. Midwestern antiques, then, include a huge variety of "primitives," that is, furniture and domestic and agricultural implements that were produced locally, sometimes by craftsmen, but often by householders for their own use. These untrained, but not unskilled, craftsmen produced wonderfully characterful pieces that are eagerly sought by today's collectors.

Many of these country pieces are "Midwestern originals," forms that originated here or were developed here in greater variety than elsewhere. The Hoosier kitchen cupboard from Indiana, the Wisconsin "jail house" cupboard, and the pie safes, dry sinks, and bucket benches found all over the region all have distinctively Midwestern characteristics. Interestingly, while all of these pieces would have been found in the kitchens and outhouses of Midwestern country homes, their front parlors and more public rooms would have been furnished with the more expensive and "better" products of the factories in Cincinnati, Grand Rapids, or Chicago.

Although most were not made in this county, another common Midwestern form is the immigrant trunk. These boxes held the few possessions that immigrants could bring on the ships and wagons that carried them across the Atlantic and the North American continent to their new homes in the Midwest. And after the journey they provided convenient household storage. The most interesting have names and destinations painted on them and are sometimes decorated in the style of their country of origin. Smaller, flat-topped ones are often used as coffee tables today, but the dome-topped ones were originally the more highly valued, for their domed shape meant that they had to travel on top of the stack, and thus were less liable to damage on the journey.

Period Antiques

Besides the early industrial goods and the primitives, there is a third category of antiques to be found in the Midwest. Period, that is pre-industrial, antiques may not have been made here, but early settlers brought them here. The Western Reserve, in northeastern Ohio, was originally granted to Connecticut, and its New England roots can be seen not only in its architecture and village greens, but also in its antiques. And while Yankees did come from the northeast, the largest immigration was from Virginia and the south. Unlike their northern Yankee cousins, Virginia and the plantation states retained close commercial and social links with England well into the nineteenth century. Consequently, their antiques were frequently either imported from England or were made to conform closely to English styles. This southern furniture can be found throughout the Midwest, but especially along the southern portions of Ohio, Indiana, and Illinois.

These settlement routes exerted a strong influence on the taste of Midwesterners, with the consequence that the antiquer will find dealers in fine Colonial and Federal American antiques, as well as ones who specialize in eighteenth-century English furniture and accessories. The antiques business in the Midwest dates only from the 1920s, when in its early days, it dealt primarily with imported English and Continental antiques for the wealthy industrialists of cities like Detroit, Chicago, Cincinnati, and Cleveland. It is still the case that some of the finest English and Continental antiques can be found in the Midwest. (See QuickCodes 53 and 54 for dealers specializing in Period Continental and Period English Furniture, and QuickCode 47 for French Antiques.)

Beginning in the 1950s, interest in the aesthetic and historical qualities of American antiques began to increase. Antiques made in the Midwest, particularly glass, ceramics, and furniture, were rescued from attics, barns, and junk shops, and primitive gadgets and make-dos were recognized as folk art. These previously neglected objects, now referred to as Americana, can be found in profusion and variety all over the region. At the same time, Midwestern collectors who wanted pre-Revolutionary American antiques turned to the northeast, and, as a consequence, there was a steady flow of Colonial period antiques into the region from New England. (See QuickCodes 1 for Americana dealers and 52 for Period American Furniture, as well as QuickCodes 41-46 for Folk Art.)

The early settlers of the Midwest came not only from the eastern United States, but also from Europe, particularly northern Europe. Michigan, Wisconsin, and Minnesota attracted large numbers of Germans, Scandinavians, and Poles who brought with them the tastes and styles of their homelands, particularly for beautifully painted pine. Many Midwesterners retain a connection to their immigrant forefathers and mothers by collecting pieces with "rose maling," a Norwegian style of painting that features elaborate flowers and foliage and which was used to decorate everything from cupboards and trunks to smaller utensils such as spoons and bowls.

This rich history of industry, agriculture, and immigration has produced a wide variety of antiques in the Midwest. There is literally something for every taste and every budget. There are dealers in every type of antique, from formal to primitive, from oriental porcelain to Depression glass and from seventeenth-century prints to twentieth-century advertising.

Where to Buy Antiques

There are many different ways to buy antiques in the Midwest. This book lists over 2,000 dealers in every corner of the region. Wherever you go you will find a number of antique shops that are worth visiting. Certain urban areas, such as Cleveland, Cincinnati, and Chicago's north shore and suburbs, have attracted large numbers of dealers in predominantly formal and period antiques. Equally, however, many smaller towns and cities are home to significant clusters of dealers, and any one of them can be chosen as a destination that offers many collecting opportunities. This book will enable you to identify "antiquing" towns like Milan and Lebanon in Ohio or Crete in Illinois. It will also help you pick out antique corridors, such as Route 151 in Wisconsin, which links the many dealers in Madison, Mount Horeb, and Mineral Point.

You will also find that the Midwest is rich in museums, historic houses, and historic sites that complement antique shops. Many of them have rooms and sometimes whole houses furnished and decorated in period. Visiting them can extend your knowledge of the antiques you collect, and it often gives fresh insights into how antiques were used in the everyday lives of our forebears. These may, in turn, give you ideas about decorating, furnishing, and living with antiques today.

The simplest way to buy antiques may be through the group shop or antique mall. Here the wares of a dozen to maybe a couple of hundred dealers are brought together under one roof. Picking through the tens of thousands of items requires a sharp eye and patience, but the chances of finding your particular treasure are high. A rule of thumb: the larger the mall, the greater the variety, the younger the stock, and the lower the prices. Smaller group shops are more selective in their dealer mix and tend to carry earlier, higher quality antiques. Each state has a handful where the quality is as high as that of the single-owner, specialist shop.

The single-owner shop rarely offers the variety of a mall but will instead reflect the tastes or special interests of the owner. Their inventories range from a more general line to carefully selected, specialist items for the serious collector. In a single-owner shop, you can talk to the owner, pick his or her brains, and learn all that you can about the piece you are considering. Most dealers will guarantee what they sell, will describe it and its origin on the sales receipt, and will buy it back if it turns out to be other than represented. In most malls and group shops, however, sales are final.

Specialist and selective dealers sometimes do not keep regular shop hours, but they welcome visitors by chance or appointment. By chance is as chancy as it sounds, particularly in the off season, and you are well advised to accept the dealer's invitation to call ahead for an appointment. Don't feel that you are under any obligation to buy because the dealer has stayed in or opened up especially for you. Dealers expect collectors, especially serious ones, to search thoroughly before buying, and they know that they may not have the item you are looking for. They do, however, get real pleasure in showing you their stock and in talking about it, even if you decide not to buy anything on this particular visit.

Other Midwestern experiences for the antiquer are offered by shows and auctions. A show gathers together dealers of comparable quality, who offer their best stock at their best prices (it is a myth that dealers raise prices for shows). Shows offer plenty of opportunity for comparison shopping, plenty of antiques to browse among, and plenty of dealers to talk to. All the major Midwestern cities have at least one "high end" show a year and numerous ones of more general interest. These are usually held indoors in the fall, winter, or spring. The summer offers a different range of shows. Outdoor, tented ones are often held on the grounds of beautiful old mansions where you can combine antiquing with admiring the gardens and the view; or they may take over a town square or the main street of a village. They may be commercially run, or held to benefit the local historical society, the library or the botanical gardens, or the hospital or the women's club. An antiques show makes a wonderful day out for the antiquer.

Auctions are an equally important part of the Midwestern antiques scene. They take various forms, from ones where major firms sell high end antiques that they have spent many months assembling, to weekly local ones where householders, farmers, and dealers consign more common country or primitive items. The auctioneer has carefully selected items in the specialist sales, but in the estate or regular sale, anything may turn up — and in any condition. Prices can be as unpredictable as the merchandise. Sometimes collectors will bid against one another and send prices far above those that you would pay in a dealer's shop; at other times, dealers are the only bidders, and the price is wholesale; and at yet others, the bidders appear to sit on their hands, and the price is a giveaway. Auctions can be great fun, so long as you learn as much as you can about an item before you bid on it. Auction sales are always "final."

All experienced antiquers know the value of the old adage "Buy the best you can afford." Be prepared to stretch your definition of affordable if you come across a piece that really "speaks to you." Writing a slightly larger check than you'd planned may make you catch your breath as you sign it, but in six months' time, you'll be glad that you did. It is always preferable to have fewer but better antiques, not least because when you wish to "trade up" (and all collectors eventually do), the higher quality piece is more likely to have held or even increased its value and will be the easier to resell.

Furnishing and Decorating with Antiques

New furniture, new decor can look good and can please our aesthetic taste, but the new has no history. Antiques do. Each has written into it the place where it was made and used. The wear on its surface tells the story of the hands that have used it, each dent or scratch is a sign of an accident that happened to it, and it alone. Antiques are not only aesthetically satisfying; they are imaginatively rich because they have a history as well as an innate beauty. Antiques are not just objects: they are objects plus history, plus locality, plus imagination.

Antiques do so much more than merely furnish or decorate a home. They link that home to the past and the future, for owning an antique is not like owning a pair of shoes. Antiques are not to be used and discarded, but to be used, cared for, and passed on to the next generation. Possessing an antique is holding something in trust for the future from the past. An antique collector is a trustee rather than an owner.

Even early manufactured goods have acquired a uniqueness through their use, for their history has added an imaginative dimension that was not there when they were new. That history may be short, it may take the form of nostalgia, of the desire to recapture something of the feel of grandmother's kitchen, or to use the toys and books of our own childhood to stop our past drifting out of reach.

Whatever your antiquing pleasure, we hope that the Green Guide will help you satisfy it. It will help you find general line group shops as well as specialist dealers; it lists show promoters and auctioneers; it suggests museums and historic homes that you will enjoy and learn from; it will put you in touch with appraisers, insurers, and restorers. We hope that you will enjoy your antiquing, enjoy your antiques, and come back again to the Midwest.

Part I

Dealer Listings
by State

Illinois

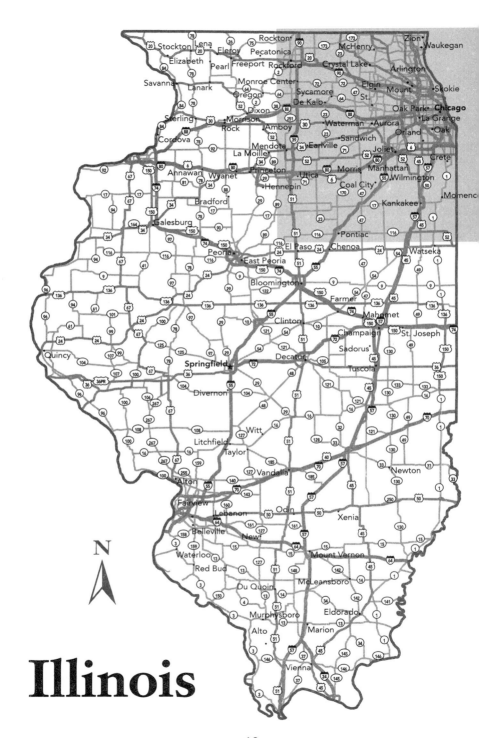

Illinois

Shaded area detail below

Chicago Area

Algonquin

Algonquin Antique Mart [G40]
113 S Main St
(847)658-1991
Hrs: Tue-Fri 10-4, Sat-Sun 10-5.

Algonquin House Antiques
321 S Main St
(847)854-2504

Furniture, tools, primitives. **Hrs:** Mon-Fri 10-4, Sat 10-5, Sun 12-5 (closed Mon-Tue in Win).

Linden Gallery of Fine Art
213 S Harrison
(847)658-3666

Paintings & prints. **Hrs:** Daily 10-4. **QC: 7 74**

Main Street Estates
115 S Main St (Rte 31)
(847)854-4444

Antiques & collectibles; estate liquidations. **Hrs:** Daily 9-7. **Own:** Darlene Fournier. **QC: S2 S12**

Alto Pass

Austin's of Alto Pass
Rte 127
(618)893-2206

Oak & walnut furniture, pottery, glassware. One-owner shop in restored 1927 brick grade school bldg. **Hrs:** Sat 10-5, Sun 1-5.

Alton

1900s Antique Company
9 E Broadway
(618)465-2711 • (618)466-6730

Furniture, primitives, collectibles, books, paper, paintings & rugs.

Alton Antique Center
401 E Broadway
(618)463-0888

American, European & Oriental antiques. **Hrs:** Call ahead for appt.

Alton Landing Antiques
110 Alton St
(618)462-0443
Hrs: Daily.

Broadway Antiques
217 E Broadway
(618)465-0423

Antiques, paintings & lamps.

Carol's Corner — Frank's Steins
318 E Broadway
(618)465-2606

Glass, china, lace, collectibles, quilts, art & clocks. **QC: 81 61 35**

Country Meadows
401 E Broadway
(618)465-1965

Antiques & primitives. **Hrs:** Mon-Sat 11-4:30, Sun 12-4:30.

Debbie's Decorative Antiques
108 George St
(618)465-6018 • (618)465-6960 (fax)
debbiesdecant@ezl.com
www.altonweb.com/antiques/debbies.htm
Hrs: Daily.

Golden Time Treasures
302 E Broadway
(618)465-9275

Collectibles, baseball cards & coins. **QC: 16 33 32**

Heartland Antiques
321 E Broadway
(618)465-6363
Furniture, art, quilts, pottery & glassware. **Hrs:** Daily 11-5.

Jack & Jeanee's Annex
319 Broadway
(618)463-0451 • (618)463-0422
Graniteware. **QC: 31**

Mineral Springs Mall
301 E Broadway

Various mostly owner-operated shops featuring antiques & collectibles, primitives, used & rare books, glassware, oak furniture, coins & ephemera. **Hrs:** Times vary.

Old Bridge Antique Mall [G]
435 E Broadway
(618)463-9907
Hrs: Mon 11-5, Wed-Sat 10-5, Sun 12-5.

The Old Post Office Mall [G]
300 Alby St
(618)462-8204
Furniture, collectibles & crafts. **Hrs:** Daily 10-5.

Plain & Fancy Emporium
112-114 E Broadway
(618)465-0742
Antiques & collectibles.

Rubenstein's Antiques
724-726 E Broadway
(618)462-5243 • (618)465-1306
Furniture, collectibles & brass. **Hrs:** Mon-Sat 9-3, Sun call ahead advised. **QC: 48 32 20**

Steve's Lighting & Antiques
323 E Broadway
(618)465-7407
Hrs: Mon-Sat 10-5, Sun 12-5.

Amboy

Country Peddler
223 E Main St
(815)857-2253 • (815)625-6909
Glassware, lamps & primitives. **Hrs:** Mon-Wed 8:30-2 (call ahead advised). **QC: 61**

Annawan

Annawan Antique Alley [G55]
309 N Canal St
(309)935-6220
Hrs: Mon-Sat 9-5:30, Sun 12-4. **CC:** V/MC.

Antioch

Another Man's Treasure
25218 Rte 173
(847)395-8513
Hrs: Wed-Sun 10-5. **Dir:** 2 mi W of Rte 83.

Channel Lake School Mall [G]
Lake Ave
(847)395-0000
Antiques & collectibles. **Hrs:** Wed-Sun 10-5.

Green Bench Antiques
924 Main St (Rte 83)
(847)838-2643
Antiques & collectibles, furniture, glass, jewelry, linen, photographs & paper. **Hrs:** Tue-Sat 10-4 (Fri til 7). **CC:** V/MC/DIS.

Past & Presents
345 Park Ave
(847)838-2600
Victorian, furniture, glassware, pottery. **Hrs:** Thu-Sat 11-5.

Williams Bros Emporium
910 Main St (Rte 83)
(847)838-2767
Furniture, stained glass, mirrors. **Hrs:** Mon-Sat 10-5, Sun 12-5.

Arlington Heights

All My Treasures
7 E Miner St
(847)394-2944

Antiques, collectibles, small furniture & accessories. **Hrs:** Wed & Sat 10-5, Thu & Fri 10-6:30.

Arlington Antiques Etc
208 N Dunton
(847)788-1481

World's Fair memorabilia, rugs, lamps, glass, furniture, costume jewelry & glassware. **Hrs:** Wed-Sat 10-5 (Thu & Fri til 7). **QC: 67**

Cobblestone Antiques
17 E Miner St
(847)259-4818

Sterling silver. **Hrs:** Tue & Sat 10-5, Thu 10-7. **QC: 78**

Collage Antiques
1005 S Arlington Heights Rd
(847)439-5253

Hrs: Mon-Fri 10-5:30, Sat 10-5, Sun 12-5.

Forgotten Times Ltd
104 N Evergreen
(847)259-8641

Restoration, sales & service of vintage & contemporary timepieces. **Hrs:** Mon-Tue & Thu-Fri 8-6 (Thu til 8), Sat 9-3. **QC: 35 S7**

Museum Country Store
112 W Fremont St
(847)255-1450

Consignment shop of the Historical Society of Arlington Heights. Antiques & collectibles. **Hrs:** Thu-Sat 10-4, Sun 1-4. **QC: S8**

P J's Antiques & Collectibles
116 N Evergreen
(847)259-7130

Bottles, Depression glass, advertising, post-cards, furniture & collectibles. **Hrs:** Tue-Sat 10-5 (Thu til 8, Fri til 6). **QC: 61 39**

Aurora

Sue Keyes Antiques
903 Garfield Ave
(630)892-8524

18th & 19th C American furniture, paintings, prints, textiles, stoneware, pottery, glass, metals & folk art. **Hrs:** By appt only. **Assn:** CSADA. **QC: S1**

Barrington

Estate Jewelers
118 W Main St
(847)382-8802

Vintage & antique jewelry. **Hrs:** Thu-Sat 11-5. **QC: 64 63**

Hypoint American Antiques & Folk Art
(847)540-0615

American country furniture & folk art. **Hrs:** By appt only. **Own:** Jane S Cieply. **QC: 41**

Romantiques
118 W Main St
(847)304-9421

Direct importers of European furniture. **Hrs:** Mon-Fri 10-5, Sat 10:30-4:30.

Silk 'n Things
308 W Main St
(847)381-3830

Antiques, linens & furniture. **Hrs:** Mon-Fri 10-5:30, Sat 10-5, Sun 12-4.

Batavia

Pedals, Pumpers & Rolls Ltd
240 E State St
(630)879-5555

Hrs: Tue, Wed, Fri & Sat 10-5.

The Savery Shops
14 N Washington St (Rte 25)
(630)879-6825
Hrs: Mon-Sat 10-5, Sun 12-5.

Village Antiques
416 E Wilson
(630)406-0905
Hrs: Tue-Sat 11-5, Sun 12-5.

Yesterdays
115 S Batavia Ave (Rte 31)
(630)406-0524
Hrs: Tue-Sat 10-5, Sun 12-5.

Beecher

Collectors Corner
501 Dixie Hwy
(708)946-2177

Specializing in sports memorabilia, old toys, comics & other collectibles as well as antiques & crafts. **Hrs:** Tue-Sat 11-5, Sun 12-5. **Assn:** BCADA **Dir:** Corner Dixie Hwy & Indiana Ave, across from the Princess Cafe.

Belleville

The Belleville Antique Mall [G50]
208 E Main St
(618)234-MALL

Pr: $1-10,000 **Est:** 1993 **Hrs:** Mon 11-4, Tue-Sat 10-5, Sun 12-4. **Sz:** H **CC:** V/MC **Dir:** I-64 exit Fairview Heights. S on Rte 159 to fountain. L at fountain. 10 min from I-64. **Own:** Robert & Rosie O'Rear. **QC:** 89 83 S6 S8 S1

The Victorian Rose [G50]
208 E Main St
(618)234-0202

Beautiful décor in a 130-year-old building with a European birdcage elevator. **Est:**

1979 **Hrs:** Mon 11-4, Tue-Sat 10-5, Sun 12-4. **Sz:** H **CC:** V/MC **Dir:** Rte 164 exit Fairview Heights, then S on Rte 159 to Fountain. Turn L. 3 blks on R. **Own:** Rosemary O'Rear. **QC:** 89 83 81 S1 S6 S8

Belvidere

John Kenneth Funderburg & Sons
2111 W Newburg Rd
(815)547-8186

Stained glass windows, European furniture, folk art, blanket chests & accessories. **Hrs:** Tue-Sat 10-5, Sun 12-5. **Assn:** NIADA **Own:** John Funderburg.

The Home Place Antiques
615 S State St
(815)544-0577 • (815)547-5128

Lamps, fixtures, lighting devices, repairs, restoration & parts, polishing & buffing, tea leaf ironstone, glass, china, and a general line. **Hrs:** Tue-Sat 10-5, Sun & eves by appt. **Assn:** NIADA **Own:** William R Durham & William J Galaway. **QC:** 65 22 S16 S1

Wooden-It-Be-Nice
419 E Pleasant
(815)544-0249

Furniture & advertising items. **Hrs:** Mon-Sat 9-6 (call ahead advised).

Berwyn

Antique Treasure Chest
6746 16th St
(708)749-1910

Collectibles & oak furniture. **Hrs:** Wed & Thu 10-3, Fri & Sat 10-4. **QC:** 32 50

BBMM Antiques & Collectibles
6710 S Cermak Rd
(708)749-1465
Hrs: Mon-Sat 10-6.

Berwyn Lawndale Pharmacy Antiques
6800 Cermak Rd
(708)749-0600
Hrs: Mon-Fri 9-6, Sat 9-3.

Josie's Antiques & Collectibles
2135 S Wisconsin Ave
(708)788-3820
Collectibles. **Hrs:** By chance/appt. **QC: 32**

Past Time Antiques
7100 W 16th St
(708)788-4804
Collectibles & oak furniture. **Hrs:** Thu-Sat 12-5.

The Silver Swan
6738 W 16th St
(708)484-7177
Silver, toys, china, glass & beer steins. **Hrs:** Tue-Sat 10-2. **QC: 78 87 61**

Bloomington

Bloomington Antique Mall [G30+]
102 N Center St
(309)828-1211
General line. **Hrs:** Mon-Sat 10-5, Sun 1-6. **CC:** V/MC.

Blue Island

Encores
13117 S Western Ave
(708)389-4121
General line. **Hrs:** Mon-Sat 10:30-5.

Three Sisters Antique Mall [G75]
13042 S Western Ave
(708)597-3331
Est: 1996 **Hrs:** Mon-Sat 10-6, Sun 11-5. **CC:** V/MC **Dir:** I-57 S to 127th St: 1 mi W to Western Ave; I-294 S to Cicero Ave/127th St: 3 mi E on 127th to Western.

Bourbonnais

Castle Antique Mall [G110]
1789 N State Rte 50
(815)936-1505
Hrs: Daily 10-5.

Indian Oaks Antique Mall [G150+]
N Rte 50
(815)933-9998
Hrs: Daily 10-5:30 (Thu & Fri til 8). **Dir:** At Larry Power Rd.

The Old Barn Antiques
1992 W State Rte 102
(815)939-4352
Hrs: Sat-Sun 10-4.

Bradford

Spoon River Antique Mall [G]
111 W Main St
(309)897-7010
Hrs: Mon-Sat 9-5, Sun 11-4. **Sz:** L **Dir:** On Rte 40 (formerly Rte 88).

Braidwood

Ye-Olde-Cane Shoppe
151 N Will Rd
(815)458-2090
Oak furniture. Chair caning, rushwork, wicker repair, baby buggy restoration. **Hrs:**

Daily 8-2:30. **Own:** Red Viano. **QC: 50 S6 S16**

Brookfield

The Olde Country Store
8420 Brookfield Ave
(708)447-7955

Hrs: Sat-Sun 12-4.

Champaign

Capricorn Antiques
720 S Neil
(217)351-6914

Furniture, 1870s-1940. **Hrs:** Tue-Sat 7:30-4. **CC:** V/MC. **QC: 48**

Partners in Time
311 S Neil
(217)352-2016

Tins, country store items, spool & dye cabinets, soda fountain items. **Hrs:** Mon-Sat.

Vintage Antiques [G11]
117 N Walnut
(217)359-8747

Glassware, china, furniture. **Hrs:** Mon-Sat 10-5. **CC:** V/MC.

Chenoa

Antique Mall of Chenoa [G32]
Old Rte 66
(815)945-7594

Advertising & children's items. **Hrs:** Mon-Sat 10-5, Sun 1-5. **CC:** V/MC **QC: 39**

Chenoa Old Rt 66 Antiques
305 Morehead
(815)945-4401

General line. **Hrs:** Wed-Sat 10-5.

Chicago

20th Century Revue
1903 W Belmont Ave
(773)472-8890

Hrs: Wed-Thu 12-5, Fri-Sun 12-6. **QC: 59**

Acorn Antiques & Uniques Ltd
5241 N Clark St
(773)506-9100 • (773)506-9191 (fax)
salimel@aol.com

Victoriana, silver, porcelain, perfume bottles. **Hrs:** Wed-Fri 11-6, Sat 10-6, Sun 10-5.

Robert Henry Adams Fine Art
715 N Franklin
(312)642-8700

American regionalist & modern paintings, prints & sculptures. **Hrs:** Tue-Fri 10-5, Sat 12-5. **QC: 7**

Aged Experience Antiques Etc

2034 N Halsted St
(773)975-9790

Country antiques. **Hrs:** Tue-Sat 12-6, Sun 12-5. **QC: 34**

An Antique Store

1450 W Webster Ave
(773)935-6060 • (773)871-6660 (fax)

Art Deco, Art Moderne, 50s furniture & smalls. Specializing in vintage Heywood-Wakefield. **Hrs:** Mon-Fri 11-7, Sat-Sun 10-6. **QC: 59 5**

The Antiquarians Building [G22]

159 W Kinzie St
(312)527-0533

Antiques, paintings, lighting, silver, rugs, decorative furnishings, Oriental antiques, Art Deco & 20th C furnishings. **Hrs:** Mon-Sat 10-6. **Sz:** H **Dir:** E of Wells. **QC: 5 65**

Antique Resources Inc

1741 W Belmont Ave
(773)871-4242 • (773)871-5671 (fax)

Large selection of early furniture (1670-1920), oil paintings, chandeliers. **Pr:** $500-110,000 **Est:** 1965 **Hrs:** Tue-Sat 11-5. **Sz:** H **CC:** V/MC/DIS **Dir:** Kennedy Expressway N to Damen, N to Belmont, then E. **Own:** Richard Weisz. **QC: 54 53 65**

The Antiques Centre at Kinzie Square [G18]

220 W Kinzie St
(312)464-1946 • (312)464-1947
(312)464-1907 (fax)

18th, 19th & early 20th C furniture, folk art, decorative accessories, porcelain, paintings, fine bindings, silver, art glass, lamps, jewelry

---

Decorating Glass

Prunt: A roundish blob of glass added as decoration to a piece of glassware.

Threading: Decorating glass by applying a thread of glass to a formed piece.

Lily pad: A coating of glass laid over a formed piece and tooled to a lily pad design. Originally Dutch, but taken up by New Jersey glassmakers.

Looping and swirls: Patterns made by incorporating threads of colored glass into a piece, particularly characteristic of Nailsea.

Engraving: Cutting a design into the surface of glass by a diamond point or a fine engraving wheel.

Etching: Using acid to "frost" a design on glass which results in whitish, opaque lines and areas.

Cutting: Cutting deeply into heavy, clear glass, usually in diamond patterns, to produce a faceted, sparkling design.

Enameling: Painting a design on glass that was then reheated to fix the enamel.

Gilding: Applying gold leaf to glass (see "Decorating with Gold").

Cranberry glass: Glass of a deep red color produced by adding gold to the glass while hot.

Prunts, threads, lily pads, loops, and swirls were all applied while the glass was still hot; engraving, etching, and cutting were performed after it had cooled. Colored glass became popular only after the Civil War. The peak period for cut glass was from about 1880 to 1915.

& Orientalia. Consignments welcome. **Pr:** $95-5,000 **Est:** 1993 **Hrs:** Mon-Fri 10-5, Sat 12-4. **Sz:** M **CC:** V/MC **Assn:** RNADA **Dir:** I-94 exit Ohio St: E on Ohio to Wells St, S on Wells to Kinzie, W on Kinzie 1/2 blk. **Own:** Elizabeth Keim. **QC: 36 53 54 S16 S19 S22**

Antiques Ltd

Merchandise Mart, 16th Fl
(312)644-6530

Carved wood, wrought iron, southwestern furniture, chandeliers, lighting. **Hrs:** Mon-Fri 9-5. **CC:** V/MC/DIS/AX **Dir:** Wells St & the Chicago River.

Antiques on the Avenue [G]

104 S Michigan Ave, 2nd Fl
(312)357-2800

Furniture, paintings, sculpture, sterling silver, jewelry, porcelain & 19th & 20th C decorative arts. **Hrs:** Mon-Fri 10-6, Sat-Sun 11-5. **CC:** AX/V/MC **Dir:** Across from the Art Institute.

Architectural Artifacts

4325 N Ravenswood Ave
(773)348-0622
Hrs: Daily 10-5. **QC: 3**

Armitage Antique Gallery [G40+]

1529 W Armitage Ave
(773)227-7727

Art Deco, textiles, lighting & clocks; furniture; toys, advertising, ephemera; art pottery, porcelain, glass & Orientalia; Bakelite, sterling & estate jewelry; costume jewelry & accessories. **Hrs:** Daily 11-6. **CC:** V/MC/DIS **Dir:** At I-90-94. **QC: 5 48 63**

Beaux Arts Gallery

106 S Michigan Ave
(312)444-1991

Bronzes, marble statuary, paintings, academic drawings, metallic art, art pottery. **Hrs:** Mon-Sat 10:30-5:30.

Mike Bell

Merchandise Mart, 18th Fl
(312)644-6848

French & English country furniture. **Hrs:** Mon-Fri 9-5. **CC:** V/MC **Dir:** At Wells St & the Chicago River.

Belmont Antique Mall [G]

2039 W Belmont Ave
(773)549-9270

Hrs: Daily 11-6. **CC:** AX/V/MC/DIS **Dir:** 2nd shop at 2229 W Belmont.

B J Furniture & Antiques

6901 N Western Ave
(773)262-1000

Hrs: Mon-Sat 10-5.

Sara Breiel Antiques

449 N Wells St
(312)923-9223

Antique English & Continental furniture & decorative accessories. **Hrs:** Mon-Fri 11-5, Sat 12-4. **QC: 53 54**

Rita Bucheit Ltd

449 N Wells St
(312)527-4080

Empire & Biedermeier furnishings from the early 19th C. **Hrs:** Mon-Sat 10-6. **QC: 52**

Carteaux Inc Jewelers

31 N Wabash
(312)782-5375

Fine antique jewelry: Victorian, Art Deco, Art Noveau. **Hrs:** Mon-Fri 10-5:30 (Thu til 6:30), Sat 10-5.

Cathay Gallery
980 N Michigan Ave
(312)951-1048
Hrs: By appt only.

Chicago Antique Centre [G35+]
3045 N Lincoln Ave
(773)929-0200
Furniture & decorative arts, Mission to modern. Paper, pottery, textiles, Black memorabilia, vintage costume jewelry, men's watches & cufflinks, oak & mahogany furniture, 50s upholstered furniture, Art Deco furnishings, kitchenware, lighting. **Hrs:** Daily 11-6. **CC:** V/MC. **QC: 6 49**

Christa's Ltd
217 W Illinois St
(312)222-2520
Fine furniture & accessories. **Hrs:** Mon-Sat 10-5.

The Crossings Antique Mall [G20]
1807 W 97th St
(773)233-0632 • (773)779-5828 (fax)
Small mall with unique items. Three shops located in a wallpaper & paint store for one-stop home decorating. Glassware, jewelry, ceramics, kitchen items. **Pr:** $2-500 **Est:** 1993 **Hrs:** Mon-Fri 10:30-6 (Mon & Thu til 7), Sat 10-5, Sun 12-3. **Sz:** S **CC:** AX/V/MC/DIS **Dir:** Metra 95th Train Station. Exit 99th/Halsted St from Dan Ryan Expressway. **Own:** Sheila Stanczak. **QC: 32 7 48**

Danger City
2129 W Belmont Ave
(773)871-1420
A wide selection from the 20th C with an emphasis on modern. Furniture, clothing, kitchenware, jewelry, lighting & everything in-between. Many unique items. Discounts available. **Pr:** $0.50-1,000 **Est:** 1995 **Hrs:** Daily 11-6 or by appt. **CC:** V/MC **Dir:** In the heart of the Belmont antique dealer district. **QC: 32 59 63 S19**

Daniels Antiques
3711 N Ashland Ave
(773)868-9355
Eclectic furnishings. **Hrs:** Wed-Sat 11-6, Sun 12-5.

Decoro Gallery
224 E Ontario
(312)943-4847
Japanese, Chinese & Korean antique furniture. **Hrs:** Mon-Sat 10:30-5:30.

Gene Douglas Antiques
4621-1/2 N Lincoln Ave
(773)561-4414
Design from 1900-1960. Mexican silver, Art Deco, glass, metalware, paintings, sculpture, pottery, objets d'art, jewelry & sterling. **Hrs:** Call for hours. **QC: 5 7**

Evanstonia Period Furniture & Restoration
4555 N Ravenswood Ave
(773)907-0101
Specializing in 19th & early 20th C traditional American & European antiques. **Hrs:** Mon-Sat 11-6, Sun 12-5. **QC: 48 S16**

Exposa Inc
230 W North Ave
(312)944-8454
Biedermeier furniture. **Hrs:** By appt only.

Father Time Antiques
2108 W Belmont Ave
(773)880-5599
Clocks, timepieces & watches. **Hrs:** Wed-Sun 12-5. **QC: 35**

Fitzsimmon's Decorative Arts
311 W Superior St
(312)787-0496
Arts & Crafts furniture & accessories. **Hrs:**

Tue-Fri 10-6, Sat 11-5. **Own:** Michael Fitzsimmon. **QC: 6**

Fly-By-Nite Gallery
714 N Wells St
(312)337-0264

Art pottery. **Hrs:** Mon-Sat 12-5. **QC: 22**

Malcolm Franklin Inc
34 E Oak St
(312)337-0202 • (312)337-8002 (fax)

Antiques from England. **Hrs:** Mon-Fri 9-5, Sat 9-3. **Assn:** NAADAA. **QC: 54 36**

Gold Coast Gallery
3020 N Lincoln
(773)327-7600

Furniture & lighting. **Hrs:** Sat-Sun 12-6.

Golden Triangle Imports
72 W Hubbard St
(312)755-1266

Asiatic country furniture. **Hrs:** Mon-Fri 10-7, Sat 10-5.

Green Acres
1464 N Milwaukee Ave
(312)292-1998

Victorian, Empire & Arts & Crafts. **Hrs:** Tue-Fri 12-6, Sat-Sun 11-5. **QC: 89 6**

Griffins & Gargoyles Ltd
2140 W Lawrence Ave
(773)769-1255

European antique furniture. **Hrs:** Thu-Mon 11-5. **QC: 53**

Harlan J Berk Ltd
31 N Clark St
(312)609-0016

Antiquities. **Hrs:** Mon-Fri 9-4:45.

Harlon's Antiques
3058 N Lincoln Ave
(773)327-3407

Lamps, paintings, prints. **Hrs:** Mon 10:30-2, Tue-Sun 10:30-4:30.

Richard Himmel Antique & Decorative Furniture
2828 N Paulina
(773)327-5500

17th, 18th, 19th & 20th C European & American furniture & decorative arts. **Hrs:** By appt. **Dir:** At Wells St & the Chicago River.

Ile de France Antiques
2009 Fremont Ave
(773)525-4890 • (773)227-0704

Direct importer of furniture & accessories from France including classic, provincial, Art Nouveau & Art Deco. Large selection of armoires, dressers, mirrors & chandeliers. Restoration, refinishing & cabinetry. Warehouse at 2222 N Elston. **Hrs:** Mon-Sat 10-5, Sun 11-4. **Dir:** Corner of Armitage, 2 blks W of Halsted. **QC: 47 S16**

International Antique Centre [G]
2300 W Diversey Pkwy
(773)227-2400

Furnishings, collectibles, rugs, jewelry & art. Pine & walnut furniture, bronze & Bakelite jewelry. **Hrs:** Daily 11-6. **Sz:** H **CC:** AX/V/MC.

Jan's Antiques
225 N Racine
(312)563-0275 • (312)243-1129

Architectural antiques, clocks, lamps, desks. **Hrs:** Tue-Sat 12:30-7, Sun 11:30-4. **Dir:** At 1200 W. **Own:** Jan Seymour. **QC: 3 35**

Jazz'E Junque
3831 N Lincoln Ave
(773)472-1500 • (773)472-1552 (fax)

Cookie jars, kitchen collectibles, salt & peppers. **Hrs:** Tue & Thu 12-5:30, Wed & Sat 11-5, Sun 12-6:30. **Own:** Mercedes Direnzo. **QC: 32**

Johnson Antiques Ltd
172 E Walton St
(312)440-9466
18th & 19th C jewelry & objets d'art. **Hrs:** Tue-Sat 10-5. **QC: 64 11**

Kedzie Koins
5909 S Kedzie Ave
(773)436-0777
Pr: $5-5,000 **Est:** 1967 **Hrs:** Mon-Fri 8-8, Sat 10-6. **Assn:** PN, AH, NAWCC, ANA, PJG **Dir:** 2 mi E of Midway Airport. **Own:** Hillery M Harrison. **QC: 2 33 35**

Kelmscott Gallery
4611 N Lincoln Ave
(773)784-2559
Hrs: Tue-Sat 11-6.

Kristina Maria Antiques
1919 W Belmont Ave
(773)472-2445
Hrs: Sat-Sun 12-5.

Lake View Antiques
3422 N Lincoln Ave
(773)935-6443
Hrs: Wed-Sat 11-5, Sun 12-4.

Lincoln Antique Mall [G]
3141 N Lincoln Ave
(773)244-1440
19th & 20th C antiques & collectibles. Victorian, Mission, Art Deco & Moderne; 50s designer & 60s style furniture. Lighting,

---

Use the Service QuickCode indexes at the back of the book to find restorers, appraisers, refinishers, and other specialty service providers.

---

prints, paintings, bronzes, pottery, porcelain, crystal, glass, silver, Bakelite, jewelry, compacts. **Hrs:** Daily 11-7. **CC:** AX/V/MC/DIS **QC: 5 6 89**

Lost Eras Antiques
1509-19 W Howard St
(773)764-7400
Furniture, rugs, paintings, prints, art glass, art pottery, jewelry, clothing, books. **Hrs:** Mon-Sat 10-6, Sun 12-5.

Midwestern Arts & Antiques
4648 N Western Ave
(773)275-8210
Furniture, oriental rugs, jewelry, clocks, oil paintings, bronzes, art glass, art pottery & art. **Hrs:** Mon-Sat 11-6, call ahead advised. **Own:** Gary Hartig. **QC: 48**

Miscellania
1800 W Belmont Ave
(773)348-9647
Hrs: Wed-Sun 12-5.

Modernism Gallery of Chicago
Antiquarian Bldg, 159 Kinzie St
(847)304-9191 • (847)304-1689 (fax)
www.modernism.com
Specializing in Art Deco, 20th C furnishings, lighting, glass art, bronzes & interesting artifacts. **Hrs:** Mon-Sat 10-6.

Modern Times
1538 N Milwaukee Ave
(773)772-8871 • (773)772-9189 (fax)
Vintage modern home furnishings, jewelry & clothing. Featuring works by the top designers of the 20th C in furniture, lighting, glass, ceramics & decorative accessories. Always buying/selling pieces by Herman Miller, Knoll, Dunbar, Widdicomb & more. **Pr:** $5-10,000 **Est:** 1991 **Hrs:** Wed-Fri 1-6, Sat-Sun 12-6, Mon-Tue by appt. **Sz:** L **CC:** AX/V/MC **Dir:** I90-94 Exit 48B (North Ave): Go W approx 10 blks to Milwaukee,

take a sharp L. 1/2 blk down on R. **Own:** Tom Clark & Martha Torno. **QC: 5 59 36 S19**

Nineteen Thirteen
1913 W Belmont Ave
(773)404-9522
Hrs: Wed-Sun 12-5.

Richard Norton Inc
222 Merchandise Mart Plaza, #612
(312)644-9359 • (312)644-8771 (fax)

Primarily French & Continental 18th & early 19th C furnishings with some English pieces. Highly decorative, striking & comfortable designs for residential & corporate environments. Our knowledgeable staff eagerly awaits you. **Est:** 1933 **Hrs:** Mon-Fri 9-5. **Sz:** L **Assn:** RNADA **Dir:** At the corner of Wells & Kinzie, 6th floor. **QC: 54 47 60 S1 S5 S9**

O'Hara's Gallery
707 N Wells St
(312)751-1286
Hrs: Mon-Sat 10-5.

Olde Chicago Antiques
2336-40 W Belmont Ave
(773)935-1200

French furniture to the trade. **Hrs:** Tue-Sat 11-5 or by appt. **QC: 47**

Oriental Treasures
159 W Kinzie St
(312)527-0533 • (773)761-2907

Chinese & Japanese antiques & appraisals. **Dir:** In the Antiquarian Bldg.

Penn Dutchman Antiques
4912 N Western Ave
(773)271-2208

Described by the *Chicago Tribune* as the most unusual store in Chicago. Movie & theater industries rent or purchase many of their props from us. You name it, we have it. **Pr:** $1-3,000 **Est:** 1968 **Hrs:** Daily 10-6 **Sz:** L

CC: AX/V/MC **Own:** James D Mowery. **QC: 32 48 67 S1 S12 S16**

Phil's Factory Antique Mall [G]
2040 W Belmont Ave
(773)528-8549

Pre-turn-of-the-century to 50s, 60s & 70s collectibles. Art Deco, Modern & Mission furniture; textiles & vintage clothing. **Hrs:** Daily 11-6. **CC:** V/MC **QC: 5 6 80**

Pilsen Gallery
2170 S Canalport
(312)829-2827 • (312)633-9322
(312)633-9322 (fax)

Architectural artifacts & antique furniture. Specializing in wood restoration, stained glass repairs & upholstery. **Pr:** $50-5,000 **Hrs:** Mon-Sat 10-6, Sun by chance/appt. **Sz:** H **Dir:** S of downtown near Halsted & Cermak. **Own:** Yury & Olga. **QC: 3 65 S16 S22**

Pimlico Antiques Ltd
500 N Wells St
(312)245-9199

17th-19th C English & Continental furniture. **Hrs:** Mon-Fri 10-5, Sat 11-5. **QC: 53 54**

Pine & Design Imports
511 W North Ave
(312)640-0100

European pine furniture. **Hrs:** Mon-Sat 10-6 (Mon & Thu til 8), Sun 11-5. **QC: 55**

Portals Ltd
742 N Wells St
(312)642-1066

19th C furniture & decorative objects, naif paintings. **Hrs:** Tue-Fri 10-5, Sat 11-5. **QC: 7 52**

Poster Plus
200 S Michigan Ave
(312)461-9277

Vintage posters prior to 1950. Turn-of-the-century French & American, travel, World War I & II. **Hrs:** Mon-Fri 10-6 (Tue & Thu til 8), Sat 9:30-6, Sun 11-6.

Powell's Book Store

2850 N Lincoln Ave
(773)248-1444

Used, rare & out-of-print books. **Hrs:** Sun-Fri 11-9, Sat 10-10. **QC: 18**

Kenneth Probst Galleries

46 E Superior St
(312)440-1991

Specializing in 19th & 20th C paintings. **Hrs:** By appt. **Own:** Kenneth A Probst. **QC: 7**

Red Eye Antiques

3050 N Lincoln Ave
(773)975-2020

Art Deco, architectural, folk art, jewelry. **Hrs:** Sat-Sun 12-6 or by chance.

Reflections Antiques

2428 N Ashland Ave
(773)871-7078

Lighting & furniture (1820-1920). **Hrs:** Mon-Fri 11-7, Sat-Sun 10-6.

Alan Robandt & Co

220 W Kinzie St (4th Fl)
(312)645-9995

18th & 19th C English & Continental furniture, mirrors, lighting, accessories & porcelain from Midwestern old monied families. Most business to dealers & design trade to the New York & Southern markets. **Pr:** $300-15,000 **Est:** 1988 **Hrs:** Mon-Fri 10-5, Sat by appt only. **Sz:** L **Dir:** Mid-block on Kinzie St behind the Merchandise Mart & 3 blks from Sotheby's. **QC: 53 54 68 S12**

Jay Robert's Antique Warehouse Inc

149 W Kinzie St
(312)222-0167

Furniture. **Hrs:** Mon-Sat 10-5. **QC: 48**

Russ's Pier W

1227 W Diversey Pkwy
(773)327-5718

Hrs: Daily.

Saito Oriental Antiques Inc

645 N Michigan Ave, Ste 428
(312)642-4366

Chinese, Japanese & Korean antiques. **Hrs:** Mon-Fri 10:30-5:30, Sat 11-5.

Schwebel

311 W Superior St
(312)280-1998

19th C furniture & accessories. **Hrs:** Mon-Fri 10-5.

Silver Moon

3337 N Halsted St
(773)883-0222
www.antique-shop.com/silvermoon

Vintage clothing from Victorian to 1960s. **Hrs:** Tue-Sun 12-6. **QC: 83**

Sonia Simone

904 Armitage Ave
(773)296-0931

Collectibles, vintage clothing, jewelry. **Hrs:** Wed-Sun 12-6.

Stanley Galleries

2118 N Clark St
(773)281-1614

Hrs: Mon-Sat 12-7.

Steve Starr Studios

2779 N Lincoln Ave
(773)525-6530

Art Deco & Moderne. **Hrs:** Mon-Fri 2-6, Sat-Sun 1-5. **QC: 5**

Studio V

672 N Dearborn
(312)440-1937
studiov@studiovchicago.com
www.studiovchicago.com

Antique & antique reproduction jewelry,

cufflinks, martini wear, perfume bottles, lamps, art glass, vintage clothing, porcelain as well as 50s kitsch, antique telephones, antique purses, scarves & hats. **Pr:** $5-1,750 **Est:** 1975 **Hrs:** Mon-Sat 12-6; Nov-Dec also open Sun 1-5. **Sz:** M **CC:** AX/V/MC **Dir:** I90-94 exit Ohio St: L at Dearborn. Studio is on L at 3rd blk between Huron & Erie. **Own:** Jack Garber. **QC:** 63 5 36 S12 S15

Taskey's Antiques
230 W Huron St (2-E)
(312)664-8400

17th, 18th & early 19th C English, Continental & American antiques to the trade only. **Hrs:** Mon-Fri 11-4. **QC:** 52 53 54

Tree Studio
613 N State St
(312)337-7541

Art Deco & American art. **Hrs:** Mon-Sat 11-6.

Turtle Creek Antiques
850 W Armitage Ave
(773)327-2630

In a renovated 1890s area of Chicago, fine antique quilts, estate linens, jewelry, fine silver, glass & porcelain. Antiques only. **Pr:** $10-2,500 **Est:** 1974 **Hrs:** Tue-Fri 11-6, Sat 10-5, Sun 12-5 (every day in Dec). **Sz:** M **CC:** AX/V/MC/DIS **Dir:** I-90/94 exit North Ave (Rte 64) E to Sheffield St, then N to Armitage, then E 2-1/2 blks. **Own:** Mary K Popma. **QC:** 84 81 64 S16 S1 S8

Urban Artifacts
2928 N Lincoln Ave
(773)404-1008

20th C furniture. **Hrs:** Wed-Sun 1-6. **QC:** 59

US #1 Antiques
1509 N Milwaukee Ave
(773)489-9428

Victorian, Art Nouveau & Art Deco. **Hrs:** Wed-Sun 12-5. **QC:** 89 5

Vintage Pine
904 W Blackhawk
(312)943-9303

European pine furniture & garden accessories. **Hrs:** Tue-Sat 10-5, Sun 12-5. **QC:** 55 60

Vintage Posters International Ltd
1551 N Wells St
(312)951-6681

Hrs: Mon-Fri 11-7, Sat 11-6, Sun 12-5. **QC:** 39

Wallner Antiques
1229 W Diversey
(773)248-6061

Hrs: Mon-Sat 11-6, Sun 12-5.

Wisteria
3715 N Southport
(773)880-5868

A vintage emporium of clothing & gifts. For the hep, swank, hot diggety, cat's meow, hip, je ne sais quoi, cool, groovy, dreamy, daddy-o, unreal, vintage threads, see our unique collection of clothing for men, women & children. **Pr:** $10-350 **Est:** 1985 **Hrs:** Thu-Fri 4-9, Sat 12-9, Sun 12-5. **Sz:** M **CC:** V/MC **Dir:** Near Wrigley Field in the Music Box Building. **Own:** Mr Koontz. **QC:** 83 63 32 S12 S8

Wrigleyville Antique Mall [G70]
3336 N Clark St
(773)868-0285 • (773)868-0683 (fax)
dannyalias@aol.com

Watches, jewelry, perfumes, compacts, chrome, Bakelite, cigarette cases, American dinnerware & pottery, World's Fair, souvenir buildings, vintage fashion, textiles, postcards/magazines; Mission, Art Deco to Fifties, H-Wakefield, dinettes, soda signs. **Pr:** $10-2,500 **Hrs:** Mon-Sat 11-6:30, Sun 12-6. **Sz:** H **CC:** AX/V/MC/DIS **Dir:** 3 mi

E of I90-94, Addison Exit, 1/3 mi S on Clark St. **Own:** Danny Alias & Jeff Nelson. **QC: 5 49 73 S19**

Yesterday
1143 W Addison St
(773)248-8087

Nostalgia shop featuring books, sports items, magazines, comics, baseball cards, non-sports cards, newspapers, movie memorabilia, toys, games, puzzles, monster items, political buttons, railroad, train items & more. **Pr:** $1-500 **Est:** 1976 **Hrs:** Mon-Sat 1-7, Sat 2-6. **Sz:** S **Dir:** 1 blk W of Wrigley Field **Own:** Tom Boyle. **QC: 16 67 87**

Zigurat Architectural Ornament
1702 N Milwaukee Ave
(773)227-6290
Hrs: Daily 11-6. **QC: 3**

Zig Zag
3419 N Lincoln Ave
(773)525-1060

20th C furnishings. **Hrs:** Wed-Fri 2-6, Sat 1-6, Sun 1-4. **QC: 59**

Gift Music, Book & Collectibles
2501 Chicago Rd
(708)754-4387 • (708)754-4387 (fax)
jntschulte@rocketmail.com

Worldwide gifts, sheet music & books (1800s to present), signed, limited & 1st eds; musical instruments; limited ed figurines & collectibles. Run by church musicians. **Pr:** $5-1,000 **Est:** 1989 **Hrs:** Mon-Tue & Fri 11-6, Wed-Thu 10-12. Call ahead advised. **Sz:** L **CC:** AX/V/MC/DIS **Dir:** 11 blks S of Rte 30 (Lincoln Hwy) on Rte 1 (Chicago Rd). Exit Rte 80/294 at Rte 1 (Halsted) S. **Own:** Gift Ministries. **QC: 18 69 32 S10 S12**

Clarendon Hills

Ebeneezer Gift House
14 S Prospect St
(630)654-8882
Hrs: Mon-Sat 10-5.

Clinton

Clinton Antique Mall [G100]
Rte 51
(217)935-8846

General line. **Hrs:** Mon-Sat 10-5, Sun 12-5. **Dir:** Intersection of Rte 51 & Rte 54.

Coal City

Collector's Corner
355 S Broadway
(815)634-3345
Militaria. **Hrs:** Mon-Fri 11-7. **QC: 4**

Sheryl's Doll Clinic
135 S Broadway
(815)634-4605

Dolls & doll accessories. Restoration. **Hrs:** Mon-Fri 10-5, Sat 10-2. **QC: 38 S11**

Victoria's
660 Division St (Rte 113)
(815)634-4563

Collectibles, carnival & Depression glass. **Hrs:** Mon-Sat 11-5.

Cordova

Antique & Treasure Trove [G]
15508 IL Hwy Rte 84N
(309)654-2669

Furniture, collectibles, crafts. **Hrs:** Wed-Sat 10-4:30, Sun 12-4:30.

Crete

Crete Antiques
502 5th St
(708)672-4188

Specializing in beer signs, automobile & railroad memorabilia & toys. Large selection of copper items & kitchen gadgets. **Hrs:** Tue-Sat 11-4, Sun 11-5. **Assn:** CBADA.

The Farmer's Daughter
1262 Lincoln St
(708)672-4588

Country antiques, primitive lighting, folk art, windsor chairs on a c 1877 homestead. **Est:** 1992 **Hrs:** Tue-Sat 10-5, Sun 12-4. **Sz:**

L **CC:** V/MC/DIS **Assn:** CBADA **Own:** Jacque Gaines. **QC: 34 41 45**

The Finishing Touch
563 W Exchange St
(708)672-9520 • (708)672-6913 (fax)
(800)866-4749

Upscale flower shop with unusual gifts & collectibles including Muffy Vanderbear & Beanie Babies. **Pr:** $0.95-500 **Est:** 1978 **Hrs:** Mon-Sat 9-5. **Sz:** M **CC:** AX/V/MC/DIS **Assn:** CBADA **Own:** Holly Milburn & Jill Hansen. **QC: 32 89 S15**

Gatherings
1375 Main St
(708)672-9880

Hand-picked cottage-style antiques, architectural fragments & decorative accessories. **Pr:** $10-1,800 **Est:** 1993 **Hrs:** Tue-Sat 10-5, Sun 12-5. **Sz:** L **CC:** V/MC/DIS **Assn:** CBADA **Dir:** I-94 to I-394 or Rte 57 to Sauk Trail exit. **Own:** Linda Grund. **QC: 3 36 51**

Indian Wheel Company

1366 Main St
(708)672-9612 • (708)748-8762 (fax)
indianwheelcompany@worldnet.att.net

Antiques, furniture, glassware, toys, tins, radios, books, political paper & old tools. Also carry Western items & Native American Indian artifacts. **Hrs:** Tue-Sat 10-5, Sun 12-5. **Assn:** CBADA **Dir:** On Main St in downtown historic Crete. **Own:** Brad Watson.

The Marketplace [G20+]

550 W Exchange St
(708)672-5556

Crete's oldest antique shop. Originally a church built in 1853 featuring a wide selection of glassware, furniture, Stieff, jewelry, crafts & collectibles. **Est:** 1968 **Hrs:** Daily 10-5. **Assn:** CBADA.

Seasons

1362 Main St
(708)672-0170

Originally built for a barbershop c 1915 with original tin ceilings & mosaic tile floors, featuring antiques & collectibles accented with botanicals. **Hrs:** Tue-Sat 10-5, Sun 12-5. **Assn:** BCADA.

Third Generation Antiques [G10]

1362 W Exchange St
(708)672-3369

Nestled on two floors of a cedar log cabin, a selection of fine furniture, lamps, clocks, prints, linens, china, glass, advertising & memorabilia from the 19th & 20th C. **Pr:** $1-2,000 **Est:** 1991 **Hrs:** Tue-Sat 10-5, Sun 12-5 (closed New Year's Day). **Sz:** L **CC:** AX/V/MC/DIS **Assn:** CBADA **Dir:** I-394 S

Domestic Arts

Fraktur: A Pennsylvanian Dutch certificate executed in traditional German gothic calligraphy, often surrounded by folk art motifs of birds, foliage, and figures. The certificates commemorated important domestic events, particularly births and deaths, and are now recognized as one of the most significant forms of folk art. After the mid-1830s, printed frakturs with spaces for handwritten names and dates gradually replaced the hand-made examples. The best are still beautiful, and many were hand-colored, but it is the earlier ones in traditional calligraphy that are obviously the most prized. "Fraktur" (literally "broken curve") is the German name for the traditional gothic script written with a broad nib that "broke" curves into thick and thin strokes.

Theorem: A stenciled painting, usually on velvet, but sometimes on Bristol board, of a still life of flowers and fruit, in a basket or urn, and occasionally with a bird or two. Theorem painting was an important accomplishment and art form for women and girls in the first half of the 19th century. It gradually replaced embroidery. The artist would first cut a number of stencils of different leaves, petals, and other motifs and design an arrangement from them. Though stenciled, no two theorems are the same. A thick, almost dry, watercolor was the preferred medium. Theorems are rarely signed, and today they are much appreciated examples of women's decorative art.

Mourning pictures: Mourning pictures were another accomplishment of girls in the early 19th century. The tomb, usually inscribed with the name of the deceased, occupied the center of the design, and was surrounded by conventional symbols of mourning — the weeping willow, the river (of life and death), a church and one or more mourners. They were either painted in water color or were worked in silk, in which case the faces and the inscription on the tomb were painted. George Washington's death provoked many mourning pictures.

to Exchange, W 5 mi, or Rte 57 to Sauk Trail exit, E to Western, S to Exchange, then E. **Own:** Francis & Amy Sheehan. **QC: 48 22 67 S7 S12**

Village Antiques & Lamp Shop
595 W Exchange St
(708)672-8980

Family-operated shop in a c 1875 home. Specializing in lamps of all kinds as well as lamp supplies & repair. Brass & copper polishing service. Also furniture, glassware & collectibles. **Est:** 1978 **Hrs:** Tue-Sat 10-5, Sun 12-5. **QC: 65**

Crystal Lake

Country Church Antiques [G10]
8509 Ridgefield Rd
(815)477-4601

English, American & pine furniture & English accessories. **Hrs:** Wed-Sun 11-4. **CC:** V/MC **QC: 55 36**

Penny Lane Antiques
6114 Lou Ave
(815)459-8828

Hrs: Wed-Sun 11-5. **CC:** V/MC/DIS.

De Kalb

Joanne Boardman
522 Joanne Ln
(815)756-9359

17th, 18th & 19th C furniture & accessories. We especially love early furniture in original paint or surface, treenware & early lighting. Your visit is always welcome. **Est:** 1975 **Hrs:** By chance/appt. Call any time. **Assn:**

> Use the Specialty QuickCode indexes at the back of the book to find dealers who specialize in your area of interest.

CSADA NIADA NHADA **Dir:** 60 mi W of Chicago. **Own:** Joanne & Jack Boardman. **QC: 1 52 88**

Cracker Jax
118 N Third St
(815)758-8178

Hrs: Mon-Sat 10-6, Sun 12-5.

Kathleen's Cupboard
323 E Locust St
(815)758-2111

Hrs: Tue-Sat 10-3.

Stephen Reed Antiques
1022 E Lincoln Hwy
(815)756-1182

19th C American furniture, oil paintings, prints, early American glass, lighting, ironstone, textiles, iron & folk art. **Hrs:** By appt only. **Assn:** CSADA.

Decatur

Nellie's Attic Antique Mall
3030 S Mt Zion Rd
(217)864-3363

Hrs: Tue-Sat 10-5, Sun 12-5.

Divernon

The Country Place Antique Mall [G7]
Frontage Rd
(217)628-3699

Hrs: Mon-Sat 9-5. **CC:** V/MC **Dir:** I-55 exit 80.

Dixon

Brinton Avenue Antique Mall [G]
725 N Brinton Ave
(815)284-4643

Furniture, lamps, smalls, dishes & toys. **Hrs:** Daily 10-5.

E & M Antique Mall [G35]
1602 S Galena
(815)288-1900
Furniture, smalls & antique cars. **Hrs:** Mon-Sat 10-6, Sun 10-5. **CC:** V/MC/DIS. **QC: 48 90**

Downers Grove

Treasures on Main
4912 Main St
(630)964-5155 • (630)963-5754

Entire second floor of old home crammed with collectibles. First floor is a tearoom. **Pr:** $1-150 **Est:** 1987 **Hrs:** Sep-May Mon-Sat 11-3, Jun-Aug Mon-Fri 11-3. **Sz:** M **CC:** V/MC **Dir:** I-88 to Highland exit. S on Highland, which becomes Main St, pass Ogden, S to 4900 block. **Own:** Diane M Schwartz & Marily Nachman. **QC: 32 38 63**

About Time Antiques & Collectibles & Neat Stuff
932 Warren Ave
(630)968-7353

Hrs: Mon, Wed, Fri, Sat 11-5, Thu 11-7 (closed Sun & Tue).

Asbury's
1626 Ogden Ave
(630)769-9191

Hrs: Mon-Fri 10-6 (Thu til 8), Sat 10-5.

Treasures on Main Street
4912 Main St
(630)964-5515

Hrs: Mon-Sat 11-3.

Duquoin

Main Street Memories [G7]
212 E Main St
(618)542-5043
Hrs: Mon-Sat 10-5.

The Mulberry Tree Antiques [G6]
24 S Mulberry St
(618)542-6621

Antiques & collectibles. **Hrs:** Tue-Fri 10-5, Sat 10-4.

Earlville

Gray Goose Antiques
139 W Railroad St
(815)246-7274
Hrs: Wed-Sat 10-4.

The Olde Mercantile in Earlville
103 W Railroad St
(815)246-9413
Hrs: Mon-Sat 10-5, Sun 9-3.

East Dundee

The Antique Emporium at the Milk Pail [G50]
Rte 25
(847)468-9667

Hrs: Daily 10-5. **Sz:** L **Dir:** 1/4 mi N of I-90 (2 min from tollway), 1/2 mi S of Rte 72.

River Street Antiques & Gallery House
314 N River St
(847)426-3149

Country antiques. **Hrs:** Thu-Sat 10:30-4:30. **QC: 34**

Treasured Memories
1 E Main St
(847)428-1833
Hrs: Tue-Sat 10-5.

Windsor Antiques
205 S Van Buren
(847)428-0291
Hrs: Sat-Sun 10-4.

East Peoria

Pleasant Hill Antique Mall [G250+]
315 S Pleasant Hill Rd
(309)694-4040

Hrs: Mon-Thu 7-7pm, Fri-Sat 7-8pm, Sun 7-5. **CC:** V/MC/DIS.

El Paso

El Paso Antique Mall [G]
800 W Main St
(309)527-3705

Hrs: Daily 10-6. **Dir:** I-39 exit 14.

Eldorado

Antique Gallery
1332 Locust
(618)273-2737

General line. **Hrs:** Mon-Sat 10-5, Sun 1-5. **CC:** V/MC/DIS.

Little Egypt Antiques
1212 State St
(618)273-9084

Glassware, Depression glass & china. **Hrs:** Tue-Sat 10:30-4 (Sat til 5), Sun 1-5.

Eleroy

Treasures of Time Antiques
101 Bridge St
(815)233-2202

Oak & walnut furniture. **Hrs:** Sat-Sun 11-5.

Elgin

P Ks Antiques & Collectibles
19 Douglas Ave
(847)742-4880

Large selection of vintage clothing, hats, gloves, purses & costume jewelry, linen. 100s of records & books, beer steins, glassware, ceramic horses, old fishing tackle & framed pictures. **Pr:** $5-350 **Est:** 1990 **Hrs:** Mon & Thu-Fri 10-6, Tue-Wed 10-5:30, Sat 10-4 (closed Sun). **Sz:** M **CC:** V/MC/DIS **Dir:** I-90 Exit 31 to downtown. In lower level of Keenup Sporting Goods. **Own:** Patricia S Kenney. **QC: 18 32 83**

Elizabeth

Main Street Mini Mall [G]
115 N Main St
(815)858-3607

Hrs: Thu-Mon 10-4:30.

Shop on the Hill
504 S Main St
(815)858-3815 • (815)858-2082 (fax)

1st floor of large Victorian home stuffed full of furniture, primitives, glass, prints, frames & stoneware. **Pr:** $5-2,000 **Est:** 1977 **Hrs:** Mon-Tue & Thu-Sat 9-5, Sun 11-5. Wed by chance/appt. **Dir:** 15 mi E of Galena on Rte 20. **Own:** Pat Schaible. **QC: 1 48 22**

Welcome Home Antiques
118 N Main St (Rte 20)
(815)858-3450

Hrs: Mon-Sat 9-4.

Elk Grove Village

Antiques Mart [G225]
1166-1170 W Devon Ave
(847)895-8900

Furniture, jewelry, art, glass, china, pottery, flow blue, silver, sporting goods, military, toys. Clock & crystal repair. **Hrs:** Mon-Fri 11-7, Sat-Sun 10-5. **QC: S7 S16**

Oakton Street Antique Centre [G75+]
2430 E Oakton St
(847)437-2514

Hrs: Mon-Sat 10-6 (Thu til 8), Sun 11-6. **Dir:** 10 min from O'Hare.

Elmhurst

Circa Antiques

549 Spring Rd
(630)834-4088
(800)79-CIRCA
circaelm@aol.com
www.circa-antiques.com

A general line of glass, china, toys, furniture & decorative accessories. Specializing in American sterling silver flatware & hollowware, children's glass & china & ladies' accessories including jewelry, compacts, purses & perfume bottles. **Pr:** $5-1,000 **Est:** 1989 **Hrs:** Tue-Sat 10-5. **Sz:** S **CC:** AX/V/MC/DIS **Assn:** ISA **Dir:** 1/2 mi E of Rte 83 & 3 blks S of St Charles Rd. **Own:** Karl & Nanette Horn. **QC: 78 63 36 S1 S12**

Evanston

Another Time, Another Place Antiques

1243 Chicago Ave
(847)866-7170

Furniture, jewelry, linens & quilts. **Hrs:** Mon-Fri 10-4.

British Collectibles of Chicago

917 Chicago Ave
(847)570-4867
Hrs: Mon-Sat 9:30-6, Sun 12:30-4.

Estate Buyers of Evanston

1917 Central St
(847)475-8363

Buying antiques, collectibles, gold, silver & watches. **QC: S12**

Eureka!

705 Washington St
(847)869-9090

Antiques, nostalgia & collectibles. Paper dolls, radios, chiming clocks, neon signs, Chicagoana & World's Fair collectibles, old store signs & tins, paper ephemera, Black memorabilia, Deco, kitsch. **Hrs:** Tue-Sat 11-5.

Evanstonia Period Furniture & Restoration

702 Main St
(847)869-0110

Specializing in 19th & early 20th C traditional American & European antiques. **Hrs:** Mon-Sat 11-6, Sun 12-5. **QC: 48**

In the Fireplace I

Andirons: Large iron supports, often faced with brass, used on either side of a fireplace to support the logs. Smaller versions are sometimes called "firedogs." Andirons often had hooks on the back of their uprights to hold a spit.

Spit: A revolving metal bar upon which meat was impaled and hung over the fire for roasting. At one end was a pulley wheel connected by a rope or chain to some form of motive power — human, animal, or mechanical.

Turnspit: A boy or a small dog trained for the tedious task of turning the spit. The dog worked in a treadmill at the side of the hearth. Dogs performed this task in England and Europe but not, as far as we know, in America.

Spit-jack: A mechanism for turning the spit that was driven by a heavy weight of stone or lead slowly descending.

Folk Works Gallery
1310-1/2 Chicago Ave
(847)328-0083

Architectural antiques, Bakelite, costume jewelry, decoys, early baskets, folk art, garden antiques, jewelry, linen, Mexican silver, primitives, quilts, textiles, pottery, purses, willow & wicker furniture, yellowware. **Hrs:** Tue-Sat 11-5, Sun 1-5. **QC: 41 37 3**

Green Bay Trail Antiques
1937 Central St
(847)328-9780

Lamps, framed prints & furniture. **Hrs:** Call for hours. **QC: 48 74**

Harvey Antiques
1231 Chicago Ave
(847)866-6766

18th & 19th C American furnishings, American Indian art & folk art. Jewelry. **Hrs:** Tue-Sat 11-5.

Hilties
1812 Central St
(847)492-1001

Mission furniture, fully restored. **Hrs:** Tue-Sat 11-5. **QC: 49**

Originals Gallery of Antique Jewelry
1511 Sherman
(847)328-4040

Ancient to modern jewelry. **Hrs:** Mon-Fri 10-6, Sat 10-5, Sun 12:30-4. **CC:** V/MC.

The Pursuit of Happiness
1524 Chicago Ave
(847)869-2040

Antiques & other decorative arts. **Hrs:** Mon-Sat 11-6.

Recollections Antiques
836 Custer Ave
(847)869-4244

Jewelry & collectibles. **Hrs:** By appt only.

Sara Bustle Antiques
921 Dempster St
(847)869-7290

Antique lighting & jewelry. **Hrs:** Mon-Tue & Thu-Sat 10-6, Sun 1-4. **QC: 65 64**

Secret Treasures
611 Dempster St
(847)866-6889

Consignment shop for glass, porcelain, pottery, vintage costume jewelry. **Hrs:** Tue-Fri 11-5, Sat 10-5, Sun 12-5. **QC: S8**

Evergreen Park
Aunt-Tiquery's
3300 W 95th St
(708)422-0677

Costume jewelry, china, furniture. **Hrs:** Mon-Sat 10-5, Sun 12-5.

Fairview Heights
St Clair Antique Mall [G200+]
315 Salem Pl
(618)628-1650

Antiques & collectibles. **Hrs:** Mon-Sat 10-8, Sun 12-6. **Sz:** H.

Farmer City

Farmer City Antiques Center [G6]
201 S Main St
(309)928-9210
General line. **Hrs:** Mon-Sat 10-5, Sun 12-5.

Main Street Antiques
115 S Main St
(309)928-9208
General line. **Hrs:** Mon-Sat 10-5, Sun 12-5.

Margaret's Attic to Basement Antiques [G8]
117 S Main St
(309)928-9100
General line. **Hrs:** Mon-Sat 11-5, Sun 12-5.

Flossmoor

Loon Lake Ltd
2557 Flossmoor Rd
(708)957-3636
Silver, folk art & paintings. **Hrs:** Tue-Sat 1-5.

Forest Park

At Home With Antiques [G]
7512-7516 Madison St
(708)771-0608
www.antique-shop.com/athome
Furniture & smalls. **Hrs:** Mon-Fri 11-6, Sat 10-5, Sun 12-5. **QC: 48**

Traveling East? Take along a copy of *Sloan's Green Guide to Antiquing in New England*. Call Toll Free (888)875-5999 or visit your local bookstore or antiques dealer.

Atlantic Crossing
7501 W Madison St
(708)771-8400
Hrs: Mon-Fri 1-5, Sat 10-4.

Curiosities, Giftware & Collectibles
7439-1/2 W Madison St
(708)366-2030
Hrs: Tue-Sat 10-6.

Forest Park Antiques
7504 Madison St
(708)366-0232
Furniture, glassware, sewing tools, railroad memorabilia & Fiestaware. **Hrs:** Daily 10-5, Tue by chance/appt.

Pieces of the Past
7500 W Madison St
(708)366-1072
Hrs: Mon-Sat 11-6, Sun 11-5.

Fox River Grove

Memories
412 Lincoln Ave
(847)639-8555
Hrs: Wed-Sat 11-4.

Frankfort

Antiques Unique
100 Kansas St
(815)469-2741
Jewelry, furniture & stained & beveled glass windows. **Hrs:** Tue-Sat 10-5, Sun 12-5. **QC: 64**

The Trolley Barn [G45]
11 S White St
(815)464-1120
In a renovated turn-of-the-century trolley barn. **Hrs:** Mon-Fri 10-8, Sat 10-6, Sun 12-6.

Freeport

Butch's Antiques
330 W Pleasant St
(815)233-4437

Country & primitives. **Hrs:** Mon-Fri 8:30-5.

Luecke's Antique Mall [G30]
10-1/2 E Main St
(815)233-0021
Hrs: Mon-Sat 10-5, Sun 12-5.

Main Street Antiques [G10]
12 E Main St
(815)233-0027
Hrs: Mon-Sat 10-5 (Fri til 8).

The Swan's Nest
Bus Rte 20
(815)234-SWAN

Country, quilts, decoys, folk art. **Hrs:** Daily 9-5 (Fri til 9). **Dir:** At Bypass 20 W. **QC: 34 84 37**

Galesburg

East Main Antiques
125 E Main St
(309)342-4424

A general line specializing in glassware. **Hrs:** Daily 10-5. **CC:** V/MC/DIS **QC: 61**

Rail City Antiques
665 E Main St
(309)343-2614

Furniture, jewelry & glassware. **Hrs:** Mon-Sat 10-5, Sun 12-4. **QC: 48 61**

Rug Beater Antiques
137 E Main St
(309)343-2001 • (309)284-4358
(309)343-0108 (fax)
rug.beater@misslink.net
www.misslink.net/rugbeaterantiques/

Specializing in quilts, dolls & furniture as well as a general line. **Est:** 1980 **Hrs:** Mon-

Sat 11-4. **Sz:** M **CC:** AX/V/MC/DIS **Assn:** GADA **Dir:** Halfway between Peoria & Quad Cities on I-74. **Own:** Evelyn & Melvin Gibson. **QC: 84 38 48 S1**

Ziggy's [G27]
674 E Main St
(309)342-9448

Mostly smalls & some furniture. **Hrs:** Mon-Sat 9-5.

Geneva

A Step in the Past
122 Hamilton St
(630)232-1611

Pine & oak furniture, glassware, linens, toys, baskets, jewelry, primitives & vintage clothing. **Hrs:** Tue-Sat 11-4, Sun 12-5. **QC: 55 50**

Circa Garden
123 S Third St
(630)208-0013
Hrs: Mon-Sat 10-5:30, Sun 12-5.

Circa Home
317 S Third St
(630)262-6222
Hrs: Mon-Sat 10-5:30, Sun 12-5.

The Country Store
28 James St
(630)232-0335
Hrs: Mon-Sat 9:30-5, Sun 12-4.

Findings of Geneva Antiques
307 W State St (Rte 38)
(630)262-0959

Linens, illustrated books & prints, flow blue, toys, ephemera, jewelry, china, silver, pottery, advertising. Single-owner shop. **Hrs:** Tue-Sat 10:30-6, Sun 12-5.

Fourth Street Galleries
327 Franklin St
(630)208-4610
Hrs: Tue-Sat 10-4.

Geneva Antique Market
227 S Third St
(630)208-1150
Hrs: Mon-Sat 10-5, Sun 12-5.

Geneva Antiques Ltd
220 S Third St
(603)208-7952
Hrs: Mon-Sat 10-5, Sun 12-4.

Bill Kohanek Antiques and Decorations
121 W State St
(630)232-0552
Hrs: Tue-Sat 11-5, Sun by chance/appt.

The Little Traveler
404 S Third St
(630)232-4200
Hrs: Mon-Fri 9:30-5, Sat 9:30-5:30.

Wesley Mansfield Ltd of Geneva
228 S Third St
(603)262-9330
Hrs: Mon-Sat 10-5, Sun 12-4.

Richard J Matson Jewelers
312 S Third St
(630)232-4500
Antique jewelry & jewelry repair. **Hrs:** Mon-Sat 10-5. **QC: 64 S1 S16**

Shirley McGill Antiques
1578 Kirkwood Dr
(630)262-8430
Antiques & appraisals. **Hrs:** By appt only. **Assn:** CSADA **QC: S1**

Order an additional copy of the Green Guide for yourself or a friend by calling Toll Free (888)875-5999 or visit your local bookstore or nearest antiques dealer.

Vintage Treasures
321 Hamilton St
(630)262-8544
Hrs: Tue-Sat 10:30-5, Sun by chance/appt.

Glen Ellyn

Marcia Crosby Antiques
477 Forest Ave
(630)858-5665
American country accessories, prints, maps & folk art. Appraisals. **Hrs:** Thu-Sat & Mon 10-5. **Assn:** CSADA **QC: 34 41 S2**

Patricia Lacock Antiques
526 Crescent Blvd
(630)858-2323
Victorian & estate jewelry, cut crystal, sterling, hand-painted porcelain & quilts. **Hrs:** Mon-Sat 10:30-4:30. **QC: 64**

Pennsylvania Place [G30]
535 Pennsylvania Ave
(630)858-1515
Furniture, china, pottery, glass, books, vintage lighting, jewelry, vintage clothing. **Hrs:** Tue-Sat 10-5 (Thu til 9:30), Sun 12-4:30.

Betty Pitts Antiques
22 W 640th Burr Oak
(630)469-3643
Toys, dolls, Chinese porcelain & Americana. **Hrs:** By appt only. **Assn:** CSADA **QC: 38 87 25**

Royal Vale View Antiques
388 Pennsylvania Ave
(630)790-3135
Architectural & furniture. **Hrs:** Sat or by appt.

Sign of the Whale Antiques [G]
558 Crescent Blvd
(630)469-5320
19th C furniture, quilts, folk art & acces-

sories. **Hrs:** Mon-Sat 10-5. **Assn:** CSADA **Own:** Virginia Larsen. **QC: 1 52 41**

Stagecoach Antiques
526 E Crescent Blvd
(630)469-0490

Antique, heirloom & estate jewelry & watches as well as glassware, china, silver & collectibles. **Hrs:** Mon-Sat 11-5.

Glencoe

It's About Time
375 Park Ave
(847)835-2012

Clocks. **Hrs:** Wed-Sat 10-5. **QC: 35**

Glenview

Antiques & Porcelain by GK Ltd
1011 Harlem Ave
(847)724-3059 • (847)724-3060 (fax)

Furniture, crystal, glassware, brass, silver, lamps, china, dolls, English antique pottery, fine arts & estate jewelry. Specializing in Meissen porcelain. Porcelain restoration. **Hrs:** Tue-Sat 10:3-5. **QC: 23 61 S16**

Grant Park

Sentimental Journey Antiques
111 S Main St
(815)465-6100

Depression glass & dolls. **Hrs:** Thu-Sun 10-5.

Grayslake

Antique Warehouse [G75]
2 S Lake St
(847)223-9554 • (847)223-2580 (fax)
sales@antiquewhse.com
www.antiquewhse.com

Featuring 19th & 20th C antiques & col-

Grayslake, IL
Rt.132 (Grand Ave.)
Washington St.
Antique Warehouse
Rt. 83
Rt. 45
94
N
Lake St.
Center St.
Rt. 120 (Belvidere Rd.)

lectibles. A Midwest favorite of dealers & collectors alike. Liberal discounts. Dealer specialties include pottery, jewelry, watches, dolls, sports, architecture, Deco, country, Victoriana, oil paintings & furniture **Est:** 1991 **Hrs:** Mon-Sat 10-5, Sun 12-5 (2nd Sun of month 10-5). **Sz:** L **CC:** V/MC **Assn:** CAGA **Dir:** I-94 W Grand Ave exit to Rte 45 S. 7 mi W of I-94. **Own:** Candyce Martens. **QC: 32 67 S1 S12 S8**

Duffy's Attic
22 Center St
(847)223-7454

Glassware, clocks, furniture & clock repair. **Hrs:** Tue-Sat 10-5, Sun 12-4. **QC: 61 35 S7**

Grayslake Trading Post
Rte 83
(847)223-2166

General line. **Hrs:** Daily 10-4. **Dir:** Off Rte 120 W to Rte 83.

Gurnee

Anamosa Antiques
19056 W Grand Ave (Rte 132)
(847)356-0832

Furniture, jewelry, paintings, clocks, glassware, toys, silver, porcelain, rugs, lamps & dolls. **Hrs:** Tue-Sun 10-5. **CC:** V/MC **Dir:** 3 min W of Gurnee Mills Mall, just W of Rte 45.

Hampshire

Olde Saint Pete's Antiques [G32]

12N950 Plank Rd
(847)464-0299

Featuring period furniture, mirrors, primitives, architectural, folk art & garden antiques. Resilvering. In an 1873 church on the Historic Register. **Hrs:** Daily 10-5. **Dir:** At Rte 47. **QC: 60 41 3 S16**

Harvard

Dairy Barn Antiques [G70]

708 W Brink St
(815)943-7030

Banks, books, bottles, crocks, furniture, glass, Griswold, marbles, Roseville, steins, tools, trains, watches, cast iron & pressed steel toys, military (Civil War through WWII). **Hrs:** Daily 10-5. **CC:** V/MC.

Hebron

Back In Time

10004 Main St
(815)648-2132

Victoriana & primitives. **Hrs:** Thu-Mon 11-4.

Grampy's Antique Store [G11]

10003 Main St
(815)648-2244

Furniture & primitives. **Hrs:** Thu-Mon 10-5.

Fat or Grease Lamps

Lamps probably predate candles. Most early civilizations had vessels that held oil or grease in which a wick was suspended.

Cruisie: The cruisie is the simplest form of lamp of all. It consists of a shallow tin or iron bowl with one, two, or four "spouts" in which the wick was laid.

Betty lamp: A betty lamp is technically a cruisie in which the spout for the wick, and sometimes the whole bowl, is covered over, but in practice the name is often used to refer to cruisies as well.

Phoebe lamp: A Phoebe lamp is a betty with a bowl under the font and shaped like it to catch the drippings. It is sometimes called a double betty lamp.

Betties, phoebies and cruisies were hanging lamps usually on chains with spikes and/or hooks to hang from, but similar lamps were made on stands. Lamps were usually made of iron or tin, and sometimes of pewter. Standing lamps were also made of earthenware.

The word "betty" derives not from the name of some archetypal housewife (as giving it a capital B would suggest), but from *betynge* — the early English word for the fat and oil left after cooking. Cruisie on the other hand refers to the vessel not its contents: a *cruse* or *crusekyn* was a 14th century vessel with a spout and handle. Where the name "Phoebe" came from is a mystery. The moon was sometimes called Phoebe, and this is a possible origin of the name.

Names for antiques, like those for people, go in and out of fashion: "Phoebe," for instance is rarely used today, whereas "cruisie's" popularity increased after 1950s. "Betty," whether used broadly to refer to all lamps of this type or specifically to ones without wick covers, is the name that never goes out of fashion, and if the technically incorrect capital B stimulates us to imagine the hard-working and highly skilled colonial women who used the lamps, then so much the better.

Hebron Antique Gallery [G12]
10002 Main St
(815)648-4794

Furniture, folk art, fine art, architectural & garden. **Hrs:** Daily 10-5.

Nancy Powers Antiques
12017 Maple St
(815)648-4804

Quirky country. **Hrs:** Fri-Mon 10-5. **Dir:** Corner Rtes 173 & 47.

Prairie Avenue Antiques
Main St & Prairie Ave
(815)648-4507

Furniture & collectibles. **Hrs:** Daily 10-5.

Scarlet's Antiques
9911 Main St
(815)648-4112

Country & primitives. **Hrs:** Mon & Wed-Sun 10-5.

Watertower Antiques
9937 Main St
(815)648-2287

Hrs: Mon & Wed-Sun 10-5.

Hennepin

Northwind Antiques
420 High
(815)925-7264

Pine furniture, graniteware, tools & tins. **Hrs:** By appt only. **CC:** V/MC **QC:** 55 86 31

Highland Park

Arthur M Feldman Gallery
1815 St Johns Ave
(847)432-8858

Fine art & Judaica. **Hrs:** Mon-Sat 10-5.

Merrimac Antiques
1905 Sheridan Rd
(847)433-0334 • (847)295-2241

Antique furnishings, fine art & decorative accessories, garden furniture & ornaments, primitives. **Hrs:** Wed-Sat 11-5 (call ahead advised). **Own:** Mary McLeod & Jim McGonagle.

Frank & Barbara Pollack
(847)433-2213

American primitive paintings, furniture in original finish & paint, folk art & textiles of the 18th & 19th C & decorative arts & jewelry of the 20th C. Oct-Apr Sunapee, NH; (603)763-2403. **Hrs:** By appt only. **Assn:** ADA NHADA **QC:** 1 41 51

George Ritzlin Maps & Prints
469 Roger Williams Ave
(847)433-2627 • (847)433-6389 (fax)

Just steps from the beautifully restored Queen Anne train station in Ravinia & overlooking Jens Jensen Park, this gallery features maps & prints c 1490-1890, botanicals, fashion plates, medieval manuscript leaves & cartographic reference books. Catalog. **Pr:** $25-5,000 **Est:** 1976 **Hrs:** Wed-Fri 10-5, Sat 10-4 or by appt. **Sz:** M **CC:** V/MC **Assn:** ABAA **Dir:** I-94/US 41 exit E (R) at Lake-Cook Rd 1 mi to light at Green Bay Rd; turn L (N) 1 mi to light at Roger Williams; turn R (E) to gallery (3-1/2 blks). **Own:** George Ritzlin. **QC:** 18 66 74 S1 S8

Highwood

Freidarica Ltd Antiques
257 Waukegan Ave
(847)433-4595 • (847)432-8858

English & French accessories. **QC:** 36

Hinsdale

David Alan Antiques & Art
52 S Washington
(630)325-6090
Hrs: Tue-Sat 11-5.

Aloha's Antiques
6 W Hinsdale Ave
(630)325-3733

Antique jewelry, china & smalls. **Pr:** $10-4,000 **Est:** 1970 **Hrs:** Sep-May Tue-Sat (closed Sun-Mon); Jun-Aug Tue-Wed & Fri-Sat (closed Mon, Thu & Sun). **Sz:** S **CC:** V/MC **Own:** Aloha Drahn. **QC: 64 23 78**

Barbara Curtis Antiques
5900 S Grant St
(630)323-7914

General line of furniture & accessories. **Hrs:** Tue-Sat 11-4. **Assn:** CSADA.

Fleming & Simpson Ltd
53 S Washington St
(630)654-1890

Fine English & French furniture, porcelain, silver, brass, picture frames, clocks & decorative accessories. **Hrs:** Tue-Sat 10-5. **Own:** Anne Stevens & Janet Urban. **QC: 54 53 36**

The Yankee Peddler
6 E Hinsdale Ave
(630)325-0085
Hrs: Mon-Sat 10-5.

Huntley

Antiques & Uniques
7214 Seeman Rd
(815)923-4495

Country furniture, tin & wooden kitchen tools & accessories, graniteware, stoneware, old toys. **Est:** 1978 **Hrs:** Tue-Sat (call ahead advised). **Assn:** NIADA **Dir:** 3 mi E of Union. **Own:** Betty & Al Young. **QC: 31 34**

Joliet

Chicago Street Mercantile
175 N Chicago St
(815)722-8955
18th C furnishings. **Hrs:** Call for appt.

Uniques Antiques Ltd
1006 W Jefferson St
(815)741-2466

Furniture, advertising, glassware, toys, dolls, jewelry & military. **Hrs:** Tue-Sat 11-5. **QC: 48 61 39**

Kankakee

Bellflower Antiques
397 S Wall St
(815)935-8242

Antiques & collectibles. **Hrs:** Mon-Fri 4-8 & Sat-Sun 10-5. **QC: S1**

Blue Dog Antiques [G12]
440 N 5th Ave
(815)936-1701
Hrs: Mon-Fri 10-5 or by appt.

Frame World & Gallery
259 S Schuyler Ave
(815)933-7263

Antique art, frames & ornaments. **Hrs:** Mon-Fri 11-5:30, Sat 10-3 or by appt. **QC: 7 S13**

Haigh Enterprises Ltd Inc
2738 E 2000N Rd
(815)939-7797

Antiques, estates & collectibles. **Hrs:** By appt only. **QC: S6**

Kankakee Antique Mall [G225]
147 S Schuyler Ave
(815)937-4957

Antiques & crafts. **Hrs:** Daily 10-6.

Little House Antiques
RR 4 & Hwy 17W
(815)937-0989

Furniture, primitives & quilts. **Hrs:** Tue-Sat 10-5 or by appt.

Kenilworth

Federalist Antiques
515 Park Dr
(847)256-1791

American Federal & Classical furniture, period accessories & works of art. **Pr:** $250-10,000 **Est:** 1972 **Hrs:** Mon-Sat 10-5. **Sz:** L **CC:** V/MC **Dir:** I-94 N from Chicago to Lake Ave Exit E to Green Bay Rd. 1 mi to stop light at Park Dr, L 1/2 block. Northwestern Metra from Chicago to Kenilworth, cross street 1/2 block. **Own:** Michael Corbett. **QC:** 52 8 12

Smith & Ciffone Antiques
630 Green Bay Rd
(847)853-0234

18th & 19th C Continental & English ceramics, Staffordshire, majolica. **Hrs:** Mon-Sat 11-5. **QC:** 23 30

La Grange

Another Time Around
10 S Stone Ave
(708)352-0400

Hrs: Wed-Sat 9:30-5:30.

Antiques & More
2 S Stone Ave
(708)352-2214

Hrs: Tue-Sat 9:30-5:30.

La Grange Antique Mall [G]
35 E Plainfield Rd
(708)352-9687

Collectibles & smalls. **Hrs:** Daily 10-5 (Mon & Thu til 9).

Plainfield Road Antiques
30 E Plainfield Rd
(708)352-8172

Hrs: Mon-Fri 11-6 (Thu til 8), Sat 10-6, Sun 11-5.

Rosebud
5349 S La Grange Rd
(708)352-7673

Furniture. **Hrs:** Mon-Sat 11-5:30, Sun 12-4. **QC:** 48

Antique & Vintage Traders
1510 W 55th St
(708)246-2415 • (708)246-3077

Furniture. **Hrs:** Mon-Sat 10-5 (Thu til 7). **QC:** 48

31st Street Antiques
1017 E 31st St
(708)352-1172

Hrs: Mon-Fri 11-6 (Thu til 8), Sat 10-6, Sun 11-5.

Almost Anything Antiques
19 E 31st St
(708)352-7001

Smalls & collectibles. **Hrs:** Tue-Fri 12-5, Sat 11-5.

Heart's Desire Antiques
1014 E 31st St
(708)354-3040

Hrs: Mon-Sat 11-5 (closed Wed), Sun 12-5.

La Grange Park Antique Mall [G]
1005 E 31st St
(708)482-3966

Hrs: Mon-Sat 11-6, Sun 11-5.

Scanlon & Tuthill Ltd
800 E 31st St
(708)482-3966

Hrs: Tue-Sat 10-5, Sun 12-5.

Lake Bluff

Lawrence Interiors Inc
109 E Scranton Ave
(847)234-7944

English furniture, reproductions & accessories. **Hrs:** Mon-Fri 9-5, Sat 9-4.

The Shops on Scranton
37 E Scranton Ave
(847)735-0001

Jewelry, antiques, ironwork & furniture. **Hrs:** Mon-Fri 10-5, Sat 10-4.

Lake Forest

Anna's of Lake Forest
950 N Western Ave
(847)295-9151

Vintage estate furniture. **Hrs:** Mon-Sat 10-5, Sun 11-4. **QC: 48**

Clockworks
560 N Western Ave
(847)234-7272

Clocks & timepieces. **Hrs:** Mon-Fri 9-5:30, Sat 9-4. **QC: 35**

The Country House Inc
179 E Deerpath Rd
(847)234-0244 • (847)234-7559 (fax)

A convenient & comfortable location to peruse English & American antiques. Large selection of porcelain & fitments. Estate division & appraisals. European-trained cabinetmakers on site for fine restorations. **Est:** 1936 **Hrs:** Mon-Fri 10-5, Sat 10-4:30 or by appt. **Dir:** I-94 to Deerpath Rd E. **QC: 23 34 54 S1 S5 S9**

Crescent Worth Art & Antiques
626 N Western Ave
(847)295-8036 • (847)295-8145 (fax)

18th, 19th & 20th C paintings, furniture, silver, jewelry & decorative accessories.

Hrs: Mon-Sat 10-5:30. **Own:** Lynda Dehler & Colleen Doyle. **QC: 7 36**

Lake Forest Antique Consignments
225 E Deerpath Rd
(847)234-0442 • (847)234-0480 (fax)

Quality consignments including furniture, crystal, silver & paintings. **Hrs:** Tue-Sat 10-5. **QC: 48 61 78**

Olden Daz Antique Jewelers
514 N Western Ave
(847)295-3333

Antique jewelry. **Est:** 1969 **Hrs:** Thu-Sat 10-4, Sun 10-2. **Own:** Florence & Jack Ross. **QC: 64**

David O'Neill Antiques Inc
139 E Woodland Rd
(847)234-9344

Porcelain, folk art & unusual pieces. **Hrs:** By appt only.

Snow-Gate Antiques
234 E Wisconsin Ave
(847)234-3450

Hrs: Tue-Sat 10-4:45 (call ahead advised).

Lamoille

LaMoille Mercantile Co Mall [G]
Rt 34 & 103 Martin St
(815)638-2710

Hrs: Tue-Sat 10-4.

Pine Stock Books and Antiques
Rt 34
(815)539-6630

Hrs: Apr-Dec: Wed-Fri 10-5.

Lanark

Jeannine Carroll
14384 Lover Spring Rd
(815)493-2521

American country furniture & accessories.
Hrs: By appt only. **Assn:** NIADA **QC: 34
51 41**

Cothren House Antiques
(815)493-6215

18th & 19th C furniture & related accessories. **Hrs:** By appt only. **Assn:** CSADA
Own: Richard L Peterson & Frank V
Colson. **QC: 52**

Lebanon

And Thistle Dew
210 W St Louis St
(618)57-4443

Furniture, pottery, art, books, paper goods
& chair caning. **QC: 48 7 39 S6**

The Cross-Eyed Elephant
201 W St Louis St
(618)537-4491

Furniture, glass, primitives, paper goods,
books & jewelry. **Hrs:** Tue-Sat 10-4:30,
Sun-Mon by chance/appt. **QC: 48 61 39**

General Store Antique Mall [G]
112 E St Louis St
(618)537-8494

Furniture, glassware, pottery, primitives,
Breweriana & paper goods. **Hrs:** Tue-Sat
10-4:30, Sun 11-4:30. **QC: 48 61 39**

Grandma's Attic
121 W St Louis St
(618)537-6730

General line. **Hrs:** Tue-Sat 10-4:30, Sun-
Mon by chance/appt.

Heritage Antiques & British Grocery Shop
218 W St Louis St
(618)537-2667

American country furniture & accessories.
Hrs: Mon-Sat 10-5. **QC: 48**

Mom & Me
200 W St Louis St
(618)537-8343

General line. **Hrs:** Mon, Thu, Fri, Sat 10-5,
Tue 10-8, Sun 12-5.

Ownings Antiques
326 W St Louis St
(618)537-6672

Furniture & glassware. **Hrs:** Tue-Sat 10-4,
Sun 12-5. **QC: 48 61**

Peddler's Books & Things
209 W St Louis St
(618)537-4026

Books, dolls & furnishings. **Hrs:** Wed-Sat
10-4:30, Sun-Tue by chance/appt. **QC: 18
38**

The Shops at One-Eleven
111 W St Louis St
(618)537-4162

Hrs: Wed-Sat 10-5, Sun-Tue by
chance/appt.

Leland

Leland Antiques & Collectibles
124 E Railroad
(815)495-9034

Hrs: Wed-Sun 11-5 (Jan-Feb by
chance/appt).

43

Lemont

Antique Parlour
316 Canal St
(630)257-0033

Victorian & country furniture in period room settings including 200+ chairs (pressbacks, windsors & balloonbacks), needlepoint, linen & lace, china, pressed glass, silverplate, jewelry, mirrors, frames, pictures, lampshades. **Hrs:** Wed-Sun 11-5. **Dir:** In a restored c 1928 Dodge Car showroom in picturesque Lemont. I-55 to Lemont Rd S Exit 271A 3.5 mi to downtown. **Own:** Fran & Bob Brindac.

Greta's Garret
408 Main St
(630)257-0021

Antiques, collectibles, art pottery, glass, jewelry, Lenox china, linens, jewelry, books. **Hrs:** Tue-Sat 11-4. **Own:** Greta Hayes.

Lemont Antiques [G]
228 Main St
(630)257-1318

Collectibles, furniture, china, glass, clocks, dolls, jewelry, linens, lamps, cookie jars, collector plates, Russian curios, primitives. Clock repair. **Hrs:** Daily 11-5. **QC: 32 S7**

Main Street Antique Emporium [G]
218-220 Main St
(630)257-3456

Antiques, collectibles, stamps, postcards, lamps, toy trains. **Hrs:** Daily 10-5. **Own:** Bill & Edie Montgomery. **QC: 48 86**

Myles Antiques
119 Stephen St
(630)243-1415

European & American furniture, home decorating accessories & Fenton glass. **Hrs:** Wed-Sun 10-4. **Own:** Samantha & Robert Myles. **QC: 48 61**

Lena

Quilted Treasures
209 E Main St
(815)369-9104

Quilts. **QC: 84**

Rebecca's Parlor Antiques
208 S Schuyler St
(815)369-4196

Glass, porcelain, collectibles. **Hrs:** Mon & Wed-Sun 10-5, Tue 10-2.

In the Fireplace II

Bottle-jack: A spring-driven mechanism for turning the spit introduced at the end of the 18th century. Named for its bottle-shaped case, which was usually made of brass. The mechanisms of spit-jacks and bottle-jacks were larger versions of those used in long-case clocks.

Chimney fan: A fan, fitted horizontally in the chimney that was turned by the rising heat. It turned the spit via a system of pulleys.

Chimney crane: A bracket of wrought iron or brass used to suspend a pot or tea kettle over an open fire. Originally from Scotland, where it is known as a swey, the crane is fixed to the wall and may come in a variety of sizes or with a device to raise, lower, or swing the pot to any position over the fire.

Trammel: A device for adjusting the height at which a pot hung over the fire. The adjustment was effected by either a peg fitting into a series of holes, or by a latch moved up and down a saw-toothed bar.

St Andrews Antiques

12075 W Oak St
(815)369-5207

Walnut, pine & original paint furniture.
Hrs: By chance/appt.

Libertyville

Armstrong's Country Connection

1757 N Milwaukee Ave
(847)816-8400

Furniture & Depression glass. **Hrs:** Mon-Sat 10-6, Sun 11-5.

Millennium Art & Antiques Gallery

541 N Milwaukee Ave
(847)918-8263

Primitive furniture, trunks, tools, boxes.
Hrs: Mon 11-5, Tue, Wed & Fri 10-6, Thu 10-7, Sat 10-5, Sun 11-4.

Neville-Sargent Gallery

406 N Milwaukee Ave
(847)680-1414 • (847)680-3366 (fax)

A gallery of constantly changing unique antiques & antique prints dating from the 1700s. Some contemporary original art as well as conservation framing services. Friendly & helpful staff. **Pr:** $15-4,000 **Est:** 1974 **Hrs:** Tue-Fri 11-6, Sat 10-5, Sun 12-4. **Sz:** M **CC:** AX/V/MC/DIS **Dir:** IL Tollway to Rte 176, W to IL 21 (or Milwaukee Ave), then R 2 blks. **Own:** Jane & Don Neville. **QC:** 7 48 74 S1 S9 S13

Use the Service QuickCode indexes at the back of the book to find restorers, appraisers, refinishers, and other specialty service providers.

The Old Garden

705 N Milwaukee Ave
(847)680-1114

Hrs: Tue-Sat 10-5. **QC: 60**

Lincolnshire

Rebecca Anne Antiques & Furniture

23346 N Milwaukee Ave
(847)634-2423

Armoires, buffets, hunt cabinets, back bars, dining & bedroom sets from Belgium, France, Germany & Holland. **Hrs:** Mon-Fri 10-6, Sat 10-5, Sun 12-5. **Dir:** I-294 Rte 22 Exit: 2-1/2 mi W, 1/4 mi N of Rte 22.

Phyllis Sibley Antiques

Milwaukee Ave
(847)634-9177

Glassware, furniture, lamps & fixtures. **Hrs:** By chance/appt. **QC: 61 48**

Lisle

Antique Bazaar Inc

924 Ogden Ave
(630)963-8282

Furniture, architectural & restoration services. **Hrs:** Mon-Sat 10-5 (Thu til 8), Sun 12-4. **QC: 48 3 S16**

Russian Shop (Maison Russe)

1720 Ogden Ave
(630)963-5160 • (630)963-5170 (fax)
russhop@mcs.com
www.mcs.com/~russhop

Maison Russe combines first-hand knowledge of Russia on the part of the parents, who came to the United States in 1949, with the American connoisseur perspective & business expertise of their American-born children. **Pr:** $10-1,000 **Est:** 1976 **Hrs:** Mon-Sat 10-5, Sun 1-4 **Sz:** M **CC:** AX/V/MC/DIS **Dir:** 1 mi from I-355 & 1 mi from I-88. **Own:** Vitaly Shukin. **QC: 11 87 41 S1 S19 S8**

Litchfield

Yesterday's Market & Chicken Coops Antique Mall [G57]

416 W Kirkham St
(217)324-4244 • (217)324-4784

Marbles, linens, bottles, books, art pottery & glass, toys, advertising, ephemera, furniture & more. **Pr:** $0.50-2,000 **Est:** 1985 **Hrs:** Daily 10-5. **Sz:** L **CC:** V/MC **Dir:** 50 mi SW of Springfield, IL, on I-55, E on IL 16 to Depot. S 1 blk. **Own:** Diane M Dudley. **QC: 1 39 S8**

Lockport

Ages Antiques, Collectibles, Etc

928 S State St
(815)838-8540

Hrs: Wed-Fri 1:30-4:30, Sat 11-5, Sun 12-4.

Antiques on State

901 S State St
(815)834-1974

Smalls & Victorian art glass. **Hrs:** Wed-Sat 11-5, Sun 12-4.

Canal House Antiques

905 S State St
(815)838-8551

18th & 19th C American furniture, folk art, hooked & braided rugs & accessories. **Hrs:** Wed-Sun 11-5. **Assn:** CSADA **Own:**

Rosemary Winters. **QC: 52 41 75**

Caroline's Antiques & Select Secondhand

103 E 10th St
(815)834-2999

Hrs: Tue-Sun 11-5 (Fri til 6).

Pastimes Cafe & Antiques

110 W 10th St
(815)834-0993

Hrs: Mon-Fri 6-3, Sat 10-5.

Station House Antique Mall [G60]

12305 W 159th St
(815)301-9400 • (708)301-9408 (fax)
www.southsidenet.com

Good selection of furniture, glassware, toys, lighting, jewelry & collectibles. **Pr:** $5-15,000 **Est:** 1995 **Hrs:** Daily 10-6. **Sz:** H **CC:** AX/V/MC/DIS **Dir:** I-80 to 96th Ave N to 159th St. W 3 mi. **Own:** Kris Hardy.

Long Grove

Bank Street Antiques

345 Old McHenry Rd
(847)634-0715

Antique English country pine furnishings, flow blue china, English pub signs, Torquay & many unusual accessories. **Dir:** Fountain Square. **QC: 55 22**

Carriage Trade

427 Coffin Rd
(847)634-3160

Pine furniture, oil paintings, rugs. **Hrs:** Tue-Sat 11-5.

The Emporium of Long Grove [G18]

Coffin Rd
(847)634-0188

Primitives to formal. **Hrs:** Daily 10-5. **Dir:** Mill Pond Blg.

Especially Maine Antiques
231 Robert Parker Coffin Rd
(847)634-3512

Estate gold & silver jewelry, pressed & cut glass, china, paintings & collectibles. **Est:** 1979 **Hrs:** Mon-Sat 10-5, Sun 11-5. **Own:** M Penney Welch.

Lyons

A Touch of Beauty, Brass & Lighting
7703 W Joliet Rd
(708)442-5535

Lighting, brass & hardware. **Hrs:** Call ahead for appt.

Mahomet

Olde Town Gallery
401 E Main St
(217)586-3211

Victoriana & primitives. **Hrs:** Mon-Sat 10-5, Sun 1-4. **QC: 89**

Victorian House
408 E Main St
(217)586-4834

Furniture. **Hrs:** Tue-Sat 10-5, Sun 12-5. **QC: 48**

Manhattan

Locker Plant Antiques
155 W North
815)478-5550

Furniture, Depression glass, pottery & crystal. **Hrs:** Sat-Sun 10-4.

Manteno

Darter's Antique Interiors
26 S Locust
815)468-3675

Furniture, hardware & stripping supplies. **Hrs:** Sat-Sun 12-5 or by appt.

Main Street Antiques
131 N Main St
(815)468-6486

Railroadiana, china & furniture. **Hrs:** Sat-Sun 1-4.

Manteno Antique Mall [G]
35 E Third St
(815)468-0114

Toys, primitives, furniture. **Hrs:** Daily 10-5.

Marion

Kerr's Antiques
213 N Hamlet
(618)993-6389

Victorian furniture & accessories. **Hrs:** By appt only. **QC: 58**

McHenry

The Crossroad Merchant [G6]
1328 N Riverside Dr
(815)344-2610
nrozee@juno.com

Victorian, primitive & country antique furniture, pottery, kitchenware, vintage clothing, jewelry, toys. Plus carefully selected goods to coordinate with antiques including lighting, dried florals, candles & cards. **Pr:** $1-2,000 **Est:** 1991 **Hrs:** Mon-Sat 10-4. **Sz:** M **CC:** V/MC/DIS **Dir:** I-90 Exit Rte 31 N to McHenry. R on Rte 120, then L on Riverside Dr (light before Fox River Bridge). **Own:** Nancy A Roozee. **QC: 34 48 80 S8 S12**

47

McLeansboro

Melba's Antiques
601 S Washington St
(618)643-3355
Furniture, dishes & crystal. **Hrs:** Tue-Sat 9-5.

Mendota

CB's Antiques
Rt 51
(815)539-5054
Hrs: Mon-Fri 9-2.

Heartland Treasures
714 Illinois Ave
(815)538-4402
Hrs: Mon-Sat 10-5, Sun 12-4.

Little Shop on the Prairie
702 Illinois Ave
(815)538-4408
Hrs: Mon-Sat 9-5.

Momence

Cal-Jean Antiques
127 E Washington
(815)472-2667
Hrs: Mon-Sat 9-5, Sun 12-5.

Days of Yesteryear
2076 N Rte 1
(815)472-4725
Antiques & collectibles. **Hrs:** Sat 10-5 & Sun 11-5.

Monroe Center

Paul Egeland
(815)393-4584
Country & formal furniture, lighting & nautical items. **Hrs:** By appt only. **Assn:** CSADA.

Morris

Allison's Cool Stuff
126 E Washington St
(815)941-2175
Hrs: Mon-Sat 9-5.

Judith Ann's
117-119 W Jackson
(815)941-2717
Hrs: Tue-Sat 10-5.

Morris Antique Emporium [G]
112 W Washington St
(815)941-0200
Furniture, clocks, jewelry, collectibles & glassware. **Hrs:** Mon-Fri 10-7 (Thu til 8), Sat 10-5, Sun 12-5. **QC: 48 35 61**

Repeat Boutique
124 E Washington St
(815)941-0253
Hrs: Mon-Sat 9-5, Sun 10-4.

Samantha Lynn's
117 W Washington St
(815)941-0366
Hrs: Mon-Sat 10-5.

Constantly Stitching n' More
13690 Lincoln Rd
(815)772-2833
Furniture, dishes, glassware & lighting. **Hrs:** Mon 12-9, Tue-Fri 10-5, Sat 10-4, Sun 12-4. **QC: 48 61**

Gallery on Main
112 E Main St
(815)772-4725
General line. **Hrs:** Mon-Fri 9-5 (closed Thu), Sat 9-2, Sun 9-5.

Morton Grove

Magazine Memories
6006 Dempster St
(847)470-9444

100,000 magazines, 10,000 posters, newspapers from 1740. **Hrs:** Mon-Fri 11-7, Sat 10-5, Sun 12-4. **QC: 39**

Mt Prospect

Chelsea Gallerie
129 W Prospect
(847)879-8332

Prints. **Hrs:** Tue-Fri 10-5, Sat 10-4. **QC: 74**

Mt Vernon

Flota's Antiques
901 S 10th St
(618)244-4877

1880s+ oak, walnut & cherry furniture, tools, books, china & lamps. **Hrs:** Mon-Sat 9-5 (closed Fri & Sun). **QC: 86 48**

Variety House Antiques
412 S 18th St
(618)242-4344

General line. **Hrs:** By chance/appt. **Dir:** Off Rte 15 (Broadway).

Murphysboro

As Time Goes By Antiques and Collectibles Mall [G]
1329 Walnut St
(618)687-3288

Gina's Antiques
1334 Walnut St
(618)687-2654

Furniture. **QC: 48**

Old & In The Way Antiques & Collectibles
1318 Walnut St
(618)687-3605

Pam's Jewelry
1601 Walnut St
(618)687-2590

Estate jewelry. **QC: 64**

Furniture Tops

Cornice: A flat, overhanging top on a tall piece of furniture, usually molded.

Pediment: An architectural element in the form of the shallow triangular end of a roof which was frequently applied to the cornices of bookcases, secretaries, and cabinets in the 18th century. More common in English than American furniture.

Broken pediment: A pediment where the apex of the triangle has been cut away to allow for a bust or finial to be set on a pedestal rising from the base of the triangle.

Bonnet top: A strongly curved pediment, shaped like a cupid's bow, and "broken" at the top to allow for a bust or finial, as in a broken pediment. Often the two broken ends are embellished with rosettes. In England, often called a "swan's neck" pediment because of its resemblance to two swans' necks. In English furniture the swan's neck pediment is frequently only a facade, whereas in America it often extends to the whole depth of the piece. Typically used on secretaries, highboys, chests on chests, and clocks.

Blind bonnet top: A bonnet top in which the space behind the central finial is closed by a vertical board.

Phoebe Jane's Antiques & Collectibles
1330 Walnut St
(618)684-5546

Virginia's Antiques
1204 Chestnut
(618)687-1194
virginia@globaleyes.net

China & glassware, furniture & silver. **Hrs:** Mon-Sat 10-5, Sun 1-5.

Naperville

Mary's Antique Mall [G]
34 W Jefferson Ave
(630)717-8899

Hrs: Mon-Sat 10-5, Sun 12-4.

Nana's Cottage
122 S Webster St, Suite 101
(630)357-5105

Hrs: Tue, Wed, Thu 10-4, Fri-Sat 10-5.

Riverwalk Lighting & Gifts
401 S Main St
(630)357-0200

Hrs: Mon-Fri 9:30-5:30 (Thu til 8), Sat 9-5.

New Minden

New Minden Antiques
367 N Main St
(618)478-5787

Furniture & smalls. **Hrs:** Daily 9-5. **QC: 48**

Newton

Country Seed House Antique Mall [G15]
604 E Jourdan
(618)783-4006

Hrs: Wed-Sat 10-5, Sun 12-5.

Niles

Antique Clock Shoppe
8043 N Milwaukee Ave
(847)965-2215

Hrs: Tue-Fri 11-6, Sat 11-3.

Northfield

Caledonian Inc
820 Frontage Rd
(847)446-6566 • (847)446-6569 (fax)
info@caledonianinc.com
www.caledonianinc.com

Celebrating 57 years as a premier purveyor of antique English furniture from the 17th, 18th & 19th C. Be it the grandeur of formal furniture or the warmth & charm of English country pieces, the same criteria of quality always apply. Decorating services. **Est:** 1941 **Hrs:** Tue-Sat 9-5, Mon by appt (closed Sun). **Sz:** H **CC:** AX/V/MC/DIS **Dir:** From I-94 N exit Willow Rd W. R at 1st light onto Central Ave to stop sign. L onto Frontage Rd. Shop is 3/4 mi on W side. From I-94 S exit Tower Rd. Shop is in front of exit. **Own:** Barrie T Heath. **QC: 54 36 56 S15 S17 S16**

Crost Furniture & Imports
1799 Willow Rd
(847)501-2550

Direct importer from England & Ireland. Furniture & smalls. **Hrs:** Mon-Fri 9:30-5, Sat 9-5:30. **CC:** V/MC **QC: 48**

Town & Country Antiques
310 S Happ Rd
(847)501-4902

Home to Circa Antiques Ltd & Rare Finds Ltd: Victorian, Edwardian, Art Nouveau jewelry. English antique accessories, flow blue, majolica & silver. Imported fine antique smallwares, fireplace furnishings, Victorian bamboo furniture. **Hrs:** Mon-Fri 11-5, Sat 11-4. **QC: 5 23 36**

Northlake

Cupid's Antiques
32 E North Ave
708)531-0333
Hrs: Tue, Thu, Fri & Sat 10-5, Sun 12-5.

Oak Lawn

Browsatorium Inc
505 S Cook Ave
708)423-0287 • (708)423-8955

Antiques, appraisals & refinishing. Hrs:
Mon-Sat 10-5, Sun 11:30-4. Assn: ASA
Own: Hilda M & Jeffery R Breuer.

Shirley's Antiques
650 S Pulaski Rd
708)499-2300

Furniture & a general line. Hrs: Tue-Sat
10-5.

Oak Park

Antiques Etc [G23]
25 N Marion St
708)386-9194

Furniture (Mission, French, Victorian,
Deco); art (old etchings, lithos, modern &
contemporary paintings, serigraphs); art
pottery (Roseville, McCoy, Van Briggle);
jewelry (fine & costume, Victorian, Deco,
contemporary); books, vintage clothing &
more. Pr: $1-10,000 Est: 1996 Sz: L CC:
V/MC/DIS Dir: 1 blk SE of intersection of
Harlem & Lake. Own: Jagna Schwartz. QC:
8 32 36

The Gold Hatpin / The Jewelry Studio
25 N Marion St
708)445-0610 • (708)848-3247
708)383-6396 (fax)

Specializing in fine antique & estate jewelry
including diamond, ruby, sapphire & other
gemstones, Mexican silver, Bakelite & costume. Also carry ladies' & gentlemen's
accessories. Pr: $10-10,000 Est: 1986 Hrs:
Apr-Dec Mon-Fri 11-7 (Mon & Thu til 8),
Sat 10-5, Sun 12-5. Jan-Mar Mon-Fri 11-6,
Sat 11-5, Sun 12-5. Sz: S CC: V/MC/DIS
Dir: I-290 exit Harlem Ave: N 1/2 mi to
North Blvd, then R 1 blk to Marion. L into
parking lot. Inside Antiques Etc. Own:
Diane Richardson & Llyn Longwell. QC:
64 78 6 S16

Kellar & Kellar
105 S Ridgeland Ave
(708)848-2882

Art glass, furniture, ceramics & prints. Hrs:
By chance/appt. QC: 48 74 S1

Treasures & Trinkets
600 Harrison Ave
(708)848-9142
Hrs: Mon-Fri 10-3, Sat 10-4.

Odin

Lincoln Trail Antiques
US Hwy 50
(618)775-8255

Direct importer from Europe. Pine furniture, pottery & glassware. Hrs: Mon-Sat 9-
5. CC: V/MC/DIS Dir: In front of water
tower. QC: 55 61

Oregon

Silo Antiques & Art Gallery [G]
1490 N IL Rte 2
(815)732-4042

Furniture, smalls & Depression glass. Hrs:
Daily 10-5.

51

Orland Park

Beacon Hill Antiques [G]
14314 S Beacon Ave
(708)460-8433 • (708)460-7970

Furniture & smalls. **Hrs:** Mon-Sat 10:30-5, Sun 12:30-5.

Cracker Barrel Antiques
9925 W 143rd Pl
(708)403-2221

American & European furniture & decorative accessories. **Hrs:** Daily 11-5. **CC:** V/MC **Dir:** 1 blk W of Beacon.

Emporium Antique Shop [G5]
143322 Beacon Ave
(708)460-5440

Vintage jewelry, glassware, furniture & collectibles. **Hrs:** Mon-Sat 10:30-5, Sun 12:30-5. **QC: 61 48**

Favorite Things
14329 S Beacon Ave
(708)403-1908

Hrs: Mon-Sat 10:30-5, Sun 12:30-5.

The General Store [G]
14314 S Union Ave
(708)349-9802

Hrs: Mon-Sat 10:30-5, Sun 12:30-5.

The Old Bank Antiques [G]
14316 S Beacon Ave
(708)460-7979

Jewelry, glass & collectibles. **Hrs:** Mon-Sat 10:30-5, Sun 12:30-5.

The Old Homestead
14330 Beacon Ave
(708)460-9096

Victorian & country furniture. **Hrs:** Mon-Sat 10:30-5, Sun 12:30-5.

Kay Shelander Antiques & Appraisers
14314 S Beacon Ave
(708)460-7980

Furniture & reference books. **Hrs:** Mon-Sat 10:30-5, Sun 12:30-5.

Oswego

Bob's Antique Toys & Collectibles
23 W Jefferson St
(630)554-3234

Toys. **Hrs:** Tue-Thu 10-5, Fri & Sat 10-4, Sun 12-4. **QC: 87**

Old Oak Creek Shoppes
4025 US Hwy 34
(630)554-3218

Furniture. **Hrs:** Mon-Sat 10-2:30. **CC:** V/MC/DIS **Dir:** Corner of Rte 34 & Rte 71. **QC: 48**

Oswego Antiques Market
Rt 34 & Main St
(630)554-3131

Art glass, dolls, lamps, furniture, jewelry, toys, clocks, Depression glass, linens, flow blue, coins & currency. **Hrs:** Mon-Sat 10-5, Sun 11-5. **QC: 48 38 33 S11**

Pennington Ltd
25 Jefferson St
(630)554-3311

Antique & estate jewelry. **Hrs:** Mon-Sat 10-5 (closed Fri), Sun 12-4. **QC: 64 S1 S16**

Use the Specialty QuickCode indexes at the back of the book to find dealers who specialize in your area of interest.

Regal Antiques [G10]
72 S Main
(630)554-3131
General line. **Hrs:** Mon-Sat 10-5, Sun 11-5.
CC: V/MC/DIS.

Palatine

A Matter of Time
25 N Brockway
(847)359-1810
Clocks, watches & music boxes. **Hrs:** Tue-Sat 10-5, Sun 12-5. **QC: 35**

Palatine Antique Center [G]
23 E Northwest Hwy
(847)359-9771
Collectibles, furniture & vintage clothing.
Hrs: Tue-Sat 10-5, Sun 12-5. **Dir:** On Rte 14, behind the Bank of Palatine.

Park Ridge

Boom Gallery
146 Northwest Hwy
(847)825-1411
Baby boomer collectibles **Hrs:** Mon-Fri 11-6, Sat 10:30-6, Sun 12-4. **QC: 32**

Jade Butterfly Antiquities
(847)825-6458
Chinese & Japanese art & antiques. **Hrs:** By appt only. **Own:** Dorothy Wallace. **QC: 71 S1**

June Moon Collectibles
245 N Northwest Hwy
(847)825-1411 • (847)825-6090 (fax)
junmoonstr@aol.com
www.junemooncollectibles.com
Specializing in baby boomer collectibles & fine antiques including toys, records, jewelry, pottery, china, glass, autographs & paintings. **Pr:** $3-900 **Est:** 1988 **Hrs:** Tue-Fri 12-6, Sat 12-5, Sun 12-3. **Sz:** M **CC:** AX/V/MC **Dir:** 3 mi E of II-294 Touhy East. 3 mi N of I-94 Cumberland N exit. 10 min from

O'Hare Airport. **Own:** Nancy Frugoli. **QC: 87 32 S12**

Pearl City

Circle H Farm Antiques
65 Hwy 73 N
(815)443-2917
General line. **Hrs:** By chance/appt.

Sew Many Antiques
160 S Main St
(815)443-2211
Hrs: Mon, Wed, Fri 11-7, Tue & Thu 3:30-7, Sat 10-5, Sun 11-5.

Pecatonica

Antiques at Hillwood Farms
498 N Farwell Bridge Rd
(815)239-2421
18th & 19th C American antiques, most in original surface. **Pr:** $25-12,000 **Est:** 1971 **Hrs:** Wed-Sun (call ahead advised). **Sz:** M **Assn:** NIADA **Dir:** I-90 Rockford Exit: 22 mi W on Rte 20. **Own:** Marion Atten. **QC: 51 34 52 S18**

Ghost Town Antiques
US Rte 20
(815)239-1188
Hrs: By chance/appt. **Dir:** Between Rockford & Freeport.

Roberta's Antiques
418 Main St
(815)239-1023
Furniture, primitives, kitchen. **Hrs:** Wed-Sat 10-4.

Peoria

Abe's Antiques
2001 N Wisconsin Ave
(309)682-8181
American antiques. **Hrs:** Tue-Sat 11-4, Sun 1-4. **CC:** V/MC/DIS **QC: 1**

Backdoor Antiques & Collectibles [L]
725 SW Washington St
(309)637-3446
Hrs: Mon-Fri 11-4:30, Sat 9-5, Sun 12-5.

Illinois Antique Center [G250+]
308 SW Commercial St
(309)673-3354
Antiques & collectibles from 1800-1970s. No crafts or reproductions. **Hrs:** Mon-Sat 9-5 (Thu til 8), Sun 12-5.

Plainfield

Bringing Back the Years
23364 Lincoln Hwy (Rte 30)
(815)439-7316
Hrs: Mon-Sat 10-5, Sun 11-5.

On the Sunny Side of the Street Antiques
515 W Lockport St
(815)436-1342
Hrs: Tue-Thu & Sat 10-5, Fri 12-5, Sun 11-5.

Plainfield Antique Mart
502 W Lockport Rd
(815)436-1778
Hrs: Mon-Sat 10-6, Sun 11-5.

R & S Antiques
23364 Lincoln Hwy (Rte 30)
Hrs: Daily 10-5.

Pontiac

Old City Hall Shoppes [G18]
321 N Main St
(815)842-1343
General line. **Hrs:** Tue-Sat 10-5, Sun 11-4. **CC:** V/MC.

Princeton

Antiques & Collectibles Village
1665 N Main St
(815)879-7027
Hrs: Daily 9-9.

Hoffman's Pattern of the Past
513 S Main St
(815)875-1944
Hrs: Mon-Sat 9-5.

Midtown Antique Mall [G60]
105 S Main St
(815)872-3435
Hrs: Mon-Sat 10-7, Sun 10-5.

Princeton Antique Center
432 S Main St
(815)875-1363 • (815)872-5031
Hrs: Daily 9-8.

Sherwood Antique Mall [G]
1661 N Main St (Rt 26)
(815)872-2580
Hrs: Daily 9-9.

Quincy

Old Town Antiques
1883 Jersey
(217)223-2963
Early furniture & smalls. **Hrs:** Mon-Sat 9-5, Sun 12-5. **Dir:** Corner 20th & Hampshire.

Yester Year Antique Mall [G50]
615 Maine St
(217)224-1871
yyam@rnet.com
Hrs: Mon-Fri 10-7. **CC:** V/MC/DIS.

Red Bud

Blossom City Antiques
131 N Main St
(618)282-3000

Furniture, glassware, dishes, jewelry & lamps. **Hrs:** Daily 10:30-5:30. **CC:** V/MC/DIS **QC: 48 61**

Richmond

The 1905 Emporium [G9]
Broadway & Main Sts
(815)678-4414

Glassware, jewelry, advertising, country store items. **Hrs:** Daily 10:30-5. **CC:** V/MC/DIS **Dir:** 1 mi S of Rtes 12 & 173.

Antiques on Broadway
Broadway & Main Sts (Rte 12)
(815)678-7951

Refinished furniture including dining room sets, bedroom sets & accessory pieces in oak, walnut, pine & mahogany. **Hrs:** Tue-Sat 11-5, Sun 12-5. **Own:** Chuck Hollenbach. **QC: 48**

Ed's Antiques
10321 Main St (Rte 12)
(815)678-2911

Hrs: Tue-Sat 10:30-5, Sun 12-5.

Happy House Antiques
5604 Broadway St
(815)678-4076

Watches, jewelry, clocks. **Hrs:** Daily 10:30-5.

Hiram's Uptown
5613 Broadway St
(815)678-4166

Hrs: Daily 10:30-5.

Kathleen's Lasting Treasures
5614 Broadway St
(815)678-4884

Hrs: Wed-Sun 12-5. **Own:** Kathleen Kelly-Meyer.

Little Bit Antiques
5603 Broadway St
(815)678-4218

Hrs: Daily 10:30-5.

The Olde Bank Antiques
5611 Broadway St
(815)678-4839

General line. **Hrs:** Daily 11-5 (Mon-Tue by chance in Win).

The Rose Peddler's Wife & Co
10315 N Main St
(815)678-3802

Vintage linens & clothing, estate & costume jewelry. **Hrs:** Tue-Sun.

Serendipity Shop
9818 Main St
(815)678-4141

Hrs: Tue-Sun 10-5.

Ridgefield

Antiques & Art Unlimited
4120 Country Club Rd
(815)356-9698

Hrs: Wed-Sun 11-4.

Aurora's Antiques [G10]
8404 Railroad St
(815)455-0710

Furniture, collectibles & primitives. **Hrs:** Daily 11-5.

Eclectic Etc
4112 Country Club Rd
(815)356-3920

Hrs: Thu-Sun 11-4.

Postal Station [G10]

4124 Country Club Rd
(815)455-1834
Hrs: Daily 11-4.

Railroad Street Market [G7]

8316 Railroad St
(815)459-4220

Country furniture & architectural artifacts.
Hrs: Wed-Sun 11-4. **QC: 48 3**

Riverside

Arcade Antiques & Jewelers

25 Forest Ave
(708)442-8110

Art glass, lamps, jewelry & bronze. **Hrs:**
Tue-Sat 11-5, Sun 12-4.

JP Antiques

36 East Ave
(708)442-6363

Eclectic antiques, smalls & collectibles. **Hrs:**
Tue-Sat 11-5, Sun 12-4.

Riverside Antique Market [G]

30 East Ave
(708)447-4425

Collectibles & smalls. **Hrs:** Mon-Sat 11-5,
Sun 12-4.

Rock Falls

Rock River Antique Center [G150+]

2105 E Rte 30
(815)625-2556 • (815)625-4868 (fax)

Great selection of furniture, lamps,
Victoriana, art, primitives & smalls. Monthly
outdoor flea markets last weekend of month
Apr-Sep. All one level. No crafts. **Pr:** $2-
55,000 **Est:** 1996 **Hrs:** Mon-Sat 10-5, Sun
12-5. **Sz:** H **CC:** AX/V/MC **Dir:** 1/2 mi off
I-88 or 1-1/4 mi E of Rte 40. **Own:** Teresa

Colley & Wayne Wright. **QC: 48 65 34
S12 S8 S10**

Rockford

Alouette

510 E State St
(815)966-8980

Antiques, collectibles, vintage clothing,
Scandinavian antiques. **Hrs:** Daily. **QC: S2**

Blue Clover Antiques

1328 Camp Ave
(815)964-1945

Flow blue china & ironstone. **Hrs:** By appt
or mail order. **Assn:** NIADA **Own:** Bill
Byers & William Miller. **QC: 22**

Chris' Antiques

5152 Harlem Rd
(815)654-1610

Country & primitives. **Hrs:** Mon-Sat 11-4.

Collin's Antiques

1012 Old Ralston Rd
(815)633-2875

Pine, oak & walnut furniture. **Hrs:** Mon-Fri
10-5, Sat-Sun by chance.

Copper Fish Galleries

402 E State St
(815)965-9221

Art, antiques, jewelry. **Hrs:** Mon-Fri 11-6,
Sat 9-6.

Eagle's Nest Antiques

7080 Old River Rd
(815)633-8410

Country furniture — refinished, rough &
original paint; eastern decorated stoneware;
country store, advertising & unusual decorative accessories. **Hrs:** By chance/appt (closed
Jul). **Assn:** NIADA **Dir:** 3 mi N of Rockford
1/2 mi off Rte 2. **Own:** Todd Franke. **QC:
48 31**

East State Street Antiques Mall I [G150+]

5411 E State St
(815)229-4004

China, pottery, jewelry, Depression glass, advertising, slot machines, trains, pianos, furniture, vintage clothing, light fixtures, radios, coins, toys, dolls, guns, clocks, books, games, hardware, plumbing fixtures, record players, juke boxes. **Hrs:** Daily 10-9. **Sz:** H.

East State Street Antiques Mall II [G150+]

5301 E State St
(815)226-1566

China, pottery, jewelry, Depression glass, advertising, slot machines, trains, pianos, furniture, vintage clothing, light fixtures, radios, coins, toys, dolls, guns, clocks, books, games, hardware, plumbing fixtures, record players, juke boxes. **Hrs:** Daily 10-9. **Sz:** H.

Forgotten Treasures

4610 E State St
(815)229-0005

Country to Victorian furniture including finished pine & original paint, country accessories, baskets, quilts. **Hrs:** Mon-Fri 10:30-6, Sat 10-5. **Sz:** L **Assn:** NIADA **Own:** Cheryl & Terry Walker. **QC: 48**

Homestead Antiques

3712 N Central Ave
(815)962-7498

Country furniture & primitives. **Hrs:** By chance/appt. **QC: 34**

Flo Jacobs Antiques

4512 E State St
(815)398-3875

Hrs: Sat, Sun & Wed 1:30-5.

Barbara A Johnson Antiques

7801 E State St
(815)397-6699

American & Scandinavian country furniture. Painted & decorated mora clocks, textiles, copper & other accessories in room settings. **Hrs:** Daily 10-5. **Assn:** CSADA NIADA **Own:** Barbara & Fred Johnson. **QC: 48 36**

Randee & John Malmberg

712 Green Meadow Ave
(815)226-8343

Early American country painted furniture, folk art & accessories. **Hrs:** By appt only. **Assn:** CSADA NIADA. **QC: 51 41**

Lighting and Dowsing Candles

Tinder: Dry flammable material such as scorched cotton designed to be ignited easily by a spark from a flint. Sometimes this happened. More often, particularly if the tinder was more than a day or two old, ignition was chancy, rarely instantaneous, and frequently frustrating.

Flint: A sliver of flint stone held in the striker.

Tinderbox: A box holding tinder, flint, and steel striker.

Tinderbottomed: A type of candleholder, usually tin, whose base is a tinderbox.

Candle snuffers: Implements used to trim the wick when a candle started smoking. They resemble scissors fitted with a small box to catch the trimmed wick. Introduced about 1725, they were made first of iron and later of silver or brass. They often stand on small trays, or, more rarely, fit vertically into elaborate holders. They range from simple, functional household tools to elaborate objects of ostentation. To snuff, we should note, originally meant to trim not to extinguish.

Candle dowser or candlecone: A conical device on a handle for extinguishing candles. Candlecones are often hung on hooks fitted to the handles of chambersticks.

New Mill Antiques
6583 11th St
(815)874-8853

Furniture, glassware, kitchen. **Hrs:** Sat-Sun 12-5.

Peddler's Attic
2609 Charles St
(815)962-8842

Vintage clothing. **Hrs:** Mon-Sat 11-5.

Rolander's Antiques
6130 Guilford Rd
(815)397-1917

Direct importers of English country pine furniture, grandfather clocks & accessories. **Hrs:** By appt only. **Assn:** WADA **Own:** Mary & Dick Rolander. **QC: 55 35**

Vintage Adventure
403 11th St
(815)227-1892

Vintage clothing. **Hrs:** Wed-Sat 12-7. **QC: 83**

Rockton

The Big D's Antiques & Vintage Fashions
110 N Blackhawk Blvd
(815)624-6300

Antiques & collectibles, vintage clothing, jewelry, linens, glassware, silver, toys, furniture, books on antiques & collectibles, old books & records, pictures, "odds 'n' ends." **Pr:** $15-100 **Est:** 1957 **Hrs:** Mon-Sat (closed Sun). **Sz:** H **CC:** V/MC **Dir:** I-90 exit at

Rockton Rd. Near WI border. **Own:** Duane J Short & Don L Rubel. **QC: 19 63 83**

Nichols Antique Shop
212 W Main St
(815)624-4137

General line. **Hrs:** Daily 10-5.

Sadorus

Antique & Curiosity Shop
101 S Vine St
(217)598-2200

Furniture, glassware, silverplate matching & linens. **Hrs:** Thu-Sat 10-5. **QC: 48 61 81**

Saint Joseph

I-74 Antique Mall [G]
302 Northgate
(217)469-7464
bobt@net66.com

Hrs: Mon-Sat 10-5, Sun 12-5. **CC:** V/MC/DIS.

Sandwich

Antique Central [G]
Rt 34 & Dayton St
(815)786-2180

Hrs: Daily 10-7.

Grace Carolyn Dahlberg
1110 N Latham St
(815)786-1890

Sandwich Antiques Market [G550+]
Rte 34
(815)227-4464
www.antiquemarkets.com

Over 500 exhibitors, all merchandise guaranteed, furniture delivery service available. Free parking. Admission $4 per person. Food. **Est:** 1987 **Hrs:** Call for schedule. **Dir:** At the Fairgrounds.

Sandwich Antique Mall [G]
108 N Main St
(815)786-7000

Hrs: Mon-Sat 10-5, Sun 12-5.

Savanna

Pulford Opera House Mall [G120]
Great River Rd (Rte 84)
(815)273-2661

Hrs: Oct-May Mon-Sat 10:30-5:30 (Fri-Sat til 8), Sun 11-6; Jun-Sep Mon-Sat 9:30-8. **Sz:** H.

Schaumburg

The Estate Inc
N-133 Woodfield Mall (Golf Rd)
(847)517-7750 • (847)517-7750 (fax)

Fine estate jewelry, antiques & objets d'art. **Hrs:** Mon-Fri 10-9, Sat 10-7, Sun 11-6. **Assn:** ISA **QC:** 64 S1

Skokie

Ashley Loren Antiques
4550 Oakton St
(847)679-9494

Fine furniture & decorative & fine art. **Hrs:** Mon-Sat 11-5, Sun 12-4. S8

Prestige Art Galleries Inc
3909 W Howard St
(847)674-2555
prestige@prestigeart.com
www.prestigeart.com

One of the largest collections of beautiful romantic European (French, Dutch, English) antique paintings on the North side of Chicago. Professional third-generation ISA appraisal services, restorations, graphic broker & custom framing. **Pr:** $500-150,000 **Est:** 1963 **Hrs:** Mon-Wed 10-5, Sat-Sun 11-5, Thu-Fri by appt. **Sz:** L **CC:** V/MC **Assn:**

ISA **Dir:** I-94 exit Touhy E to Crawford. L (N) to Howard, R (E) 1/2 blk. **Own:** Louis Schutz. **QC:** 7 74 5 S1 S16 S13

Somonauk

Country Corners Antiques
100 S Depot St
(815)498-1105

Hrs: Mon-Fri 9-4 (closed Wed), Sat & Sun 11-5.

Harmon's Attic
115 W Rte 34
(815)498-9533

Hrs: Mon-Sat 10-4 (closed Wed), Sun 11-3.

House of 7 Fables
300 E Dale St
(815)498-2289

American country furniture, glass, textiles, lamps, pottery, baskets, toys. **Hrs:** Daily 9-5, call ahead advised. **Assn:** CSADA **Own:** M A Shaw. **QC:** 48 61 81

Springfield

Abe's Tradin' Post
2704 Peoria Rd
(217)753-2237

Collectibles & primitives. **Hrs:** Daily 9:30-5:30. **CC:** V/MC **Dir:** E of Fairgrounds.

The Barrel Antique Mall [G125]
5850 S 6th St Rd
(217)585-1438

Hrs: Daily 9:30-5:30. **CC:** V/MC **Dir:** Rte 55 exit 90.

Eastnor Gallery of Antiques
700 E Miller
(217)523-0998

18th & 19th C furniture. **Est:** 1975 **Hrs:** Tue-Sat 11-4. **CC:** V/MC **Assn:** ISA.

Old Georgian Antique Mall [G37]
9th at S Grand
(217)753-8110

Furniture, jewelry & primitives. **Hrs:** Mon-Sat 10-4, Sun 12-4. **CC:** V/MC/DIS **QC:** 48

Pasttime Antiques
6279 N Walnut
(217)487-7200

Primitive furniture. **Hrs:** Tue-Sat 10-5, Sun by appt. **QC:** 48

St Charles

American International
221 W Main St
(630)584-3112

Antique Emporium
10 S Third St
(630)443-6570

Glass, pottery, linens, textiles, furniture, tools. **Hrs:** Daily 10-5. **Own:** Bob Hines, Jane Hoban, Don Jobe & Terri Johnson. **QC:** 34

Antique Market I [G50+]
11 N Third St
(630)377-1868

Art & Depression glass, pottery, porcelain, country to formal furniture, tin, sterling, jewelry, Art Deco, primitives, books & ephemera, prints & paintings, rugs, dolls, toys, linens, quilts, textiles, tools, vintage clothing & collectibles. **Hrs:** Daily 10-5 **Sz:** L **CC:** V/MC.

Antique Market II [G50+]
301-303 W Main St
(630)377-5798

Art & Depression glass, pottery, porcelain, country to formal furniture, tin, sterling, jewelry, Art Deco, primitives, books & ephemera, prints & paintings, rugs, dolls, toys, linens, quilts, textiles, tools, vintage clothing & collectibles. **Hrs:** Daily 10-5. **Sz:** L **CC:** V/MC.

Antique Market III [G80]
413 W Main St
(630)377-5599

Art & Depression glass, pottery, porcelain, country to formal furniture, tin, sterling, jewelry, Art Deco, primitives, books & ephemera, prints & paintings, rugs, dolls, toys, linens, quilts, textiles, tools, vintage clothing & collectibles. **Hrs:** Daily 10-5.

The Art Shoppe
211 W Main St
(630)443-4086

Brown Beaver Antiques
219 W Main St
(630)443-9430

Brass & iron beds, furniture. **Hrs:** Tue-Sat 11-5.

Consign Tiques
15 S Third St
(630)584-7535

Cottage Interiors
210 Cedar Ave
(630)377-6844

Primitives & pine furniture. **Hrs:** Tue-Sat 10-5.

Fritz Gallery
404 S Second St
(630)584-5131

La Vie en Rose
11 N 2nd Ave
(630)377-9770

Antiques & accessories. **Hrs:** Mon & Wed-Sat 10-5.

The Market
12 N Third St
(630)584-3899

Old Stone House Shops
20 N Second Ave
(630)377-6406

Vintage fabrics, garden & architectural.
Hrs: Mon-Sat 10-5, Sun 12-4.

Pariscope
116 Cedar Ave
(630)513-8979 • (630)513-8993 (fax)

Out-of-the-ordinary antique furnishings,
garden accessories & fun finds from Parisian
flea markets. **Pr:** $5-8,000 **Hrs:** Wed-Sat 10-
5. **CC:** AX/V/MC **Dir:** On E side of Rover,
2 blks W of Rte 25, 1 blk N of Rte 64. **Own:**
Madeline Roth. **QC: 47 36 60 S15**

Riverside Antiques
410 S First St
(630)377-7730

St Charles Antiques Shoppe
113 E Main St
(630)443-7414

Antiques, fine collectibles & home decor.
Hrs: Wed-Sat 10-5, Sun 12-5, Tue by
chance/appt.

Shrivenhan Antiques Co
125 N Eleventh Ave
(630)584-5843

Importers of European antiques including
armoires in pine, walnut, oak & mahogany
from England & France, painted pieces from
Germany. Buffets, tables, chairs, hall stands,
stained glass & collectibles from 1780-
1940s. **Hrs:** Wed-Sun 11-5. **Sz:** H **CC:**
AX/V/MC/DIS **QC: 48**

St Charles Resale Shoppe
111 W Main St
(630)513-0244

Hrs: Daily.

Studio Posh
17 N 2nd Ave
(630)443-0227

Garden & architectural. **Hrs:** Wed-Sat 10-
5, Sun 12-5. **QC: 3 60**

The Warehouse Antiques
16 N First Ave
(630)584-6368

The What Not Shoppe
106 E Main St
(630)587-8750

European antiques, vintage & estate jewelry.
Hrs: Tue-Sat 10-5, Sun 11-5.

St Joseph

The Village Shoppe
228 Lincoln St
(217)469-8836

Furniture & primitives. **Hrs:** Tue-Sat 10-5,
Sun 12-5, Mon by chance/appt. **QC: 48**

Steger

Now & Then Shops
3725-29 Chicago Rd (Rte 1)
(708)755-9591

Hrs: Tue-Sat 10:30-4:30, Sun 12-4.

Sterling

American Heritage Antique Center
202 First Ave
(815)622-3000

Victorian walnut furniture. **Hrs:** Mon-Sat
10-5, Sun 12-5. **QC: 58**

Stockton

Tredegar Antique Market [G25]
208 E North Ave (US Rte 20)
(815)947-2360 • (815)858-2452 (fax)

A wide selection of smalls, pottery, glassware
& primitives. **Pr:** $5-1,000 **Hrs:** Thu-Tue
10-5, Wed 12-5. **Sz:** L **Dir:** 30 min E of
Dubuque, IA, on Rte 20. **Own:** Miles Breed.
QC: 22 34 36

Sycamore

Bygone Era Inc
249 W State St
(815)895-6538

Hrs: Mon-Sat 9-5:30 (Mon, Thu & Fri til 9), Sun 12-4.

The Humble Peddler
1210 E State St
(815)899-5095

Hrs: Daily by chance/appt.

Storeybook Antiques & Books
1325 E State St (Hwy 64)
(815)895-5910

Hrs: By chance/appt.

Taylor Springs

Back When Antique & Collectible Mall
Rte 127 (S Hilsboro)
(618)283-3610

Primitives, toys, tools & petroliana. **Hrs:** Mon-Sat 10-5, Sun 1-5 (closed Tue). **QC:** 87 86

Tuscola

Prairie Sisters Antique Mall [G]
102 W Sale St
(217)253-5211

General line. **Hrs:** Mon-Thu 9-5, Fri 9-6, Sat 9-4 (closed Sun). **CC:** V/MC/DIS.

Utica

Blue Heron Antiques
106 Mill St
(815)667-4325

Textiles, furniture, jewelry, art glass,

Depression & crocks. **Hrs:** Sat 10-5, Sun 12-5. **QC: 80 61**

Vandalia

Cuppy's Antique Mall [G19]
Gallatin St
(618)283-0080

General line. **Hrs:** Mon-Sat 10-5. **CC:** V/MC.

Treasure Cove Antique Mall [G30]
302 W Gallatin
(618)283-8704

General line. **Hrs:** Mon-Sat 10-5, Sun 12:30-5. **CC:** V/MC.

Vienna

From The Past Antiques
118 N 4th St
(618)658-2097

General line. **Hrs:** Thu-Sat 10-4.

Villa Park

Astorville Antiques
51 S Village Ave
(630)279-5311

Restored & refinished turn-of-the-century oak & Victorian walnut furniture, accessories & linens. **Pr:** $5-3,000 **Est:** 1993 **Hrs:** Wed-Fri 12-5, Sat 11-4. **Sz:** M **CC:** V/MC/DIS **Dir:** 1st light W of Rte 83 & 1 blk S of St Charles Rd. **Own:** Sandra S Dollinger. **QC: 50 58 49**

Volo

Portobello Road Antiques

27616 W Rte 120
(815)385-6707
Hrs: Daily 11-5.

Volo Antique Malls [G300]

Volo Village Rd
(815)344-6062

Three malls. **Hrs:** Daily 10-5. **Sz:** H **Dir:** At Rte 12 & 120, exit Volo Village Rd. **Own:** Carolyn Grams, Mgr. **QC: 90**

Warrenville

Elizabeth J Antiques at Butterfield Garden Center

29W036 Butterfield Rd
(630)393-1062

Hrs: Mon-Sat 10-5, Sun 10-4.

Lil' Red Schoolhouse Antiques [G14]

3 S 463 Batavia Rd
(630)969-4620

In Warrenville's first schoolhouse, built in 1836, antiques & collectibles at reasonable prices. **Est:** 1981 **Hrs:** Mon-Sat 10-5, Sun 11-5 (closed Xmas & Easter). **CC:** V/MC **Dir:** I-88 Winfield Rd exit: N to Warrenville Rd, then L to Batavia Rd. R on Batavia. Shop is 3rd bldg on R. **Own:** Louise Collins & Marge Bradshaw. **QC: 22 48 80 S8**

Route 59 Antique Mall [G60]

3 S 450 Rte 59
(630)393-0100

The premier mall in Chicago's western suburbs. Excellent selection of furniture, home accents, primitives & more. **Pr:** $1-1,000 **Est:** 1996 **Hrs:** Mon-Sat 10-5, Sun 11-5. **Sz:** H **CC:** V/MC/DIS **Dir:** I-88 exit Rte 59: 1 mi N, just S of Butterfield Rd. **QC: 67 69 1 S12**

Joiners, Turners & Cabinetmakers

Joiner: A 17th century carpenter who made houses, barns, wagons, ships, caskets, and furniture. He used the same woodworking techniques for all projects and relied largely on the pinned mortise-and-tenon joint, though, when he had to join planks, as in drawers, he would rabbet and nail them. By the end of the century, he began to use large, crude dovetails in drawer fronts. Almost all American "joined," or "joynt," furniture was made in New England.

Arkwright: A maker of arks, or chests in medieval England. The earliest term for a furniture maker, sometimes used interchangeably with joiner.

Turner: An early craftsman who worked on a lathe. Before about 1700, furniture was all joined and/or turned (sometimes called "thrown"). The earliest chairs were either wainscot (joined) or thrown (turned).

Wainscot: A high-quality oak used in making wagons, ships, and houses. Wainscoting was paneling made by a joiner. A thin piece of board was set into grooves in a frame made of mortised-and-tenoned "stiles" (vertical) and "'rails" (horizontal). The board could move within the grooves, and thus could accommodate the swelling and shrinking caused by humidity and temperature changes, or the movement of a wagon or ship. Wainscot panels are found on chests, cupboards, chair backs, beds, and walls.

Cabinetmaker: A specialist furniture maker who rapidly displaced the joiner beginning around 1700. His work is characterized by the dovetail joint (which is not used in making houses, ships, or wagons).

63

Waterloo

Echoes of the Past Antiques
116 E Third St
(618)939-6160

Victorian & primitive furniture, dishes & glassware. **Hrs:** Tue-Fri 10-5, Sat 9-4. **Dir:** Across from the courthouse. **QC: 58**

Waterman

Country Mill Square — Looking Back Antiques and Collectibles
140 W Lincoln Hwy
(815)264-7771

Hrs: Daily 10-5 (closed Tue).

Whistlestop Antique Shoppe [G]
248 W Lincoln Hwy
(815)264-9003

Hrs: Daily 10-5 (closed Tue).

Watseka

Watseka Antique Mall [G60+]
1790 E Walnut St
(815)432-2280

Hrs: Mon-Sat 10-5, Sun 12-5. **CC:** V/MC.

Wauconda

Tin Horse Antiques
451 W Liberty St (Rte 176)
(847)487-7973

Furniture, primitives, antiques, collectibles, pottery. **Hrs:** Mon-Sat 10:30-5, Sun 1-5. **Dir:** 2 blks E of Rte 12.

Whippletree Farms Antiques Inc
210 Main St
(847)526-7808 • (847)526-7812 (fax)
mail@antiquex.com
www.antiquex.com

An eclectic mix of quality antiques including

Victorian, European, oak, primitives, glassware, fireplace mantels, stained glass, art glass, bronzes, sterling plate, light fixtures, handpainted china & more. **Est:** 1968 **Hrs:** Mon-Sat 10-5, Sun 11-4. **Sz:** L **CC:** V/MC **Own:** Gerry Lorenz.

Waukegan

Ancestor's Antiques
709 North Ave
(847)623-4700

Hrs: Tue-Sat 1-5:30.

The Antique Connection
608 & 612 North Ave
(847)623-4008

Smalls & collectibles. **Hrs:** Tue-Sat 1-6.

Irene's Treasure House
942 North Ave
(847)336-3838

Glassware, smalls & collectibles. **Hrs:** By appt only. **QC: 61**

West Dundee

Adornments
125 W Main St
(847)428-8323

Estate jewelry & vintage linens. **Hrs:** Mon-Sat 10:30-5, Sun 12:30-4:30.

Antiques & Decorative Arts of Dundee
105 W Main St
(847)426-0409 • (847)426-0417 (fax)

Furniture, glass, porcelain, pottery, folk art, textiles, sculpture, silver, garden & outdoor

statuary & Americana. **Hrs:** Fri-Sat 11-5 (call ahead advised) or by appt. **CC:** AX/V/MC/DIS **Dir:** 25 mi from O'Hare. **Own:** Wyona Burns. **QC: 1 48 22**

Westmont

Old Plank Road Antiques
233 W Ogden Ave
(630)654-8882

English & Irish pine furniture, French faience, majolica & garden statuary. **Hrs:** Tue-Sat 10-5, Sun 12-5. **QC: 27 55 60**

Tony's Antiques & Collectibles
141 S Cass Ave
(630)515-8510

Hrs: By chance/appt.

Wheaton

Gabriel's Trumpet
229 Rice Lake Sq
(630)871-9500

Furniture, china, oils, prints, mirrors & tapestries. **Hrs:** Tue 10-6, Thu-Fri 10-8, Sat 10-5, Sun 12-4. **CC:** V/MC **Dir:** In the Rice Square Mall. Intersection of Butterfield Rd & Naperville Rd. **QC: 48 74**

Wheaton Antique Mall [G75]
1621 N Main St
(630)717-5511

Hrs: Mon-Sat 10-5 (Thu til 8), Sun 12-5. **Sz:** H **CC:** V/MC/DIS.

Wheeling

O'Kelly's Art, Antiques & Jewelry
971 N Milwaukee Ave
(847)537-1656

Hrs: Tue-Sun 11-5.

Antiques Center of Illinois [G58]

1920 S Wolf Rd
(847)215-9418

Crystal, china, pottery, lamps, jewelry, clocks, toys, sports, flow blue, glassware, dolls, books, porcelain, silver, watches & Depression glass. **Pr:** $1-5,000 **Est:** 1993 **Hrs:** Daily 10-5. **Sz:** L **CC:** V/MC **Dir:** At Wolf & Camp McDonald Rds. **Own:** Irwin Brill.

Antiques of Northbrook

971 N Milwaukee Ave
(847)215-4994

Hrs: Daily 10-5.

County Faire Inc

971 N Milwaukee Ave
(847)537-9987
www.countryfaire.com

General line of china, silver & glass, semi-precious jewelry. Specializing in books & fine art, unusual home decoratives & small furniture. **Pr:** $10-3,000 **Est:** 1990 **Hrs:** Daily 10-5. **Sz:** H **CC:** V/MC/DIS **Dir:** Hwy 294 exit Deerfield: W to Milwaukee Ave (Rte 21) S to 1st light. Enger Sale Barn Square. **Own:** Bernard & Joan Lucas. **QC:** 7 18 36 S12

Echoes Antiques in the Coach House

971 N Milwaukee Ave
(847)808-1324

Linens, quilts, vintage jewelry, chandeliers, lamps. Sets of tableware, silver & silverplate. Artwork. **Hrs:** Daily 10-5. **QC:** 84 81 78

Use the Service QuickCode indexes at the back of the book to find restorers, appraisers, refinishers, and other specialty service providers.

Lundgren's

971 N Milwaukee Ave
(847)541-2299

Antiques & accessories. **Hrs:** Tue-Sun 10:30-5.

Shirley's Doll House

971 N Milwaukee Ave
(847)537-1632 • (847)537-1691 (fax)

Dolls, doll houses, doll furniture. Appraisals & mail order. **Hrs:** Mon-Sat 10-5, Sun 11-4. **QC:** 38

Wheeling Sale Barn

971 N Milwaukee Ave
(847)537-9886

Furniture & antiques. **Est:** 1963 **Hrs:** Daily 9-5. **Dir:** 1-1/2 mi N of Rte 68.

Willow Springs

Nancy Fayes Inc

8260 Archer Ave
(708)839-2155

Jewelry & accessories. **Hrs:** Mon-Sat 10-5. **CC:** V/MC.

Glassware Matching Service

(708)839-5231

Depression, Cambridge, Heisey & Fostoria. **Hrs:** Call for appt.

Wilmette

Buggy Wheel Antiques

1143 Greenleaf Ave
(847)251-2100

Est: 1961 **Hrs:** Tue-Sat 10-4.

The Collected Works

1405 Lake Ave
(847)251-6897 • (847)251-6898

Restored antique American wicker, decorative accessories, lighting, iron & brass beds, quilts, garden furniture, vintage toys. Full service wicker restoration. **Hrs:** Tue-Fri 12-

5, Sat 10-5. **Dir:** Lake Ave at Green Bay Rd. **QC: 91 S16**

Elizabeth Ferguson Inc
1135 Greenleaf Ave
(847)853-0580 • (847)853-0860 (fax)

Botanical, natural history & architectural prints; etchings, woodcuts & lithographs; charcoals, pen & ink, watercolors; children's art; Art Deco/Art Noveau; sporting. Custom matting. **Hrs:** Tue-Sat 11-4 or by appt. **Own:** Elizabeth Yntema. **QC: 74 S9**

Heritage Trail Mall Ltd [G70+]
410 Ridge Rd
(847)256-6208
htmlto@compuserve.com

A general line including artwork, books, collectibles, European furniture & artifacts, gifts, dolls, furniture, glassware, jewelry, hats, beaded purses, toys, miniatures, primitives, linens. China & crystal repair, clock repair. **Hrs:** Mon-Sat 10-5, Sun 12-5. **Dir:** E of I-94, W of Green Bay Rd, S of Lake Ave, N of Wilmette Ave.

Josie's
545 Ridge Rd
(847)256-7646

20th C, Art Deco & Art Nouveau jewelry & small furniture. **Hrs:** Tue-Wed 11-5, Thu-Sat 12-6, Sun 12-4. **QC: 5 59**

Raven & Dove Antique Gallery
1409 Lake Ave
(847)251-9550

Majolica, Staffordshire, Quimper, silver perfumes, frames, Victorian silver serving pieces & gold & silver jewelry. **Est:** 1978 **Hrs:** Tue-Sat 12-5. **CC:** V/MC **QC: 23 78 64 S8 S16**

West End Antiques
619 Green Bay Rd
(847)256-2291

Oriental, tribal & pre-Columbian artifacts. **Hrs:** Tue-Sat 10:30-5. **QC: 2**

Wilmington

Abacus Antiques
113 N Water St
(815)476-5727 • (815)476-2092

Sports memorabilia, Art Deco & Nouveau lighting, pottery. **Hrs:** Daily 10-5.

Faulkners Emporium
605 E Baltimore St
(815)476-2210

Prints, paintings, primitives. **Hrs:** Mon, Wed & Fri 10-5 or by chance/appt. **Own:** Kathy Zavada.

Mill Race Emporium [G20]
110 N Water St
(815)476-7660

Hrs: Mon-Sat 10-5, Sun 11-5.

Mill Town Market [G]
508 N Kankakee St
(815)476-0386

Hrs: Mon-Sat 10-4, Sun 11-4.

O'Koniewski Treasures
117 N Water St
(815)476-1039

General line. **Hrs:** Daily 10-5.

The Old Theatre Antique Mall [G]
114 S Water St
(815)476-7525

Hrs: Mon-Sat 10-4, Sun 11-4.

The Opera House Collections
203 N Water St
(815)476-0872

Hrs: Daily 10-5. **CC:** V/MC.

Paraphernalia Antiques

112, 114 & 124 N Water St
(815)476-9841 • (815)476-9862
(815)476-6599 (fax)

General line. Direct importers from British Isles & France. Vast selection & generous dealer discounts. Three buildings full, hundreds of pieces of furniture & thousands of smalls. Fine jewelry a specialty. **Hrs:** Mon-Fri 9-5, Sat 9-5:30, Sun 11-5:30. **Sz:** H **Own:** Chuck & Sue Jeffries. **QC: 48 64**

R J's Relics [G30]

120 N Water St
(815)476-6273 • (815)476-5061
(815)476-6273 (fax)
relics@chcast.com

General line including books, jewelry, knives, military, swords, Fostoria, Depression glass, Hummels, furniture & trains. **Pr:** $5-3,000 **Est:** 1990 **Hrs:** Daily 10-5. **Sz:** H **CC:** V/MC/DIS **Dir:** I-55 Exit 238. I-57 Peatone exit (14 mi). **Own:** Robert & Rosalee Jameson. **QC: 4 32 50 S12**

Second Time Around

115 N Water St
(815)476-6379

Turn-of-the-century oak furniture. **Hrs:** Mon-Sat 10-5, Sun 11-5. **QC: 50**

Water Street Antique Mall [G]

121 N Water St
(815)476-5900
www.onvillage.com/wsam

General line featuring Roseville, VanBriggle, Weller, Fenter, Carnival & Heisey, pottery, toys, furniture. **Hrs:** Daily 10-5. **Sz:** H **CC:** V/MC/DIS **QC: 22 61**

Winnetka

Antique Emporium

915 Green Bay Rd
(847)446-0584

English & French country furniture. **Hrs:** Mon-Fri 9:30-5:30, Sat 10-5. **QC: 47 55**

Antique Heaven

982 Green Bay Rd
(847)446-0343 • (847)446-3392 (fax)
www.antiqnet.com/da/heaven.html

18th & 19th C American & French furniture & accessories. China, glass, silver, paintings, dolls, linens & lighting. **Hrs:** Mon-Fri 11-5, Sat 10-5. **QC: 47 48 36 S8**

Arts 220

895-1/2 Green Bay Rd
(847)501-3084 • (847)501-4758 (fax)

20th C decorative arts including jewelry & furniture. Art Deco, Arts & Crafts. **Hrs:** Tue-Sat 10:30-5:30. **Own:** Fern Simon. **QC: 5 6 36**

Bick's

964-1/2 Green Bay Rd
(847)441-7744

Coins & collectibles. **Hrs:** Mon-Sat 10-5. **QC: 33 32**

The Country Shop

710 Oak St
(847)441-8690

Country furniture, copper, pottery, folk art. **Hrs:** Tue-Sat 10-5.

T J Cullen, Jeweler

730 Elm St
(847)446-6468

Antique & estate jewelry & silver. **Hrs:** Mon-Sat 9-5:15. **QC: 64 78**

Ex Floreus at the Greenhouse

897-1/2 Green Bay Rd
(847)441-8808

Antique garden accessories including urns.
Hrs: Mon-Fri 9:30-5. **QC: 60**

Heather Higgins Antiques

567 Lincoln Ave
(847)446-3455 • (847)446-5343 (fax)

A varied inventory of period English & other furniture, brass, copper, china, paintings. Garden urns in season. Other quirky things. **Pr:** $30-30,000 **Est:** 1970 **Hrs:** Mon 10:30-4, Tue-Sat 10:30-5. **CC:** V/MC **Assn:** CSADA **Dir:** Rte 41 E of Edens Expressway, across railroad tracks. **Own:** Heather & Geoff Higgins. **QC: 54 23 20 S12**

Hubbard Woods Antiques

913 Green Bay Rd
(847)446-4353

Specializing in Mission & 19th & 20th C decorative arts. Furniture, pottery, metalwork & accessories; Stickley, Roycroft, Rookwood & Roseville. **Hrs:** Tue-Sat 11-5. **QC: 6 49**

Kamp Gallery Inc

563 Lincoln Ave
(847)441-7999

16th-20th C works of art. Period frames & painting restoration. **Hrs:** Mon-Sat 11-5, eves by appt. **QC: 7 S16**

In the Library

The earliest bookcases date to the late 17th century, but these are very rare. In England few houses had enough books to warrant furniture or a room dedicated to them until the middle of the next century. In America, bookcases and library furniture are less common and later.

Library steps: A step ladder on casters to enable readers to reach the topmost shelves of bookcases. As only the wealthiest households had large quantities of books, library steps are always of the highest quality design and craftsmanship. They were introduced in the Chippendale period and were made until the Victorian. Presumably the books on the upper shelves were the least often consulted, so library steps were not heavily used pieces of furniture. These expensive pieces were often made more useful by being made metamorphic (see below).

Library chair: A metamorphic chair that through ingenious design could be unfolded and transformed into a set of library steps. Stools and side tables were also designed to metamorphose into steps when necessary. Some of these pieces are so elaborate that we have to suspect that their owner's pleasure in their ingenuity outweighed their usefulness as dual-purpose furniture. Today, we assume too, that while they might maintain their primary use as chairs or tables, their secondary use would be as conversation pieces.

Library table: A table for writing and reading in the library, usually designed to stand in the center of the room and to be used from at least two sides. Library tables were made in three forms. (1) A large writing surface supported on two pedestals that were fitted with drawers and/or cupboards. This form was typically massive, ornate, and often architectural. (2) A comparatively simple rectangular table, with shallow drawers, raised on four legs, or, in the Regency and Federal periods, on lyre-shaped ends. (3) An octagonal table on a central pedestal, usually fitted with shallow drawers, and sometimes with sloped surfaces. Today the term sometimes refers to drop-leaf tables on a central pedestal: this is inaccurate, as libraries were large rooms whose furniture did not need to fold up when not in use.

Rent table: A library table of the third form (see above) whose drawers were fitted with small compartments for money and bills, at which the land agent sat to collect rent from tenants.

Knightsbridge Antiques

909 Green Bay Rd
(847)441-5105

18th C English furniture & decorative accessories. Chinese export porcelain, boxes, lamps, English blue-and-white, prints & rugs.. **Hrs:** Tue-Sat 11-4:30. **QC: 54 36 25**

Maclund Gallery

1101 Tower Rd
(847)441-7890

American & European paintings, silver, 17th-20th C decorative arts, china, jewelry. **Hrs:** Tue-Sat 10-5, Thu eve by appt. **QC: 7**

Pied-à-Terre Antiques

554 Lincoln Ave
(847)441-5161 • (847)256-9179 (fax)

Direct importers of country French antiques including armoires, buffets, farm tables, desks, lamps, paintings, Gien porcelain, grape baskets, Provencal pottery, santons, needlepoint rugs, linens, wine bottle dryers, oriental carpets, books, pillows. **Pr:** $20-18,000 **Est:** 1993 **Hrs:** Tue-Sat 10:30-4:30, call ahead advised. **Sz:** M **CC:** V/MC **Dir:** I-94 N exit Willow Rd E to Greenbay Rd. L to 1st stoplight (Oak St), R over bridge to Lincoln, then L. Shop is past 1st stop sign on L **Own:** Diane D Phelan. **QC: 32 62**

Robertson-Jones Antiques

569 Lincoln Ave
(847)501-5006

Set in the charming village of Winnetka, specializing in late 18th & early 19th C British antiques & accessories including sideboards, occasional tables, bookcases, chairs, mirrors, desks, mantles, country pieces, boxes & brass & copper accessories. **Pr:** $50-15,000 **Est:** 1973 **Hrs:** Mon-Sat 10-5. **Sz:** M **CC:** V/MC **Dir:** I-294 Willow Rd exit E to dead end at Green Bay Rd. L on Green Bay to 1st stop light (Cherry St), R over bridge to Lincoln, then L two blocks on R. **Own:** John Robertson-Jones. **QC: 20 36 54**

Sandcastle Interiors

557 Lincoln Ave
(847)446-5559

English antiques, period furniture, miniatures, lamps, Staffordshire, writing tables, fine art, mirrors. **Hrs:** Mon-Sat 10-4.

M Stefanich Antiques Ltd

549 Lincoln Ave
(847)446-4955 • (847)446-5062 (fax)

Fine antique English silver & old Sheffield plate, antique brass, copper & Chinese export porcelain. **Hrs:** Tue-Sat 10:30-5. **Own:** Michael Stefanich. **QC: 78 20 25**

Donald Stuart Antiques

571 Lincoln Ave
(847)501-4454

Period English & Continental furniture, porcelain, Staffordshire, oriental rugs & silver. **Hrs:** Mon-Fri 10-5. **QC: 54 30 78**

The Victorian Emphasis

918 Green Bay Rd
(847)441-6675

Textiles, purses, buttons, linens, lace, shawls, needlework, tapestries, trims, hankies & decorative accessories. **Hrs:** Tue-Wed & Fri-Sat 11:30-5. **QC: 80 89**

Ken Young Antiques

920 Green Bay Rd
(847)441-6670

Antique jewelry & watches, silver, paintings, prints, children's books. **Hrs:** Tue-Sat 10-5. **QC: 64 35**

Witt

Mystique Antiques

510 N Main
(217)594-2802

Furniture & glassware. **Hrs:** Daily 10-5. **QC: 48 61**

Woodstock

Colonial Antique Mall [G150]
890 Lake Ave
(815)334-8960 • (815)334-8353 (fax)

Quality antiques, architecturals, built-ins, mantles, lamps & fixtures, furniture, primitives, dolls, clocks, watches, glassware, porcelain, ceramics, stained glass, jewelry, collectibles. All items guaranteed authentic, no reproductions or crafts. **Pr:** $5-25,000 **Est:** 1997 **Hrs:** Daily 10-5, Fri til 7. **Sz:** H **CC:** V/MC/DIS **Dir:** I-90 exit Rte 47 N to 2nd light in Woodstock, then L on Lake Ave. 200 ft on L. **Own:** Lee Muto. **QC: 48 34 S1 S12 S16**

Merchant Antique Mall [G14]
214 Main St
(815)337-0275

Specializing in furniture, glassware, jewelry, kitchenware, books, prints, toys & collectibles on 2 floors in a historic hotel. **Pr:** $1-7,500 **Est:** 1975 **Hrs:** Mon-Fri 11-5, Sat 11-8, Sun 12-5 (closed major hols). **Sz:** L **Dir:** 1/2 blk off town square in scenic downtown Woodstock. 10 blks W of Rte 47. **Own:** Don Beth & Corrine Schreiber. **QC: 32 48 86 S12**

Standau's Gallery
110-1/4 N Benton
(815)337-1490

Art including Currier & Ives, posters, & photography; militaria; American & European antiques. **Hrs:** Tue-Sat 11-5. **Dir:** On the Square. **Own:** Shelley Standau. **QC: 74 4 73**

Wyanet

Century Cottage Antiques
220 W Main St
(815)699-7256
Hrs: By chance/appt.

Classic Collectibles
102 W Main St
(815)699-2653
Hrs: Wed-Sun 10-4.

Main Street Emporium
101 E Main St
(815)699-2526
Hrs: By chance/appt.

Wyanet Antique Mall [G]
320 W Main St
(815)699-7256
Hrs: Daily 9-5.

Xenia

Charley's Antiques
Church St
(618)678-4132

Oak & walnut furniture, glassware & stoneware. **Hrs:** By chance/appt. **QC: 50 61**

Goff's Antiques
Church St
(618)678-2651

General line. **Hrs:** By chance/appt.

Yorkville

Lenore's Antiques
708 S Bridge St
(630)553-9133

Art glass, lamps & cut glass. **Hrs:** Daily 10-5.

Yorkville Antique Center [G]
708 S Bridge St (Rte 47)
(630)553-0418
Hrs: Daily 10-5.

Zion

Zion Antique Mall [G8]
2754 Sheridan Rd
(847)731-2060
Hrs: Tue-Sat 9:30-5, Sun 1-5.

Indiana

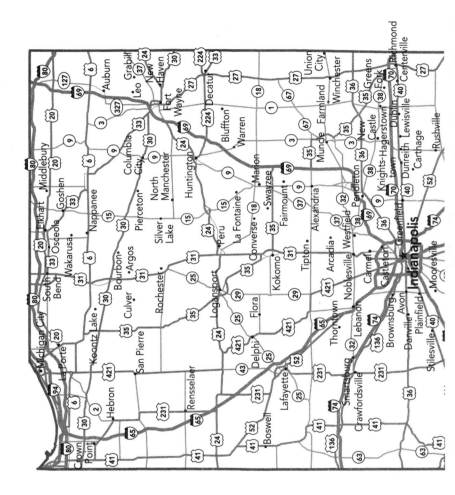

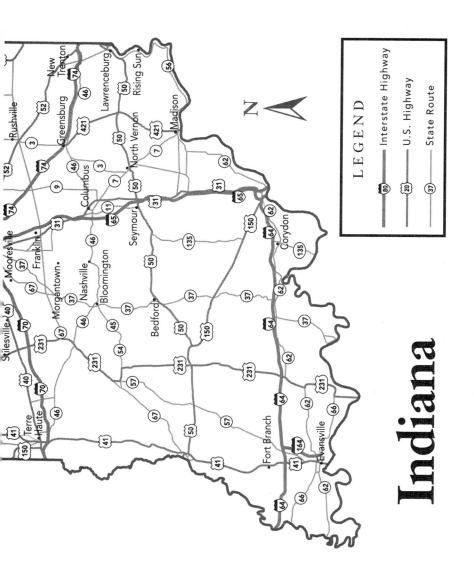

LEGEND

Interstate Highway

U.S. Highway

State Route

N

Indiana

Alexandria

A Place In Time
610 Park Ave
(765)724-7196

Furniture, jewelry, linens & dolls. **Hrs:** Mon-Sat 10-6. **Dir:** State Rd 9. **QC: 38 81 48**

Grandma's Attic Antiques
113 N Harrison St
(765)724-0314

Hrs: Mon-Sat 10-5. **CC:** V/MC.

Arcadia

Arcadia Antique Mall [G]
101 W Main St
(317)984-7107

Hrs: Mon-Sat 10-5, Sun 11-5. **Sz:** L **CC:** AX/V/MC/DIS **Dir:** 5-1/2 mi E of US 31 on 266th St, halfway between Noblesville & Tipton.

Argos

Argos Antiques
122 N Michigan St
(219)892-5135

Hrs: Wed-Sat 10-5, Sun 1-5. **Own:** Doug Howard.

Auburn

Serendipity Antiques
127 W 7th St
(219)925-5616
wagon@locl.net

Specializing in vintage jewelry — Victorian through the 1970s. Also carry a general line of affordable antiques & collectibles including furniture, linens, books, toys, glassware, kitchenware. **Pr:** $1-1,500 **Est:** 1991 **Hrs:** Mon-Tue & Thu-Sat 10-5, Wed 12:30-4:30, Sun 12-5. **CC:** V/MC/DIS **Dir:** I-69 Exit 129 E 1 mi on St Rd 8 (1 blk W of the square in downtown Auburn). **Own:** L Weigand. **QC: 64 63**

Sixth Street Emporium
106 W 6th St
(219)925-2563

Antiques & collectibles. **Hrs:** Tue-Sat 10-5, Sun 1-5.

Avon

Avon Antiques
7673 E Hwy 36
(317)272-4842

A nice selection of primitives, pre-1930s furniture (oak, walnut, cherry & pine), quilts, children's items, advertising & some glassware & wicker. A two-owner shop with a personal touch. No reproduction or newer "used" items. **Est:** 1992 **Hrs:** Mon-Sat 10-5, Sun by chance. **Sz:** M **Dir:** I-465 Danville exit (Rockville Rd): 6 mi W in Monty's Market Shopping Center. **Own:** Gail Medcalf & Debbie Herbert. **QC: 55 84 50**

Avon Haunted Bridge Antique Mall [G86]
184 N State Rd 267
(317)272-6957

Hrs: Daily 10-5. **Sz:** H.

Bedford

Brown Hen Antique Mall [G33]
Rte 11
(812)279-9172

Hrs: Mon-Sat 10-5, Sun 12-5. **CC:** V/MC/DIS **Dir:** At junction of Rtes 50 & 37. **Own:** Gerry Clark.

Pandora's Box Antique Mall [G14]

3300 W 16th St
(812)275-6534

Hrs: Mon-Sat 10-5, Sun 12-5. **Dir:** In the Stone City Mall.

Bloomington

Bloomington Antique Mall [G]

311 W Seventh St
(812)332-2290

Hrs: Mon-Sat 10-5, Sun 12-5 (EST). **CC:** V/MC/DIS **Dir:** 1 blk NW of City Square. **Own:** Becky Clayton, Mgr.

Elegant Options Antique & Design Gallery

403 N Walnut St
(812)332-5662

Specializing in silver, vintage lighting & European furniture. **Hrs:** Mon-Sat 10-6.

Bluffton

Antique & Collectible Mall [G]

101 N Main St
(219)824-1618

Hrs: Mon-Thu 8:30-5:30, Fri 8:30-6, Sat 9-5, Sun 1-5. **Dir:** In the 1882 brick bldg at Main & Market.

Boswell

Antique Mall of Boswell [G]

111 N Old US Rte 41
(765)869-5525

Antiques & collectibles: primitives, furniture, jewelry, pottery, glassware (Cambridge, Fenton & St Clair). **Hrs:** Mon-Sat 10-5 (EST), Sun 12-5. **Dir:** 90 mi S of Chicago. **QC: 61**

Bourbon

Vintage & Vine Antiques

112 E Center St (Old US 30)
(219)342-2028 • (219)342-3915

Refinished oak furniture, Nappanee & Hoosier cupboards. **Hrs:** Thu 12-5, Fri 10-5, Sat 9-5 or by appt. **Dir:** Exit State Rd 331 S, 1/2 blk E at light. **QC: 50**

Brownsburg

Deja Vu Antique Mall [G100]

1060 E Main St
(317)858-1961

Furniture, glassware, collectibles. **Hrs:** Daily 10-7. **Sz:** H **CC:** AX/V/MC/DIS **Dir:** 7 mi W of Indianapolis on I-74, Brownsburg Exit, S 1 mi to Hwy 136, E 1 mi to Mall, next to Pizza Hut.

Total Recall Antiques

8 E Main St (State Rd 136)
(317)852-0050 • (317)852-1936 (fax)
debbie@pop.oaktree.net
www.web-tek/net

Antiques, collectibles, glass, furniture. **Hrs:** Mon-Sat 10-5. **CC:** V/MC **Dir:** I-74 Exit at Brownsburg, 1 mi S to State Rd 136.

Carmel

Acorn Farm Country Store

15466 Oak Rd
(317)846-OAKS

Lamps, accessories, country furnishings. **Hrs:** Wed-Sun 11-5, Mon-Tue by chance. **Dir:** E from US Rte 31 & 151st.

Antique Emporium of Carmel [G]

1055 Rangeline Rd
(317)844-8351

Furniture, silver, linens, china & glassware. **Hrs:** Mon-Sat 10-5, Sun 12-5. **Own:** Peg Durrer.

Carthage

Red Kettle Antiques
8378 N 800 W
(765)565-6067

Early country & primitive furniture & accessories. Very large selection. **Est:** 1965 **Hrs:** By appt only. **Sz:** L **Dir:** Call for directions. **Own:** Robert & Carole Closser. **QC:** 31 34 51

Castleton

Castleton Antiques
6822 E 82nd St
(317)841-9171

Specializing in quality oak, mahogany, walnut & cherry antique furniture. Large selection of glassware, china, lamps, chandeliers, mirrors, collectibles & decorator items. **Pr:** $5-5,000 **Est:** 1994 **Hrs:** Mon-Tue & Thu-Sat 10-6, Sun 12-5 (closed Wed). **Sz:** M **CC:** V/MC/DIS **Dir:** 1 blk W of I-69/State Rd 37 on 82nd St. **Own:** Susan T Zook. **QC:** 48 36 32 S12

Centerville

The Oak Leaf
205 W Main St
(765)855-2623
xxocc@globalsite.net

Historic paintings, antique art & furniture. **Hrs:** By chance/appt. **QC:** 7

The Tin Pig Antiques
130 W Main St
(765)855-5313

Purveyors of country furniture & accessories. **Hrs:** Daily 9-5. **Own:** Pam Frantz & Ron Dixon. **QC:** 34

Tom's Antique Center [G20+]
117 E Main St (US RTE 40)
(765)855-3296

In a refurbished 1850s building, antique furniture, antique lighting & other specialty items. Stained glass studio on premises. **Est:** 1989 **Hrs:** Mon-Sat 10-5, Sun 1-5. **Dir:** Just E of downtown stoplight. **Own:** Thomas E Kurtz. **QC:** S16

Beds Great and Small I

In 1430 the Duke of Burgundy had a bed made for his wedding to Princess Isabella of Portugal. It was 19 feet long and 12 feet 6 inches wide. The Duke was presumably able to consummate his marriage and then take his dog for a walk before getting dressed. The Great Bed of Ware, now in the Victoria and Albert Museum, London, is, by comparison, a mere 10 feet 8 inches square. It was made c. 1590 for Sir Henry Fanshaw of Ware, but by 1612 it had been bought by the local inn, the White Hart. Here it must have been a good money maker — in 1700, for instance, Sir Henry Chauncey records that "six citizens and their wives came from London and slept in it." Hopefully these marriages had already been consummated, otherwise the crowding might have led to regrettable errors.

In this country master beds were not confined to private bedrooms until late in the 18th century. Before then they were commonly set in the parlor where the richness of their hangings could be admired by guests.

Tester: The canopy over a four-poster bed, originally of wood, but, by the 18th century, of fabric.

Bed hangings: Curtains surrounding a four-poster bed that not only ensured warmth and privacy but also displayed the family's wealth and good taste. Bed hangings were among the most expensive linens in a colonial household.

Webb's Antique Mall [G600+]

200 W Union St
(765)855-5542 • (765)855-5551

Furniture, glass, china, primitives, quilts & coverlets, collectibles, toys & games, baskets, paintings, metalware, silver, advertising materials, records & sheet music, kitchenware, enamelware, baseball cards & sports memorabilia, lamps, jewelry. **Hrs:** Mar-Nov daily 9-6; Dec-Feb daily 9-5. **Sz:** H **Dir:** I-70 exit Centerville: S 2 mi to Union St, R into parking lot. From Rte 40, N at light 4 blks to Union St.

Wheeler's Antiques

106-107-108 W Main St
(765)855-3400

Hrs: By appt/chance. **Own:** Sue Wheeler.

Columbia City

Hayloft Antique Mall [G25]

224 W Van Buren
(219)244-4005

Primitives, furniture, pottery, glassware, postcards. **Hrs:** Mon-Sat 10-5, Sun 12-5.

Columbus

Columbus Antique Mall [G120]

12th & Washington St
(812)375-2904

Hrs: Daily 10:30-5:30. **Sz:** H.

Little Creek Antique Mall [G]

2875 N State Rd 9
(812)546-5580
antygranny@webtv.net

Collectibles, glassware, old books, tools, quilts, baskets, furniture, primitives, crafts. **Hrs:** Mon-Sat 10-5:30, Sun 12-5. **Dir:** 2nd bldg on R from State Rd 46 & 9.

Victorian Parlour Antique Mall [G60+]

7270 State Rte 7
(812)376-0260

Hrs: Mon-Sat 10-5:30, Sun 1-5. **Sz:** L **Dir:** Jct Rte 7 & 31. **Own:** Jack Nedra & Laura Spinks.

Converse

Journey's End

202 E Railroad St
(765)395-3376

Antiques & mercantile. Bldg on National Register of Historic Places. **Hrs:** Tue-Sat 10-5.

Corydon

Griffin Building Antique Mall [G40]

113 E Beaver St
(812)738-3302

A general line including furniture, glassware, tools, quilts, jewelry, holiday collectibles. **Pr:** $5-1,500 **Est:** 1987 **Hrs:** Mon-Sat. **Sz:** L **CC:** V/MC/DIS **Dir:** I-64 W exit Corydon. Downtown on square across from Courtyard. **Own:** Bonnie Hayes. **QC: 34 48 S12 S10**

Red Barn Antique Mall [G]

215 Hwy 62 W
(812)738-2276

Furniture, Aladdin lamps, Depression glass, toys, collectibles, quilts. **Hrs:** Mon-Sat 10-5, Sun 1-5 (EDT). **Dir:** 3 blks off Old Capital Square.

Crawfordsville

Cabbages & Kings Antique Mall [G65]
124 S Washington St
(765)362-2577
Hrs: Mon-Sat 10-5, Sun 1-5.

Crown Point

Gard Gallery
700 N Sherman St
(219)663-0547 • (219)663-8702 (fax)

A mixed line of antiques, with lamps a specialty. Open to the public but primarily a wholesaler to the trade. **Pr:** $10+ **Hrs:** Mon-Fri 10-5. **Sz:** L **Dir:** I-65 to Rte 231 to Crown Point. **Own:** Bob & Rosemary Gard. **QC: 18 32 65 S1 S12 S16**

Culver

The Collectors
110 S Main St
(219)842-3398

Antique furniture, jewelry, books, primitives & glass. **Hrs:** Mon-Sat 10-5, Sun by chance.

Danville

Danville Antique Mall [G]
132 W Main St
(317)745-1774

Victorian walnut & oak furniture & accessories, fine porcelain & glass, primitives, quilts, art pottery, toys, dolls, vintage collectibles, used & rare books. **Hrs:** Mon-Sat 10-5, Sun 12-5. **Sz:** L **Dir:** 1/2 blk W of the Courthouse on Rte 36.

Heritage Antique Mall [G]
Rte 36
(317)539-4233

Antiques & collectibles; large selection of furniture. **Hrs:** Tue-Sat 10-5, Sun 12-5, Mon by chance. **Dir:** 10 mi W of Danville on Rte 36 at Groveland.

Decatur

Aumann's Antique Mall [G40+]
208 W Monroe St
(219)724-7472
Hrs: Mon-Sat 10-5, Sun 12-5. **Dir:** Corner 2nd & Monroe.

Memories Past Antique Mall [G50+]
111 W Jefferson St
(219)728-2643
Hrs: Mon-Sat 9-5, Sun 12-4.

Red Duck Antiques
132 N 2nd St
(219)728-2643

Country furniture, quilts, primitives, country smalls. Single-owner shop. **Hrs:** Mon-Sat 10-5, 1st Sun 11-3. **QC: 34 84**

2nd at Court Street Antiques
140 S 2nd St
(219)724-8019

Firearms, furniture, glass, pottery, textiles, primitives, reference books. **Hrs:** Mon-Sat 10-6, 1st Sun 10-6.

Yvonne Marie's Antique Mall [G76]
152 S 2nd St
(219)724-2001
Hrs: Mon-Sat 10-5, Sun 1-5.

Delphi

Delphi Antique Mall [G]
117 S Washington St
(765)564-3990

Furniture, toys, linens, glassware. **Hrs:** Mon-Sat 10-5, Sun 12-5.

Lil' Bit of Country
125 S Washington St
(765)564-6231

Furniture & Monon railroad items, glassware & general merchandise. **Hrs:** Mon-Sat 11-4, Sun 1-5. **Dir:** At the stoplight on the square.

Dublin

Old Storefront Antiques
1827 Main St
(765)987-8603

Hrs: By chance/appt.

Dunreith

Antiques Dunreith Junk-tion
US Rte 40
(765)987-8360

Hrs: By chance/appt.

Olde National Trail Antiques
113 Washington St (Rte 40)
(765)987-8519

Single-owner shop. **Hrs:** Thu-Mon 9-5. **CC:** V/MC/DIS **Dir:** I-70 Exit 123: State Rd 3 S to US 40. Turn R 1 blk. **Own:** Bruce & Mabel Haltom.

Elkhart

The Caverns of Elkhart [G]
111 Prairie Ct
(219)293-1484

Antiques & collectibles. **Hrs:** Mon-Sat 10-6, Sun 12-5.

Elkhart Antique Mall [G]
51772 State Rd 19 N
(219)262-8763 • (219)262-3030

Hrs: Mon-Sat 10-5, Sun 12-5. **Dir:** 1/4 N of Indiana Toll Rd exit for Elkhart. **Own:** Wayne & Kay Hostetler.

Evansville

Franklin Street Antique Mall [G103]
2123 W Franklin St
(812)428-0988

A variety of quality antiques, collectibles, crafts, glassware, books, furniture, cards & gifts, Amish wares. **Pr:** $1-2,500 **Est:** 1996 **Hrs:** Tue-Thu 10-5, Fri 10-7, Sat 10-5, Sun 12-4. **Sz:** H **CC:** AX/V/MC/DIS **Dir:** I-64 to I-164 S to Lloyd Expressway, W to Wabash Ave, then R at 1st light & L onto Franklin. 2nd blk on R. **Own:** Michael E Brank. **QC: 32 48 84**

Fairmount

Fairmount Antique Mall [G6]
115 N Main St
(765)948-5550
antique@comteck.com

"Tons of weird stuff," nice glass & paintings. **Pr:** $1-5,000 **Est:** 1992 **Hrs:** Daily 10-6. **Sz:** L **CC:** V/MC **Dir:** I-69 Fairmount exit to downtown. 40 mi N of Indianapolis in the hometown of James Dean. **Own:** Anthony & Jon Tucker. **QC: 67 87 61 S1 S8 S12**

Let's Talk Antiques & Toys
105 S Main St
(765)948-3329

Antiques & toys. **Hrs:** Daily 10-6. **Own:** Glen & Judy Cox.

Farmland

H & S Antiques
115 N Main St
(765)468-6910
Hrs: Mon-Thu & Sat 10-4, Fri by chance.

Fort Branch

Grace's Antiques
Hwy 41
(812)753-3595 • (812)768-6085

American furniture & accessories including formal & Victorian as well as country walnut, cherry, mahogany, poplar, pine & oak. **Hrs:** Mon-Sat 9-5. **Dir:** 6 mi N of I-64.

Fort Wayne

Aaron's Oriental Rug Gallery
1217 Broadway
(219)422-5184

Featuring one of the largest & finest selections of handwoven oriental rugs in the US. Extensive collection of kilims, dhurries, hooked rugs & needlepoint pillows — all affordably priced. Antique, semi-antique & new. **Pr:** $250-50,000 **Est:** 1973 **Hrs:** Mon-Sat 10-5:30. **Sz:** L **CC:** AX/MC/DIS **Dir:** I-69 Exit 102: E into city to Broadway, then R 2 blks. **Own:** Robert Doyle Anderson. **QC:** 75 76 SS1 SS8 SS12

Baxter's on Broadway Antique Mall [G25]
1115 Broadway
(219)422-6505

Furniture, sporting collectibles, paper items, pottery & advertising are specialties. On two floors. **Pr:** $5-3,000 **Est:** 1996 **Hrs:** Mon-Sat

10-6, Sun 11-5 exc major hols. **Sz:** L **CC:** AX/V/MC/DIS **Assn:** FWADA **Dir:** 1/2 blk S of Jefferson in downtown Ft Wayne. **Own:** Jeff Hoeppner. **QC:** 34 48 79 S1 S8 S22

Calhoun Street Antiques
2730 Calhoun St
(219)745-8164

Hrs: Mon-Sat 10-6, Sun 10-3. **Own:** Middy & Jim Kever.

Candlelight Antiques
3205 Broadway
(219)456-3150

Hrs: Mon-Sat 10-5, Sun 1-5.

Karen's Antique Mall [G]
1510 Fairfield
(219)422-4030

Antiques & collectibles. **Hrs:** Mon-Sat 10-6, Sun 1-5. **CC:** V/MC/DIS.

Nature's Corner Antique Mall [G]
2305 Spy Run Ave
(219)483-5236 • (219)471-9821 (fax)

Antiques, collectibles, furniture, glassware. **Hrs:** Mon-Sat 10-6, Sun 1-5.

Old House Galleries
701 Columbia Ave
(219)424-3737

Modernism & American & Indiana paintings. **Hrs:** Mon-Sat 10-5. **QC:** 7

Franklin

Lighthouse Antiques
62 W Jefferson St
(317)738-3344 • (317)736-5800
(317)736-6070 (fax)
john169jeff@worldnet.att.net

A well-lighted store located near the Courthouse in downtown Franklin featuring lighting, photography, furniture, collectibles, Longaberger, glass & china & other unique items. Currently expanding to a second floor. **Pr:** $1-6,000 **Est:** 1990 **Hrs:**

Mon-Sat 10-5, Sun 12-5. **Sz:** L **CC:** AX/V/MC/DIS **Assn:** ACDA CPCS **Dir:** I-65 Exit 90: W on State Rd 44 to downtown Franklin, 1/2 blk past Main St just off NW corner of the Courthouse Square on the N side of Jefferson St. **Own:** John & Bette Emry. **QC:** 48 65 73 S12 S19

Goshen

Carriage Barn Antiques

1100 Chicago Ave
(219)533-6353

18th & 19th C antiques & furniture in room settings. Old quilts, ironstone. Also quality antique replica lighting in copper, brass & tin, candle or electric, for indoors or out. **Pr:** $2-2,000 **Est:** 1990 **Hrs:** Mon-Fri 9:30-5, Sat 9:30-4. **Sz:** M **CC:** V/MC/DIS **Dir:** I-80/90 (Indiana Toll Rd) Bristol exit. S on State Rd 15 to Goshen, then US 33 W to Indiana Ave, then N 2 blks to the Old Bag Factory. **Own:** Mary Ann Ryman. **QC:** 51 52 34

Goshen Antique Mall [G40]

107 S Main St
(219)534-6141

Country furniture (original paint & refinished), smalls, textiles, yellowware, tinware, glassware, Roseville, Adirondack, pine/oak furniture, primitives & fine tools. **Hrs:** Mon-Sat 10-5 (Tue til 6). **CC:** V/MC **Dir:** I-80 Exit 101, S 15 mi on State Rd 15. Near Shipshewana & Nappanee.

Mustard Seed Antiques

1100 Chicago Ave
(219)534-6475 • (219)533-2345

Country antiques & primitives. **Hrs:** Mon-Fri 10-5, Sat 10-4. **Own:** Christine Waugman.

American Innovations

Hadley chest: An American dower chest made in and around the town of Hadley, Massachusetts, at the turn of the 18th century, characterized by elaborate decoration of flowers, vines, and foliage that was incised or painted or both. Considered to be the earliest form of furniture to have originated in America, though its roots in Jacobean England are quite clear.

Butterfly table: A small drop-leaf table made in New England around the turn of the 18th century. The top is raised on four turned and splayed legs joined by floor-level stretchers. The drop leaves are supported on shaped brackets that are set into the side stretchers and the underside of the table top. When open, the brackets lend the table somewhat the appearance of a butterfly. One of the earliest forms of furniture to have originated in America.

Hunt board: A small sideboard made in the southern Atlantic states between about 1800 and 1850 that is distinguished by its height, between 40 and 48 inches. After a day's fox hunt, the returning hunters would have buffet-style refreshments as they stood around the hunt board. These informal meals took place in the back hall or in the plantation office, so hunt boards are relatively unsophisticated in design.

Sugar chest: A small chest, often fitted with a lower drawer or drawers, and raised on four legs. Cherry and walnut were the most favored woods for these pieces, which were made throughout the south, though particularly in Kentucky and Tennessee. Most date from the early 19th century and were made in Sheraton or Empire styles. Some sophisticated examples were made by professional cabinetmakers, but many, simpler ones were plantation-made. A uniquely American form of furniture.

Sawbuck table: A country table made in New England and Pennsylvania with a planked top on two X-form supports joined by stretchers.

Grabill

The Country Shops of Grabill [G]

(800)626-8608 • (219)627-6311 (fax)

Hrs: Mon-Sat 9-5, Sun 12-5. **CC:** V/MC/DIS **Dir:** I-69 to exit 116: Rte 1 E 6 mi to 4 way stop at Leo, IN, then R 2 mi. **Own:** Thom Blake.

Greenfield

Reflections of Time

15 W Main St
(317)462-3878

Victorian & country furnishings. **Hrs:** Tue-Sat 10-5, Sun 12-5. **CC:** V/MC/DIS **Own:** Steve & Anita Hiser.

Sugar Creek Antique Mall [G]

2224 W US Rte 40
(317)467-4938

Rough & "as found" furniture building. **Hrs:** Daily 9-6. **Dir:** 4 mi W of Greenfield.

Greens Fork

Greens Fork Antique Shop

10 Pearl St (State Rd 38)
(765)886-6120

Hrs: Daily 10-6. **Dir:** I-70 Exit 145 N to State Rd 38.

Happy Days

24 Pearl St (State Rd 38)
(765)886-5633
(800)215-7269

Comic books, records, baseball cards, move

magazines & posters. **Hrs:** Tue-Sun 10-6. **Dir:** I-70 Exit 145 N to State Rd 38. **QC: 39**

Now and Then Collectibles

14 Pearl St (State Rd 38)
(765)886-5563

Hrs: Daily 7-5. **Dir:** I-70 Exit 145 N to State Rd 38.

Remember ?

20 Pearl St (State Rd 38)
(765)886-5633

Hrs: Daily 10-5. **Dir:** I-70 Exit 145 N to State Rd 38.

Greensburg

Stonebridge Collections [G10]

1440 S County Rd 600 E
(812)662-6533 • (812)591-3042
(888)395-0695

General line including furniture, primitives & smalls. **Pr:** $5-3,500 **Est:** 1993 **Hrs:** Mon-Sat 10-5:30, Sun 12-5. **Sz:** L **CC:** V/MC/DIS **Dir:** I-74 Newpoint exit (County Rd 850E) to Hwy 46. R on Hwy 46 2.5 mi to County Rd 600E. On corner. **Own:** Morris Kennedy. **QC: 1 32 48 S6 S7 S8**

Hagerstown

As The Crow Flies

98 E Main St
(765)489-4910 • (765)766-5266

Hrs: Thu-Fri 3-8:30, Sat 10-8:30, Sun 1-5. **Dir:** I-70 exit Hagerstown: Rte 1 N to Rte 38.

Found Treasures of Hagerstown

51 E Main St
(765)489-5335

Antiques & collectibles. **Hrs:** Thu-Fri &

Sun 1-9; Sat 10-9. **Dir:** I-70 exit Hagerstown: Rte 1 N to Rte 38.

Main Street Antiques Uniques
96 E Main St
(765)489-5792

A general line of antiques & collectibles including furniture, glassware, china, lamps, kitchen tools, books, postcards & much more. Buy & sell. **Est:** 1976 **Hrs:** Thu-Sat 1-8:30, Sun 12-8:30 or by appt. Closed Xmas & New Year's. **Sz:** M **Dir:** I-70 exit Hagerstown: Rte 1 N to Rte 38 W. Main St is Rte 38. **Own:** Jim & Becky Reed. **QC:** 32 48 S1 S12

Zachary's Antiquities & Collectibles
61 E Main St
(765)489-5335

Hrs: Thu-Sat 12:30-9:30, Sun 1-9. **Dir:** I-70 exit Hagerstown: Rte 1 N to Rte 38.

Hebron

Carol's Antique Mall [G]
108A N Main St
(219)996-4655

Tobacco items, civil war guns, dolls, glassware, jewelry. **Hrs:** Daily 9-6. **QC:** 61 63 4

Huntington

Antiques & Not Mall & B & D Crafts
515 N Jefferson St
(219)359-9824

Hrs: Tue-Sat 9-4.

Indianapolis

Allisonville Road Antique Mall [G100]
6230 N Allisonville Rd
(317)259-7318 • (317)259-7322 (fax)

Furniture, artwork, decoys, Native American art & artifacts. **Hrs:** Mon-Sat 10-8, Sun 12-5. **Sz:** H **Dir:** I-465 exit State Rd 37S, then R on 62nd St. In Sylvan Ridge Shoppes on NW corner of 62nd & Allisonville Rd. **Own:** Steve & Patti Kirk & Wayne & Brinda Corrigan.

Books, Antiques & More
1048 Virginia Ave
(317)636-1595 • (317)359-3519

Books (hardback, paperback, old & new), collectible ephemera, magazines & postcards. Dealer & repeat customer discounts. **Pr:** $0.10-2,200 **Est:** 1989 **Hrs:** Mon-Sat 10-6, Sun 12-5. **Sz:** M **Assn:** IABA **Dir:** From St Louis: I-70 E Exit 79A: R on West St to light, L on Morris St 1.5 mi to Shelby St, L on Shelby, fork L at fountain to Virginia Ave 1 blk. From Chicago: I-65 Exit 110A. **Own:** Paul & Carrie Walker. **QC:** 18 74 39 S1 S19

Colby Antiques
1111 E 61st St
(317)253-2148

Specializing in 18th & 19th C English & Continental furniture. Personal shopping available for clients at the European sources. **Est:** 1994 **Hrs:** Tue-Sat 10-4. **Sz:** M **CC:** V/MC **Dir:** I-465 N to Keystone exit: Keystone S to 62nd St; R (W) on 62nd to 3rd light (Compton); L on Compton to 61st St; R on 61st to McNamara Bldg. **Own:** Cherri Colby. **QC:** 53 59 47 S9

D & D Antique Mall
6971 W Washington St
(317)486-9760

Antiques & collectibles. **Hrs:** Mon-Sat 10-5, Sun 1-5.

Fountain Square Antique Mall [G40]

1056 Virginia Ave
(317)636-1056 • (317)933-7459 (fax)

Antiques & collectibles. Furniture, glassware, pottery, toys, sport memorabilia & vintage clothing. **Pr:** $1-2,500 **Est:** 1989 **Hrs:** Mon-Wed & Sat 10-5, Thu-Fri 10-8, Sun 12-5. **Sz:** L **CC:** AX/V/MC/DIS **Dir:** I-65 Exit 110. **Own:** Don & Jewell Resener. **QC: 32 48 83 S1 S2 S8**

Hope's Shop — Antiques

116 E 49th St
(317)283-3004

Glass & china a specialty. General line of smalls including pottery, Fiestaware, Belleek, silver, costume jewelry & some collectibles. No Beanie Babies. **Pr:** $2-1,000 **Est:** 1978 **Hrs:** Tue-Fri 12-6, Sat 10-5. **Sz:** M **CC:** AX/V/MC/DIS **Dir:** 1 blk E of Meridan St (US 31) at corner of 49th & Pennsylvania. **Own:** Vari Scudi. **QC: 30 61 89**

Laura Ann's Antiques & Collectibles [G]

3422 N Shadeland
(317)568-1950

Furniture, glassware, vintage dolls, jewelry. **Hrs:** Daily 10-5:30. **CC:** V/MC/DIS **QC: 38 48 63**

Manor House Antique Mall [G125]

5454 S East St (US Rte 31 S)
(317)782-1358 • (317)782-1371 (fax)
www.inet.net/manorhouseantiques

Quality antiques & collectibles. Showroom-style displays & glass showcases with china, porcelain, pottery, linens, books, dolls, jewelry, tools & furniture. **Pr:** $5-10,000 **Est:** 1997 **Hrs:** Mon-Fri 10-6, Sat 10-8, Sun 12-5. **Sz:** H **CC:** V/MC/DIS **Dir:** I-465 Exit 2B: 1/2 mi S on US Rte 31. **Own:** Mr & Mrs Doyal "Jake" Merrill. **QC: 36 48 S7 S12 S19**

Michigan Street Antique Center [G]

1049 E Michigan St
(317)972-8990

Antiques, 20th C modern, collectibles, artwork, furniture, glassware, 1950s, pottery, vintage clothing & ephemera. **Hrs:** Mon-Sat 10-6, Sun 12-5. **Sz:** H.

The Mobile Merchant

1052 Virginia Ave
(317)264-0868 • (317)264-0868 (fax)

Hrs: Fri, Sat & Mon 10-5, Sun 12-5. **Own:** Stephen Lietz.

Red Barn Antique & Flea Market

325 E 106th St
(317)846-8928

Primitives, collectibles, tools, books, junk, antiques, small furniture. Dealers love us! **Pr:** $25-300 **Est:** 1969 **Hrs:** Tue-Sat 12-6. **Sz:** L **Dir:** 3 blks E of US 31 on 106th St (S side). **Own:** Robert Hunter & Marion Lang. **QC: 17 32 20**

Southport Antique Mall [G210+]

2028 E Southport Rd
(317)786-8246 • (317)786-9926 (fax)
antique@iquest.net

One of the midwest's largest & finest antique malls, fully staff & alarmed. **Pr:** $1-10,000 Est: 1994 **Hrs:** Mon-Sat 10-8, Sun 12-5. **Sz:** H **CC:** V/MC/DIS **Dir:** I-65 S Exit 103, 1-3/4 mi W in the old Gerdt Furniture Bldg. **Own:** David Davis, James Haganman, Jane Haganman & Mary Mulinaro. **QC: 32 S12**

Surroundings

1111 E 61st St
(317)254-8883 • (317)254-8885 (fax)

18th, 19th & 20th C European & American antiques, select consignments, interior & garden accessories, custom silk & dried floral arrangements & topiaries.

Pr: $50-10,000 **Hrs:** Tue-Sat. **Sz:** M **CC:** V/MC **Dir:** I-465 N to Keystone exit: Keystone S to 62nd St; R (W) on 62nd to 3rd light (Compton); L on Compton to 61st St; R on 61st to McNamara Bldg. **Own:** David L Robichaud & Gary R Johnson. **QC: 54 53 23**

Knightstown

The Glass Cupboard
115 E Main St
(765)345-7572
Hrs: Wed-Sat 11-5, Sun-Tue by chance/appt.

Knightstown Antique Mall [G80]
136 W Carey
(765)345-5665

In an old furniture factory complex. Three bldgs full of antiques & collectibles. Specializing in furniture, cast iron, banks & toys, primitives, advertising, porcelain, pottery & stoneware, Depression glass & books. **Pr:** $2-4,000 **Est:** 1982 **Hrs:** Mon-Sat 10-5, Sun 12-5. **Sz:** H **CC:** V/MC/DIS **Dir:** I70 Exit 115 S or US Rte 40 E. 30 min

from Indianapolis. **Own:** Barry & Barbara Carter. **QC: 32 34 48**

Lindon's Antique Mall
32 E Main St (Rte 40)
(765)345-2545

Antiques & collectibles. **Hrs:** Mon-Sat 10-5, Sun 12-5. **CC:** AX/V/MC/DIS **Dir:** 30 min E of Indianapolis on US Rte 40 or I-70 Exit 115.

Nostalgia Nook
6 E Main St
(765)345-7937
tlong@spitfire.net

Victorian to 1930s clothing, accessories, antiques & collectibles. **Hrs:** Thu-Sat 10-5, Sun 1-5. **Dir:** I-70 Exit 115. **QC: 83**

Kokomo

Calico Cat Antiques
(765)455-3669

18th & 19th C furniture & accessories. **Hrs:** By appt only. **Own:** Laurie & Dave Wardrop. **Hrs:** Tue 1-5, Wed-Sat 10-5, Sun 12-5. **Dir:** 4 mi N of US Rte 30, 4 mi S of US Rte 6.

Alcoholic Antiques I

Cellaret: An 18th century lidded case for wine bottles, often of the highest craftsmanship, usually on casters. Cellarets were fitted with locks to keep bibulous servants at bay and were typically kept under serving tables in the dining room. Sideboards, introduced at the end of the century, included cupboards for storing bottles. They rapidly replaced cellarets.

Wine cistern: An elaborate tub of silver, pewter or, most often, of wood lined with lead for cooling wine in ice.

Wine coaster: Originally, in the 18th century, a small wagon on wheels used for circulating wine around a large dining table. Often a coaster would be fitted with decanters for port, claret, and madeira. Coasters were made of silver or mahogany and later were made to slide on baize rather than roll on wheels. It is this form that evolved into the modern coaster.

Tantalus: A lockable liquor rack, usually holding three cut-glass decanters, that allowed the liquor to be seen but not drunk. A Victorian invention designed to ensure that the master of the house controlled its alcohol.

Pieces of the Past
200 E Hoffer St
(765)456-3000

A wide variety of smalls, antique furniture from oak to walnut, country crafts. Hard-to-find unique gifts, candles, pottery, woodcrafts. Silk & dried arrangements. **Pr:** $1-1,500 **Est:** 1993 **Hrs:** May-Aug Tues-Fri 10-5, Sat 10-3; Sep-Apr Mon-Sat 10-6; open Sun 10-6 in Dec. **Sz:** M **CC:** V/MC **Dir:** US Rte 31 to Hoffer St. Turn W and go through 4 lights. 1 blk on N side of street. **QC: 58 34 80 S12 S16 S17**

Treasure Mart Mall [G]
US 31 S
(765)455-9855

Antiques, new & used furniture, decorative accessories, glassware, books & collectibles. Also consignment shop at 1020 E Sycamore St. **Hrs:** Mon-Sat 10-8, Sun 12-5. **Sz:** H **Dir:** US 31 Bypass S at Alto Rd. **Own:** Don Wilhelm. **QC: S8**

White Bungalow Antique Mall [G]
906 S Main St
(965)459-0789

Antiques & collectibles. **Hrs:** Mon-Sat 9-5. **Dir:** Just N of Markland Ave.

Wild Ostrich Antiques
928 S Main St
(765)452-3990 • (765)457-9529

Antiques, collectibles, dirilyte, Tiffany, advertising, circus, furniture, vintage luggage. **Hrs:** Thu-Sat 10-5. **Dir:** just N of Markland Ave.

La Fontaine

Shades of Yesteryear
Corner Branson & Main Sts
(765)981-2223

Featuring Victorian & traditional lamps, shades & collectibles. **Hrs:** Tue-Sat 10-4. **Own:** Brad & Connie Crump. **QC: 65**

La Porte

Coachman Antique Mall [G100]
500 Lincolnway
(219)326-5933

Hrs: Mon-Sat 9-5, Sun 12-5. **Dir:** 3 blks E of courthouse.

It's a Wonderful Life Antique Mall [G100+]
708 Lincolnway
(219)326-7432 • (616)382-4833 (fax)
beerstatue@aol.com

Antiques, collectibles, furniture, glass, sports, breweriana, vintage clothing, advertising, price guides. Four floors. **Pr:** $1-1,000 **Est:** 1995 **Hrs:** Mon-Sat 10-5, Sun 12-5. **Sz:** H **CC:** V/MC/DIS **Dir:** From Detroit, Michigan Exit 1; from Chicago, Indiana Exit 43. **Own:** George Baley. **QC: 48 67 32 S4 S8 S1**

Plain & Fancy Antiques
5395 W Johnson Rd
(219)362-5277
sensow@netnitco.net

A small, privately owned shop located in the country with a general line of antiques including country primitives, horse-drawn sleighs, buggies & carts. **Pr:** $2-3,000 **Est:** 1988 **Hrs:** May-Oct Mon-Sat 9-5, Sun 11-5; Nov-Apr Mon-Sat 10-4:30, Sun 12-4:30. **Sz:** M **Assn:** LCADA **Dir:** Halfway between LaPorte & Michigan City in La Porte County on a main county road. **Own:** Bob & Lorie Sensow. **QC: 34 48 67**

Visit our web site at www.antiquesource.com for more information about antiquing in the Midwest and New England.

Lafayette

Buck's Collectibles & Antiques [G45]
310 S 16th St
(765)742-2192

Primitives, Coca-cola, dolls, furniture, pottery, occupied Japan, railroad, advertising, tools & knives supplied by a mix of dealers from around the Lafayette area. A must stop if you are interested in browsing or purchasing the unique & unusual. **Pr:** $5-300 **Est:** 1994 **Hrs:** Mon-Sat 10-5. **Sz:** L **Dir:** I-65 exit on State Rd 26 W. Cross State Rd 52 to 5-points intersection, then L on 16th St 2 blks to Center St. Store on corner. **Own:** Wayne Buck. **QC:** 34 48 32 S8 S5

Lawrenceburg

Livery Stable Antique Mall [G]
318 Walnut St
(812)537-4364

Hrs: Mon-Sat 10-6, Sun 12-6. **Dir:** I-275 Exit 16: L on US 50 W to 2nd light. L onto Walnut St 2 blks.

Shumway's Olde Mill Antique Mall [G]
232 W High St
(812)537-1709
(888)321-1709

Hrs: Daily 10-6. **Dir:** I-275 Exit 16 (Lawrenceburg/Greendale): L onto US 50 W to 2nd light. L onto Walnut St to High St (R), 3 blks.

Tri-State Antique Market [G300]
Lawrenceburg Fairgrounds, US Rte 50
(513)738-7256
www.jsite.com/showz

Outdoor antique & vintage-only market. **Hrs:** Six Sundays per year, 7-3, rain or shine.

Call for dates. **Dir:** I-275 Exit 16, 1 mi W. **Own:** Bruce Metzger.

Lebanon

Bits & Pieces
210 W Washington St
(765)482-1823

Furniture, jewelry & collectibles; Depression glass, McCoy, Roseville, art glass, pottery, china, old books, artwork, home accessories, cut glass, cranberry glass, silver, toys & dolls. **Hrs:** Tue-Sat 11-6, Sat 12-5.

Leo

Cellar Antique Mall
15004 State Rd 1 N
(219)627-6565

Furniture, vintage clothing, glass & china. **Hrs:** Tue-Sat 10-5. **CC:** V/MC/DIS.

Shades of Country
15004 State Rd 1
(219)627-2189

Furniture, glass, collectibles. **Hrs:** Tue-Sat 10-5. **Own:** Mary Lou Wisler.

Lewisville

Apple Butter Creek Antiques
304 E Main St (Rte 40)
(765)987-8603

Furniture & primitives. **Hrs:** Apr-Dec Mon-Sat 11-5, Sun by chance/appt.

Highway 40 Antiques
303 E Main St (Rte 40)
(765)987-8116

Hrs: Apr-Nov daily 11-5.

Use the Specialty QuickCode indexes at the back of the book to find dealers who specialize in your area of interest.

Lewisville Antique Mall
102 W Main St (Rte 40)
(765)345-2545
Hrs: Daily 10-5.

Logansport

Cluttered Closet Old & New Stuff
811 Burlington Ave
(219)753-5196
(888)789-5460
debweb@netusa1.net

Antiques, collectibles & miscellaneous. **Pr:** $50-100+ **Est:** 1982 **Hrs:** Mon-Sat 10-6, Sun 12-5. **Sz:** L **CC:** AX/V/MC/DIS **Dir:** State Rd 329 to S side of Logansport. **Own:** Deborah A Hulsey. **QC: 17 36 48 S8**

Madison

507 Antiques
507 Jefferson St
(812)265-2799

Antiques & collectibles. **Hrs:** Daily 10-5.

Antiques on Main
129 E Main St
(812)265-2240

Antiques, collectibles, costume jewelry. **Hrs:** Mon-Sat 9-5, Sun 10-5.

Broadway Antique Mall
701 N Broadway
(812)265-6606
Hrs: Mon-Sat 10-5, Sun 12-5.

Carita's Antique Shoppee
108 W Main St
(812)265-6606
Hrs: Sat & Sun.

D & J's Antiques & More
313 Mulberry St
(812)265-2324
Hrs: Mon-Sat 9-5.

Jefferson Street Antique Mall & Flea Market
200 Jefferson St
(812)265-6464
Hrs: Tue-Fri 10-6, Sat 9-5, Sun 12-5.

Lumber Mill Antique Mall [G]
721 W First St
(812)273-3040
Hrs: Mon-Sat 10-5, Sun 12-5.

Main Cross Antiques & Gifts
630 W Main St
(812)273-5378
Hrs: Tue-Sat 10-5, Sun 12-5.

Old Town Emporium
113 E Second St
(812)273-4394 • (812)265-2026
(812)273-5495 (fax)
esommerf@seidata.com
www.antiqnet.com/sommerfeld

18th, 19th & 20th C furniture & accessories: English, Dutch, American. Direct European importers. Located in a c 1820 Federal home with a cook-in kitchen of the period. See also Evan Sommerfeld Antiques. **Hrs:** Mon-Sat 10-5, Sun 12-5 (EST). **Sz:** H **CC:** AX/V/MC/DIS **Own:** Evan Sommerfeld. **QC: 53 27 9**

The Purple Strawberry
326 Mulberry St
(812)265-9090

Glassware, china, holiday collectibles, furniture, folk art, vintage toys. **Hrs:** Mon-Sat 10-5.

Snicklefritz Antiques & Accessories
128 E Main St
(812)273-0646
Hrs: Tue-Sat 9-5, Sun 10-5.

EVAN SOMMERFELD ANTIQUES, INC.

118 East Main Street
Madison, Indiana 47250
812-265-2026

🐾 18 & 19th Century Furniture And Accessories

🐾 English - Dutch - American

Monday - Saturday
10 to 5 (EST)
Sunday
12 to 5 (EST)
Other times
by appointment

OLD TOWN EMPORIUM

113 East Second Street
Madison, Indiana 47250
812-273-4394

Evan Sommerfeld Antiques Inc

118 E Main St
(812)265-2026 • (812)273-4394
(812)273-5495 (fax)
esommerf@seidata.com
www.antiqnet.com/sommerfeld

18th & 19th C furniture & accessories: English, Dutch, American. Direct European importers. Located in a c 1850 hardware store. Serves lunch. Contemporary art gallery with framing service on premises. See also Old Town Emporium. **Hrs:** Mon-Sat 10-5, Sun 12-5 (EST). **CC:** AX/V/MC/DIS **Dir:** On the Ohio River between Louisville & Cincinnati. **QC: 53 27 7 S13**

Wallace's Antiques

125 E Main St
(812)265-2473

Hrs: Mon-Sun 11-5.

Marion

Hummel Hill Antiques & Collectibles

2210 N Huntington Rd
(765)668-7488

Antiques & collectibles. Specializing in Civil

War memorabilia. **Hrs:** Mon-Sat 10-6, Sun 12-5.

Jake's Antiques [G30+]

1440 Winona Ave
(765)664-9765

Antiques, collectibles & necessities. **Hrs:** Tue-Sat 9-5, Sun 12-5.

Ol' Hickory and Lace

913 S Main St
(765)452-6026 • (765)459-0208

Hrs: Wed-Sat 10-5, Sun 1-5. **Own:** Betty Moore & Gustua Wallace.

Michigan City

The Antique Market [G85]

3707 N Frontage Rd
(219)879-4084

Antiques & collectibles. **Hrs:** Mon-Sat 10-5, Sun 12-5. **Dir:** At I-94 & US 421, just S of the Holiday Inn.

Middlebury

Main Street Antique Mall

511 S Main St
(219)825-9533

Antiques, collectibles, quilts, jewelry, lamps, furniture, old toys, tools, glassware & iron. **Hrs:** Mon-Sat 8-5:30. **Dir:** 10 min from Shipshewana or the tollroad on State Rd 13.

Unique Antique Mall [G40]

106 Wayne St
(219)825-1900

Hrs: Mon-Sat 10-5. **Sz:** L **Dir:** 7 mi from IN
Toll Road & Shipshewana Flea Market.

Mooresville

Buffalo Gal Antique Mall [G40]

22 E Main St
(317)831-6020

Furniture, jewelry, old toys, music &
American collectibles. **Hrs:** Mon-Thu 10-6,
Fri-Sat 10-8, Sun 12-6.

Morgantown

Miller's Antiques

13 W Washington St
(812)597-6024

Furniture, china, collectibles. **Hrs:** Seasonal
hours.

Muncie

Off Broadway Antique Mall [G70+]

2404 N Broadway
(765)747-5000

Funiture, political, glassware, toys, vintage
clothing, coins, pottery, books, collectibles,

Antique or Not

Antique: Properly an object, at least 100 years old, of decorative, aesthetic, or historical value, which is desired and appreciated for its beauty, its craftsmanship, its antiquity, its heritage, or its curiosity. Now the word can, apparently, be used to refer to anything that is older than its owner.

Collectable, Collectible (both spellings given in *Webster's Dictionary*): An object, usually less than 100 years old, that is desired for nostalgic or sentimental reasons. Collectibles were mass manufactured and thus are comparatively easily found today. Their qualities are functional and domestic, rather than aesthetic. There is also a category of collectibles that have no function other than to be collected.

Period: A term used to refer to an antique that was made in the period when its design originated, and to distinguish it from later revival versions. The term thus refers particularly to furniture made before the 1830s, that is, during the periods of hand craftsmanship.

Revival: A later version of an earlier style. Sometimes revival styles are very close to period ones, as in the best of colonial revival: sometimes the resemblance is distant, as with gothic revival. Mass-manufactured revival styles are often a horrendous hodge-podge of period features, sometimes from different periods. Colonial revival furniture was popular from c 1875 to c 1940 and is still being made today.

Reproduction: A piece made by hand in an earlier style in the period manner. A good reproduction is an act of homage to the original and is not intended to deceive the purchaser.

Copy: An exact copy of a specific period piece. Copies are often made to complete or enlarge a set of chairs, or to make a single piece into a pair.

Fake: A reproduction intended to deceive, either by its maker, or its seller, or both. What began life as an honest reproduction may be turned into a fake by ignorant or unscrupulous sellers.

Custom or bench made: A piece made by hand in a period style, but not always in the period manner. Usually not as faithful to the original as a reproduction.

gasoline collectibles. **Hrs:** Daily 9-5. **Sz:** H.

Nappanee

Antiques on Six Antique Mall [G]

26358 Market St (Rte 6)
(219)773-7755

Antiques & collectibles. **Hrs:** Mon-Sat 10-6, Sun 1-5. **Dir:** 1-1/2 mi E of downtown Nappanee.

Borkholder Dutch Village

(219)773-2828

Flea market & group shop. Auction every Tue 8:00 a.m. **Hrs:** Mon-Sat 10-5.

Si's Son - Dan Antiques & Collectibles

110 S Main

Furniture, books, glassware, quilts, primitives & military memorabilia. **Hrs:** Mon-Sat 9:30-4:30. **QC: 4 48 61**

Nashville

Brown County Antique Mall [G]

3288 E State Rd 46
(812)988-1025

Hrs: Mon-Sat 9-5:30, Sun 11-5:30. **Dir:** 12 mi W of I-65.

New Castle

Imperial Antique Mall

1318 Broad St
(765)521-7418

Hrs: Mon-Wed 11-5, Thu-Sat 11-8, Sun 1-5.

Traveling East? Take along a copy of *Sloan's Green Guide to Antiquing in New England.* Call Toll Free (888)875-5999 or visit your local bookstore or antiques dealer.

Raintree Antique Emporium

1331 Broad St
(765)529-7548

Hrs: Wed 11-5:30, Thu-Sat 11-8:30, Sun 1-5.

Recollections & Collections

1431 Broad St
(765)521-8960

Hrs: Fri-Sat 9-4 by appt.

St Clair's Trash to Treasures

111 N 6th St
(765)521-8218

Hrs: Daily 2-6.

New Haven

Antique Treasures

613 & 621 Broadway
(219)493-4128

Furniture, pottery, china, Depression glass, Fiesta, Jewel Tea, pressed & cut glass, toys & collectibles. **Hrs:** Mon-Sat 10-5.

New Trenton

Hawkins' Antiques

(812)637-1679

Three buildings of antiques & country primitives. **Hrs:** Sun only (Mon-Sat by chance). **Dir:** Between Harrison (OH) & Brookville (IN), 3 mi W of I-74 on Rte 52. **Own:** Bob & Donnie Hawkins. **QC: 34**

Noblesville

Lazy Acres

77 Metsker Ln
(317)773-7387

Specializing in English pine furniture, wicker & art. **Hrs:** Mon-Sat 10-5, Sun 12-5. **Sz:** H **CC:** AX/V/MC/DIS **Dir:** 1/2 mi W of Noblesville on State Rd 32. **Own:** Scott Jefferson & Mark Fineberg.

Noblesville Antique Mall [G70]
20 N Ninth St
(317)773-5095

Three floors of antiques, furniture, glassware & collectibles, large library & a "ruff room." **Pr:** $5-10,000 **Est:** 1989 **Hrs:** Mon-Sat 9-6, Sun 12-6. **Sz:** H **CC:** V/MC/DIS **Dir:** On the Courthouse Square in historic downtown Noblesville. 20 min N of Indianapolis, 7 mi E of Hwy 31 or 1 mi W of Hwy 37, 1/2 blk N of Hwy 32. **Own:** Roger & Diane Crim. **QC: 32 50 67**

The Noblesville Emporium
950 Logan St
(317)773-4444

Hrs: Mon-Wed 10-6, Thu-Fri 10-8, Sat 10-6, Sun 12-6.

North Manchester

Antique Market [G]
135 E Main St
(219)982-8446

Hrs: Daily (call ahead advised).

Main Street Antiques
118 E Main St
(219)982-1118

Hrs: Mon-Thu 10-4, Fri-Sat 10-7, Sun 12-5. **CC:** V/MC/DIS.

Manchester Antique Mall [G]
209 E Main St
(219)982-1455

Hrs: Tue-Sat 10-5, Sun 1-5. **Own:** Marcia Van.

North Vernon

North Vernon Antique Mall
247 E Walnut St
(812)346-8604

Furniture, churns, Red Wing, Uhl pottery. **Hrs:** Mon-Sat 10-5.

Osceola

Classic Antiques
10775 Kern Rd
(219)633-4421
tmebrown@mvillage.com

Early 19th C period & country furniture, folk art, paintings, lighting & tinware. Located in an 1850 Greek Revival house. **Pr:** $10-10,000 **Est:** 1995 **Hrs:** By appt only. **Dir:** 20 min SE of South Bend. **Own:** Thomas & Marcia Brown. **QC: 1 52 41**

Pendleton

Dick & Jane's Antiques
112 S Franklin St
(765)778-2330

Strictly country furniture & smalls. **Hrs:** By chance/appt. **Own:** Dick & Jane Wallace. **QC: 34 48**

Heritage Antique Mall [G30+]
231 S Pendleton Ave
(765)778-4726

Furniture, glass, lamps, trunks, textiles. **Hrs:** Mon-Sat 10-5, Sun 1-5. **Dir:** I-69 Exit 19: E on Rte 38 to light in downtown Pendleton. Turn R 1-1/2 blks, shop on L.

Pendleton Antique Mall [G30]
123 W State St
(765)778-2303

Complete line of antiques including country, quilts & primitives as well as a good selection of furniture & reference books. **Pr:** $1-3,000 **Est:** 1984 **Hrs:** Mon-Sat 10-5, Sun 1-5. **Sz:** L **CC:** V/MC/DIS **Dir:** I-69 N

Use the Service QuickCode indexes at the back of the book to find restorers, appraisers, refinishers, and other specialty service providers.

Exit 19: E 1.5 mi on Rte 38. 20 mi NE of Indianapolis. **Own:** Joe & Jo-Anna Hanshew. **QC: 1 34 48 S8 S19**

Bob Post Antiques
104 W State St
(765)778-7778

Books, records, furniture, glassware, architectural. **Hrs:** Mon-Sat 10-5, Sun 12-5.

Peru

Annie's Attic
57 N Broadway
(765)473-4400

Quality antiques & collectibles. **Hrs:** Mon-Sat 9:30-5.

Peru Antique Mall [G]
21 E Main St
(765)473-8179

Hrs: Mon-Tue & Thu-Sat 10-5, Sun 1-5 (closed Wed).

Pierceton

Antique Town Mall
107-109 N First St
(219)594-9665

Hrs: Mon-Sat 10-5, Sun 12-5.

The Curiosity Shop
112 S First St
(219)594-2785

Est: 1980 **Hrs:** Mon-Sat 10-5, Sun 12-5.

Gregory's Antique Mall [G]
306-308 N First St
(219)594-5718

Hrs: Mon-Sat 10-5.

Visit our web site at
www.antiquesource.com for more
information about antiquing in the
Midwest and New England.

Huntington House Antiques
123 N First St
(219)594-5074

Collectibles, glassware. **Hrs:** Mon 10-5, Fri 1-5, Sat 10-5, Tue-Thu by chance. **QC: 32 61**

Old Theater Antique Mall
103 N 1st St
(219)594-2533

Hrs: Mon-Sat 10-5, Sun 1-5.

Roberta's Antiques
117 S First St
(219)594-2081

Est: 1986 **Hrs:** Mon-Sat 10-5, Sun 12-5.

Plainfield

Gilley's Antique Mall [G400]
Rte 40
(317)839-8779

Antiques & collectibles. **Hrs:** Daily 10-5. **Sz:** H **Dir:** 10 min W of Indianapolis off I-70, 1 mi W of Plainfield.

Rensselaer

Rensselaer Antiques & More [G17]
100 W Washington St
(219)866-2777

A small mall on the NE corner of courthouse square. Furniture, teapots, books, sport cards, hats & more. **Pr:** $1-1,000 **Est:** 1993 **Hrs:** Tue-Sat 10-5, Sun 12-4. **Sz:** M **Dir:** Intersection of IN Rte 114 & US Rte 231 4 mi E of I-65. **Own:** Judy Kanne.

Richmond

Foster's "E" St Gallery
825 N "E" St
(765)935-9055

Art, antiques & jewelry. **Hrs:** Tue-Sat 10-4. **Own:** Charles A Foster & Elizabeth Brittenham Foster. **QC: 7**

Terry Harkleroad Antiques

1110 Sylvan Nook Dr
(765)966-5353

Garden & architectural antiques, country furniture, primitives, folk art, quilts. **Hrs:** By appt only. **QC: 3 60 41**

Top Drawer Antique Mall

801 E Main St
(765)939-0349
(888)I-BUY-OLD

Antiques & collectibles. **Hrs:** Mon-Sun 11-6. **Own:** John Johnson & Steve Markley.

Rising Sun

The Front Parlor

307 S Walnut (IN 56)
(812)438-3751
rross@venus.net

Located along the Ohio River scenic route, this shop is housed in a "painted lady" Victorian home & features glass, linens & quilts as well as gifts & decorative accessories. A friendly place to browse. **Pr:** $50-400 **Est:** 1988 **Hrs:** Mon-Tue & Fri-Sat 10-5:30, Thu 10-7, Wed & Sun by chance. **Sz:** M **CC:** V/MC **Dir:** I-275 exit US 50 W to Aurora, then take IN 56 to Rising Sun. 3rd blk on L after 2nd 4-way stop. **Own:** Nanci C Ross. **QC: 81 36 22 S8**

Rochester

Green Oak Antiques

4166 E 300 S
(219)223-5702

Dressers, tables, cupboards, armoires, dining sets, benches, sideboards, chairs. **Est:** 1978 **Hrs:** Mon-Wed & Fri-Sun 10-5 (closed Thu). **Dir:** 3 mi S of Rochester on US Rte 31, 1/4 mi E on 300 S. **QC: 48**

Rushville

Rushville Antique Mall [G]

309 N Main St
(765)938-4093

Antiques, collectibles & decorator items. **Hrs:** Mon-Sat 9-6, Sun 12-5. **Sz:** H.

San Pierre

San Pierre Market Inc [G]

Rte 421
(219)828-4411 • (219)828-3023
(219)828-3381 (fax)

Furniture restoration shop on premises. **QC: S16**

Around the Fire

Fireboard: A decorated board used to hide the fireplace opening in summer.

Fireback: Cast iron plate standing behind the fire to protect the brick or stone and to throw the heat forward into the room.

Firescreen: A small screen, usually of fine needlework in a frame, that can be moved up and down a pole rising from a tripod base. Firescreens were used to protect ladies' faces from the direct heat of the fire in order to preserve their fine complexions. As only the complexions of the upper classes appeared to be susceptible to such damage, firescreens are invariably high-quality pieces of furniture.

Fireboards, firebacks, and firescreens were all beautifully decorated and are thus very collectible today.

Seymour

Crossroads Antique Mall [G]
311 Holiday Sq
(812)522-5675

Smalls, primitives, advertising, toys, pottery, Flow Blue. **Hrs:** Daily 9-5 CST.

Remember When
317 N Broadway
(812)522-5099

Hrs: Tues-Sat 10-5 or by appt. **Dir:** State Rd 11, 3-1/2 blocks N of State Hwy 50.

Silver Lake

D & J Antique Mall [G]
State Rd 14
(219)352-2400

Hrs: Mon-Sat 10-5, Sun 12-5. **Sz:** H.

Smartsburg

The Fireside Antique Mall
4035 St Rte 32
(765)362-8711

Hrs: Mon-Sat 10-5, Sun 1-5. **Dir:** 3-1/2 mi E of Crawfordsville. Near I-74 Exit 39.

South Bend

Dixie Way South Antiques
63760 Rte 31
(219)291-3931

Furniture & collectibles. **Hrs:** Daily 10-5 (closed Wed). **QC: 48**

Unique Antique Mall [G]
50981 US Rte 33 N
(219)271-1799

Furniture (oak, walnut, cherry), country primitives, glassware, pottery, jewelry, dolls, toys, clocks, books, flow blue, Belleek. **Hrs:** Daily 10-5. **QC: 50 61 35**

Stilesville

Old Gym Antique Mall
Johnsons Corner
(317)539-6111 • (317)539-2031

Furniture, toys, collectibles. **Hrs:** Wed-Sun 12-5. **QC: 48 87**

Swayzee

Swayzee Antique Mall [G]
115 N Washington (State Rd 13)
(765)922-7903

General line. **Hrs:** Mon, Wed, Thu 10-5, Fri-Sat 10-5, Sun 12-6. **Sz:** L.

Terre Haute

Shady Lane Antique Mall [G100+]
9247 S US Hwy 41
(812)299-1625

Wide selection of antiques & collectibles including jewelry, silver, Indian artifacts, furniture, banks, Roseville, clocks, flow blue, R S Prussia, Royal Doulton, advertising, reference books on antiques. **Pr:** $1-3,000 **Est:** 1983 **Hrs:** Mon-Sat 10-6, Sun 1-5. **Sz:** H **CC:** AX/V/MC/DIS **Dir:** 6 mi S of I-70 (Exit 7) on US Hwy 41. **Own:** Darrell & Jeanne Bemis. **QC: 34 32 22 S12**

Thorntown

Countryside Antique Mall [G]
4889 N US Hwy 52
(765)436-7200

Furniture, primitives, glassware, collectibles. **Hrs:** Daily 10-5. **Sz:** H.

Tipton

Tipton Antique Center [G]
114-116 S Main St
(765)675-8993

Antiques & collectibles. **Hrs:** Mon-Sat 10-6, Sun 10-5. **Own:** Ron LaVassaur.

Union City

Union City Antique Mall [G]
201 N Columbia
(765)964-3203

Hrs: Mon-Sat 10-5 (Fri til 8), Sun 12-5.

Wakarusa

Yoder Brothers Antique Mall
114 S Elkhart St
(219)862-2270

Warren

The Racketty Packetty Shop
118 Wayne St

Books, jugs, glassware & ceramic. **Hrs:** Fri-Sat 11-6. **QC: 61 18**

Westfield

Antiques Galore & More
110 E Main St
(317)867-1228

Victoriana, Indian art, art glass & pottery. **Hrs:** Tue-Sat 11-4.

R Beauchamp Antiques Inc
16405 Westfield Blvd
(317)896-3717

Direct importers of English & French 18th-

20th C furniture & accessories. **Hrs:** Tue-Sat 12-5. **Own:** Bob & Michelle Beauchamp.

Westfield Antique Mall [G]
800 E Main St
(317)867-3327

Furniture, toys, tools, Coca-cola, glass, Art Deco. **Hrs:** Mon-Fri 10-6, Sat 10-5, Sun 12-5. **Sz:** H **Dir:** 1-1/2 mi E of Hwy 31 on State Rd 32.

Winchester

White Barn Antiques
3908 E State Rte 28
(765)584-2823

General line. **Hrs:** Daily 10-5.

Wolcottville

Wolcottville Antique Mall [G]
106 N Main St
(219)854-3111 • (219)854-4226 (fax)

Furniture, glassware, primitives, pottery, memorabilia. **Hrs:** Mon-Sat 9-5 (12-4 in Sum). **Sz:** H **Dir:** 18 mi from Shipshewana.

Michigan

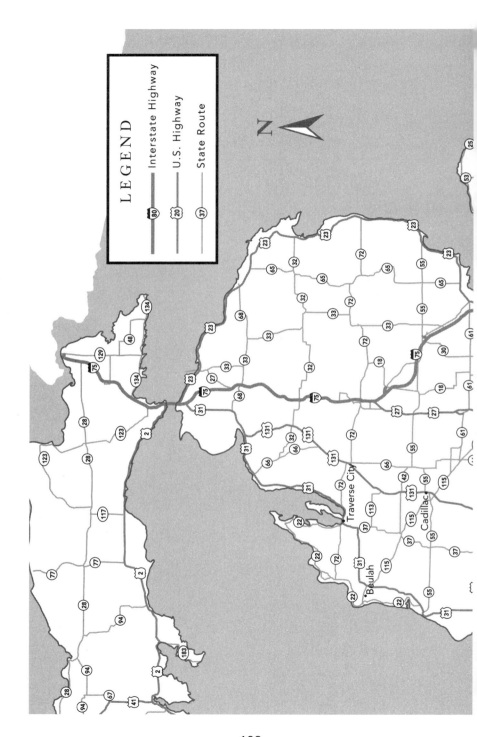

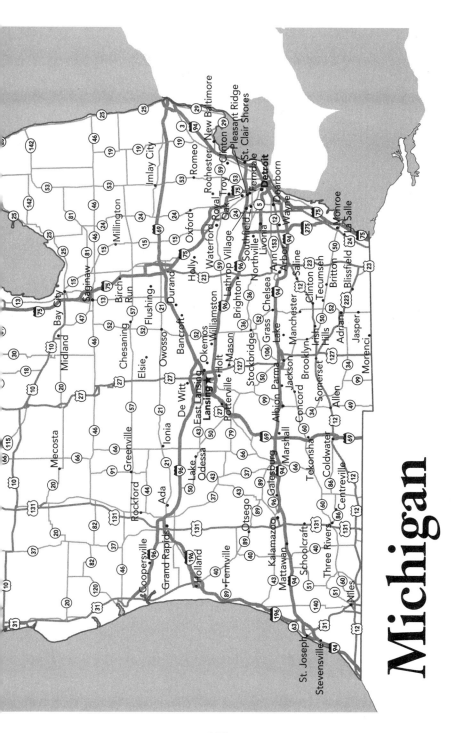

Michigan

Ada

Mad Anthony Books
(800)743-5404

Reference books on antiques, art & collectibles as well as out-of-print books on the decorative arts & antique bookends. **Pr:** $9.95-550 **Hrs:** At shows & mail order only. **CC:** V/MC **Own:** Linda Roggow & Carole Chenevert. **QC: 19 18**

Adrian

Aureas Oriental Boutique Ltd
128 S Main St
(517)263-5111

Jade carvings, oriental antiques, rosewood & wood carvings. **Hrs:** Mon-Sat 10-7.

Birdsall Depot
4106 N Adrian Hwy
(517)265-7107

Primitives & collectibles. **Hrs:** Mon-Fri 8-5, Sat 10-5, Sun 12-5.

Albion

Harley's Antique Mall [G95]
13789 Donovon Rd
(517)531-5300

Fine furnishings & unique treasures. **Hrs:** Daily 10-8. **Dir:** I-94 Exit 127 (Concord Rd). 10 mi W of Jackson.

Allen

Allen Antique Mall [G242]
9011 E Chicago Rd (Old Rte 12)
(517)869-2788

Furniture, Indian artifacts, sports memorabilia. 50s style restaurant on premises. **Hrs:** Mon-Sat 10-5, Sun 12-5.

Andy's Antiques
118 W Chicago Rd
(517)869-2182

Oldest established shop in Allen. Furniture, copper, brass & primitives. **Hrs:** Mon, Tue & Thu-Sat 10-5.

Antique East Side Mall [G100+]
237 E Chicago Rd (US Rte 12)
(517)869-2039

Antiques & collectibles. **Hrs:** Daily 10-5.

Chicago Pike Antiques [G]
211 W Chicago Rd
(517)869-2719

Glass, Victorian & Depression, china, pictures, lamps, furniture, sports memorabilia. **Hrs:** Daily 11-5 (Win Tue-Wed by chance).

Grandpa's Attic Antiques
222 E Chicago Rd
(517)523-2993

Glassware, tins, primitives & tools. **Hrs:** Mar-Oct daily 9-1:30 (closed Wed), Sat-Sun 9-5; Nov-Feb Thu-Sun 9-5.

Hand & Heart Antiques
109 W Chicago
(517)869-2553

Early Americana, folk art, country, Victorian, decoys & folk art carvings by Brent Baribeau. Buy & sell. **Hrs:** Daily 12-5 in Sum, Win by chance/appt. **QC: 1 41 34**

A Horse of Course
106 Prentiss St
(517)869-2527 • (517)524-6402

Primitives, trunks & music. **Hrs:** Mon-Tue & Thu-Fri til 4, Sat-Sun til 5.

Peddlers Alley
162 W Chicago Rd
(517)869-2280

Oak, walnut & pine furniture. Cupboards, glass & jewelry. **Hrs:** Mon-Tue & Thu-Sun 11-5 (also closed Thu in Win).

Ann Arbor

Ann Arbor Antiques Marketplace [G]
210-212 S First St
(734)913-8890
Hrs: Mon-Sun 10-6.

Ann Arbor Antiques Market [G350+]
5055 Ann Arbor - Saline Rd
(734)662-9453

Antiques & vintage collectibles. All items guaranteed as represented. Delivery service, snack bars with custom-made food. **Est:** 1968 **Hrs:** Call for show dates. **Dir:** I-75 Exit 7: S 3 mi. **Own:** Margaret Brusher.

Bancroft

Roune Galleries
104 S Main
(517)634-9111
Hrs: Fri-Tue 11-6.

Bay City

Bay City Antiques Center [G200]
1010 N Water St
(517)893-0251 • (517)893-1116
(517)893-1424 (fax)
antique@antiquecenteronline.com
www.antiquecenteronline.com

Michigan's largest. Voted #1 antique mall in Michigan by AAA readers. A full city block of antiques on 3 floors along the historic river in downtown Bay City. Barrier-free, climate-controlled, lots of parking. **Pr:** $1-9,000 **Est:** 1983 **Hrs:** Mon-Sat 10-5, Sun 12-5. **Sz:** H **CC:** AX/V/MC/DIS **Dir:** I-75 Exit 162A to downtown Bay City. L at 1st light after river, then N 6 blks to Third St. L 1 blk to Water St. **Own:** Bill & Elaine Fournier. **QC: 55 20 48 S9 S12 S19**

Beulah

Myers Granary Antique Market [G]
7300 Crystal Ave
(616)882-4299

General line including collectibles, glassware, jewelry, primitives, furniture, accessories, paintings & books. **Hrs:** May-Oct Mon-Sat 10-5, Sun 12-5. **Sz:** H.

Birch Run

Collector's Corner [G8]
11900 S Gera Rd
(517)624-4388

General line of antiques & collectibles, specializing in cookie jars. **Pr:** $2-2,000 **Est:** 1980 **Hrs:** Daily 10-5. **Sz:** M **CC:** V/MC/DIS **Dir:** I-75 exit 136: L at Gerard, L at 1st driveway. 4 mi S of Frankenmuth. **Own:** Patt Helmsmeier. **QC: 67 61 32**

Blissfield

Blissfield Antique Mall [G75+]
101 & 103 US 223
(517)486-2236

Largest selection of Depression glass in the area. Also a general line of antiques from Victorian to 1950s. Worldwide shipping. **Pr:** $0.10-8,000 **Est:** 1986 **Hrs:** Tue-Sat 10-5, Sun 12-5. **Sz:** H **CC:** V/MC/DIS **Assn:** TAADA SMADA **Dir:** US 23 N Exit 5: W 10 mi on US 223. Shop at SW corner of 1st light. **Own:** Matt Koester. **QC: 61 32 50 S12 S1 S14**

Estes Antiques Mall [G]
116-118 S Lane St
(517)486-4616

Large selection of cookie jars, jewelry, trains, glassware, lunchboxes, toys & a general line. **Hrs:** Tue-Sat 10:30-5, Sun 12-5. **Dir:** Downtown.

Green's Gallery of Antiques

115 S Lane St
(517)486-3080

Quality American antiques, Mission, Victorian, primitives, architecturals plus a general line. **Hrs:** Tue-Fri 11-5, Sat 10-5:30, Sun 12-5 or by appt. **Sz:** H **QC: 6 89**

J & B Antique Mall

109 W Adrian St
(517)486-3544

Furniture, china, fine glass & tools. **Hrs:** Tue-Sat 10-5, Sun 12-5. **Dir:** On Rte 223.

Memories on Lane St

104 S Lane St
(517)486-2327

Modern to antique dolls, bears, furniture, glassware, pottery & 1950s collectibles. **Hrs:** Daily 10-5.

Triple Bridge Antiques [G70+]

321 W Adrian St
(517)486-3777

Large selection of antiques, gifts & furniture. **Hrs:** Daily.

Williams Crossroads Antiques & Collectibles [G65]

10003 US Rte 223
(517)486-3315 • (517)486-2618 (fax)

Large selection of fine quality antique furniture & collectibles, silhouettes, china, artwork, glassware, records, vintage jukeboxes, jewelry & railroad memorabilia. **Pr:** $5-6,000 **Est:** 1996 **Hrs:** Mon-Sat 10-6, Sun 11-6. **Sz:** L **CC:** V/MC **Dir:** 8 mi W of US Rte 23 on US Rte 223 at the Blissfield village limits. **Own:** Anne & Vernon Williams. **QC: 50 58 32**

Brighton

Mill Pond Antique Galleries

217 W Main St
(810)229-8686

Furniture, art glass, oil paintings & oriental rugs. **Hrs:** Mon-Sat 10-5. **QC: 61 48 76 S2 S7 S9**

The Quaker Shoppe

210 Hyne St
(810)231-3530 • (810)229-6558

Primitives, tools, crocks & cupboards. **Hrs:**

Beds Great and Small II

Four-poster: A bed with four tall corner posts, that may, or may not, support a tester.

Campaign bed: A four poster bed, easily demountable, for use by military officers in the field.

Trundle bed or truckle bed: A low bed on wheels that was kept under a large bed and trundled out at night for use, probably by a child.

Hired man's bed: A narrow slatted bed, often spool turned, produced in quantity by factories in the Midwest and New England between about 1840 and 1890. Despite its name, it was designed as cottage furniture, not for servants.

Bed bench or bed settle: A wooden bench or settle whose box-like seat opened out to form a bed.

Sleigh bed: Bed with curved head- and foot-boards resembling a sleigh. An Empire period design, showing the French influence whose popularity at the time reflected the belief that the French Revolution and the American Revolution were twins.

Thu-Sat by chance/appt. **Own:** Rita Altenburg. **QC: 86**

Britton

Britton Village Antiques
126 E Chicago Blvd
(517)451-8129

Hrs: Thu-Sun 10-5 or by chance. **Dir:** M-50 W of railroad tracks.

McKinney's Collectibles
108 E Chicago Blvd
(517)451-2155

Beer steins, signs, neons, baseball cards, sets & comics, beer cans. **Hrs:** Mon-Fri 2:30-6, Sat 10-5 or by appt.

YesterYears Antiques
208 E Chicago
(517)451-8600

Quality line of gnarl antiques. **Hrs:** Thu-Sun 11-5:30 & Sum hols.

Brooklyn

Brooklyn Depot Antiques / Brosamer's Bells
207 Irwin St
(517)592-6885

Bells of all kinds, unusual items, antique office furniture. **Hrs:** By chance/appt.

Memory Lane Antiques [G]
12939 S M-50
(517)592-4218

Antiques & collectibles including toys, pottery, cast iron cookware, glassware & dairy items. Also oak furniture. **Hrs:** Daily 10:30-6. **CC:** V/MC/DIS

Pinetree Centre Antique Mall [G60+]
129 N Main St
(517)592-3808

Antiques & collectibles. **Hrs:** Mon-Sat 10-5, Sun 12-6. **Dir:** M-50 downtown.

Cadillac

Royer's Antique Mall [G]
211 Bell Ave
(616)779-2434

Specializing in Depression glass, toys, tins, china, pottery, furniture, fishing tackle & lures. **Est:** 1978 **Hrs:** Jun-Labor Day daily 12-5, Labor Day-May 10-5.

Centreville

Centreville Antiques Market [G550+]
State Rte 86
(773)227-4464
www.antiquemarkets.com

Over 500 exhibitors, all merchandise guaranteed, furniture delivery service available. Free parking. Admission $4 per person. Food. **Hrs:** Call for schedule. **Dir:** At the Fairgrounds.

Chelsea

Fireside Antiques
1196 S Main St (M-52)
(313)475-9390 • (313)475-7113

Hrs: Thu-Fri 12-5, Sat 10-5 or by appt. **Dir:** Off I-94 on M-52. **Own:** Mary Jo Miller.

Chesaning

Fancy That Antiques & Uniques
324 W Broad
(517)845-7775 • (517)845-4190 (fax)
(800)752-0532

Antiques & collectibles. Perfume & atomizer repair. **Hrs:** Mon-Sat 10-6, Sun 12-5. **QC: 32 S1 S8 S16**

Clinton

First Class Antique Mall
112 E Michigan Ave
(517)456-6410 • (517)456-6339 (fax)

General line of high-quality antiques, garment buttons & motorcycle memorabilia. **Hrs:** Tue-Sat 10-6, Sun 11-5. **Sz:** H.

Oak City Antiques
1101 US Rte 12
(517)456-4444

Antiques, reproductions & collectibles. **Hrs:** Daily 10-6 (closed Mon in Win).

The Rose Patch Antiques
162 W Michigan Ave
(517)456-6473

Furniture, collectibles, guy stuff & the unusual. All affordably priced. **Pr:** $5-2,500 **Est:** 1992 **Hrs:** Mon-Tue & Fri-Sat 10:30-5, Sun 11-5, Wed by chance (closed Thu). **Sz:** L **Dir:** On US 12, 20 mi W of US 23, in downtown Clinton. **Own:** Marty & Kathy Sugierski. **QC: 3 32 48 S12**

The Turn of the Century Lighting Co
116 W Michiagn Ave
(517)456-6019

Hundreds of antique fixtures. Specializing in gas & electric lighting from the Victorian era. **Hrs:** Sat-Sun 10-5 or by appt. **QC: 65**

The Wooden Box
141 W Michigan Ave
(517)456-7556

General line of antiques & collectibles, pianos, dolls & toys. **Hrs:** Sum Wed-Sat 11-4, Win Fri-Sun 11-4. **QC: 38 87**

Coldwater

Faith Baribeau's Fairfields Farm Antiques
868 Marshall Rd
(517)278-6485

General line. **Hrs:** Daily 10-4 by chance/appt (closed Win).

Concord

The Antique Cellar [G]
102 S Main
(517)524-8675 • (517)524-8872 (fax)

Vintage clothing, furniture, collectibles. **Hrs:** Thu-Sat 10-6. **QC: 48 32**

Fuzzy's Old Toys & Antiques [G]
12123 M-60
(517)524-9027

Buy, sell & trade. **Hrs:** Mon-Sat 10-6, Sun 12-6. **Dir:** I-94 to exit 127 or exit 136. **Own:** Richard & Mildred. **QC: 87**

King Road Granary
12700 King Rd
(517)524-6006

Antiques, collectibles, furniture & gifts. **Hrs:** Daily 10-6.

Mother 'n Sons Antiques & Collectibles
119 M-60
(517)524-8017

Specializing in quality furniture, trunks & select smalls. **Hrs:** Tue-Sat 10-5, Sun 12-5.

Coopersville

Coopersville Antiques & Collectibles [G]
6862 Arthur Rd W
(616)837-8547

Hrs: Mon-Sat 10-6, Sun 12-5. Dir: I-96 to exit 16. QC: S12

Dearborn

Howard Street Antiques
921 Howard
(313)563-9352

Hrs: Mon-Fri 10-6, Sat 10-4, Sun 12-4 (by chance). Dir: N of Michigan Ave.

Village Antiques [G35]
22630 Michigan Ave
(313)563-1230

Hrs: Mon-Sat 10:30-5:50 (Thu til 7:30), Sun 12-5. Dir: On US Rte 12 between US 24 & M-39.

Dewitt

Liberty Antique Mall [G]
1161 E Clark Rd
(517)646-0626 • (517)669-2624

Hrs: Mon-Sat 10-9, Sun 12-5. Dir: Rt 27 & I-69 exit 87: S of exit. Own: Pam Bogi.

Durand

The Country Cupboard
10260 E Bennington Rd
(517)288-3659

Hrs: Thu-Sat 10-5 by chance/appt.

Our Place
122 N Saginaw St
(517)288-5856

Hrs: Mon-Sat 10-6, Sun 11-5.

East Lansing

The Archives Book Shop
517-519 W Grand River
(517)332-8444

Large selection of scholarly books & collectibles. Hrs: Mon-Sat 11-6, Sun 12-5. QC: 19 32

Elsie

Melvin Antique & Clock Shop
8401 Island Rd
(517)862-4322

Furniture, clocks, glassware & collectibles. Hrs: Daily 10-8 by chance/appt. Dir: 3/4 mi W of stoplight on W Main St. QC: 35 48 32 S7

Fennville

Bird Cage Antiques [G]
Blue Star Hwy
(616)543-4732

Specializing in diningroom sets & English style wardrobes. Hrs: Fri-Mon 12-5. Dir: At the int with M-89.

Flushing

R & J Needful Things [G170+]
6398 W Pierson Rd
(810)659-2663
www.antiqueit.com

Antiques & collectibles. Also carry Lightning Stripper, brass hardware, Briwax, Never-Dull Polish & a selection of antique reference books. Hrs: Daily 10-5. CC: V/MC

Galesburg

Grant's Antique Market [G30]
33 W Battle Creek St
(616)665-4300

Furniture, glassware & collectibles. **Hrs:** Tue-Sat 10-5, Sun 12-5. **Dir:** I-94 Exit 85 or 88 just E of Kalamazoo, then N approx 2 mi to Galesburg.

Grand Rapids

All Era Antiques & Classics
2 Jefferson Ave SE
(616)454-9955

Hrs: Mon-Sat 1-7.

Antiques by the Bridge [G]
445 Bridge St NW
(616)451-3430

Quality furniture (Victorian, Deco, Mission), primitives, vintage clothing, pottery, art, china, glass, textiles & lighting. **Hrs:** Tue-Sat 10-5, Sun 12-5. **CC:** V/MC **QC: 49**

Lamplight & Old Glass Ltd
(616)942-0645

Extensive inventory of American pressed pattern glass, children's toy pattern glass & kerosene lamps. Free search service. **Pr:** $10-1,000 **Hrs:** By appt only. **Dir:** Call for directions. **Own:** Nancy E Smith. **QC: 65 61 1 S1 S9**

Perception Gallery
7 Ionia SW
(616)451-2393

19th-20th C paintings, watercolors & prints; period & period reproduction framing; painting & print restoration services. **Pr:** $100-50,000 **Est:** 1989 **Hrs:** Sep-May 20 Tue-Fri 10-5:30, Sat 10-2; May 21-Aug Tue-Fri 10-5:30. **Sz:** M **CC:** V/MC **Dir:** 131 N to downtown exit, L on Ionia, 2 blks N on L. **Own:** Kim Smith. **QC: 7 74 S1 S13 S16**

Plaza Antique Mall
1410 28th St SE
(616)243-2465

Glass, china, pottery, primitives, furniture & reference books. **Hrs:** Mon-Sat 10-7, Sun 1-5. **QC: 48 61 19**

Yarrington Antiques
6718 Old 27th St SE
(616)956-6800 • (616)954-1455

A quality shop packed full with art, pattern, Depression & finer glasswares; pottery, porcelain & dinnerware; tools, furniture, paper items, pictures, jewelry, lighting, buttons, metalwares. Quaint & beautiful, odd & unusual, treasures arriving daily. **Pr:** $1-1,600 **Est:** 1996 **Hrs:** Tue-Fri 12:30-5:30, Sat 10-5. **Sz:** M **CC:** V/MC **Dir:** I-96/28th St interchange: 28th St 1.7 mi E, then R (S) onto Old 28th St, just before Cascade Rd. **Own:** Bob & Peggy Boverhof. **QC: 22 48 61 S12**

Greenville

Greenville Antique Center [G75+]
400 S Lafayette
(616)754-5540

Featuring toy trains, reference books, old stoves, tools, pedal cars, furniture, glassware, jewelry, light fixtures, oil lamps, linens & pottery. **Hrs:** Sun-Wed 11-6, Thu-Fri 11-8, Sat 10-8. **Sz:** H **CC:** V/MC/DIS **QC: 65 87 48**

Holland

Nob Hill Antique Mall [G25]
1261 Graafschap Rd
(616)392-1424

Unique 130-year-old building housing 25

dealers and 1 clock repair person. **Pr:** $3-3,000 **Est:** 1985 **Hrs:** Mon-Sat 10-5:30. **Sz:** L **CC:** V/MC **Dir:** US 31 Exit 47B: 1 mi W on Matt Urban Dr (48th St) to village of Graffschap. **Own:** Jack Piers. **QC:** 22 32 48 S7

Tulip City Antique Mall [G200+]

3500 US Rte 31
(616)786-4424 • (616)786-4426 (fax)
www.classic-link.com/tulipcity.htm

Dolls, glass, fine china, pottery, restored radios, Indian artifacts, vintage clothing, advertising, toys, collectible books, jewelry. **Hrs:** Mon-Sat 10-6, Sun 12-6 (closed Xmas, Thanks, Easter). **Sz:** H **CC:** V/MC **Dir:** 1-1/2 mi N of Westshore Mall.

Holly

Battle Alley Arcade Antiques Mall [G25]

108 Historic Battle Alley
(248)634-8800

Victoriana, dolls, primitives, ephemera, books, jewelry, furniture, glassware & vintage clothing. **Hrs:** Tue-Sat 10:30-5:30, Sun 12-5 (closed Mon). **Dir:** Exit 98 off I-75 or Exit 79 off US 23. **QC:** 39 38 89

Holly Antiques on Main

118 S Saginaw St
(248)634-7696

Furniture, glass, pottery, toys, country store, primitives, advertising, Victoriana. **Hrs:** Tue-Sat 10-5, Sun 11-4 (closed Mon). **QC:** 48 61

Holly Water Tower Antiques Mall

310 S Broad St
(248)634-3500

Hrs: Tue-Sat 10-5 (Fri til 7), Sun 12-5 (closed Mon).

Imlay City

Memory Junction Antiques & Collectibles [G6]

244 E Third St
(810)724-4811 • (810)724-6590 (fax)
antiques@cardina.net

Quality collection of English porcelain, Depression glass, jewelry, militaria & postcards. Buy, sell & handle estates. **Pr:** $25-3,000 **Est:** 1993 **Hrs:** Mon-Sat 10-5. **Sz:** L **CC:** V/MC/DIS **Dir:** I-69 Exit 168: 1-1/2 mi N on M-53, then 1 blk W on Third St. **Own:** Robert & Melanie Norberg. **QC:** 23 30 48 S12 S1

Ionia

Grand River Antiques

7050 S State
(616)527-8880

Vintage clothing, primitives, linens, quilts, oak furniture, painted furniture, jewelry, Indian artifacts. **Hrs:** Daily 10-5. **Dir:** 1/4 mi N of I-96 on Hwy 66 exit 67.

Ionia Antique Mall [G]

415 W Main St
(616)527-6720

Hrs: Mon-Sat 10-5 (Fri til 9), Sun 12-5. **Sz:** L.

Irish Hills

Artesian Wells Antique Mall [G100+]

18707 W Toledo Rd
(517)547-7422

Specializing in antique furniture, advertising, primitives, books & lamps as well as art glass, clocks, fine art, jewelry, pottery, Royal Doulton, Tiffany, trunks, Winchester & reference books. **Hrs:** Daily 10-6. **Sz:** H **Dir:** At the intersection of Rtes 12, 127 & 223, 15 min S of Jackson.

The Enchanted Schoolhouse
14012 US Rte 12
(517)592-4365
General line of quality antiques, folk art, primitives & artist originals. **Hrs:** Mon-Sat 10-6, Sun 12-5; Jan-Mar closed Tue-Wed. By chance/appt. **Dir:** 2 mi W of M-50, 5 mi E of US 127.

Gateway Antiques Irish Hills
2519 W US Rte 12
(517)456-4532
Hrs: Seasonal. Mon-Fri by chance/appt, Sat-Sun 12-6. **CC:** V/MC **Dir:** 1 mi W of M-52.

Irish Hills Antiques
10600 US Rte 12
(517)467-4646
General line specializing in antique wood & coal-burning parlor & kitchen stoves. **Hrs:** Daily 10-6 or by chance/appt. **Dir:** 1 mi E of M-50.

Muggsie's Antiques & Collectibles
12982 W US Rte 12
(517)592-2659 • (517)467-4725
General line, children's items & furniture. **Hrs:** Fri-Mon 12-5.

Jackson

Ann's Copper, Brass & Glass
218 S Mechanic St
(517)782-8817
Hrs: Mon-Sat 12-5, Sun by appt only. **QC: 20**

The Antique Shop
340 Otsego
(517)787-2033
Old guns & ammo, military items, fishing tackle, musical instruments. **Hrs:** Mon-Fr 8-5, Sat 8-12. **QC: 4 79 69**

The Camp Gallery [G]
109 W Washington
(517)780-0606
(800)962-5038
Antiques, collectibles, crafts. The beautiful the unique, the perfect gifts. **Hrs:** Mon-Sa 9-6, Sun 12-5. **Sz:** H.

Drinking Glasses I

Cordial glass: A small glass made in the late 17th and throughout the 18th centuries for drinking sweet liqueurs, or cordials. In the 18th century, cordials were commonly drunk with tea.

Surfeit water glass: Surfeit water was a very strong 18th century brandy, so the glasses from which to drink it were small, about three-quarters of an inch in diameter, and usually flute shaped.

Toasting glass or firing glass: A short, stubby glass made strong enough to be knocked loudly on the table when toasts were drunk. As toasts tended to be numerous, and the rapping increased in volume as they progressed, the glasses had to be strong indeed. Another type of toasting glass was made with a slender stem that could easily be snapped to mark a special occasion. Predictably, these are difficult to collect.

Dram: Today a measure of liquid, an eighth of a fluid ounce. Our forefathers were untroubled by such precision and used the word more loosely as a measure of the smallest amount of liquor that was worth drinking.

Jackson Antique Mall [G]
201 N Jackson St
(517)784-3333

Quality antiques & collectibles. **Hrs:** Mon-Sat 10-6, Sun 12-5. **CC:** V/MC.

Treasurable Finds Antiques Etc
145 N Jackson St
(517)768-1120

Specializing in Depression glass. **Hrs:** Mon-Fri 9:30-5:30, Sat 10-4. **QC:** 61

Jasper

Jasper Trading Post
8380 S M-52
(517)436-3107

Affordable antiques & collectibles. Pre-1940s items bought & sold. **Hrs:** Thu-Sun 9-6, closed Jan-Mar.

Kalamazoo

Alamo Depot
6187 W "D" Ave
(616)373-3885

Hrs: Mon-Sat 10-6, Sun 12-6. **Dir:** 131 to exit 44 then W 1/2 mi.

Kalamazoo Antiques Market [G30]
120 N Edwards St
(616)226-9788 • (616)343-1259 (fax)

In the early 1890s, the Kalamazoo Antiques Market was a carriage maker's shop. Today it holds the wares of 30 dealers who offer a broad selection of high-quality antiques from Victorian to early country to collectibles. **Pr:** $5-250 **Est:** 1995 **Hrs:**

Mon-Sat 11-6, Sun 1-5. **Sz:** L **CC:** V/MC **QC: 6 23 63 S4 S8 S18**

Kalamazoo Antiques Market
100 N. Edwards St. (behind Wendy's)
Kalamazoo Ave.
Michigan Ave.
Westnedge Ave.
Park St.
Portage St.
BUS 131
BUS 131
M43
M43
BUS 94
BUS 94
N
DOWNTOWN KALAMAZOO

Lake Odessa

Lake-O-Antique Mall [G]
1014 4th Ave
(616)374-3078

Hrs: Wed 10-8, Sat & Sun 10-5.

Lansing

Antique Connection [G100+]
5411 S Cedar St
(517)882-8700

Antiques, collectibles, dolls & jewelry. **Hrs:** Mon-Fri 10-9, Sat 10-6, Sun 12-5. **Dir:** 1 mi N of I-96, Cedar St exit 104, across from K-Mart. **QC: 38**

Mid-Michigan Mega Mall [G200+]
15487 S Rte 27
(517)487-3275

Hrs: Daily 11-6 (Thu til 8:30). **Dir:** 2 mi S of I-69.

Triola's
1114 E Mt Hope Rd
(517)484-5414

Classic modern furniture & decorative objects from Art Deco to 60s. Herman

Miller, Knoll, Widdicomb, Dunbar, Heywood, Wakefield furniture; Russel Wright & Eva Zeisel dinnerware; nostalgia & popular culture. **Hrs:** Mon-Sat 12-5 or by appt. **Own:** Bill Triola. **QC: 5 59**

LaSalle

American Heritage Antique Mall [G50]
5228 S Otter Creek Rd
(313)242-3430

Wide & varied assortment of antiques & collectibles. **Hrs:** Daily 10-5. **Dir:** I-75 Exit 9.

Lathrup Village

Michael's Lamp Shop
17621 W 12 Mile Rd
(810)557-8828

Antique style shades, antique lamps, wall sconces, chandeliers, floor & table lamps. Lamp & shade repair. **QC: 65**

Livonia

Town & Country Antiques Mall [G48+]
31630 Plymouth Rd
(313)425-4344

General line including furniture, glassware, lamps & toys. **Hrs:** Daily 11-6 (Thu-Sat til 8). **Sz:** L **CC:** V/MC **Dir:** Behind Eastside Mario's. **QC: 34 38**

Manchester

Manchester Antique Mall [G]
116 E Main St
(313)428-9357

Furniture, porcelain, glass, rugs, primitives, silver & collectibles. **Hrs:** Daily 10-5.

Marshall

Hildor House Antiques
105 W Michigan Avenue
(616)789-0009

Hrs: Mon-Sat 10-5, Sun 12-5.

J H Cronin Antique Center
101 W Michigan Ave
(616)789-0077

Hrs: Mon-Sat 10-5, Sun 12-5. **Own:** Ted Tear.

Marshall House Antique Center [G]
100 Exchange St
(616)781-7841

Hrs: Mon-Sat 11-5, Sun 12-5.

Pineapple Lane Antiques
209 W Michigan Ave
(616)789-1445

Hrs: Mon-Sat 11-5, Sun 12-5. **Own:** Mike Masters & Mary Trimner.

Mason

Mason Antiques District [G45+]
111-208 Mason St
(517)676-9753

Furniture, primitives, jewelry, toys, dolls, glass, art glass lamps, paper, linens, clothing, old coins, paper money, fishing, sporting & collectibles. **Hrs:** Daily 10-6. **CC:** V/MC

Mattawan

Halsey Dean
24028 Front St
(616)668-3510

18th & 19th C American, French, English & Italian furniture, accessories, linens, silver & primitives. **Hrs:** Wed-Sun 12-5. **QC: 52 53 54**

William Lesterhouse Antiques
24020 Front St
(616)668-3229

Period American furniture, oriental art & glass. **Hrs:** Wed-Sun 12-5. **Dir:** I-94 exit 66: 1 mi S to 2nd light. **QC: 52 61**

Mecosta

The Browse Around Antique Mall [G7]
301 W Main St
(616)972-2990

China, furniture, pictures, primitives, glass, jewelry, hardware & refinishing supplies. **Hrs:** Mon-Sat 10-5, Sun 12-5.

Millington

Millington Antique Co-Op Mall [G40+]
8549 State St
(517)871-4597

Hrs: Daily 10-5 (Fri & Sat til 6). **Sz:** L **CC:** V/MC/DIS **Dir:** 25 mi from Flint & Saginaw, 30 mi from Bay City & 12 mi from Birch Run & Frankenmuth.

Millington Antique Depot [G40+]
8484 State St
(517)871-3300

Hrs: Daily 10-5 (Fri & Sat til 6). **CC:** V/MC/DIS **Dir:** 25 mi from Flint & Saginaw, 30 mi from Bay City & 12 mi from Birch Run & Frankenmuth.

Monroe

Sauer Furniture & Antiques
15300 S Dixie Hwy (M-125)
(313)242-6284

A full-service store featuring quality antiques & collectibles. **Hrs:** Tue-Fri 10-6, Sat 10-5. **Dir:** 1 mi S of Monroe.

Morenci

Brick Treasure House
118 W Main St
(800)762-8234

Quality antiques & collectibles — over 50,000 items. **Hrs:** Daily.

New Baltimore

Heritage Square Antique Mall [G20]
36821 Green St
(810)725-2453

Hrs: Tue-Sat 10-5, Sun 11-5. **CC:** V/MC **Dir:** I-94 E to 23 Mile Rd exit. **QC: S12**

Niles

Four Flags Antique Mall [G]
218 N 2nd St
(616)683-6681

Hrs: Mon-Fri 10-5, Sat 10-6, Sun 12-6.

Michiana Antique Mall [G89]
2423 S 11th St
(616)684-7001
(800)559-4694
michianaantiquemall@compuserve.com

Quality antiques & collectibles. **Pr:** $1-10,000 **Est:** 1973 **Hrs:** Daily 10-6. **Sz:** H **CC:** V/MC/DIS **Dir:** I-80/90 Exit 77 N 5 mi on E side of hwy. **QC: 61 22 50**

Pickers Paradise Antique Mall [G]
2809 S 11th St
(616)683-6644

Hrs: Daily 10-6.

Northville

The Barn Antiques [G25+]
48120 W 8 Mile Rd
(248)349-0117

Specializing in intricate glass, unique lamps, beautiful furniture & a wide variety of primitives in a barn re-built in the 1920s on a historic farmstead property dating from 1827. **Pr:** $5-5,000 **Est:** 1994 **Hrs:** Tue-Sat 10-5, Sun 12-5. **Sz:** L **CC:** V/MC **Dir:** I-96 Beck Rd Exit, S to 8 Mile Rd, W 1/4 mi. **Own:** Russ & Judy Elvy. **QC:** 34 52 36 S1 S8 S12

Knightsbridge Antique Mall [G150+]
42305 W 7 Mile Rd
(248)344-7200 • (248)471-9944

2nd location 32315 Grand River Ave, Farmington.

Okemos

Farm Village Antique Mall [G45+]
3448 Hagadorn Rd
(517)337-4988

Hrs: Mon-Sat 11-6, Sun 12-6. **CC:** V/MC/DIS **Dir:** I-96 exit 110 Okemos: N to 1st light (Jolly Rd), then W 1.6 mi to Hagadorn.

Otsego

Otsego Antiques Mall [G35]
114 W Allegan St
(616)694-6440

Decoys, dolls, furniture (oak & Victorian),

> Use the Specialty QuickCode indexes at the back of the book to find dealers who specialize in your area of interest.

garden antiques, glass/bottles, jewelry, memorabilia, mirrors, prints, sporting, textiles, toys & tools. **Est:** 1992 **Hrs:** Tue-Sat 10-6, Sun 1-5. **Sz:** L **CC:** V/MC/DIS **Dir:** Hwy 131 Exit 49B W on M89. **QC:** S6 S7 S8

Owosso

"I Remember That"!
2085 E Main (M-21)
(517)723-9397

Glassware, furniture, textiles, kitsch. **Hrs:** Mon-Sat 10-7, Sun 12-5. **QC:** 61 48 80

Owosso Midtown Antiques Mall [G]
1426 N M-52
(517)723-8604

Hrs: Mon-Sat 10:30-5:30, Sun 11-4:30. **Dir:** 2 mi N of M-21.

Oxford

Oxford Antique Mall [G]
18 N Washington St (M24)
(248)969-1951

Hrs: Sun-Wed 11-6, Thu-Sat 11-9.

Parma

Cracker Hill Antique Mall [G]
1200 Norton Rd
(517)531-4200

Furniture, primitives, tools, glass, graniteware, prints, paintings, collectibles. **Hrs:** Mon-Sat 10-6, Sun 12-6. **Sz:** M **CC:** V/MC/DIS **Dir:** I-94 exit 128. **QC:** 55 61 74

Pleasant Ridge

Denise Scott Antiques
(248)398-9745

18th & 19th C American furniture & decorative arts. **Pr:** $10-5,000 **Est:** 1991 **Hrs:** By appt only. **Own:** Sam & Denise Scott. **QC:** 1 52 51

Potterville

Elliott's Emporium

6976 Windsor Hwy
(517)645-4545
(800)864-5380

McCoy pottery, antler art, hunting & fishing, canoes & boats, primitives, bottles. **Hrs:** Mon-Sat 10-6, Sun 12-6. **CC:** AX/V/MC/DIS **Own:** Bill Elliott & Steve Swain.

Rochester

Antiques by Pamela

319 Main St
(248)652-0866

Specializing in Victorian, Nouveau & Edwardian jewelry. **Hrs:** Mon-Fri 10-6

(Thu til 8), Sat 10-5. **Own:** Pamela Krampf. **QC:** 63

Tally Ho! Antiques

404 Main St
(248)652-6860

Period furniture, vintage books, paintings, rugs & decorative accessories. **Hrs:** Mon-Fri 12-6 (Thu 12-8), Sat 10-5. **QC:** 54 36

Rockford

Rockford Antique Mall [G40]

54 Courtland St
(616)866-8240
tsc@x2.alliance.net

Furniture, glassware, silver, jewelry, toys, vintage clothing, linens, primitives, paper items, memorabilia, books, pottery & more. **Est:** 1996 **Hrs:** Daily. **Sz:** L **CC:** V/MC **Dir:** Rte 131 Rockford exit: 10 min N of Grand Rapids. **Own:** Tom Chamberlin. **QC:** 19 48

Alcoholic Antiques II

Monteith: A bowl used to cool drinking glasses in iced water. Its rim had notches into which stemmed glasses were slotted. Named after the 17th century Earl of Monteith, a court fop noted for the elaborately scalloped hems on his cloaks which the rim of the monteith resembled, the first British examples date to around 1680, while the first American one was made about 1700 by the Boston silversmith John Coney. Later monteiths were also made of porcelain and glass, sometimes with a removeable silver rim, in which case the bowl doubled as a punch bowl.

Wine stand: A small stand with a dish or tray top. It resembles a candlestand, but is two or three inches lower, making it a convenient height for a wine glass when placed at the arm of one's easy chair.

Toddy table: An 18th century name, now fallen into disuse, for a side table for holding drinks. Its alliterative aptness makes it a term worth reviving. The interior design guru David Hicks advises readers of *Antique Interiors International* that drinks should always be served on a marble- or stone-topped table and never from a cocktail cabinet, which he disdains as suitable only for the outer reaches of suburbia.

Can or wine can: A small handleless cup of silver or porcelain, usually a straight-sided or slightly flared cylinder, used for drinking wine in the 18th century.

Romeo

Town Hall Antiques [G50]
205 N Main St
(810)752-5422 • (810)752-5414 (fax)

A general line in two buildings on two floors. **Pr:** $5-5,000 **Est:** 1990 **Hrs:** Daily 10-6 exc Thanks, Xmas, New Years. **Sz:** H **CC:** V/MC/DIS **Dir:** M53 (Old Van Dyke) & 32 Mile Rd in downtown historic Romeo. **Own:** Kit Dimambro. **QC: 1 48 79 S10 S19**

Royal Oak

Antiques on Main
115 S Main St
(248)545-4663

Hrs: Mon-Sat 10-6.

Antiques Unlimited
831 E 11 Mile Rd
(248)545-4488

Tiffany, Handel & Pairpoint lamps; music boxes; oil paintings; clocks; oak & Victorian furniture; architectural & toys. **Hrs:** Thu-Sun 11-5. **QC: 65**

Jeffrey's 4th Street Antique Mall [G40]
404 E 4th St
(248)584-2220

Vintage American art pottery, art glass & estate jewelry as well as Art Deco, 50s & 60s Modern & Mission furniture & accessories. **Hrs:** Tue-Sat 10-6, Sun 12-5. **QC: 22 64**

Lovejoy's Antiques [G]
720 E 11 Mile Rd
(248)545-9060

From Victorian to Art Deco. **Hrs:** Tue-Thu 10-5, Fri 12-5, Sat-Sun 10-5. **Sz:** L **CC:** V/MC/DIS.

The Yellow House
125 N Washington
(248)541-2866

Country, folk art, primitives, tramp art, art pottery, vintage textiles & quilts. **Hrs:** Mon-Sat 11-5, Sun 12-5. **QC: 22 41 84**

Saginaw

Antique Warehouse [G70]
1910 N Michigan Ave
(517)755-4343

Lighting, oak furniture, pottery. **Hrs:** Mon-Sat 10-5, Sun 12-5. **Sz:** H **Dir:** I-75 exit N to I-675, then exit Davenport St. L on Michigan 2 blks (look for blue awning).

Saline

Attic Treasures
10360 Moon Rd
(313)429-4242

General line of collectibles & country items. **Hrs:** Wed-Sun 11-5.

Pineapple House Ltd
101 E Michigan Ave
(313)429-1174

Fine American & European antiques. **Hrs:** Mon-Sat 10-5, Sun 12-4.

Saline Crossings
107 E Michigan Ave
(313)429-4400

Fine antiques & collectibles. China & out-of-print collectible books. **Hrs:** Mon-Sat 10-5, Sun 12-5.

Salt City Antiques
116 W Michigan Ave
(313)429-3997

Quality antiques, collectibles, furniture, glass & primitives. **Hrs:** Mon-Sat 10-5, Sun 11-5.

Schoolcraft

Norma's Antiques & Collectibles [G]
231 Grand St
(616)679-4030 • (616)679-5406 (fax)
(800)575-6476
nt1933@aol.com

Furniture, smalls & reference books; glassware & china; advertising; primitives, baskets, paper items, postcards, coins & jewelry. **Hrs:** Tue-Sat 10:30-6. **Sz:** H **CC:** AX/V/MC/DIS.

Prairie Home Antiques
240 N Grand St (Rte 131)
(616)679-2062

Quality antiques in room settings. Furniture (1800-1950s), mirrors, art, textiles, china, children's items, antiques for your home & office. Sewing tools our specialty. Browsers welcome, buyers adored. **Pr:** $5-3,000 **Est:** 1995 **Hrs:** Mon-Tue & Thu-Sat 11-5, Sun 12-5, Wed by chance. **Sz:** L **CC:** V/MC/DIS **Dir:** 10 mi S of Kalamazoo on Hwy 131. **Own:** Beth Pulsipher. **QC: 34 36 52 S15 S8 S12**

Ron's Grand Street Antiques & Mom's Memories [G2]
205 N Grand St (Rte 131)
(616)679-4774 • (616)327-2056
grandstant@aol.com

A quality selection with an occasional hard-to-find item sprinkled in. Bridal registry & glass repair. **Pr:** $5-3,500 **Est:** 1991 **Hrs:** Tue-Sat 10-5, Sun 12-5. **Sz:** M **CC:** V/MC/DIS **Dir:** I-94 exit US 131 10 mi S. **Own:** Ronald G Harding. **QC: 22 48 S16 S22**

Somerset

Oak Hill Antiques
10250 Somerset Rd (Rte 12)
(517)547-4195

Quality antiques & collectibles. Picture frame restoration & framing, lamp restoration (oil & electric). Complete line of fabric & glass shades. **Pr:** $2-6,500 **Est:** 1974 **Hrs:** Mon & Wed-Sun 10-6:30 (closed Tue). **Sz:** M **Dir:** 1 mi W of the junction of US 127 & US 12. **Own:** Jeanne Donaldson & Ralph Trujillo. **QC: 48 65 68 S16 S13 S6**

Southfield

The McDonnell House
19860 W 12 Mile Rd
(810)559-9120

Antiques & collectibles. **Hrs:** Mon-Sat 10-5, Sun 12-5.

St Clair Shores

Adams English Antiques
19717 E Nine Mile Rd
(810)777-1652

Direct importer of English antiques. Furniture, collectibles, smalls. **Hrs:** Mon-Fri 9-5, Sat 10-5. **QC: 55**

St Joseph

Days of Yore Antiques [G12]
215 State St
(616)983-4144

Antiques, collectibles & memorabilia. Specializing in 50s nostalgia, Victoriana, jewelry, furniture, autographs, reference books, political memorabilia. **Pr:** $0.50-2,000 **Est:** 1998 **Hrs:** Mon-Sat 10-5:30. **Sz:** M **CC:** AX/V/MC/DIS **Dir:** 1 blk off Business 94 in downtown St Joseph. **Own:** Connie Yore. **QC: 63 89 67 S1 S8 S12**

Stevensville

Bill's Real Antiques
7566 Red Arrow Hwy
(616)465-3246

Art glass, silver, pottery, furniture, china, jewelry. Actively purchasing antiques daily

— 1 piece to entire estates & you always deal with the owner. **Pr:** $1-10,000 **Hrs:** Daily 12-6. **Sz:** L **CC:** AX/V/MC **Dir:** I-94 Exit 16: 3-1/2 mi N on Red Arrow Hwy. **Own:** Chris Prentice. **QC: 22 48 64 S12**

Stockbridge

Thomas R Forshee Antiques
119 W Main St
(517)851-8114 • (313)475-7178

Specializing in fine oriental porcelain. **Hrs:** Fri-Sat 10-4, Sun 12-4. **QC: 24**

Hafner Antique & Craft Mall [G22]
5000 S Clinton
(517)851-7677

Furniture, collectibles, glassware & primitives. **Hrs:** Daily 10-6. **QC: 32 48 61**

Tecumseh

Hitching Post Antique Mall [G40+]
1322 E Monroe Rd
(517)423-8277

General line of quality antiques, books on antiques. Giant flea market on ground Mem Day, July 4th & Labor Day. **Hrs:** Daily 10-5:30. **CC:** V/MC **Dir:** 2 mi W of Tecumseh on M-50 & M-52. **Own:** The Nelson Family.

L & M Antique Mall
7811 E Monroe Rd
(517)423-7346

General line of antiques & collectibles. Specialties include marbles, Aladdin lamps, china & books. **Hrs:** Tue-Thu 11-5, Fri-Sun 11-6.

Visit our web site at www.antiquesource.com for more information about antiquing in the Midwest and New England.

Tecumseh Antique Mall I [G30]
112 E Chicago Blvd
(517)423-6441

General line of antique furniture, primitives, glass & collectibles. **Hrs:** Mon-Sat 10-5, Sun 12-5. **CC:** V/MC.

Tecumseh Antique Mall II [G100]
1111 W Chicago Blvd
(517)423-6082

Antiques & collectibles. **Hrs:** Mon-Sat 10-5, Sun 12-5.

Wood's Antiques
140 E Chicago Blvd
(517)423-9545

Single-owner shop offering quality Victorian furniture, glassware & other 19th C antiques. **Hrs:** Daily 10-6.

Tekonsha

Antique Stove Shop
415 Fleming Rd
(517)278-2214

Kitchen ranges, parlor stoves, museum-quality restorations. **Hrs:** Daily 10-5 by chance/appt. **QC: S16**

Kempton's Country Classics
1129 Marshall Rd
(517)279-8130

Specializing in primitive & fine country furnishings. **Hrs:** Tue-Sat 10-5, Sun-Mon by chance/appt. **Dir:** 8 mi N of Coldwater, 16 mi S of Marshall. **QC: 34 48**

Three Rivers

Links to the Past Antiques, Books & Collectibles
52631 US Rte 131 N
(616)279-7310 • (616)345-3910 (fax)

An entire house & connecting pole barn

filled to the brim with quality antiques, thousands of collectibles & advertising memorabilia, plus six rooms of rare, used & collectible books. Fiction/nonfiction but specialize in older children's books. **Pr:** $1-2,500 **Hrs:** Mon-Tue & Thu-Sat 10-6, Sun 11-5 (closed Wed). **Sz:** L **Dir:** 6 mi S of Schoolcraft or 6 mi N of Three Rivers on Rte 131 N. Near M216 on E side of hwy. **Own:** Pam Blackburn. **QC: 18 32 67 S12**

Nettie Dee's Antiques

25 N Main St
(616)273-9579

Cherry, walnut, maple, oak & Victorian furniture; RS Prussia, Rubina, Nippon, Moser. Cranberry, carnival & Steuben glass. **Hrs:** Tue-Sat 10:30-5:30.

Traverse City

Chum's Corner Antique Mall [G]

Rte 31
(616)943-4200

Furniture, primitives, collectibles & glass. **Hrs:** Daily 10-6. **Dir:** On Rte 31 1/4 mi W of the Rte 31 & M-37 corner.

Walt's Antiques

2513 Nelson Rd
(616)223-7386 • (616)223-4123

Hrs: Daily 10-6.

Wilson Antiques

123 S Union
(616)946-4177

Antiques & collectibles. **Hrs:** Mon-Sat 10-6, Sun 11-5. **Sz:** H. **QC: 38**

Troy

Judy Frankel Antiques

2900 W Maple, Ste 111
(248)648-4399

Antique decorative items, textiles &

furniture. **Hrs:** Mon-Wed 10-4, Thu 10-12 by chance/appt. **QC: 36 48 80**

Waterford

The Great Midwestern Antique Emporium [G50]

5233 Dixie Hwy (Rte 24)
(248)623-7460 • (248)625-4326 (fax)

Top-quality, affordable antique & collectible merchandise in a relaxed & friendly atmosphere. Furniture, glass, pottery, advertising & a general line. **Pr:** $1-5,000 **Est:** 1984 **Hrs:** Tue-Sun (closed Mon & New Year's). **Sz:** L **CC:** AX/V/MC **Dir:** I-75 Exit 93, 4 mi S. **Own:** Nan Dangel. **QC: 50 79 39 S1 S7 S16**

Wayne

Sanders Antiques & Auction Gallery

35118 Michigan Ave
(313)721-3029

Specializing in jewelry, furniture, paper, dolls, toys, radios, guns & knives, coins, lamps, china & pottery. **Hrs:** Daily 10-6. **Sz:** H **CC:** V/MC/DIS **QC: 48 61 S2**

Williamston

Antiques Market of Williamston [G75]

2991 Williamston Rd
(517)655-1350

Est: 1982 **Hrs:** Daily 10-6. **Dir:** 1/3 mi N of I-96.

Canterbury Antiques
150 S Putnam St
(517)655-6518

Furniture, porcelain. **Hrs:** Mon-Sat 10:30-5, Sun 12:30-5.

Lyon's Den Antiques
132 S Putnam
(517)655-2622 • (517)655-6225

Flow blue, Victorian & fancy oak furniture. **Hrs:** Wed-Sat 11-5 (Thu til 8), Sun 12-5, Mon-Tue by appt. **Own:** Ted & Loretta Lyon. **QC: 22 50**

Old Village Antiques
125 E Grand River Ave
(517)655-4827

Specializing in walnut & cherry furniture, glass, China & Wallace Nutting prints. **Hrs:** Oct-May Tue-Sat 10-5, Sun by chance/appt; Jun-Sep Mon 11-4, Tue-Sat 10-5, Sun by chance/appt. **QC: 48 61**

Putnam Street Antiques
122 S Putnam St
(517)655-4521

Hrs: Tue-Sat 10:30-5, Sun-Mon 12-4. **CC:** V/MC/DIS.

Sign of the Pineapple Antiques [G10]
137 E Grand River
(517)655-1905 • (517)655-1376

Fine antiques with an emphasis on country furnishings, primitives, oak, Mission, Victorian, glassware & graniteware. **Pr:** $5-2,000 **Est:** 1998 **Hrs:** Tue-Sat 10-5, Sun 1-5. **Sz:** L **CC:** V/MC **Assn:** ACDA **Dir:** I-96 Exit 117: 1-1/2 mi N. **QC: 1 34 48**

Minnesota

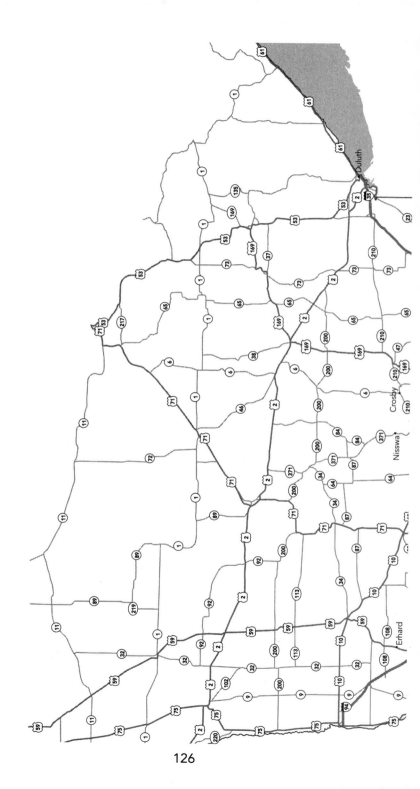

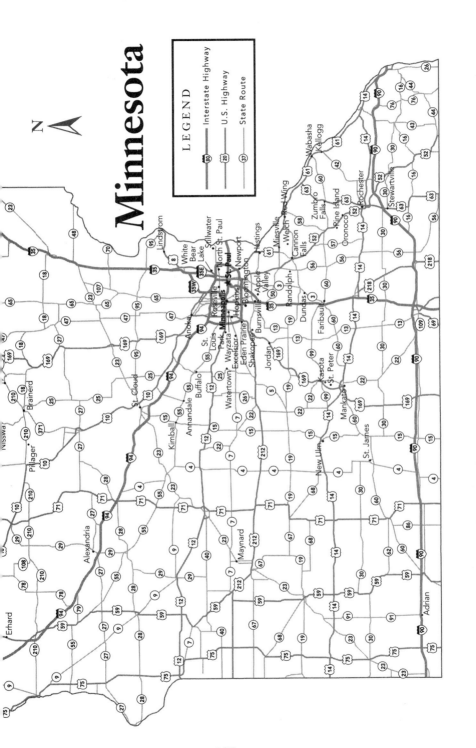

Minnesota

LEGEND

80		Interstate Highway
20		U.S. Highway
37		State Route

Adrian

Marsh's Antique Mall

138 S Winter St
(517)263-8826

Oak & Victorian furniture, general line of antiques & collectibles. **Hrs:** Thu-Sat 10-5:30, Sun 12-5. **CC:** V/MC/DIS. **QC: 50 58**

Alexandria

Alexandria's Antiques on Broadway

523 Broadway
(320)763-9996

Glassware, furniture, coin-op machines, advertising, fishing & hunting items, primitives, paper, pottery & decorative accessories. **Hrs:** Mon-Sat 10-5:30, Sun 12-5.

Three Havens General Store Inc

3907 County Rd 42 NE
(320)846-3764

Furniture, glassware, primitives. **Hrs:** May-Aug daily 7-10; Sep-Apr daily 7-8. **Dir:** 4 mi N of Alexandria on County Rd 42.

Annandale

Annandale Antiques

70 Maple Ave
(320)274-8260

Hrs: Daily 10-5. **Dir:** 1 blk N of Hwy 55.

Anoka

Amore Antiques [G62]

2008 2nd Ave
(612)576-1871 • (612)420-7774 (fax)
nsmeaton@compuserve.com
www.usucceed.com/amore/

A bright, clean & positive environment dedicated to your shopping pleasure. **Pr:** $5-3,000 **Est:** 1994 **Hrs:** Mon-Sat 10-5:30, Sun

11-5. **Sz:** L **CC:** V/MC/DIS **Dir:** Hwy 169 to Anoka. E onto Main St 1 blk, then N onto 2nd Ave. **Own:** Kay Jensen, Marilyn Mertens, Carolyn & Neil Smeaton. **QC: 48 89 64 S1 S8 S12**

Antiques on Main [G50+]

212 E Main St
(612)323-3990

Hrs: Daily 9-6 exc hols. **CC:** AX/V/MC/DIS

Apple Valley

Granny Smith's Antiques & Collectibles [G175]

7600 W 147th St
(612)891-1686

Antiques & collectibles. **Hrs:** Mon-Fri 11-6, Sat 10-6, Sun 12-5. **Sz:** H **Dir:** S of the Mall of America.

Bloomington

Antiques at Anthonie's [G]

801 E 78th St
(612)854-4855

Hrs: Mon-Sat 10-5, Sun 12-5. **Dir:** S Service Rd of I-494, Portland Ave exit, near Mall of America.

Brainerd

Hyland Antiques

1466 Hwy 371 N
(218)828-8838

Quality antique furniture, glassware & china. Extensive general line. Also warehouse with furniture in the rough. **Hrs:**

Mon-Sat 10-5, Sun 1-5 (Sum only). **Dir:** 1-1/2 mi N of Paul Bunyan. **Own:** Debra & Myron Hyland Jr.

Buffalo

Waldon Woods Antiques

2612 Hwy 55 SE
(612)682-5667 • (612)338-2545

Antique furniture, architectural items, stained glass, antique clocks, collectibles a specialty. **Pr:** $2-10,000 **Est:** 1972 **Hrs:** Mon-Sat 10-5, Sun 12-5. **Sz:** H **CC:** V/MC **Assn:** NAWCC **Dir:** Hwy 55 3 mi SE of Buffalo. **Own:** Lee & Marian Waldon. **QC:** 35 3 32

Burnsville

Antiques Minnesota [G100+]

Hwy 13

Est: 1979 **Hrs:** Mon-Sat 10-5, Sun 12-5 (closed Tue). **Sz:** H **CC:** V/MC/DIS **Dir:** Just off I-35W.

Kitsch 'n Kaboodle

14607 County Rd 11
(612)953-0606 • (612)953-0606 (fax)

Offers a unique & comfortable atmosphere while you search for treasures. Specialize in kitchen & dining antiques. Coffee & kitchen shop. **Pr:** $5-2,500 **Est:** 1995 **Hrs:** Mar 15-Jan 15 Mon-Fri 10-6 (Thu til 8), Sat 9-4, Sun 12-4. **Sz:** M **CC:** AX/V/MC/DIS **Dir:** 1 mi E of Burnsville Ctr on County Rd 42. **Own:** Peggie A Fern. **QC:** 61 36 32 S19 S12 S8

Cannon Falls

Country Side Antique Mall [G45]

31752 65th Ave
(507)263-0352

General line of antiques & collectibles. **Est:**

1991 **Hrs:** Mon-Sat 9:30-5:30, Sun 11-5:30 (closed Easter, Xmas, Thanks). **Sz:** H **CC:** V/MC **Dir:** 1 blk E of Hwy 52 stoplight or 1 mi S of downtown Cannon Falls.

Danielson Antiques

33615 Hwy 52 Blvd
(507)263-4608

General line, primitives, glass, china, linens, jewelry & furniture. **Hrs:** By chance/appt. **Dir:** Look for the red plow. **Own:** Marlene & Don Mattson.

Fourth Street Antiques [G12]

106 S 4th St
(507)263-7249

Hrs: Tue-Sat 10:30-5:30, Sun 12-5.

Schaffer's Antiques

111 N Fourth St
(507)263-5200

Owner-operated shop featuring a general line of quality antiques, furniture, primitives, tools, pottery, pictures & stoneware. **Hrs:** Tue-Sat 10-5.

Thora Mae's Antique [G]

In the Mall of Cannon Falls
(507)263-2073

Antiques & collectibles, quality furniture, jewelry, hats, books, toys, Depression glass, kitchen bric-a-brac, Red Wing stoneware, art pottery & dinnerware. **Est:** 1998 **Hrs:** Mon-Fri 9:30-5:30, Sat 9:30-5, Sun 12-5. **Dir:** Just off Hwy 52.

THE COUNTRY LOOK IN ANTIQUES

240 Water Street, Excelsior, MN 55331

Visit the charm of Colonial New England...

Featuring primitives, original painted furniture, quilts, braided and loomed rugs, country lamps, folk art and lighting.

Monday to Saturday	**(612) 474-0050**
10:00 to 5:00	**Sunday: Seasonal**

Crosby

Hallett Antique Emporium [G36+]
28 W Main St
(218)546-5444

Primitives, furniture, glass, pottery, jewelry, china & coins. **Hrs:** Daily 10-5.

Duluth

Antique Centre Duluth [G]
335 Canal Park Dr
(218)726-1994

Hrs: Mon-Sat 10-5, Sun 11-5. **Dir:** I-35 Lake exit.

Canal Park Antique Mall [G]
310 S Lake Ave
(218)720-3940

Hrs: Daily 10-5 (Sat til 8).

Old Town Antiques & Books [G]
102 E Superior St
(218)722-5426

Hrs: Mon-Sat 10-5 (Fri & Sat til 6), Sun 12-5. **Sz:** L

Eden Prairie

Bruda Collectables
(612)935-3848

Silver, porcelain, jewelry, furniture, glass & decorative accessories. American, European & Oriental. **Est:** 1970 **Hrs:** By appt only. **Own:** Marian Dennis & George Dodds. **QC:** 78 64 22

Erhard

Dakota Antiques
County Rd 3
(218)736-6818

Handmade pine cupboards, pine & oak furniture, primitives, trunks & a general line. **Hrs:** May-Sep Tue-Sat 9-5, Sun 11-5; Oct-Apr Thu-Sat 9-5, Sun 11-5 or by chance/appt. **Sz:** L **Dir:** 10 mi S of Pelican Rapids.

Excelsior

The Collector's Choice
223 Water St
(612)474-6117

Hrs: Mon-Sat 10-5, Sun 11-5.

The Country Look in Antiques [G]
240 Water St
(612)474-0050

Colonial New England antiques: 18th, 19th & early 20th C furniture, primitives, original painted furniture, quilts, braided & loomed rugs, country lamps, lighting, folk art, books & sports memorabilia. Seven large rooms. **Est:** 1980 **Hrs:** Mon-Sat 10-5, Sun 12-4 (seasonal). **CC:** V/MC **Dir:** 30

mi W of the Twin Cities on Lake Minnetonka. **Own:** Mark & Audrey Jackson. **QC: 1 34**

Leipold's

239 Water St
(612)474-5880

Lighting, lamp parts, lamp repair, glass shades. **Hrs:** Mon-Fri 9:30-7, Sat 10-5, Sun 10-4. **QC: 65**

Mary O'Neal & Co

221 Water St
(612)470-0205

Consignment household furnishings, art & antiques. **Hrs:** Mon-Sat 10-5, Sun 12-5. **QC: S8**

Faribault

The Dimestore Antique Mall [G60]

310 Central Ave N
(507)332-8699

One of Minnesota's largest antique malls & the largest Frankoma display in the Midwest. Depression glass, pottery & furniture. **Pr:** $1-1,000 **Est:** 1995 **Hrs:** Apr-Jan 15 Mon-Sat 10-6, Sun 12-5; Jan 15-Mar Mon-Thu 11-5, Fri-Sat 9:30-6, Sun 12-5. **Sz:** H **CC:** V/MC **Dir:** 2 mi E of I-35 on Hwy 60 to Central Ave, then 1/2 blk S, in historic downtown. **Own:** Jim & Shelley Tholen. **QC: 32 48 22**

Stoeckel's Antiques

615 NW 3rd St
(507)334-7772

Antique clocks & dolls, refinishing & repair. **Hrs:** Mon-Fri 9:30-12 & 1-5, Sat by chance/appt. **Own:** Fritz & Pat Stoeckel. **QC: 35 38 S16**

> Use the Specialty QuickCode indexes at the back of the book to find dealers who specialize in your area of interest.

Hastings

Carroll's Antiques

107 E 2nd St
(612)437-1912

Furniture, china, glass, jewelry, stained glass, tools, linens, books, paper. **Hrs:** Mon-Sat 10-5, Sun 12-5. **Dir:** Downtown by the Mississippi. **Own:** Mary & Don Carroll.

Cherished Treasures

116 E 2nd St
(612)480-8881

Primitives, furniture, jewelry, Roseville, Hull, Watts, Shawnee, Red Wing, quilts, linens, candles, dolls, tea sets, many gift items. **Hrs:** Mon-Sat 10-5, Sun 12-4.

Hastings Antique Mall [G25]

33rd St & Hwy 61
(612)437-7412

Featuring antique furniture, glass collectibles, crafts, fishing tackle, primitives, Barbie doll clothes, coins. **Hrs:** Mon & Wed-Sun 9-5, Fri til 8 (closed Tue). **Sz:** H **Dir:** Next to Farm & Country C/T Tractor.

Towered House Antiques

207 W 2nd St
(612)480-3358

Small shop located in historic home featuring antique furniture, primitives, glassware, vintage linens & unique decorating items for home & garden. **Hrs:** Mon & Thu-Sat 10-5, Sun 12-5, Tue-Wed by chance/appt.

Hopkins

Blake Antiques [G]

1115 Excelsior Blvd E
(612)930-0477

Furniture, orientalia, decorative art, fine art, bronzes, sterling silver, porcelain, pottery, glass, collectibles & fine antique jewelry. **Hrs:** Mon-Sat 11-6, Sun 12-5. **Dir:** E of Hwy 169.

Mary Frances Antiques [G]
901 Main St
(612)930-3283
Hrs: Mon-Sat 11-6, Sun 12-5.

Hopkins Antique Mall [G68+]
1008 Main St
(612)931-9748
Hrs: Mon-Sat 11-6, Sun 11-5. Sz: H.

Isanti

Isanti Antiques [G25+]
16 W Main St
(612)444-5522

Depression glass, china, Shawnee, McCoy, Fiesta, toys, dolls, games, prints, jewelry, Red Wing, Fostoria, Fenton & furniture. Hrs: Mon-Sat 10-5, Sun 12-5. Dir: 40 mi N of Twin Cities on Hwy 65.

Jordan

Mother Jordan Antiques
108 Creek Ln
(612)492-6897

Antiques, collectibles & home decorations. Lots of furniture, fancy to primitives, unusual new fabrics, ceramics & china. Pr: $1-4,800 Est: 1995 Hrs: Jun-Sep Tue-Sun 12-5; Oct-May Sat-Sun 12-5. Sz: M CC: V/MC Dir: Behind the Community Bank. Own: Phyllis & Evan Hopkins. QC: 48 32 36 S22

Water Street Antiques [G12]
240 Water St
(612)492-6918 • (612)447-8320

Charming multi-dealer antique & collectible

> Use the Service QuickCode indexes at the back of the book to find restorers, appraisers, refinishers, and other specialty service providers.

shop nestled on Sand Creek. Pr: $1-2,50C Est: 1991 Hrs: Tue-Sat 10-5, Sun 12-5. Sz: L Dir: Hwy 169S to Jordan, MN. Hwy 21 & Water St. 30 min from Twin Cities. Own: Pat & Dave Johnston. QC: 34 48 32 S12

Kasota

Wild Goose Chase Antiques
Hwy 22
(507)931-9434 • (507)931-9255

Country pine cupboards, pie safes, dry sinks, trunks, wardrobes, quilts, glassware (1800-1940s), stoneware, linens. Hrs: Wed-Sat 11-4, Sun 12-4. Dir: Hwy 22 S from St Peter 4 mi or Hwy 22 N from Mankato 6 mi, then W on Township Rd (T-140).

Kellogg

AJ's Antiques [G]
207 Baldwin St
(507)767-4930

A little bit of everything. Hrs: Mon-Sat 10-5 or by chance/appt. Dir: From Hwy 61, turn E at Kwik Trip 5 blks to Shepard, turn R (S) 2 blks & watch for signs.

Kimball

The New & Used Company of Kimball Inc
11 E Hazel St
(320)398-2956 • (320)398-2957 (fax)
toynucol@espressocom.com

A delightful mix of old & new. General line, large toy inventory, farm toys & memorabilia. Advertising & character collectibles, unique one-of-a-kind items. Pr: $0.25-2,000 Est: 1990 Hrs: Mon-Sat 10-5:30, Sun 12-5:30. Sz: L CC: V/MC Dir: I-94 W from Twin Cities to Kimball exit (Hwy 15). S 15 mi to Hazel St. Own: Lee & Gracka Gruis. QC: 87 32 36 S12 S19

Lindstrom

Lindstrom Antique Mall
Hwy 8
(612)257-3340 • (612)257-0779

Furniture, glassware, dolls, jewelry, china, toys, primitives & vintage clothing. **Hrs:** May-Oct Mon-Sat 10-6, Sun 12-5; Nov-Apr Mon-Sat 10-5, Sun 12-5.

Mankato

Earthly Remains Antique Mall [G50+]
731 S Front St
(507)388-5063
ertiques@ic.mankato.mn.us
www.mankato.mn.us/~ertiques

Furniture, glassware, pictures/frames, toys, dolls, Star Wars, coins, jewelry, paper advertising, 1000s of books, fishing lures, many more collectibles & memorabilia. **Pr:** $1-2,000 **Est:** 1983 **Hrs:** Mon-Sat 10-5. **Sz:** H **CC:** V/MC/DIS **Dir:** 3 blks S of downtown Civic Center. **Own:** Jim & Jordan Kagermeir. **QC:** 32 67 74 S3 S8 S12

Maynard

Corky's Corner Antiques
Hwy 23
(320)367-2930

General line. Lots of dolls & toys, advertising & memorabilia, RR items, farm items, lightening rods & accessories. Primitives. Toy repairs, missing parts. **Pr:** $1-1,000 **Est:** 1996 **Hrs:** Apr-Oct daily 9-5, Nov-Mar daily 11-5. **Sz:** M **Dir:** Near corner of Hwy 23 & Maynard. **Own:** Corky & Bev Lauritsen. **QC:** 32 34 87 S1 S12 S16

Miesville

Village General Antiques
Hwy 61
(612)437-8150

Country furniture, quilts, rugs, stoneware, primitives & a general line. **Hrs:** Daily.

Minneapolis

American Classics
4944 Xerxes Ave S
(612)926-2509

Furniture, glass, china, pottery, sporting collectibles, new books on antiques. **Hrs:** Mon-Sat 10:30-5, Sun 12-4. **Sz:** G **Assn:** MADA **Own:** Marge & Kerrie Drogue. **QC:** S1 S12

Antiques Riverwalk [G50+]
210 3rd Ave N
(612)339-9352

In a restored warehouse in Minneapolis's warehouse district. American, Asian & European furniture, decorative arts & design from the 18th through the 20th C. **Hrs:** Mon-Sat 10-5, Sun 11-5. **Sz:** H **CC:** V/MC **Own:** Sarah Randol.

James E Billings, Antiquarian
(612)788-7890

Orientalia, period furniture & fine antique art. **Hrs:** By appt only. **Assn:** AAA. **QC:** 71 54 7 S1

Birdsall-Haase Antiques
(612)224-3669

18th & 19th C American & European furniture & paintings. **Hrs:** By appt only. **Own:** Michael Birdsall & Roger Haase. **QC:** 52 54 7

Cupboard Collectables
3022 W 50th St
(612)929-9244

Glassware, collectibles, country antiques. Estate & moving sales. **Hrs:** By appt. **Own:** Barbara Gilham & Sue Trebtoske.

Finishing Touches Antiques & Design

2520 Hennepin Ave S
(612)377-8033

18th, 19th & 20th C fine & decorative furniture & accessories. **Hrs:** Tue-Sat 10-5, Sun 12-5, Mon by appt. **QC: 36 48 S15**

Great Northern Antiques

5159 Bloomington Ave S
(612)721-8731

Large selection of vintage radios, plus a variety of antiques & collectibles. **Hrs:** Wed-Fri 12-5:30, Sat 11-5 (Mon-Tue by chance). **Dir:** 4 blks W of Cedar Ave on 52nd St.

Hennepin Avenue Antiques Center Inc [G50+]

2801 Hennepin Ave S
(612)879-5140

Hrs: Daily 11-6. **Dir:** 2 blks N of Lake St.

Kramer Gallery

800 La Salle Ave, Ste 240
(612)338-2911

American & European oil paintings, sculpture & graphics of the 19th & early 20th C. Specializing in American Indian artifacts. Fine art appraisals & restoration. **Assn:** AAA **Dir:** In La Salle Plaza. **Own:** Wes & Leon Kramer. **QC: 7 42 S1 S16**

Blue and White Porcelain I

Blue-and-white Staffordshire: Staffordshire was the center of the pottery industry in England, and many factories operated there from the mid-18th century to the present day. The development of transfer printing (see below) allowed these potteries to become among the earliest mass manufacturers, and their affordable products rapidly swept pewter and treen off the tables of the English and American middle-class households. From the 1780s, Staffordshire factories produced huge quantities of transferware for the domestic and export markets. English colonial laws forbad the development of ceramic factories in America so as to protect the Staffordshire industries, so shiploads of blue and white crossed the Atlantic. Blue was the most popular color, partly because cobalt was the easiest pigment to fire, but transferware was also produced in green, magenta, and black. Designs that required fine lines, such as a ship's rigging, reproduced most clearly in black.

Transfer printing: Before the development of transfer printing in the 1750s, all china was decorated by hand. Transfer printing enabled decoration to be industrialized, though semi-skilled handwork was still involved. A copper engraving was inked with metallic inks, and the design transferred by a sheet of tissue paper, or later a "bat" of gelatin, to the chinaware while the inks were still wet. This was an easy process on flatware, such as plates and chargers, but on hollowware it was impossible to fit the transfers exactly, and the edges of the sheets can always be seen.

Blue willow: The most common of all transfer patterns, blue willow was first produced at the Caughley Pottery in 1780 and is still made today. The pattern was derived from the Chinese by Thomas Turner. His busy, crowded composition is a westernization of the sparer, more economical Chinese design (oriental wares made for export were always more heavily decorated than those made for domestic use), and it caught European taste so well that it was widely produced by factories in England, Germany, Holland, Japan, and, later on, America. The pattern depicts three figures, a bridge, a pagoda, birds, and trees in a Chinese landscape. According to legend, it tells the story of a pair of lovers fleeing from an angry father: the gods changed them into birds to enable them to escape him. A nice, romantic nineteenth century story that is purely European in concept: China is a land of arranged marriages, not of romantic love.

The Loft Antiques [G14]
3022 W 50th St
(612)922-4200

Antiques & collectibles. **Hrs:** Mon-Sat 10-5, Sun 12-4.

Lyndale House Antiques
2225 Lyndale Ave S
(612)871-3491

Country pine & formal furniture from England & the Continent. Specializing in armoires & wardrobes. Also collectibles, country accessories, jewelry & vintage clothing. **Hrs:** Tue-Thu 11-7, Fri 11-5, Sat 10-5.

J Oliver Antiques [G]
2730 Hennepin Ave S
(612)872-8952

Fine furniture, silver, porcelain & decorative accessories.

Park Avenue Antiques
4944 Xerxes Ave S
(612)925-5850 • (612)922-0887

Fine furniture, pottery, art glass, porcelain, paintings. **Hrs:** Tue-Sat 11-5, Sun 12-4. **Dir:** 2nd location at 3004 W 50th St, Mpls. **Own:** Stephen & Charles Mozey.

Plaza Antiques
1758 Hennepin Ave
(612)377-7331 • (612)455-8971

Furniture, oriental art objects & rugs, prints, oils, engravings, silver, china, crystal & bronzes. **Hrs:** Tue-Sat 11-4. **Own:** James C Lau. **QC: 71 7 36 S8**

Anthony Scornavacco
(612)699-4375

Fine early silver, glass, period furniture, porcelain & pottery. **Hrs:** By appt only. **QC: 77 61 S1**

Shades on the Lake
921 W Lake St
(612)822-6427

Antique lamps & contemporary, traditional & antique lampshades. **Hrs:** Mon 12-8, Tue-Fri 10-5, Fri 10-3. **Own:** Jeffrey & Faye Bies. **QC: 65**

Theatre Antiques
2934 Lyndale Ave S
(612)822-4884

Victorian, Arts & Crafts, Deco & mid-century. **Hrs:** Mon-Sat 11-6, Sun 12-6. **QC: 89 6 5**

Tiques & Treasures Antiques
117 N 4th St, Ste 100
(612)359-0915 • (612)359-0083 (fax)

Specializing in nautical, transportation, sporting goods, hunting & fishing equipment, fine arts, lodge & Mission furniture & accessories. **Pr:** $1-10,000 **Est:** 1990 **Hrs:** Mon-Fri 11-6, Sat 10-4. **Sz:** L **CC:** V/MC/DIS **Assn:** MADA **Dir:** In the Minneapolis Warehouse District. **Own:** James Jurgens. **QC: 7 79 70 S1 S12 S19**

Victorian Memories
3208 Hennepin Ave S
(612)824-1080

Victoriana. **Hrs:** Tue-Thu 10-8, Fri 9-5, Sat 9-5 (closed Mon). **QC: 89**

Waldon Woods Antiques
213 Washington Ave N
(612)682-5667 • (612)338-2545

Antique furniture, architectural items, stained glass, antique clocks, collectibles a specialty. **Pr:** $2-10,000 **Est:** 1972 **Hrs:** Mon-Fri 12-5, Sat 10-5 (closed Sun). **Sz:** L **CC:** V/MC **Assn:** NAWCC **Dir:** 2 blks N of Hennepin Ave on Washington. **Own:** Lee & Marian Waldon. **QC: 35 32 3**

New Ulm

Antique Haus [G16]
327 N Broadway (Hwy 15)
(507)354-2450

Two floors of a historic home filled with quality antiques & collectibles. Furniture, glassware, pottery, crocks, clocks & lighting, jewelry, prints, linens & primitives, with furniture in-the-rough in the garage. **Pr:** $10-3,000 **Est:** 1994 **Hrs:** Mon-Sat 10-5, Sun 12-4 (closed major hols). **Sz:** L **Dir:** Hwy 15 through town (1 blk W of Glockenspiel). **QC: 48 32**

Newport

Antiques, Décor & More [G70+]
Hwy 61S & I-494
(612)458-0729

Unique items for your decorating or collecting needs. **Hrs:** Mon-Sat 9:30-6:30, Sun 11-5. **Dir:** At the Newport Center.

Nisswa

Lake Country Antiques
Nisswa Square
(218)963-4615

Hrs: May-Oct daily 10-5 (shorter hrs in May & Oct).

Times Remembered
E Clark Lake Rd
(218)963-2432 • (612)588-3415

General line with emphasis on porcelain, crystal & silver. **Hrs:** May 23-Sep 1 Wed & Sat. **Own:** Leanne M Carlson.

North St Paul

Fireside Antiques
2569 E 7th Ave
(612)770-6106

Large selection of Depression & elegant glass plus a general line of antiques. **Hrs:** Mon-Tue & Thu-Sat 10-5.

Visit our web site at www.antiquesource.com for more information about antiquing in the Midwest and New England.

Oronoco

Antiques Etcetera
15 1st St NE
(507)753-2398

Quality furniture, primitives, pottery, toys, lures, Amish gifts & quilts, hickory furniture, dolls, vintage clothing & baskets. **Hrs:** Tue, Thu, Fri 12:30-4:30, Sat 10:30-4:30 or by chance/appt.

Antiques Oronoco
Hwy 52
(507)367-2220
cariveau@infonet.isl.net

Huge showroom, old book area & building with as-found & architectural items. Furniture refinished or in original condition plus dolls, toys, pottery, glassware, stoneware & more. **Pr:** $1-6,000 **Hrs:** Feb-Dec Wed-Sun. **Sz:** L **CC:** AX/V/MC/DIS **Own:** Gordon & Yvonne Cariveau. **QC: 48 24 18 S12 S16**

Berg's Antique Store
50/420 Minnesota Ave S
(507)367-4413 • (507)367-4588

Original finish oak & pine furniture, original parts, kitchenware, paper, toys, advertising, frames, lighting. Wholesale/retail. **Pr:** $1-4,000 **Est:** 1963 **Hrs:** Apr 9-Dec 5 Tue-Sat 9-5; call ahead advised. **Sz:** L **Dir:** Hwy 52 6 mi N of Rochester to Minnesota Ave. **Own:** Mary Lou Berg. **QC: 34 50 1 S12**

Pillager

Sebasky's Pinecrest Antiques
Otto Kober Rd
(218)746-3936

Furniture, glassware & reference books. **Hrs:** May-Nov Mon-Sat 10-6; Dec-Apr Sat 10-6, Mon-Fri by chance/appt. **Dir:** From Pillager, N 4-1/2 mi on Rte 1, then W 3-1/2 mi on Rte 34, then N 1 mi on Otto Kober Rd. **Own:** Andre Sebasky.

Pine Island

Country Treasures
235 S Main St
(507)356-2244

Antique furniture, glassware, crafts, paintings, quilts, woven rugs. **Hrs:** Mon-Fri 10-6, Sat 9-3. **Own:** Kim Hanson.

Green's Stripping & Antiques
Main St
(507)356-4903

Furniture, "as is" or refinished, some smalls, wholesale/retail. Also furniture stripping. **Hrs:** Mon-Sat (closed Sun). **Own:** Jerry & Gloria Green. **QC: S16**

Lantern Antiques
100 E Frontage Rd
(507)356-4215

Log cabin & summer kitchen full of quality refinished, painted & "as-is" furniture, primitives & accessories. Wholesale & retail. **Hrs:** Daily. **Dir:** On Hwy 52. **Own:** Evon & Pete Bushman.

Randolph

Deutch Hollow Antiques & Collectibles
954 260th St E
(507)263-2745

Glassware (collectible & usable), Fiestaware, furniture (refinished & primitive), handcrafted & custom furniture, farm memorabilia, farm tools & implements, cast iron & pottery, linens & doilies, jewelry & hats, rugs

& quilts. **Hrs:** Daily 8-8. **Dir:** 4 mi N of Cannon Falls.

Red Wing

Al's Antique Mall [G40]
1314 Old W Main St
(612)388-0572
(888)388-0572

Wide variety of antiques & collectibles. **Pr:** $1-1,000 **Est:** 1990 **Hrs:** Apr-Nov Mon-Sat 9-6, Sun 10-6; Dec-Mar Mon-Sat 9-5, Sun 10-5. **Sz:** H **CC:** AX/V/MC/DIS **Dir:** 1 blk off Hwy 61 on Old W Main St. **Own:** Al Novek. **QC: 31 22 67 S19 S12 S10**

Harry & Jewel's Victorian Antiques
1010 Hallstrom Dr
(612)388-5989

Walnut & rosewood furniture, many marble-topped, clocks, lamps & unique accessories. **Hrs:** By chance/appt. **Own:** Harry & Jewel Lindrud. **QC: 58**

Hill Street Antiques
212 Hill St
(612)388-0736

General line, dealer friendly. Specializing in Red Wing dinnerware, art pottery & stoneware — over 5,000 pieces. **Hrs:** Sum daily 9-6; Win Sat-Sun 10-5 or by chance/appt. **Dir:** 3 blks E of Al's Antique Mall across from Kwik Trip. **QC: 31 22**

Ice House Antiques
1811 Old W Main St
(612)388-9839

Quality antiques, collectibles & gifts, quilts, estate jewelry, glass, furniture & stoneware on 2 floors. **Hrs:** Hours vary by season.

Larry's Jugs
751 Wilkinson St
(612)388-3331

Specializing in Red Wing stoneware & art pottery. **Hrs:** Sat 11-5 in Jun & Oct. **QC: 31**

Memory Maker Antiques
419 Main St
(612)385-5914

A general line of quality antiques including toys, furniture, Red Wing, primitives & a large selection of tools. **Hrs:** Daily 9-5. **Dir:** Across from the St James Hotel in downtown.

Mona Lisa Antiques & Gardens
1228 Old W Main St
(612)388-4027
(800)405-4027

Fine furniture, jewelry, advertising items & toys in the oldest building on W Main St. **Hrs:** Mon-Fri 10-5:30, Sat 10-6, Sun 11-5:30.

Old Main Street Antiques / Memories Antiques / Pottery Place Antiques [G50+]
2000 Old W Main St
(612)388-1371 • (612)388-7765
(612)388-6446

Three shops on one floor featuring furniture, quality smalls, and a large pottery line, including Red Wing. **Est:** 1983 **Hrs:** Mon-Sat 10-6, Sun 11-6. **Dir:** On the 3rd floor of the Pottery Place Outlet Center. **QC:** 31

Teahouse Antiques in the Octagon House
927 W Third St
(612)388-3669

A general line of antiques in the 1857 Octagon House. **Est:** 1967 **Hrs:** Daily. **Dir:** 1 blk off Hwy 61 (turn at Kwik Trip).

Rochester

Blondell Antiques
1406 2nd St W
(507)282-1872

Early American & Scandinavian peasant art, furniture & accessories. **Hrs:** Daily 8 am-10 pm (call ahead advised). **Own:** Doris Blondell. **QC:** 41 48

Mayowood Galleries
In the Kahler Hotel
(507)288-6791 • (507)288-2695

Importer of fine English antiques, 17th-19th C, for both country & formal settings. Furniture, mirrors & decorative accessories. **Hrs:** Mon-Fri 10:30-5:30 or by appt. **Dir:** Downtown Rochester. **Own:** Rita H Mayo. **QC:** 54 68 36

Shakopee

Lady Di Antiques [G24]
126 S Holmes
(612)445-1238
(800)6-LADY-DI

Furnishings, lamps, jewelry, pottery, tools, linens, glass, prints, kitchenware, clocks, magazines, dolls, toys, vintage clothing, collectible books, books on collectibles. **Hrs:** Mon-Thu & Sun 10-5, Fri-Sat 10-6. **CC:** AX/V/MC/DIS.

St Cloud

Kay's Antiques
713 Mall Germain
(320)255-1220

Art pottery, Tiffany & furniture. **Hrs:** Mon-Sat 10-7, Sun 12-5. **Dir:** 45 min from Mpls. **QC:** 22 61

St James

Precious Things Estate Buyers
510 1st Ave S
(507)375-5076 • (507)375-3426 (fax)

Glass, pottery, postcards, gold, silver, costume & antique jewelry, furniture, linens & other antique & collectible items. **Pr:** $2-1,000 **Est:** 1995 **Hrs:** Mon-Fri 10-5, Sat 10-3. **Sz:** L **Dir:** On Hwy 60 in SW Minnesota. **Own:** Lenora Heller. **QC:** 63 64 S12

St Louis Park

C W Smith Inc

4424 Excelsior Blvd
(612)922-8542

Direct importer of quality 18th & 19th furniture & accessories. English, Chinese, Anglo-Indian, Colonial Dutch & Portuguese. **Hrs:** By appt only. **Own:** Carol Smith. **QC: 54 71 53**

St Paul

Anderson's Lampshades

263 W 7th St
(612)222-6131

Antique lamps & lighting. Lampshades of all types. **Own:** Glen G Anderson. **QC: 65**

Antique Lane [G20+]

946 Payne Ave
(612)771-6544

General line. Victoriana, lighting & chandeliers a specialty. **Hrs:** Mon-Sat 10:30-5, Sun 12-5. **Sz:** H **Own:** Jim & Nadia Hennessy. **QC: 89 65**

The Antique Mart

941 Payne Ave
(612)771-0860

Military, collectibles, toys, glass, furniture. **Hrs:** Mon-Sat 10-5.

Antiques Minnesota [G100+]

1197 University Ave
(612)646-0037

Hrs: Mon-Sat 10-5, Sun 12-5 (closed Tue). **Sz:** H **CC:** V/MC/DIS.

Decorating with Gold

Gold leaf: A thin skin of gold. Gold's malleability enables it to be beaten to microscopic thickness and still be workable.

Gilding: The application of gold leaf by one of two processes. One was water-based, in which the gilding was applied to a specially treated plaster that had been formed into often elaborate rococo shapes. In the other, oil-based process, the gilding was applied directly to a piece of furniture that had been primed with a gold size.

Gesso: A plaster made of chalk, plaster, and various clays that was often the ground for gilding. When wet it could be pressed into molds, and when dry it could be carved or engraved. In the 18th and 19th centuries it was stiffened with wire and used to make elaborate mirror frames.

Parcel gilt: Partially gilded.

Silver-gilt: Silver fused with a thin coating of gold, either for decoration or to protect the silver from attack by substances such as salt. Silver salt cellars and spoons are always gilded.

Vermeil: French word for silver-gilt.

Eglomise: The process by which the reverse of a glass panel is gilded, and the gilt decorated by hair pencils dipped in asphaltum or by etching with fine needles. Commonly used on the upper panel of tabernacle mirrors from the Sheraton through the Empire periods.

Gilded glass: Glassware was decorated with gold by two methods. From the 13th century, gold was fired onto the surface of glass; in the early 18th century gold leaf was applied after firing. Fired gold is more durable, but the applied gold leaf is brighter. Porcelain was decorated with gold leaf by a similar method.

Antiques-To-Go
1129 Payne Ave
(612)771-5309 • (612)771-7116

Furniture, glass, china, lamps. **Hrs:** Mon-Wed 1-5:30, Tue & Thu-Sat 10-5:30. **Own:** Eleanor K Hovelsrud.

Crescent Moon Antiques
864 Randolph St
(612)293-9202

Art pottery, linens, primitives, furniture, ephemera, glass. **Hrs:** Tue-Fri 11-5:30 (Thu til 8), Sat 10-5:30, Sun 12-4:30.

CW Exchange
978 Payne Ave
(612)772-9080

Furniture, collectibles, dishes, glassware. **Hrs:** Mon-Sat 10-5, Sun 12-4.

French Antiques
174 W 7th St
(612)293-0388 • (612)825-2504

Specialists in French antiques & other fine items. **Hrs:** Tue-Sat 12-5. **Dir:** Across from the St Paul Civic Center. **Own:** Peggy & Marc Giunta. **QC: 47**

Golden Lion Antiques
983 Payne Ave
(612)778-1977

A general line including oriental items, cut glass, oil paintings, Victoriana. **Hrs:** Mon-Sat 10-5:30. **Own:** Ralph Kromarek. **QC: S1**

Grand Remnants
1692 Grand Ave
(612)698-3233

Vintage fabric, furnishings, linens, lace, but-tons, vintage clothes, jewelry, pottery, glass-ware. **Hrs:** Mon-Wed 10-6, Thu 11-8, Fri-Sat 11-6, Sun 12-5. **QC: 80**

Hudgins Gallery
250 W 7th St
(612)291-1185 • (612)291-7879 (fax)

18th, 19th & 20th C antiques & works of art including porcelain, bronze, Oriental, Continental & American. Some furniture, but specialize in decorative accessories. **Est:** 1970 **Hrs:** Wed-Thu 12-3 or by appt. **Sz:** L **CC:** V/MC **Assn:** MADA **Dir:** I-94 in downtown St Paul to River Centre Auditorium, then 2 blks W on 7th St. **Own:** Charles J Hudgins. **QC: 7 30 36**

John's Antiques
261 W 7th St
(612)222-6131

Extensive selection of antique lighting from the 19th & 20th C including chandeliers, sconces, floor lamps, table lamps. Lamp parts & repairs. Also a general line. **Hrs:** Mon 10-8, Tue-Fri 10-5:30, Sat 10-3. **Own:** John Remackel. **QC: 65**

The Mall of St Paul [G40]
1817 Selby Ave
(612)647-6163

Period furniture & furnishings, memorabilia & collectibles, glassware, china, jewelry, art, dolls & toys, vintage linens. **Hrs:** Tue-Sun 10-6 (closed Mon).

Missouri Mouse [G45]
1750 Selby Ave
(612)642-1938

Hrs: Tue-Fri 11-5, Sat 10-5, Sun 11-5. **Dir:** I-94 Snelling Ave exit.

Nakashian-O'Neil Inc
23 W 6th St
(612)224-5465

Antiques & interiors. **Hrs:** Mon-Sat 9:30-5:30 (closed Sat Jun-Aug). **Own:** Daniel F O'Neill.

Robert J Riesberg Antiques

(612)457-1772 • (612)450-6014 (fax)

Specializing in American, English & Continental furniture, objects & paintings of the 17th, 18th & early 19th C. **Est:** 1971 **Hrs:** By appt only. **Sz:** L **CC:** V/MC **Assn:** MADA **QC: 52 53 54 S1 S8 S12**

Teheran Oriental Rug Gallery

723 Grand Ave
(612)292-1777

Oriental rug specialist. Buy, sell, trade. Expert cleaning, repair & appraisals. **Own:** Jahan Zademehran. **QC: 76 S1 S16**

Wescott Station

226 W 7th St
(612)227-2469

Furniture, stained glass, collectibles in seven rooms. **Hrs:** Mon-Sat 10-6 (Mon til 7:30). **Dir:** 1 blk W of Civic Center.

Wooden Trunk Antiques & Collectibles

1091 Payne Ave
(612)776-1837

General line of antiques & collectibles. **Hrs:** Wed & Thu 11-4, Sat 11-4:30. **Own:** Pat & Duke Ramsey.

St Peter

Collective Memories

216 S Minnesota
(507)931-6445
(888)931-6445

Vintage clothing, hats & accessories. **Hrs:** Mon-Tue & Thu-Fri 10-5:30, Sat 10-5, Sun 12-5. **CC:** V/MC **QC: 83**

Tate Antiques [G]

317 N Minnesota Ave
(507)931-5678

Antiques & collectibles. **Hrs:** Mon-Sat 9-5,

Sun 10-5. **Sz:** L **Dir:** On Hwy 169 at N end of St Peter.

Stewartville

Antique Manor

Hwy 63
(507)533-9300

Glassware, pottery, toys, primitives, advertising, room-ready furniture, holiday items & paper goods. **Hrs:** Mon-Sat 9-5, Sun 12-4. **Dir:** 7 mi S of Rochester on Hwy 63. I-90 Exit 209A: 1 mi S. Next to Americinn Motel.

Stillwater

American Gothic Antiques

236 S Main St
(612)439-7709

Hrs: Mon-Thu 10-6, Fri-Sat 10-8, Sun 11-6 (daily til 8 in Sum).

Architectural Antiques Inc

316 N Main St

Architectural & garden antiques as well as lighting. **Hrs:** Mon-Tue & Thu-Sat 10-5, Sun 12-5 (closed Wed). **QC: 3 60 65**

Country Charm Antiques [G]

124 S Main St
(612)439-8202

Hrs: Mon-Thu 10-5, Fri-Sat 10-6, Sun 12-5.

A Glimpse of Yesterday

115 Union St
(612)351-0060

China repair & antique doll restoration. **Hrs:** Mon-Fri 10-5 (call ahead advised). **Dir:** On the alley between Chestnut & Myrtle. S16 S11

Main Street Antiques

118 N Main St
(612)430-3110

Hrs: Open Sat-Sun; Wed-Fri by chance (closed Mon-Tue).

Mid-Town Antique Mall [G80+]

301 S Main St
(612)430-0808

Hrs: Mon-Thu 10-6, Fri 10-8, Sun 11-6 (extended hrs in Sum). **Sz:** H.

The Mill Antiques [G80+]

410 N Main St
(612)430-1816

Hrs: Daily 10-6. **Sz:** H **CC:** V/MC/DIS **Dir:** In the restored Isaac Staples Sawmill.

More Antiques [G65]

312 N Main St
(612)439-1110 • (612)430-0856 (fax)
mail@moreantiques.com
www.moreantiques.com

An mall where quality is the rule rather than the exception. Specialties include lighting, quality 19th C furniture, American art pottery, sporting items, stoneware, clocks, Victoriana & Carnival, elegant, art & Depression glass. No reproductions. **Pr:** $1-10,000 **Est:** 1990 **Hrs:** Mon-Sat 10-5, Sun

---

Candleholders I

Candles shed faint light and thus needed to be a close as possible to what their user wanted to see. Apart from sconces and chandeliers, the devices for holding them, then, were portable, sometimes adjustable, and often equipped with hooks, spikes, or other means of placing them where they were needed.

Candlestick or candleholder: A device to hold a candle, made of metal, porcelain, or wood in many forms.

Chamberstick: A candleholder with a handle, designed for carrying from room to room, particularly to the bedroom.

Taper stick: A holder for a rigid taper, like a small candlestick.

Taper jack or wax jack: A small, footed reel on which a flexible taper was coiled. Fitted with a pincer device for holding the end that was lit. An 18th century desk implement that was often highly elaborate, especially when made of silver.

Hogscraper: A simple iron candlestick on a circular base. Its shape and strength enabled farmers to use it for scraping the hair off pigskin.

Candelabra: A multiple-branched candleholder, often very ornate.

Sconce: A wall-mounted candleholder.

1-5. **Sz:** H **CC:** V/MC/DIS **Assn:** MADA **Dir:** I-94 to I-694 N to Hwy 36E to Stillwater & the St Croix River. Hwy 36 curves & becomes Hwy 95. Hwy 95 becomes Main St. Continue N through town to shop on L. **Own:** Tim Spreck. **QC: 52 89 65**

Mulberry Point Antiques [G65]
70 N Main St
(612)430-3630

Quality antiques including oak, pine, Mission & country furniture, china, porcelain, glass, linens, books & decorative accessories. Specializing in American country furniture, textiles & American pattern glass. **Hrs:** Mon-Sat 10-5, Sun 11-5. **Sz:** L **CC:** V/MC **Own:** Dianne Rollie.

River City Antiques & Collectibles
19 S Main St
(612)439-3889

Hrs: Mon-Sat 10-5, Sun 1-5.

Stillwater Antiques Mall [G60+]
101 S Main St
(612)439-6281

Furniture, lighting, glass & china, pens & inkwells, linens, books, vintage dolls, toys. **Hrs:** Daily 10-5.

Deanna Zink's Antiques
344 60th St N
(612)770-1987
(888)770-1987
www.gazlay.com/zink
Hrs: Thu-Sat 12-6 or by appt. **Dir:** On Hwy 36.

Wabasha

Wabasha's Old City Hall Antiques
57 W Main St
(612)565-2585

Furniture, glassware, paper items, books, sports, collectibles, stoneware & pottery in a historic building. **Hrs:** Daily (Fri-Sat til 8 in Sum). **Dir:** 1 blk from Anderson house.

Watertown

Oak Lake School House Antiques [G]
County Rd 20
(612)955-1365

Wind-up & cast iron toys, Watt ware, Red Wing, Depression glass, advertising, Shawnee, Hull, Roseville, flow blue, R S Prussia, oak furniture & ephemera. **Hrs:** Sum Tue-Sat 10-6; Win Sat 10-6 or by appt. **Dir:** 2-1/2 mi E of Watertown. **QC: 87 22**

Wayzata

Antiques Wayzata [G]
1250 E Wayzata Blvd
(612)449-9440

Hrs: Mon-Sat 10-5, Sun 12-5. **Dir:** In the Wayzata Home Center.

Carrousel Antiques Inc
1250 E Wayzata Blvd
(612)449-0678

Furniture (especially dining sets), accessories & mirrors. Glassware, porcelain & many unusual items. **Dir:** In the Wayzata Home Center. **Own:** Iris Berg & Stephen Berg.

The Corner Door
1250 E Wayzata Blvd
(612)473-2274

Antiques & quality consigned furnishings. **Hrs:** Mon-Sat 10-4:30. **Dir:** In the Wayzata Home Center. **QC: S8**

Gold Mine Antiques
332 S Broadway
(612)473-7719

General line of fine antiques including American & English furniture, paintings, silver, porcelain, glass, Oriental items & decorative accessories. **Est:** 1960 **Hrs:** Mon-Sat 10-4:30. **QC: 23 7 78 S1 S8**

Marilyn Simmons Antiques

17620 Copperwood Ln
(612)473-5638 • (612)473-5638 (fax)
fdsimmons@worldnet.att.net

18th & 19th C American country painted
furniture, folk art & related accessories with
an emphasis on form & surface. **Pr:** $50-
5,000 **Est:** 1976 **Hrs:** By appt. **Sz:** M **CC:**
V/MC **Dir:** I-94W to I-494 S to
Minnetonka Blvd W to Hwy 101 N. L on
Copperwood. **QC: 1 41 51 S1 S8 S15**

Welch

Mark & Audrey Jackson at Hungry Point Farm

(612)438-9949

New England country furniture & accessories. Featured in *Decorating with American
Country*. **Hrs:** By appt only. **QC: 52 34**

White Bear Lake

Antiques White Bear Inc

4903 Long Ave
(612)426-3834

General line of antiques & collectibles
including china, cut glass & dolls. **Hrs:**
Mon-Sat 10-5, Sun 11-5.

Zumbro Falls

The Wicker Woman

531 Main St
(507)753-2006

Specializing in the sale & restoration of
antique (c 1880-1930) cane & wicker furniture. Chairs, tables, rockers, lamps, tea carts,
plant stands, buggies. **Hrs:** By chance/appt.
QC: 91 S16

Ohio

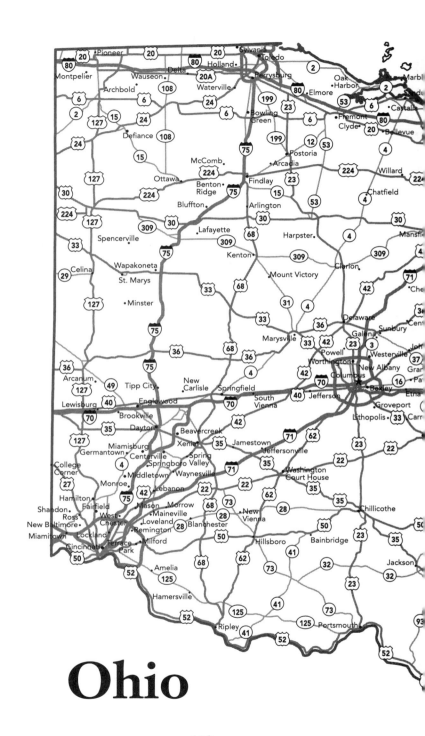

Ohio

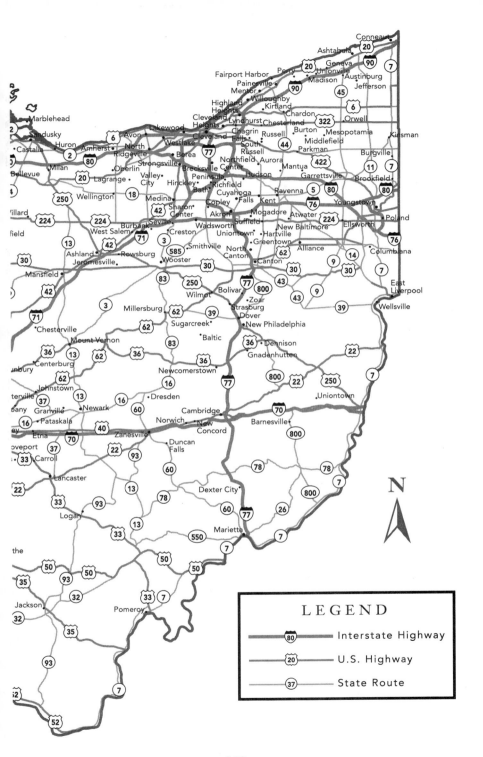

Akron

Abbey Ann's Second Hand Store
1773 State Rd
(330)940-3337

Collectibles. **Hrs:** Mon-Sat 10:30-7. **QC: 32**

Althea's Attic
1203 Canton Rd
(330)794-2845

Antiques, crafts & collectibles. **Hrs:** Mon-Sat 10-5. **QC: 32**

Ashley's Antiques & Interiors
443 W Market St
(330)535-1944

Antiques, furniture & accessories. **Hrs:** Mon-Sat 10-4.

Barberton Antique Mall [G150+]
135 Snyder Ave
(330)848-1549

General line. **Hrs:** Daily 10-5. **CC:** V/MC/DIS.

The Corner House
3220 Massillon Rd
(330)644-6950

Oak furniture, collectibles & Victoriana. **Hrs:** Mon-Fri 11-5, Sat 10-6, Sun 12-6. **Own:** Fred Carr. **QC: 50 32 89**

Market Antiques
439 Market St
(330)762-6343

Glassware, china & small furniture. **Hrs:** Mon-Sat 10-4, Sun 10-5. **CC:** V/MC/DIS **QC: 61**

Norton Antique Mall
2980 S Hametown Rd
(330)825-8695

Hrs: Thu-Sat 12-5.

Stagecoach Antiques
449 W Market St
(330)762-5422

Furniture, china, glassware, jewelry, books & linens. **Hrs:** Mon-Sat 10-8, Sun 12-5. **CC:** V/MC.

West Hill Antiques [G]
461 W Market St
(330)762-6633

Furniture, Depression glass, pottery, books, magazines, records. **Hrs:** Daily 10-6.

Alliance

Alliance Antiques
319 E Main St
(330)821-0606

Furniture & glassware. **Hrs:** Mon-Sat 10-5 or by appt. **QC: 48 61**

Attic Treasures Antiques
248 E Main St
(330)823-8920

Furniture & glassware. **Hrs:** Mon-Fri 10-4. **QC: 48 61**

Aunt Polly's Antiques
Corner E State & Freedom
(330)821-9136

Hrs: Mon-Sat 10-5.

Bruce's Place
14722 Ravenna Ave NE
(330)935-0523

General line. **Hrs:** Sun, Mon & Wed 11-5.

Lazy Acres
1360 W Main St
(330)823-8783

General line. **Hrs:** By chance/appt.

Memory Lane Antiques
(330)823-8568

Hrs: By appt only.

Towne Hall Antiques
12347 Marlboro Ave NE
(330)935-0114

General line. **Hrs:** Mon-Sat 10-5, Sun 12-5 (closed Tue).

Amelia

Cannonball Express Antiques
3430 Moria Dr
(513)753-8400

Cherry furniture, lamps & country accessories. **Hrs:** By appt only. **Own:** Cecil & Betty / Greg & Peggy Beckett. **QC:** 48

Amherst

The Mermaid's Tale
201 Church St
(440)988-7826

Furniture, jewelry & smalls. **Hrs:** Mon-Sat 10-5. **CC:** V/MC **QC:** 48

Arcadia

Little House Antiques
19706 Township Rd
(419)894-6888

Quilts, pattern glass, candlewick, flow blue, primitives. **Hrs:** By chance/appt. Closed Jan-Feb. **Dir:** State Rd 12 E to TR 214 2 mi E. **QC:** 84 61

Arcanum

Colonial Antiques
1905 US Rte 127
(937)678-4284

Located in a rural setting with a period log house on the premises. Late 17th to early 19th C American furniture specializing in rare & unusual pieces (some with orig surface) including highboys, tall clocks, pewter, china, oil paintings, textiles. **Pr:** $100-35,000 **Est:** 1979 **Hrs:** By chance/appt. **Sz:** M **CC:** V/MC **Dir:** I-70 Exit 10, 9-1/2 mi N on Rte 127 on R. **Own:** Phil & Judee Harbaugh. **QC:** 12 52 72

Smith's Antique Store [G50+]
109 W George St
(937)692-8540

Ohio's oldest general store (c 1851). **Hrs:** Tue-Sat 10-5, Sun 12-5. **Own:** Ned & Deb Brown.

Staley's Antiques & Woodworking
7 N Sycamore St
(937)692-8050

Furniture. **Hrs:** Tue-Sat 10-5, Sun 12-5, call ahead advised. **QC:** 48

Victorian Babes Antique Mall [G8]
20 W George St
(937)548-3349 (eves)

General line. **Hrs:** Tue-Thu 11-5, Fri by chance/appt.

Archbold

Primitive Pig Antiques & Soda Fountain
214 N Defiance St
(419)445-2323

General line. **Hrs:** Mon-Fri 10-9, Sat 10-5. **CC:** V/MC.

Arlington

Arlington Antique & Flower
112A N Main St
(419)365-7008

Antique furniture, collectibles, gifts, flowers. **Hrs:** Mon-Fri 9:30-5:30, Sat 9-1. **CC:** V/MC **Own:** Jayme Inbody & Julie Snyder.

Morrow's Antiques

526 N Main St
(419)365-5171

Depression & Heisey glass. **Hrs:** Mon-Fri 8-9pm.

Ashland

Antiques on Main

143 W Main St
(419)289-8599

Antiques & collectibles. **Hrs:** Mon-Sat 10-5.

The Gleaner

1488 County Rd 995
(419)281-2849

Country, primitives & furniture. **Hrs:** Mon-Sat 10-5, Sun 1-5. **QC: 48**

Susie's Antiques

59 South St
(419)281-3685

General line. **Hrs:** Tue-Sat 10-5 (Fri til 8), Sun 1-5 (closed Mon). **CC:** V/MC/DIS.

Ashtabula

Moses Antiques Mall [G]

4135 State Ave
(440)992-5556

Furniture, linens, jewelry, paper Americana, posters, vintage clothing, advertising, primitives, collectibles, glassware, pottery, china, lamps, dolls, books, toys, silver, autographs. **Hrs:** Mon-Sat 10-5, Sun 12-4. **Dir:** Near the Ashtabula Mall, Rte 20, Rte 11 & I-90. **Own:** Jane Anderson & Jane Moses.

Traveling East? Take along a copy of *Sloan's Green Guide to Antiquing in New England.* Call Toll Free (888)875-5999 or visit your local bookstore or antiques dealer.

Trash & Treasures Barn

5020 N Ridge Rd E
(440)998-2946

General line. **Hrs:** Mar-Oct Mon-Sat 10-7, Sun 1-5; Nov-Feb 11-3 or by appt.

The Way We Were

1837 Walnut Blvd
(440)964-7576

Paper antiques & advertising items. **Hrs:** By appt only. **Own:** Lynda & Dick Dunbar. **QC: 39**

Atwater

Floyd's Antiques

1131 Stroup Rd
(330)947-2151

Specializing in model trains. Furniture, stoneware, glassware, reproduction hardware, refinishing. **Hrs:** Daily 10-4. **Own:** Bob Floyd.

Aurora

Aurora Antiques

334 E Garfield Rd
(330)562-2626

Collectibles & antiques 1800-1950s. **Hrs:** Daily 11-6, Thu til 8. **CC:** V/MC **Dir:** On Rte 82 1/2 mi E of Rte 306.

Kent Farm Antiques

(330)562-5781

18th & early 19th C New England country furniture, many pieces in paint, as well as decorative accessories. **Pr:** $5-5,000 **Est:** 1991 **Hrs:** Shows only. **Own:** Nancy L Fetzer. **QC: 1 51**

Western Reserve Antiques [G8]

214 S Chillicothe Rd
(330)562-5950 • (440)247-6169

Located in a 9-room farmhouse built in

1830, 8 dealers offering quality country & formal antiques as well as unusual primitives including porcelains, silver, furniture, textiles, glass, artwork, jewelry & advertising. **Pr:** $1-6,000 **Est:** 1996 **Hrs:** Daily 11-5. **Sz:** M **Dir:** I-80 Ohio Tpke Exit 13: 5 mi N on Rte 43. **Own:** Vivan & Hank Platek & Sandy Seaman. **QC: 34 32 48 S1 S8 S12**

Avon

The Antique Arcade

36840 Detroit Rd
(440)934-0808 • (440)245-6127

Hrs: Tue-Sat 11-5, Sun 12-5. **Own:** Cathy & Gary Cummings.

Antique Gallery of Avon [G6]

36923 Detroit Rd
(440)934-4797

Furniture, pottery, glassware & collectibles. **Hrs:** Mon-Sat 10-5, Sun 11-5. **Own:** Bill Dineen. **QC: 48 61**

Applewood Antiques and Upholstery

37319 Detroit Rd
(440)934-5090

Furniture, clocks & watches. **Own:** Jim Murphy. **QC: 48 35 S16**

Coffee-An-Tiques [G15]

37321 Detroit Rd
(440)934-3131

Furniture, glassware, jewelry, military, toys, sports & books. **Hrs:** Daily 10-6. **Own:** Millie Harley & Peggy O'Rourke. **QC: 48 4 79**

Country Heirs [G]

35800 Detroit Rd (Rte 254)
(440)937-5544

Twenty-two room country home. **Hrs:** Mon-Sat 10-5, Sun 12-5.

Country Lady Interiors

2536 Stoney Ridge Rd
(440)934-5096 • (440)322-6721

English pine furniture & accessories. **Hrs:** Tue-Sat 11-5. **Dir:** Junction of Rte 254 & Rte 611. **QC: 55**

Countryside Antiques [G9]

37290 Detroit Rd (Knights Farmhouse)
(440)937-5204

Hrs: Mon-Sat 11-5, Sun 12-5. **Dir:** Rte 254: W of Rte 83.

Curiosity Shoppe

36145 Detroit Rd
(440)934-4795

Antiques & collectibles. **Hrs:** Tue-Fri 9:30-4:30, Sat 10-3.

Grinders Switch Antiques [G5]

37110 Colorado Ave (Rte 611)
(440)934-1315

Hrs: Daily 11-5. **Dir:** Rte 611 off Detroit Rd. **Own:** Lowell & Judy Neal.

Jameson Homestead Antiques [G30]

36675 Detroit Rd
(440)934-6977

In a 1906 farmhouse & barn, antiques & collectibles in room settings. **Hrs:** Mon-Sat 11-5, Sun 12-5; Nov-Dec til 8 on Thu. **Own:** Mary Ann Brown.

Remember When Antiques

2535 Hale St
(440)934-1544 • (440)779-7907

Glassware, dolls, jewelry & laces. **Hrs:** Mon-Sat 10-5, Sun 12-5. **Dir:** S off Detroit Rd. **Own:** Ruth Smith. **QC: 61 81 38**

Robin's Nest [G]

37298 Detroit Rd
(440)934-6950

Furniture, jewelry, vintage clothing, ephemera, militaria & collectibles. **Hrs:**

Mon-Sat 11-6, Sun 12-6. **Own:** Robin & Jim Collins. **QC: 48 4 83**

Shinko's Country Store [G]
2536 Stoney Ridge Rd
(440)934-6119 • (440)937-5204
Est: 1896 **Hrs:** Mon-Sat 11-5, Sun 12-5.

Sweet Caroline's at the Williams House [G30]
37300 Detroit Rd
(440)934-1800 • (440)934-4605

Furniture, glassware, primitives, pottery, books, toys & sporting memorabilia in a c 1836 registered historic site. **Hrs:** Mon-Sat 10-5, Sun 12-5. **Dir:** Rte 254, W of Rte 611, S of I-90. **Own:** Carole & Bob Nelson. **QC: 48 79 61**

Tree House and the Rooster Crows
36840 Detroit Rd
(440)934-1636

Antiques & collectibles. **Hrs:** Daily 11-5.

Bainbridge

Antiques at Hixson's [G]
16381 Chillicothe Rd
(440)543-5858

Furniture, accessories, glass, primitives, lamps, linens, quilts & jewelry. **Hrs:** Mon-Sat 10-5, Sun 12-5. **Dir:** 2 1/2 mi N of Rte 422. **Own:** Barbara Wells, Mgr. **QC: 48 84 61**

The Trading Post
401 S Maple St
(740)634-2867

Furniture, tools & glassware. **Hrs:** Mon-Fri 12-6, Sat-Sun 12-5. **Sz:** H. **QC: 48 61 86**

Baltic

Hershberger Antique Mall [G]
3245 State Rte 557
(800)893-3702

Glassware, furniture, quilts, pottery & tools. **Hrs:** Mon-Sat 9-8. **Dir:** 1 mi W of Farmerstown, 3 mi E of Charm & 15 mi E of Millersburg. **QC: 61 48 84**

Barnesville

Antiques on the Main
108 N Chestnut St
(740)425-3406

General line. **Hrs:** Mon-Sat 10-5. **CC:** V/MC.

Barnesville Antique Mall [G68]
202 N Chestnut St
(740)425-2435

General line. **Hrs:** Daily 8-5. **CC:** V/MC/DIS.

This Old House
118 N Chestnut St
(740)425-4444

Furniture, decorative accessories & crafts. **Hrs:** Mon-Sat 10-5, Sun 1-5. **CC:** V/MC **QC: 48 36**

Bath

Yellow Creek Barn
794 Wye Rd
(330)666-8843

Country antiques & collectibles. **Hrs:** Mon-Sat 10-5. **CC:** V/MC.

Beavercreek

Bevercreek Antique Mall [G55]
3854A Kemp Rd
(513)320-1910

General line. **Hrs:** Mon-Fri 11-6, Sat 9-7, Sun 1-5. **CC:** V/MC/DIS.

Bellevue

Junction Antique Mall
127 E Main St
(419)483-8227

Hrs: Daily 10-6. **Sz:** H **CC:** V/MC **Own:** Scott & Renee Carroll.

Berea

Bank of Berea
46 Front St
(440)234-7285

General line including advertising & trade cards. **Hrs:** Daily exc Mon.

Colonial House Antiques
182 Front St
(440)826-4169
(800)344-9299

Glass, porcelain, stoneware, collectibles. **Hrs:** Mon-Sat 10-5 or by appt. **CC:** AX/V/MC/DIS.

Bexley

David Franklin Ltd
2216 E Main St
(614)338-0833

Interior design & fine antiques. Specializing in period English furniture & decorative accessories. **Hrs:** Mon-Fri 10-5. **Dir:** I-70 Main St/Bexley Exit: A deadend at Main St, across from Bexley Square Shopping Plaza. **QC: 54 36 S15**

Joseph M Hayes Antiques
2264 E Main St
(614)238-3000 • (614)238-0093 (fax)

Fine period English & Continental 18th & 19th C furniture & accessories displayed in an attractive fine arts gallery. **Hrs:** Tue, Wed & Sat 10-6, Fri 10-8, Sun 12-5. **QC: 54 53 7**

The Bryan H Roberts Gallery
539 S Drexel Ave
(614)236-1245 • (614)236-1252 (fax)
brobert3@ix.netcom.com
www.robertsgallery.com

Fine paintings of the 19th & 20th C. A few pieces of early furniture & a selection of decorative accessories are always on hand as well. Worldwide shipping available. **Pr:** $200-10,000 **Hrs:** Tue-Sat 1-5, Sun by chance in p.m. **Sz:** M **CC:** V/MC **Dir:** I-70 E: Bexley/Main St exit N to Main; R on Main to Drexel. I-70 W: Livingston Ave exit. L at bottom of ramp, then N on Alum Creek Dr to Main; R on Main to Drexel. **QC: 7 S1 S13 S16**

Blanchester

Broadway Antique Mall [G]
102 S Broadway
(937)783-2271

Furniture, toys, dolls, pottery, primitives, glassware, clocks, linens, advertising & jewelry. **Hrs:** Mon-Sat 10-5, Sun 12:30-5. **QC: 38 81 87**

Bluffton

Deer Creek Shoppes [G30]
124 N Main St
(419)358-7467

A unique combination of antiques ranging from country furniture to fine collectibles, all in a quaint Main Street building. **Pr:** $1-5,000 **Est:** 1995 **Hrs:** Tue-Fri 11-5, Sat 10-5. **Sz:** M **CC:** V/MC **Dir:** I-75 N exit

Bluffton. **Own:** Steve & Jan Shaw. **QC: 32 34 S8**

Bolivar

Central Avenue Antiques [G]
127 Central Ave
(330)874-4136

Glassware, furniture & primitives. **Hrs:** Daily 10-5. **Dir:** I-77 exit 93, State Rte 212 W 6 blocks. **QC: 61 48**

Bowling Green

B G Antiques Mall [G25]
182 S Main St
(419)353-6300

Dolls, arrowheads, furniture. **Hrs:** Mon-Fri 11:30-9, Sat 11:30-8, Sun 1-6 (closed Wed). **CC:** V/MC/DIS **QC: 29 33**

Millikin Antique Mall [G46]
101 S Main St
(419)354-6606

Antiques & collectibles in the historic Hotel Millikin. **Hrs:** Mon-Sat 10-5; Sun 12-5 **Dir:** Crn S Main & E Wooster. Easy access off I-75. **QC: 23**

Quality Steins & Collectibles
133 E Wooster
(419)353-6847

Die-cast, neons, beer advertising, antiques, primitives. **Hrs:** Mon-Thu 3:30-8; Fri-Sun by chance/appt. **QC: 23 30**

Brecksville

Riverview House Antiques
12929 Chippewa Rd
(440)838-5661

General line. **Hrs:** Mon-Fri 9-5, Sat-Sun 12-5. **Dir:** Rte 82 at Riverview Rd, 2 mi E of Rte 21 (Brecksville Ctr) and 4 mi W of Rte 8, between I-77 and I-271.

Brookfield

Valley View Antique Mall [G]
7281 Warren Sharon Rd
(330)448-6866 • (330)448-2570 (fax)
(800)587-2535

General line of antiques & collectibles including glass, furniture, jewelry, linens, pocket watches, books, tools, kitchen items, old coins, paper & vintage clothing. **Hrs:** Mon-Sat 10-8, Sun 10-6. **Sz:** H **CC:** V/MC/DIS **Assn:** NOADA **Dir:** I-80 Exit 234: Rte 7 N 4 mi to Brookfield Ctr. R on Warren Sharon Rd (old Rte 82). **QC: 35 48 61 S2 S6 S7**

Brookville

Baltimore House
11632 Baltimore-Phillipsburg Rd
(937)884-5240

Furniture, primitives & decorator items. **Hrs:** Fri-Sun 11-5. **CC:** V/MC/DIS **Dir:** I-70 exit 24. Rte 49 to 2nd light, turn L at light shop is 4.5 mi from light on L. **QC: 48**

Burbank

The Rose & Thistle Antique Mall [G]
27 Front St (Rte 83)
(330)624-0106

Antiques & collectibles. **Hrs:** Wed-Sat 11-5, Sun 11-4. **Own:** Laura & Keith Enoch.

Burghill

Lane Tavern Antiques
5330 Rte 7
(330)772-3807

Vintage clothing, country furniture, primitives, farm tools, glassware, quilts & clocks. **Hrs:** Thu-Sun 1-5 or by appt. **Own:** Mary Novelli. **QC: 84 83 86**

Burton

Apple Butter Antiques
East Park St
(440)834-1426

General line. **Hrs:** Tue-Sat 11-5, Sun 12-5.
Own: Linda Nagy & Mamie Tompkins.

Burton Square Antiques & Gifts
14576 W Park St
(440)834-1426

General line. **Hrs:** Mar-Dec Wed-Sun 12-5:30; Jan-Feb Sat-Sun 12-5:30. **CC:** V/MC/DIS **Own:** Bonnie & Gary Gordon.

Spring Street Antiques
13822 Spring St
(440)834-0155

General line. **Hrs:** Tue-Sat 11-5, Sun 12-5. **CC:** V/MC/DIS **Own:** Ronald Wright & Harry Jones.

Cambridge

10th Street Antique Mall [G10]
127 S 10th St
(740)432-3364
hcherry@cambridgeoh.com
www.cambridgeoh.com/users/hcherry/

General line. **Hrs:** Mon-Sat 10-5 (closed Sun). **CC:** V/MC/DIS.

Judy's Antiques
422 S 9th St
(740)432-5855 • (740)432-3045

Quilts, furniture & glass. **Hrs:** Mon-Fri 1-5, Sat by chance. **QC: 48 84 61**

Penny Court Antiques [G50]
637 Wheeling Ave
(740)432-4369

Hrs: Mon-Sat 10-6, Sun 12-5 (closed holidays). **CC:** V/MC/DIS/AX.

Canton

Just Resale
1126 30th St NW
(330)493-1103

General line. **Hrs:** Mon-Sat 10-7.

Memory Lane Antiques [G20]
929 Wertz Ave NW
(330)452-5700 • (330)455-5580

Excellent selection of clean antiques & collectibles including furniture, glassware, pottery, advertising, military, petroliana, sports, kitchenware, toys, Coke & Pepsi items. Shop is air-conditioned & wheelchair accessible with ample parking. **Pr:** $1-10,000 **Est:** 1995 **Hrs:** Mon & Wed-Sat 10-5, Thu til 7, Sun 12-5. **Sz:** L **CC:** V/MC **Assn:** ACDA **Dir:** I-77 Exit 106: follow signs to Stark County Fairgrounds. Shop is 2 blks N. **Own:** Milan W Dolanski. **QC: 48 32 87**

Somewhere in Time Antiques [G]
3823 Cleveland Ave NW
(330)493-0372

General line. **Hrs:** Mon-Fri 10-4, Sat 10-5, Sun 12-5 (closed Tue).

Treasure Trove Antiques
4313 Tuscarawas St W
(330)477-9099

Furniture, quilts & china. **Hrs:** Mon-Sat 10-6. **CC:** V/MC **QC: 48 84**

Carroll

Antique Palace Mall [G]
4250 Coonpath
(614)756-4411
General line. **Hrs:** Wed-Sun 11-5.

Castalia

Cloud's Antique Mall [G]
510 N Washington St (Rte 269)
(419)684-7566

Glassware, china, furniture, lamps, quilts, art glass, decorator items, books, smalls & reference books on antiques. **Dir:** Midway between Toledo & Cleveland. OH Tpke Exit 6A. **Own:** Mark & Trina Cloud.

Celina

The American Shoppe
215 S Main St
(419)586-8897
Furniture. **Hrs:** Mon, Wed, Fri 9:30-5, Sat 9:30-1 or by appt. **QC: 48**

Michael's Antique Mall [G35]
125 W Fayette St
(419)586-7973
Hrs: Mon-Sat 10-5, Sun 1-5.

Centerburg

Coach's Corner Antiques & Oak [G4]
26 E Main St
(740)625-6222

Antiques & reproduction. **Hrs:** Mon-Sat 11-6, Sun 10-5. **Own:** Denny & Kathy Stevens.

> Visiting one of our advertisers? Please remember to tell them that you "found them in the Green Guide."

Centerville

Barn Antiques Gallery & World Imports
548 St Rte 725
(800)800-7998

Import French & Italian furniture, clocks & accessories. **Hrs:** Mon-Fri 10-8, Sat 10-5, Sun12-4. **Sz:** H.

Phil & Jeanne Jessee
(513)434-1364 • (937)434-1364 (fax)

Specializing in leather books, 18th & early 19th C furniture & appropriate accessories. **Pr:** $200-10,000 **Est:** 1989 **Hrs:** By appt only. **QC: 18 7 52**

Chagrin Falls

Bell Corner Shop [G5]
5197 Chilicothe Rd
(440)338-1101

Period & Victorian furniture, glassware, jewelry, prints & tools. **Hrs:** Daily 11-5. **Dir:** Rte 306.

Chagrin Antiques
516 E Washington St
(440)247-1080

English porcelain, sterling silver, glassware & furniture. **Hrs:** Mon-Sat 11-5. **QC: 78 61 48**

Chagrin's Fine Jewelry
42 N Main St
(440)247-7688

Estate jewelry. **Hrs:** Mon-Sat 10-5. **QC: 64**

Chagrin Valley Antiques
15605 Chillicothe Rd (Rte 306)
(440)338-1800

A historic Western Reserve home with 11 rooms decorated with period American painted & country primitive, Victorian, country French & European furniture. Quimper, ceramics, textiles, early & repro-

duction lighting, books, mirrors, clocks, brass & more. **Pr:** $5-12,000 **Est:** 1995 **Hrs:** Tue-Sat 11-5, Sun 12-5 (closed Mon). **Sz:** L **Assn:** NOADA NAACD **Dir:** Rte 422 W to Rte 306 N (1 mi S of Rte 87). **Own:** Diana L Rossi & Thomas A Colucci. **QC:** 34 52 1 S12 S15 S18

Tim & Barb Martien / Choice American Antiques

1229 Bell St
(440)338-3666

American "high country" furniture 1740-1890. Specializing in cherry, tiger maple & walnut. Emphasis on top quality & eye appeal. American 8-day tall clocks, signed/dated jacquard coverlets, graphic American samplers, brass student lamps w/orig shades. **Pr:** $150-15,000 **Est:** 1968 **Hrs:** By appt at your convenience. Pls call ahead. **Sz:** M **Dir:** I-271 Exit 27A (US 422E — Solon). E 10 min to OH 306, L at exit then N exactly 3 mi to Bell. Turn R to 2nd

drive on L. Sign on lamp post, gallery to rear of house. **QC:** 1 52 82 S8 S15 S9

Martines' Antiques

516 E Washington St
(440)247-6421 • (216)371-5255
(440)247-6421 (fax)
martines@stratos.net

Specialists in silver, silver flatware matching, silver miniatures, clocks & Russian appoint-

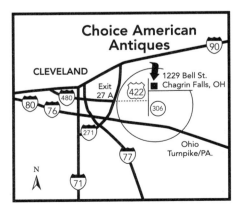

Choice American Antiques

1229 Bell St. Chagrin Falls, OH

CLEVELAND

Exit 27 A

90 480 80 76 422 306 271 77 71

Ohio Turnpike/PA.

N

ments & smalls. **Pr:** $15-150,000 **Est:** 1975 **Hrs:** Mon-Sat 11-5, call ahead advised. **Sz:** M **Assn:** NAWCC **Dir:** I-271 Exit Chagrin Blvd E approx 6 mi thru the Village of Chagrin. 1 mi E on E Washington St. **Own:** Peggy & Joseph Martines. **QC: 78 10 35 S7**

The Silk Road
49 W Orange St
(440)247-8810

Chinese antiques & collectibles. **Hrs:** Tue-Sat 10-5 or by appt.

Chardon

Antiques on the Square [G21]
101 Main St
(440)286-1912

Oak, country & Victorian furniture, glass, jewelry, linens & advertising. **Hrs:** Mon-Sat 10-5, Sun 12-5. **CC:** V/MC/DIS **Own:** Pat & Greg Martin. **QC: 39 81 61**

Bostwick Antiques
310 South St (Rte 44)
(440)285-4701

General line of antiques. One-owner shop. Wheelchair accessible. **Pr:** $3-2,000 **Est:** 1963 **Hrs:** Daily. **Sz:** S **CC:** V/MC **Assn:** NEODA **Dir:** E of Cleveland, S 7 mi of I-90 on Rte 44. **Own:** Jeanne Bostwick. **QC: 1 32 48**

Elaine's Antiques & Stained Glass
11970 Ravenna Rd (Rte 44)
(440)285-8041

Victorian, oak & country furniture, lighting, smalls & glassware. **Hrs:** Tue-Sat 11-5. **Dir:** 1 mi N of Rte 322. **Own:** Elaine Berkebile.

> Use the Service QuickCode indexes at the back of the book to find restorers, appraisers, refinishers, and other specialty service providers.

QC: 58 65 61

Olden Dayes Shoppe
129 Main St
(440)285-3307

General line. **Hrs:** Mon-Sat 11-5, Sun 12-5.

Steeplechase Antiques [G]
111 Main St (Rte 44)
(440)286-7473

Country & Victorian furniture, vintage jewelry, dolls, linens & postcards. **Hrs:** Mon-Sat 10-5, Sun 12-5. **Own:** Kathy & Jim Willis. **QC: 58 81 39**

Wedgewood Etc
304 Park Ave
(440)285-5601

Period furniture, tools & collectibles. **Hrs:** By chance/appt. **Dir:** 1 block S of square, off Rte 44, corner of Park & Tilden Ave. **Own:** Dottie Wedge. **QC: 86**

Chatfield

Chatfield Country Antiques
6786 State Rte 4
(419)465-2483

General line of country antiques, furniture a specialty. **Hrs:** Apr-May Fri & Sun 12-5; Jun-Aug Wed-Fri & Sun 12-5.

Chesterland

Antiques of Chester [G13]
7976 Mayfield Rd (Rte 322)
(440)729-3395

Victorian, country, oak & primitive furniture, tools & quilts. **Hrs:** Tue-Sat 11-5, Sun 12-5. **Dir:** 5 min E of I-271, W of Rte 306. **Own:** Kay Previte, Mgr. **QC: 58 84 86**

The Second Time Around
11579 Chillicothe Rd (Rte 306)
(440)729-6555

Antiques & collectibles. Furniture repair &

refinishing available. **Hrs:** Tue 10-2, Wed-Sun 11-5. **Dir:** N of Rte 322, between Wilson Mills Rd and Rte 6. **Own:** Barb & Bob Golob **QC: S16**

Chesterville

Chesterville Antiques
Corner Rtes 95 & 314
(419)768-3979

Early American pattern glass & Victorian art glass. **Hrs:** Wed-Sun 12-5. **Dir:** 2 mi E of I-71 Exit 151.

Chillicothe

Antiques on Main St
145 E Main St
(740)775-4802

Glassware, furniture, jewelry & books. **Hrs:** Tue-Sat 11-5. **CC:** V/MC/DIS **QC: 61 48 18**

The Cellar Room Corner
203 W Water St
(740)775-9848

Antiques, collectibles & gifts. **Hrs:** Tue-Sat 10:30-5:30. **CC:** V/MC/DIS **Dir:** Crn High & Water Sts.

Tygert House
245 Arch
(740)775-0222

Furniture & glassware. **Hrs:** Mon-Sat 9:30-5. **QC: 48 61**

Cincinnati

Acanthus Antique & Decorative Arts
3446 Edwards Rd
(513)533-1662

Architectural antiques & European furniture. **Hrs:** Mon-Sat 10:30-5. **CC:** V/MC/AX **QC: 3 53**

Berg Brothers Antiques
4923 Whetsel Ave
(513)561-5054

Furniture. **Hrs:** By appt only. **QC: 48**

Briarpatch Antiques
1006 Delta Ave
(513)321-0308

Primitives, country & furniture. **Hrs:** Mon-Sat 11-5. **CC:** V/MC. **QC: 34 48**

Byrd/Braman
338 Ludlow Ave
(513)872-0200

Vintage furnishings 1920-1960: 50s, Art Deco, Herman Miller, Knoll, Noguchi, Eames, Nelson, Frankl, Rohde, Saarinen, Bertoia, Bakelite, lighting, chrome, silver & glass. **Hrs:** Wed-Sat 12-6. **QC: 5 59**

Cincinnati Art Galleries
635 Main St
(513)381-2128 • (513)381-7527 (fax)
www.cincinnatiartgalleries.com

Specializing in quality paintings & American art pottery as well as books about American art pottery & American Arts & Crafts. **QC: 7 22 19 S1 S2**

Country Manor
7754 Camargo Rd
(513)271-3979

Furniture & accessories. **Hrs:** Mon-Fri 11:30-4:30, Sat 10:30-4:30. **QC: 48**

Crackle
1999 Madison Rd
(513)321-3339

Accessories, architectural & garden antiques. **Hrs:** Tue-Sat 11-5, Sun 12-5. **QC: 3 60**

Duck Creek Antique Mall [G170+]
3715 Madison Rd
(513)321-0900

Furniture, toys, jewelry, paper, primitives, textiles, pottery, advertising, china. **Hrs:**

Grosvenor Brant Antiques

Fine Period Accessories & Furniture

3407 Monteith Avenue
Cincinnati, Ohio 45208

Phone: (513) 871-1333
Fax: (513) 871-9212

Margy & Bill Gale

Mon-Sat 10-5, Sun 12-5. **Dir:** I-71 Exit 9 (Red Bank Rd): R at 2nd light. 1 mi on L. **Own:** Nancy Martin.

English Traditions

2041 Madison Rd
(513)321-4730 • (513)321-4730 (fax)

English, Irish & French fruitwood antiques, garden artifacts, European hotel silver & decorative arts. **Pr:** $30-8,500 **Est:** 1992 **Hrs:** Tue-Sat 10-5, Sun 12-4. **Sz:** M **CC:** AX/V/MC **Dir:** N-71 to Dana Exit. L off exit 2 lights, then R at Madison. Shop at 3rd light on L. **Own:** Mary Cordill & Casey Cordill. **QC:** 36 47 55 S15 S19

Federation Antiques Inc

2124 Madison Rd
(513)321-2671 • (513)321-7059 (fax)

Fine English & American 18th & 19th C furniture & decorative accessories. **Hrs:** Tue-Sat 10-5. **Own:** Charles E Bolton. **QC:** 54 7 36 S15

Bill Ferguson's Antique Mall [G90]

3742 Kellogg Ave (Rte 52)
(513)321-0919

General line. **Hrs:** Wed-Fri 10-5, Sat-Sun 9-6.

Denise Deloach Goble Antiques

2009 Madison Rd
(513)321-5312

Architectural & garden items, china & silver, linens & lace, antiques & accessories. **Hrs:** Tue-Sat. **Sz:** M **CC:** V/MC **Dir:** I-71 to Dana (Exit 5): 1 blk to Madison Rd. Turn R to O'Bryonville Antique District (3rd through 5th traffic light). **QC:** 78 81 60

Grand Antique Mall Ltd [G175+]

9701 Reading Rd (State Rte 42)
(513)554-1919

Antiques & collectibles: jewelry, china/glass-

ware, pottery, antique toys, furniture, silver. **Hrs:** Mon-Sat 10-6, Sun 12-6. **Sz:** H **Dir:** Evendale area.

Greg's Antiques

925 Main St
(513)241-5487

Victorian furniture. **Hrs:** Mon-Fri 11-5, Sat 10-4. **CC:** V/MC **QC:** 58

Grosvenor Brant Antiques

3407 Monteith Ave
(513)871-1333 • (513)871-9212 (fax)
wmggba@att.net

Fine period antiques in a 19th C carriage house. English & Continental furniture & porcelains, Chinese export, early brass & copper, silver, prints & other quality smalls. **Pr:** $100-20,000 **Est:** 1993 **Hrs:** Tue-Sat 10-5 or by appt. **Sz:** M **CC:** AX/V/MC **Dir:** I-71 Exit 5 (Dana Ave): E 2 mi to Monteith. L on Monteith to 1st driveway on L. **Own:** Bill & Margy Gale. **QC:** 20 23 54

Raul Hass

2709 Erie Ave
(513)321-7679

Jewelry & smalls. **Hrs:** Mon-Sat 9:30-5.

Les Trouvailles

2031 Madison Rd
(513)533-9380

Handpainted furniture. **Hrs:** Tue-Fri 10:30-5, Sat 11:30-5. **CC:** V/MC

Nicholson Antiques

1999 Madison Rd
(513)871-2466 • (513)231-9371 (fax)

Carefully selected English, Irish & French country antiques: armoires, buffets, tables, cupboards, scent bottles, blue & white, brass, silver & decorative architectural & garden items. Direct importer. **Pr:** $100-16,000 **Est:** 1973 **Hrs:** Tue-Sat 11-5, Sun-Mon 12-4. **Sz:** L **CC:** AX/V/MC/DIS **Dir:** I-71 to Dana (Exit 5): 1 blk to Madison Rd. Turn R to O'Bryonville Antique District (3rd through 5th traffic light). Across from Franklin Savings. **Own:** Kathleen & Joyce Nicholson. **QC: 55 47 60 S12**

Parlor Antiques by Benjamin

6063 Montgomery Rd
(513)731-5550

Restored upholstered antiques. **Hrs:** By appt only. **QC: 48 S22 S1 S16**

Professional Clockery Inc

7600 Hamilton Ave
(513)931-8463 • (513)530-9921 (fax)
bob@proclocks.comm
www.proclocks.com

Over 350 antique clocks on display & over 3,000 in our warehouse. Clock repairs, manufacture of mystery clocks & porcelain clock dials. Dealer specials. **Pr:** $2-14,000 **Est:** 1972 **Hrs:** Mon-Fri 11-5, Sat 10-4. **Sz:** H **CC:** V/MC/DIS **Assn:** NAWCC **Dir:** I-75 to Ronald Regan Hwy. Exit at Mt Healthy, 1/2 mi N. **Own:** Robert Crowder. **QC: 35 S7**

Special Things Antique Mall [G]

5701 Cheviot Rd
(513)741-9127

Rookwood, Roseville & art pottery; furniture, Fiesta, glassware, china, country, linens, quilts, jewelry, books, postcards, trains, tools, toys, advertising, collectibles. **Hrs:** Mon-Sat 10-5, Sun 12-5. **Dir:** I-74 Exit 14 or I-275 Exit 31. **Own:** Mary E Mecklenborg.

Statzer Gallery & Antiques

2003 Madison Rd
(513)533-9377

Antiques, art, home accents, gifts. Original landscapes by Statzer. **Own:** Steve Statzer.

Treadway Gallery Inc

2029 Madison Rd
(513)321-6742 • (513)871-7722 (fax)
www.treadwaygallery.com

Rookwood & American art pottery. **Hrs:** By appt only. **QC: 22**

Treasures Inc Art & Antique Gallery

1971 Madison Rd
(513)871-8555

Art, antiques, collectibles, furniture, jewelry, textiles. **Hrs:** Wed-Sat 11-5, Sun 12-4. **Dir:** I-71 to Dana Ave exit. S 1 blk to Madison Rd, then R to 5th traffic light. In O'Bryonville. **Own:** Barbara Huenefeld LeBlond. **QC: 48 S8**

Westwood Antiques & Fine Furniture

3245 Harrison Ave
(513)481-8517

Victorian furniture & glassware. **Hrs:** By chance/appt. **CC:** V/MC **QC: 61 58**

Woodward Antiques

1404 Main St
(513)241-0040

Continental antiques & glassware. **Hrs:** Wed-Sat 11-4. **CC:** V/MC.

Claridon

Claridon Antiques

13868 Mayfield Rd (Rte 322)
(440)635-0359

China, furniture & glass. **Hrs:** Daily 12-5 (closed Tue). **Own:** Richard & Janet Beuck. **QC: 61 48**

Tamarack Farm Antiques

(440)286-6992

Country furniture, accessories & stoneware. **Hrs:** By appt only. **Own:** Karl & Sue Kronk.

Cleveland

Alanna Antiques

3441 Tuttle Ave
(216)671-8190

General line. **Hrs:** Mon-Sat 12-5.

Larchmere Antiques District

↑
Shaker Square

North Moreland Boulevard

**Shaker Heights
Antique Mall** ■

Chesire

E. 130th Street

■ **Bischoff Galleries**

**Rachel Davis
Fine Arts** ■

Bingham & Vance ■

■ **John L. Young Antiques**

Kendall

**Shaker Square
Antiques** ■

■ **Elegant Extras**

E. 128th Street

Larchmere Boulevard

■ **Ashley's Antiques & Interiors**

E. 127th Street

**Dede Moore
Oriental Rugs** ■

**Heide Rivchun
Furniture Conservation**
■ (see p. 269)

(see p. 269)

E. 127th Street

Downtown Cleveland
↓

Ambrose Antiques
1867 Prospect Ave E
(216)771-4874

Furniture & glassware. **Hrs:** Mon-Fri 9-5.
QC: 48 61

American Antiques
3107 Mayfield Rd
(216)932-6380

General line. **Hrs:** Mon-Sat 12-7.

Ameriflag Antiques
4240 Pearl Rd
(216)661-2608

General line. **Hrs:** Mon-Fri 9-5, Sat 9-3.

Annie's
10024 Lorain Ave
(216)961-3777

Furniture. **Hrs:** Mon-Sat 11-4. **CC:** V/MC
QC: 48

Antique Arcade & Antiques in the Bank
4125 Lorain Ave
(216)281-6040

Furniture, accessories & architectural antiques. **Hrs:** Wed-Sun 12-5. **Own:** Virginia Skala.

Antiques Gallery at the Bijou
7806 Lorain Ave
(216)961-4432

Furniture, silver, china, glassware & linens. **Hrs:** Wed-Sun 12-5. **QC: 81 78 61**

Ashley's Antiques & Interiors
12726 Larchmere Blvd
(216)229-1970 • (216)229-8100 (fax)

Fine formal furniture & antiques. Reproduction 18th C Chippendale, French & Queen Anne styles. Complete dining & bedroom sets, oriental rugs, Dresden, Meissen, porcelain & accessories. **Pr:** $50-10,000 **Est:** 1976 **Hrs:** Tue-Sat 12-5. **Sz:** M

CC: V/MC **Dir:** E on Carnegie to Stokes Blvd. R onto Stokes. R onto MLK Blvd turn L at stop light onto Larchmere Blvd. **Own:** Daniel Jerome Billeter.

Bingham & Vance
12801 Larchmere Blvd
(216)721-1711 • (330)928-0281 (fax)

Unique smalls, folk art & uncommon objects. Native American, jewelry, furniture & 20th C decorative arts. **Est:** 1991 **Hrs:** Wed-Sat 12-4. **Sz:** M **CC:** V/MC **Own:** Sherrie Bingham Chicatelli & Jeffrey Chicatelli. **QC: 41 42 63**

Bischoff Galleries
12910 Larchmere Blvd
(216)231-8313

Buy & sell antique & estate jewelry. Jewelry repair. **Est:** 1979 **Hrs:** Tue-Sat 11-5. **CC:** AX/V/MC **QC: 64 S16**

Century Antiques
7410 Lorain Ave
(216)281-9145

Furniture & accessories. **Hrs:** Mon-Sat 10-5. **CC:** V/MC/AX.

Cleveland Antiquarian Books
13127 Shaker Sq
(216)561-2665
www.clevelandbooks.com

Specializing in antique books, antique maps & antique library furnishings & located in the historic Shaker Square shopping district. Also autographs, vintage photographs, prints & manuscripts. **Pr:** $1-30,000 **Est:** 1979 **Hrs:** Mon-Sat 10-8, Sun 12-6. **Sz:** L **CC:** V/MC **Dir:** I-271 Chagrin exit: R on Richmond Rd, L on Shaker Blvd to Shaker Sq. Shop on NW side of Square. **Own:** William Chrisant. **QC: 18 66 39**

Rachel Davis Fine Arts
12803 Larchmere Blvd
(216)791-6040

Fine & decorative art, c 1850-1950. **Hrs:** Tue-Sat 11-5. **QC: 7**

Elegant Extras

2900 Larchmere Blvd
(216)791-3017

Decorative antiques for the art of entertaining, porcelain, crystal, textiles, fashion & estate jewelry, small items of furniture & distinctive accessory gifts. **Pr:** $5-5,000 **Hrs:** Tue-Sat 11-5. **Sz:** M **CC:** AX/V/MC **Own:** Allan J Hodges & William J Santabarbara. **QC: 1 23 63 S1 S8 S15**

Federal House Antiques

7106 Detroit Ave
(216)221-2149

Victorian furniture. **Hrs:** Tue-Sun 12-5. **Own:** Drew Bolda. **QC: 58**

Marc Goodman Antiques

2736 Larchmere Blvd
(216)229-8919 • (216)961-4231

Antiques, collectibles, furniture, linens & pianos. **Hrs:** Tue-Sat 12-6, Sun by appt.

Gwynby Antiques

483 Fairmount Blvd
(216)229-2526

Fine period American & English furniture & appropriate accessories. **Hrs:** Tue 10-5, Thu-Sat 10-5 (closed Mon, Wed & Sun). **CC:** V/MC **Own:** Eleanor Wilkins. **QC: 54 30 36**

Jordan-Etzler Vintage Gallery

7900B Lorain Ave
(216)961-0775

Hrs: Wed-Sat 12-5 or by appt.

Lakewood Antique Mall [G]

16928 Detroit Ave
(216)221-7650

General line. **Hrs:** Tue-Sun 12-5 (closed Mon).

Larchmere Antiques/Paulette's [G]

12204 Larchmere Blvd
(216)231-8181

Jewelry, china, glass, furniture, buttons & vintage clothing. **Hrs:** Tue-Sat 11-5. **Own:** Jim & Paulette Batt. **QC: 83**

Repairs and Restorations I

Restoration: The attempt to return a damaged antique to its original condition so skillfully that the restoration is invisible to all but the expert eye. The restorer often uses new materials but makes them look old.

Repair: Work done on a damaged object that enables it to continue to serve its original function. Often a repairer uses no new material, but glues or mends the original. A good repair is unobtrusive, but not invisible. The line between restoration and faking can sometimes be a fine one: good repairs are open and "honest."

Replacement: The replacement of working parts, such as handles, hinges, and latches, that become worn and broken with use. Also used to refer to the restoration of a whole component of a piece of furniture, such as the top of a candlestand or the base of a chest on frame.

Refinish: The replacement of an original surface that has become worn with a new one that makes the piece look like it did when it was new. A "finish" is a protective coat, such as varnish or French polish, that allows the natural wood to show through. Refinishing involves stripping the piece back to the bare wood and putting on a new finish. This is an irrecoverable process that destroys patina and reduces the value of an American piece by at least 50% and probably more (on an English piece it may have little or no effect on value).

Loganberry Books

12633 Larchmere Blvd
(216)795-9800

Used & rare books. **Hrs:** Mon-Sat 11-5, Sun 1-5. **QC: 18**

Dede Moore Oriental Rugs & Accessories

12633 Larchmere Blvd
(216)795-9802
dede@logan.com
www.logan.com/dede

New & old decorative rugs & kilims. **Hrs:** Tue-Sat 11-5, Sun 1-5. **QC: 76**

Anne Narosny Antiques

2118 S Taylor Rd
(216)371-2551

General line. **Hrs:** Mon-Sat 12:30-3:30.

Nook "n" Cranny Antiques

5201 Lorain Ave
(216)281-6665

General line. **Hrs:** Thu-Mon 10-5. **Own:** Paul Gibbons.

Old Brooklyn Antiques

2010 W Schaaf Rd
(216)351-8500

General line. **Hrs:** Wed-Sun 12-5. **CC:** V/MC.

Play Things of Past

3552 W 105th St
(216)251-3714 • (216)251-3714 (fax)
gbsptop@aol.com

Specialize in vintage radios, phonographs, jukeboxes & telephones. Also repair & restore these items. **Pr:** $10-200 **Est:** 1991 **Hrs:** Wed 12-9 & Sat 12-6 or by chance (closed Sun). **Sz:** M **Dir:** I-90 exit W 117th St or I-71 exit Belaire Rd. **Own:** Gary B Schneider. **QC: 77 69 S9 S12 S16**

Princeton Antiques & Photographica

12805 Larchmere Blvd
(216)231-8855
princeton@antiquesworld.com
www.photographica.com

Cameras, watches, jewelry & collectible **Hrs:** Wed-Sat 11-4:30 or by appt. **Ow**r Steven Sagri & Marian Dieter. **QC: 35 73**

Shaker Heights Antiques Mall [G]

13015 Larchmere Blvd
(216)231-6255

Quality group shop in the Larchmer antiques district. **Hrs:** Tue-Sun 10-6. **Ow**r Jennifer Emery.

Shaker Square Antiques Inc

12733 Larchmere Blvd
(216)231-8804 • (216)231-1146 (fax)

18th & early 19th C English & America furniture & decorative arts. **Hrs:** Mon-S; 10-4:30. **Own:** Mary M & Fred J Bentof **QC: 52 54**

A Sisser Jewelers Inc

2044 E 4th St
(216)621-3524
www.spectreint.com/sisser

Jewelry, autographs, slots, collectibles ; sports memorabilia. **Hrs:** Mon-Sat 10-5:3(**CC:** V/MC **QC: 32 67**

South Hills Antique Gallery [G]

2010 W Schaaf Rd
(216)351-8500

Furniture, primitives, clocks, quilts, lamp jewelry & prints. **Hrs:** Wed-Sun 12-5. **Q**C **48 35 74**

Studio Moderne

13002 Larchmere Blvd
(216)721-2274

20th C furnishings, decorative accessories ;

vintage clothing. **Hrs:** Tue-Sat 12-5, Sun 1-5. **QC: 59 36**

Suite Lorain [G14]
7105 Lorain Ave
(216)281-1959

Vintage clothing. **Hrs:** Daily 11-5. **CC:** V/MC/DIS **QC: 83**

Sutter Antiques Inc
16850 Lorain Ave
(216)251-9500

Victorian, Art Nouveau, Art Deco & Mission furniture, art glass shades, pottery, windows. From the very affordable to the exquisite, pricey & rare. Also buying. **Pr:** $2-20,000 **Est:** 1983 **Hrs:** Sep-May Tue-Sat 10-6; Jun-Aug Tue-Fri 10-6, Sat 10-4. **Sz:** L **CC:** V/MC/DIS **Dir:** I-71, I-480, I-90 exit 150th St. OH Tpke Exit 10, 3 mi. **Own:** Conni Wood. **QC: 5 19 48 S9 S18 S19**

Wolf's
1239 W 6th St
(216)575-9653 • (216)621-8011 (fax)
(800)526-1991

Art, decorations & furnishings, silver & porcelain, oriental rugs & jewelry. **Hrs:** Mon-Fri 10-5, or by appt. **CC:** V/MC **Own:** Dennis Eberhart, CAI. **QC: 7 78 36**

Yesterdays Treasures Antiques
4829 Turney Rd
(216)441-1920

Furniture, glassware & smalls. **Hrs:** Wed-Sat 12-5. **CC:** V/MC/DIS **QC: 48 61**

John L Young Antiques
12908 Larchmere Blvd
(216)721-3123

Jewelry & fine art. Specializing in oriental art, unique furniture & accessories. **Hrs:** Wed-Sat 11-5. **QC: 64 9**

Cleveland Heights

Artisan Antiques & Jewelry
3095 Mayfield Rd
(216)371-8639

Art Noveau, Art Deco, architectural artifacts. **Hrs:** Mon-Sat 2-7. **CC:** V/MC/DIS **QC: 3 5**

Attenson's Coventry Antiques
1771 Coventry Rd
(216)321-2515

Costume & fine jewelry, toys, prints, oils, linens, furniture & silver. **Hrs:** Mon-Sat 11:30-5:30. **CC:** V/MC **QC: 63 74 78**

Greenwald Antiques
3096 Mayfield
(216)932-5535

19th & early 20th C arts. **Hrs:** Mon-Fri 10-5, Sat 10-4. **CC:** V/MC **Own:** Joan & Ron Greenwald.

Clyde

Farmstead Antique Mall [G50+]
2005 W McPherson Hwy (Rte 20)
(419)332-9628 • (419)332-9628

Furniture, glassware, paper items, silverware, jewelry, lamps & toys. **Hrs:** Mon-Sat 10-5, Sun 12-5. **Own:** Robert & Martha Lanz.

Maplewood Gallery [G]
1012 E US Rte 20
(419)547-9175

Hrs: Mon-Fri 10-6 (Thu til 8), Sat 10-5, Sun 1-5. **Sz:** H.

College Corner

Victorian House Antiques
2 Main St (Rte 27)
(513)523-3881

General line. **Hrs:** Daily 9-5.

Columbiana

Columbiana Antiques Gallery
103 S Main St
(330)482-2240

Furniture, glassware & smalls. **Hrs:** Mon-Fri 10-4:30, Sat 11-5, Sun 12-5. **CC:** V/MC **QC: 48 61**

Mainstreet Antiques [G14]
13 E Park Ave
(330)482-5202

Victorian, oak & country furniture; glassware, china & toys. **Hrs:** Mon-Sat 10-4:30, Sun 12-5. **Dir:** On the square.

Vivian's Antiques & Collectibles
21 S Main St
(330)482-3144

Collectibles. **Hrs:** Mon-Sat 10-5 (Fri til 7), Sun 1-5. **CC:** V/MC/AX **QC: 32**

Columbus

Akers & Akers
(614)836-5225

Featuring original works by American & European artists of the 19th & early 20th C. Period-style framing services. **Pr:** $200+ **Est:** 1985 **Hrs:** By appt only. **Dir:** SE of Columbus on Rte 33. **Own:** Rick & Jo Akers. **QC: 7 8 9 S15 S13 S18**

Antiques & Uniques
247 W 5th Ave
(614)294-9663

Glassware, mirrors, home accessories & furniture. New gift & garden items added to the inventory for a classic yet eclectic look. **Pr:** $5-3,000 **Est:** 1997 **Hrs:** Tue-Sat 11-7, Sun 12-7. **Sz:** M **CC:** AX/V/MC/DIS **Dir:** I-71 5th Ave exit. W on 5th 3 blks past High St. **Own:** Jo Leatherman. **QC: 36 58 6 S8 S16 S15**

Antiques Etc
3521 N High St
(614)262-7211

Silver, lamps & chandeliers. **Hrs:** Mon-Tue & Thu-Sat 11-6, Sun 12-6 (closed Wed). **CC:** V/MC/DIS **QC: 78**

Antiques Etc Mall [G]
3265 N High St
(614)447-2242

Furniture, glassware, jewelry & dolls. **Hrs:** Daily 12-6. **QC: 38 48 61**

Bella Casa
2116 Arlington Ave
(614)488-6002

Art & furniture. **Hrs:** Mon-Fri 10-6, Sat 10-5. **CC:** V/MC/DIS. **QC: 7 48**

Down Memory Lane
3250 N High St
(614)262-6390

Furniture, frames, glassware, prints & ceramics. **Hrs:** Mon-Sat 1-6 (closed Thu & Sun). **QC: 22 74 61**

Echoes of Americana — Antiques
3165 N High St
(614)263-9600
echoes@ds.net
www.ds.net/~echoes

Always a unique selection of fine antiques & collectibles in the American tradition. **Pr:** $10-10,000 **Est:** 1993 **Hrs:** Mon-Sat 10-5, Sun 12-5. **Sz:** L **CC:** V/MC/DIS **Dir:** I-71 exit at Weber. W to High St & N 2 blks. Shop at NW corner of Pacemont & High. **Own:** Tim Baker & Ken Naponiello. **QC: 1 22 67**

Euro Classics
3317 N High St
(614)447-8108

Mission, Victorian & turn-of-the-century furniture. **Hrs:** Tue-Fri 12:30-5, Sat 10:30-

4, Sun 12-4. **Sz:** L **CC:** V/MC/DIS **QC:** 49 58

Fireside Book Co
503 City Park Ave
(614)621-1928
fireside@infinet.com
www.infinet.com/~fireside

Used, out-of-print & vintage books for readers, scholars & collectors. Free book search service. **Pr:** $1-250 **Est:** 1993 **Hrs:** Tue-Sat 1-7, Sun 12-5. **Sz:** M **CC:** V/MC/DIS **Dir:** In German Village. **Own:** Jane Landwehr & Bryan Saums. **QC:** 18

German Village Antique Mall [G]
716 S High St
(614)443-2511

Furniture, paintings & collectibles. **Hrs:** Daily 11-4. **Sz:** H **Own:** Jim Langley. **QC:** 48 32

German Village Furniture
764 Parson Ave
(614)444-5252

Furniture. **Hrs:** Mon-Sat 9-6. **QC:** 48

Greater Columbus Antique Mall [G70+]
1045 S High St
(614)443-7858

Wide range of inventory on five floors including furniture, glass, china, pottery, coins, oil paintings, oriental rugs, art glass, quilts, jewelry, sterling silver, toys, advertising & slot machines. **Est:** 1979 **Hrs:** Daily 11-8. **Sz:** H **CC:** V/MC/DIS **Dir:** In German Village. **Own:** Fred Altevogt.

Heritage on High Antique Mall [G60+]
1224-1226 S High St
(614)444-2950

Glassware, pottery, furniture, fine art, Fiesta, prints, jewelry, art pottery, architecturals, advertising, collectibles & reference books.

Hrs: Mon-Sat 10-6, Sun 12-6. **Sz:** L **CC:** V/MC **Own:** Jackie Murphy.

Kathryn's Quality Vintage Fashion
1247 N High St
(614)299-7923

Vintage clothing. **Hrs:** Sat 12-6, weekdays by appt. **QC:** 83

Mary Catherine's Antiques
1128-1130 N High St
(614)291-4837 • (614)268-1539
Hrs: Mon-Fri 11-5, Sat 10-5.

Midwest Quilt Exchange
495 S Third St
(614)221-8400

Antiques quilts. **Hrs:** Mon-Sat 10:30-4:30, Sun by appt. **Own:** Sandra Mitchell. **QC:** 84

Minerva Park Furniture Gallery
5200 Cleveland Ave
(614)890-5235

Victorian furniture. **Hrs:** Mon, Tue, Fri & Sat 12-7 (closed Wed & Sun). **CC:** V/MC/DIS **QC:** 58

Myra's Antiques & Collectibles Inc
2799 Winchester Pike
(614)238-0520

Furniture, dolls, Depression & vintage clothing. **Hrs:** Tue-Sun 10:30-5 or by appt. **CC:** V/MC **QC:** 83 38 61

Peddler's Village Craft & Antique Mall [G314]
1881 W Henderson Rd
(614)326-0022
www.peddlersmall.com

Wide range of antiques from primitives to fine furniture, collectibles & jewelry. New stock arriving daily. **Pr:** $1-3,000 **Est:** 1993 **Hrs:** Mon-Fri 10-8, Sat 10-6, Sun 12-5. **Sz:**

H **CC:** V/MC **Dir:** From State Rd 315, take Henderson Rd exit W. At corner of Reed & Henderson. **QC: 32 48 6 S8 S12 S15**

Petro Annie's

595 E Weber Rd
(614)263-7867

Advertising, memorabilia & toys. **Hrs:** Tues-Fri 12-6, Sat-Sun 12-5, Mon by appt. **QC: 39 87 67**

Thompson's Haus of Antiques

499 S Third St
(614)224-1740

Furniture, cut glass, Flow blue & silver. **Hrs:** Tue, Wed, Fri-Sun 10-4 (closed Mon & Thu). **CC:** V/MC **QC: 48 78 61**

Unique Treasures

3514 N High St
(614)262-5428

Furniture & glassware. **Hrs:** Tue & Wed 11-3, Fri 11-5, Sat 12-5. **CC:** V/MC/DIS **QC: 48 61**

Vintage Jewels

65 E State St
(614)464-0921

Estate jewelry. **Hrs:** Mon-Fri 10-6, Sat 10-4. **CC:** V/MC/DIS **QC: 64**

Vintage Treasures

580 Oakland Park Ave
(614)263-2822

Kitchenware, toys & lamps. **Hrs:** Mon-Fri 12-6, Sat 11-4 (closed Sun). **QC: 87**

Repairs and Restorations II

Repaint: The application of a coat of paint over the original. Some repainted pieces can be stripped back to their original paint and will still be desirable, though they will have lost some patina and therefore some value. Pieces that have had heavy use, such as windsor chairs, have often been repainted more than once, and, if the final coat is not recent, and the older and/or original coat(s) can be detected where the paint has been worn or chipped, the chair will be valued for its "paint history," though it will still be less valuable than one in original paint.

Reconfiguration: Changing the structure or appearance of a piece to make it more useful or fashionable. A not-uncommon example of major reconfiguration is the conversion of large and almost useless 19th century wardrobes into breakfront bookcases or display cabinets. Some larger Hepplewhite and Sheraton sideboards have had their original depth of 28 or 30 inches reduced by six or eight inches to make them fit better into smaller rooms, and some highboys and chests on chests have had their height reduced by the removal of one drawer level for similar reasons. Less major examples of reconfiguration include glazing the blind doors of a secretary, scalloping the apron of a Queen Anne tavern table, or carving the knees or top of a Chippendale tilt top tea table — all of which were, in the 19th or early 20th centuries, common ways of enhancing unfashionably plain pieces.

Marriage: The creation of a piece of antique furniture by joining two parts that were originally from different pieces. Tables or candlestands sometimes have tops married to bases, but the most common marriages are found in large two-part case pieces such as highboys, secretaries, and chests on chests. A good marriage is when the two parts are of the same period and each was originally a part of the same form. A bad marriage is when the periods are not the same. The worst marriages of all are those that create a new form, as when as slant front desk is given a bookcase top that it was never designed to have, or when the bottom of a chest on chest is fitted with the top of a secretary to make a linen press.

Yesteryear Antiques
268 S 4th St
(614)224-4232

General line. **Hrs:** Tue-Fri 10-5, Sat 10-5:30, Sun 11-5 (closed Mon). **CC:** V/MC/DIS.

Conneaut

Ferguson Antique Shop
282 E Main Rd (Rte 20)
(440)599-7162

Furniture, lamps, art glass, china. **Hrs:** Daily 10-5, eves by appt. **Own:** Jack Coville. **QC:** 48 61

Studio Antiques
242 W Main Rd
(440)599-7614

Furniture, lamps, railroad items & china. **Hrs:** Sat-Sun afternoons or by appt. **Own:** Bob Goldsmith. **QC:** 48

Copley

Copley Antique Mall [G]
1451 S Cleveland-Massillon Rd
(330)665-5581
www.tfweb.com/copley

Glass, pottery, furniture, advertising & primitives. **Hrs:** Daily 11-4. **CC:** V/MC **Dir:** 4 min S of Montrose, 30-45 min from Akron, Canton & Cleveland at the intersection of Rte 162 & old Rte 21. **QC:** 48 61 39

Creston

Harbor Hill Inn & Antiques
10285 Wooster Pike
(330)334-9051

A country inn offering antique chandeliers, Victorian furniture, china, silver & stemware in a restored c 1908 B&B. **Hrs:** Daily 8-5.

Cuyahoga Falls

The Hidden Pearl
2206 Front St Mall
(330)928-8230

Victorian through the 1960s. Vintage clothing (men's & women's), luggage, linens, pottery. **Hrs:** Tue, Thu, Sat 12-7, Wed & Fri 12-7, 2nd Sun of month 1-5.

River Walk Antiques [G5]
2237 Front St
(330)945-6898

General line. **Hrs:** Mon-Sat 11-5. **CC:** V/MC/DIS.

Silver Eagle
2215 Front St
(330)929-0066

Antiques, art, collectibles, sports & toys. **Hrs:** Tue-Sat 12-5. **Dir:** Riverfront Centre Mall.

Dayton

Little Cottage Antiques
100 Watervliet Ave
(937)252-6809

Glassware & furniture. **Hrs:** Mon-Sat 12-5, by chance/appt. **CC:** DIS **QC:** 61 48

Old World Antiques and Estate Jewel
4017 N Main St
(937)275-3226

Estate jewelry. **Hrs:** Mon-Sat 10-5. **CC:** V/MC **QC:** 64

Traveling East? Take along a copy of *Sloan's Green Guide to Antiquing in New England.* Call Toll Free (888)875-5999 or visit your local bookstore or antiques dealer.

Remember When Antiques
1111 Wayne Ave
(937)222-7005

Furniture, glassware, gifts. **Hrs:** Wed-Fri 12-6, Sat 12-5. **CC:** V/MC **QC: 48 61**

Serendipity Antiques [G]
1942 N Main St (Rte 48)
(937)277-8001

Primitives, smalls, pottery, furniture & glass. **Hrs:** Tue-Sat 12-5:30. **QC: 48 61**

Springhouse Antiques
49 S Main St
(937)433-2822

Period & country furniture & rugs. **Hrs:** Sum: Tue-Wed 9:30-4:30, Thu-Sat 10:30-4:30; Win: Tue-Sat 10:30-4:30. **CC:** V/MC **QC: 48**

Then & Now
436 E 5th St
(937)461-5859

Deco, 50s modern, vintage. **Hrs:** Mon-Thu 12-5, Fri & Sat 12-12am, by chance/appt.

Uptown Downtown
343 E Fifth St
(937)223-9495 • (937)461-4568

Hrs: Thu-Sat 12:30-8.

Defiance

Heller Heaven Antiques
Rte 1 Evansport Rd
(419)784-1199

Two barns full of furniture & general line. **Hrs:** Daily 9-5 (appt suggested). **Dir:** N on State Rd 66 to Banner School Rd; 3 mi W to

Evansport Rd; then S 1/4 mi. **Own:** L & J Heller.

Delaware

Delaware Antiques
27 Troy Rd Shopping Ctr
(740)363-3165

General line. **Hrs:** Mon-Sat 10-6 (Fri til 8), Sun 12-6. **CC:** V/MC/DIS.

Essentials / King Tut's Antiques
43 N Sandusky St
(740)369-7003 • (740)369-9726 (fax)

Large assortment of antique furniture from several periods displayed on 2 floors with eclectic decorative accessories. Hand-made curly maple furniture in the style of the 1800s. Show-quality antique smalls: glassware, stoneware, silver, tools, pottery. **Pr:** $5-5000 **Hrs:** Mon-Sat 10-6, Fri til 8, Sun 11-5. **Dir:** Corner Winter St & Sandusky St in downtown Delaware. 6 mi W of I-71, intersection of State Rd 23, 42, 37 & 36. **Own:** Connie Hoffman & Bob Tuttle. **QC: 36 52 58 S12**

Delta

Delta Antiques Market [G]
301 Main St
(419)822-3012

Specializing in Victorian, primitive, painted, oak & country pine furniture. **Hrs:** Mon-Sat 10:30-5, Sun 12:30-5. **Dir:** State Rte 2, exit 3B Ohio Turnpike. **QC: 58 51 50**

Dennison

250 Antique Mall [G50]
9043 St Rte 250 SE
(740)922-3811
www.tusco.net

General line. **Hrs:** Daily 10-5. **CC:** V/MC/DIS.

Dexter City

Dexter City School House Antiques [G75]
Rte 821
(740)783-5921

General line. **Hrs:** Mon-Sat 10-6, Sun 12-6. **CC:** V/MC/DIS.

Yellow Rose Antique Mall [G]
Rte 821
(740)783-4300

General line. **Hrs:** Mon-Sat 10-5, Sun 12-5. **Dir:** I-77 exit 16.

Dover

Dover Antique Mall [G]
416 W 8th St
(330)343-3336

"Antique, unique, authentic." **Hrs:** Mon-Sat 10-5. **Dir:** I-77 Exit 83: 1 blk from Warther Museum. **Own:** Tom & Ann Harmon.

Dresden

M & M Antiques and Crafts
14976 County Rd 439
(740)754-6163

Duncan Falls

Corner Cupboard Antiques
357 Elm St
(740)453-3246 • (740)674-6169

Antiques & collectibles. **Hrs:** Mon-Fri by chance/appt. **Dir:** Off I-70, N of Zanesville.

Hamilton's Antiques
524 Main St
(740)674-6010

Furniture, lamps, glass, pottery & clocks. **Hrs:** Mon-Sat 10-4, Sun 1-4. **Dir:** Located on State Rte 60, S of Zanesville. **QC: 48 35 61**

East Liverpool

East Liverpool Antique Mall [G200]
4th & Washington St
(330)385-6933

Hrs: Mon-Sat 10-6, Sun 12-6. **Sz:** H **Dir:** Rte 30-39 exit.

Ellsworth

Antiques at Ellsworth
10985 Akron-Canfield Rd
(330)533-3000

Antiques & gifts. **Hrs:** Mon-Sat 11-5, Sun 1-5. **Own:** Bev & Jim Porter.

Elmore

Elmore 5 & 10 Antiques [G45+]
346 rice St
(419)862-3058

Antiques & collectibles on two floors of a 114-year-old general store. **Hrs:** Mon, Wed & Sat 10-5, Sun 12-5.

Lazy Dog Antiques
366 Rice St

General line. Specializing in restored trunks. Smalls, Roseville & Hull. **Hrs:** Mon-Fri 12-5.

Englewood

Country Collectibles & Affordable Antiques
202 N Main St
(937)832-1531

Single-owner business in a small-town setting. Wide range of general antiques including furniture, pottery, kitchen items, linens, buttons & vintage clothing. **Pr:** $1-800 **Est:** 1986 **Hrs:** Tue-Sat 12-6. **Sz:** M **CC:** V/MC/DIS **Dir:** I-70 Exit 29: 2 mi N. **Own:** Robert & Brenda Shearer. **QC: 34 81 83 SS12 S8**

Etna

Nook & Cranny [G12]
9380 Hazelton-Etna Rd
(740)927-2700

Antiques, crafts, dolls, giftware, concrete geese & "goose gear." Primitives, beanies, Victoriana & more. **Est:** 1992 **Hrs:** Tue & Thu-Sat 10-6, Wed & Sun 12-6. **Sz:** L **CC:** AX/V/MC/DIS **Dir:** I-70 Exit 118N on State Rd 310 1/2 mi on L. **Own:** L Terry & C Mesarvey. **QC: 32 38 S8 S10**

Fairfield

Pumpkin Vine Line
4800 Holiday Dr
(513)829-4796 • (513)894-3089

Country antiques. **Hrs:** Sat 10-5 or by appt. **QC: 34**

Fairport Harbor

Treasure Shop
213 High St
(440)354-3552

Antiques, collectibles, jewelry & glassware. **Hrs:** Mon-Sat 11-6, Sun by appt. **Own:** Joy Carpenter. **QC: 61 32**

Findlay

Books on Main
220 S Main St
(419)424-3773

10,000+ used, out-of-print & antiquarian books. General stock with emphasis on

Ohioana. **Hrs:** Mon 12-8, Tue-Fri 9:30-5:30, Sat 9:30-4. **Own:** Marjorie & Bob Weaver. **QC: 18**

Jeffrey's Antique Gallery [G250]
11326 Township Rd 99
(419)423-7500
findit@spfldantique.com

NW Ohio's largest antiques gallery with 40,000 sq ft of showroom. Furniture, dolls, toys, china, glassware, pottery, books, tools, lamps, jewelry, advertising, tins, guns, clocks, postcards, primitives, figurines & coins. **Hrs:** Daily 10-6. **CC:** V/MC/DIS **Dir:** I-75 exit 161: 2 mi N of State Rte 224, 30 min S of Toledo. **QC: 48 38 39**

Kate's Corner Antiques
540 S Main St (Ste C)
(419)423-2653

Pottery, jewelry, art glass, pattern glass (including Findlay & Fostoria) plus interesting collectibles. **Hrs:** Thu-Fri 10-3, by chance/appt. **QC: 22 61**

Fostoria

Copper Kettle Antiques
544 N County Line St (Rte 23N)
(419)435-3828

General line. **Hrs:** Daily 11-5, Sun 12-5.

Fluted Ribbon Antiques [G4]
111 N Main St
(419)435-7011

General line. **Hrs:** Tue-Fri 10-5, Sat 10-4, Sun by chance/appt. **CC:** V/MC.

Unique Antiques
3409 Fostoria Rd (US Rte 23 N)
(419)435-6961

Antiques, furniture repaired/refinished. **Hrs:** Mon-Fri 8-5, Sat 8-12 (closed Sun).

Fremont

M & T Antiques
427 W State St
(419)334-2836

Specializing in antique lamps & repair. **Hrs:** Mon-Fri 10-5, Sat-Sun by chance. **QC: 65**

Galena

Eileen Russell at The Acres
7035 Dustin Rd
(740)965-5344
eileenqlts@aol.com

Antique American quilts, linens & other textiles. **Hrs:** By chance/appt. **Dir:** In Home Gallery N of Columbus. 7 mi from Polaris exit or 4 mi from I-71 Rte 36-37 exit. **QC: 84 81**

Garrettsville

Susan's Antiques & Treasures
2702 State Rte 88
(330)527-5159

Furniture, primitives & smalls. **Hrs:** Mon-Sat 10-6. **Dir:** 3 mi S of Rte 422.

Waterfall Antiques
8130 Main St
(330)527-5340

Furniture, glassware, jewelry, pottery, toys. **Hrs:** Tue-Sat 10-6, Sun 1-6. **Own:** Judy & Nelson Bisard.

Geneva

Broadway Antiques & Collectibles [G]
1 N Broadway
(440)466-7754

Glassware, china, pottery, postcards, furniture & clocks. **Hrs:** Wed-Sat 10-5, Sun 12-5, or by chance. **QC: 61 35 39**

Geneva Antiques [G]
28 N Broadway
(440)446-0880

General line of furniture & smalls. **Hrs:** Mon-Sat 10-5, Sun 12-4. **Own:** Chris Quickel & Mary Lou Williams.

Germantown

Pastime Antiques & Collectibles
24 W Market St
(937)855-3115

Glassware, Victorian, country & primitive furniture. **Hrs:** Wed-Sun 10-5. **QC: 61 58**

Gnadenhutten

K & K Antiques
(740)254-9229

Country furniture: dry sinks, glass-door corner cupboards, jelly cupboards, schoolmaster's desks, pie safes, cupboards, stands. **Hrs:** By chance/appt. **Dir:** 15 min S of New Philadelphia. **QC: 34 48**

Granville

The Crown and Cushion
230 E Broadway
(740)587-2769

Reproductions. **Hrs:** Mon-Sat 10-5, Sun 12-4. **CC:** V/MC.

Granville Cherry Tradition
1630 Columbus Rd
(740)587-3414

Hrs: Tue-Sat 10-5, Sun 12-5.

Greystone Country House
128 S Main St
(740)587-2243

Primitives & quilts. **Hrs:** Mon-Sat 10-5:30, Sun 12-5. **CC:** V/MC/DIS **QC: 84**

Our Place Antiques
121 S Prospect St
(740)587-4601
Hrs: Wed-Sun 12-5.

Wee Antique Gallery
1630 Columbus Rd
(740)587-2270
Fine antique furniture. **Hrs:** Sun-Fri 10-5.
CC: V **QC: 48**

Greentown

Union Station Antiques Inc [G15]
9817 Cleveland Ave NW
(440)966-0568
Hrs: Mon-Sat 10-5, Sun 12-5. **CC:** V/MC.

Groveport

The Hanson House
549 Main St
(614)836-7258
Antique & reproduction toys & furniture.
Hrs: Wed-Fri 12-5, Sat 11-4.

Hamilton

1848 House Antiques
5137 Waynes Trace Rd
(513)726-5496
Country & painted furniture & companion
smalls. **Hrs:** By appt only. **Own:** Sharon &
Claude Baker. **QC: 34 51**

Harpster

Old General Store Antique Mall [G9]
7223 State Rte 294 Box 67
(740)496-9004
General line. **Hrs:** Mon-Sat 11-5, Sun 1-5.

Hartville

Elmarna Antiques & Treasures
788 Edison St NE
(330)877-8767
nanctique@aol.com
A "gallery of yesterday's memories," featuring a general line of antiques, collectibles &
decorative accessories including furniture,
pottery, china, glassware, silver, costume
jewelry, pocket watches, bottles, candles &
ornaments. **Pr:** $5-1,200 **Est:** 1991 **Hrs:**
Mon-Fri 10-5, Sat 10-6. **Sz:** M **CC:**
V/MC/DIS **Dir:** I-77 exit Rte 241N to Rte
619E to Hartville. **Own:** Nancy S Feller.
QC: 32 36 48 S6 S8

Hartville Antique Mall [G]
749 Edison St NW
(3300)877-3364 • (440)877-9034
Dir: Corner of Rte 619 & Market Ave.
Own: Gertrude Miller.

Hartville Antique Mall & Flea Market [G60+]
788 Edison St
(330)877-9860
Antique mall & one of Ohio's largest weekly
flea markets (Mon & Thur). **Est:** 1998 **Hrs:**
Mon-Sat. **Sz:** H **Own:** Marlon Coblentz,
Mgr.

Hartville Square Antiques [G]
107 W Maple St (Rte 619)
(330)877-3317
Furniture & collectibles. **Hrs:** Mon-Sat 10-
5 (closed Tue & Sun). **QC: 48**

New Baltimore Antique Center [G14]
14275 Ravenna Ave
(330)935-3300
Quality antiques & collectibles. **Hrs:** Mon,
Wed, Thu, Fri, Sat 11-5, Sun 12-5. **CC:**

V/MC **Dir:** At Rte 44 & Pontius. **QC:S7 S22**

Past Memories
751 Edison St
(330)877-4141
Hard-to-find items & antiques for nostalgia lovers. **Hrs:** Mon-Sat 10-5.

Victorian Rose Antiques
238 Kent Ave (Rte 43)
(330)877-8400 • (330)877-8781 (fax)
Elegant antique Victorian furniture, fine porcelain, rare beaded & mesh purses, old & new lamps & lighting fixtures, architectural items including stained & leaded glass windows, fireplace mantels, doors & reproduction brass hardware, gifts & cards. **Pr:** $10-20,000 **Est:** 1996 **Hrs:** Mon-Sat 10-5. **Sz:** L **CC:** V/MC **Dir:** I-76 Exit 33: S 10 mi on Rte 43. I-77 Exit 118: N on State Rd 619 10 mi to Hartville, then L on State Rd 43. In North Plaza. **QC: 58 89**

Highland Heights

Highland Antique Mall [G]
6119 Highland Rd
(440)446-0937
Antiques & collectibles. **Hrs:** Tue, Wed, Sat 10-5, Thu-Fri 10-6, Sun 12-5. **Sz:** L **Dir:** I-271 at Wilson Mills exit, W 2 streets to Miner Rd, then N to Highland. **Own:** Dan Bookshar, Mgr.

Hillsboro

Antique Haven
7030 Beechwood Rd
(937)393-4735
Depression glassware, lamps, phonographs,

dishes & books. **Hrs:** Mon-Sat 12-5. **QC: 61 18**

Gable House Antiques
240 E Main St
(937)393-1255
Glassware & china. **Hrs:** Mon-Sat 9-5, Sun by chance/appt. **QC: 61**

Old Pants Factory Mall [G]
125 N West St
(937)393-9934
Antiques & collectibles. Dealers welcome. **Hrs:** Mon & Wed-Sat 10-6, Sun 1-5 (closed Tue). **CC:** V/MC/DIS.

Hinckley

A Few Years Back
1353 Ridge Rd
(330)278-2788
Antiques & collectibles. **Hrs:** Daily 11:30-5.

Jeanette's Antiques
1369 Ridge Rd
(330)278-2090
Glassware, pottery, furniture, books, jewelry, prints & dolls. **Hrs:** Mon-Sat 11-5. **Dir:** Corner of Rte 3 and Rte 303. **Own:** Jeanette Painting. **QC: 74 48 61**

Holland

Holland Antiques
7154 Front St
(419)865-6094
Glassware (Fenton, Heisey, Depression, milk glass, cut & pattern), pottery & kitchen smalls. **Hrs:** Wed-Sun 12-5. **Dir:**

Rte 2 to Holloway Rd, then turn L over RR tracks to intersection. **Own:** Helen Damon. **QC: 61**

Hudson

The Cross-Eyed Crow Antiques
186 N Main St
(330)342-0101
Hrs: Mon, Thu, Fri & Sat 11-5.

Hudson Antiques [G]
72 N Main St
(330)656-5689
American country & period antiques, English country & garden antiques. **Hrs:** Tue-Fri 11-5, Sat 11-3. **QC: 34**

Gus Knapp Antiques
(216)653-6141
American country furniture & accessories. **Hrs:** By appt only. **Dir:** 3 mi W of village. Rte 8 under OH Tpke, R at next red light (2nd bldg on R). **QC: 48**

Huron

Huron Antiques on Main
511 S Main St
(419)433-8135
Carnival & elegant glass, 50s collectibles, Art

Oddities in Glass History

Mary Gregory glass: A colored glass decorated by white enameled sentimental figures of children and foliage. Mary Gregory was employed by the Boston and Sandwich Glass Company to decorate their wares; she painted naturalistic landscapes. Neither she, nor her company, had anything to do with the glass that is now named after her. "Mary Gregory" glass was actually made in Bohemia from about 1880 until well into this century and was exported in large quantities to both America and Britain.

Coin glass: In 1892 the Central Glass Company of Wheeling, West Virginia, produced a line of pressed glass tableware that was decorated with molds of U.S. coins. Within four or five months the U.S. Treasury stretched its imagination to the limit and accused the company of counterfeiting American coinage. Then, as now, common sense was no use in dealing with a government department, and the offending line was withdrawn. The company quickly replaced the U.S. coins with Colombian ones showing Christopher Columbus and Americus Vespucius. This "Colombian Coin" was produced until the end of the century. Technically, coin glass is inferior glass, but its rarity and its history of government stupidity have pushed prices of its less common items, such as the compote, up to $1,000 — not bad for a piece that retailed at 80 cents. While cheaper, Colombian coin is still very collectible. Collectors should be aware that a modern "coin glass" with no dates on the coins was produced in the 1960s, and that the Fostoria Company produced a line with coin lookalikes instead of real coins from 1958 to 1982.

Witch ball: A hollow glass ball, from two to eight inches in diameter, made in 18th century England and hung in the windows of glassmakers' cottages to ward off the evil eye. They were usually made of swirled, parti-colored glass. Small witch balls were made to hang on candletrows at twelfth night, and later, at Christmas (a candletrow is a tree-like wooden frame supporting a number of candles burned during the Christmas season). The glass balls decorating today's Christmas trees are direct descendents of the witch ball.

Witch ball and stand: A clear or colored glass bowl supported on a vase- or goblet-shaped stand. A 19th century whimsy made in America for domestic decoration not supernatural protection.

Deco, small furniture, pottery. **Hrs:** Mon-Fri 10-5, Sat-Sun 12-5. **QC: 61**

TC & Co
3512 Cleveland Rd E (Rte 6)
(419)433-2756

Glass, pottery, figures, baskets, jewelry, furniture, lamps & other collectibles. **Hrs:** Mon-Tue & Thu-Fri 10-6, Sat-Sun 12-6.

Jackson

Jackson Antique Mall [G70+]
(614)286-0172

Hrs: Mon-Sat 10-7, Sun 12-5 (closed major hols). **CC:** V/MC **Dir:** At Burlington Rd & Rte 32.

Jamestown

Country Village Antique Mall [G]
27 N Limestone St
(937)675-6333

General line. **Hrs:** Daily 12-5. **CC:** V/MC.

Jefferson

Carriage House Antiques
2550 Griggs Rd
(440)576-2158

Furniture, glassware & collectibles. **Hrs:** Fri 1-5, Sat 10-5 or by appt (closed Jan & Feb). **Dir:** 3 mi S of I-90 on Rte 46, then left on Griggs Rd 3-1/2 mi. **Own:** Lee & Evelyn Smith. **QC: 48 61**

Farm Market Antiques
9 S Main St
(740)426-6233

Furniture. **Hrs:** Daily 9-4. **QC: 48**

South Main Street Antiques
24 S Main St
Smalls. **Hrs:** Tue-Sat 10-5.

Village Antiques & Stuff
1 W High St
(740)426-6848

Furniture, pottery, glassware & graniteware. **Hrs:** Tue-Sat 10-6. **CC:** V/MC **QC: 48 61**

Jeromesville

Delagrange Antiques
12 N High St
(419)368-8371
www.ohioantiques.com

Early 19th C American furniture in walnut, cherry & original paint & complementary accessories. **Hrs:** Sat-Sun 12-5 or by appt. **Own:** George & Susan Delagrange.

Johnstown

Village Antique Mall [G]
42 S Main
(740)967-0048

General line. **Hrs:** Mon-Sat 9:30-6. **CC:** V/MC.

Kent

City Bank Antiques
115 S Water St
(330)677-1479

Specializing in fine time pieces & antiques: vintage jewelry, wristwatches, pocket watches; regulator, grandfather & mantle clocks; music boxes, Native American artifacts. **Hrs:** Tue, Thu, Fri & Sat 10:30-5, Wed 12-6.

Olde Country Store Antiques
508 W Columbus St
(419)675-1027

Country furniture, primitives, glassware & tools. **Hrs:** Mon-Thu by chance/appt. **QC: 48 61 86**

Kinsman

Antiques of Kinsman
8374 Main St (Rte 7)
(330)876-3511

Antiques & collectibles. **Hrs:** Daily 11-5.

Heart's Desire Antiques
8227 Main St (Rte 7)
(330)876-8234

Victorian & early 20th C oak & walnut furniture, jewelry, glassware, quilts & linens. **Hrs:** Tue-Sat 10-5, Sun by appt. **Own:** Judith Leonard. **QC: 58 59 61**

The Hickory Tree
8426 State St
(330)876-3175

Nice selection of country & formal antique furniture & accessories. Sheraton dressers, nightstands, blanket chests, corner & wall cupboards, paintings, prints, Oriental rugs, woven coverlets, quilts, iron gates & small accessories. **Pr:** $5-2,000 **Hrs:** Apr-Nov by chance/appt. **Dir:** 30 mi S of I-90, 25 mi N of I-80, 6 mi E of Rte 11, 1 blk from junction Rtes 5 & 7, 5 mi W of Penn border. **Own:** Richard & Susan Webb. **QC: 34 52 15 SS1 S8 S12**

Kirtland

Canterbury Station
9081 Chillicothe Rd (Rte 306)
(440)256-0321

Furniture, glassware, linens. **Hrs:** Tue-Sat 10-5, Sun 12-4. **Dir:** 1-1/4 mi S of I-90. **Own:** Kathy Alexander. **QC: 81 48 61**

Yesteryear Shop
7603 Chardon Rd (Rte 6)
(440)256-8293

Antiques & restoration/repair of furniture & metal items. **Hrs:** Wed-Sun 12-5. **Dir:** 1 mi W of Rte 306. **Own:** Victor & Bernice Nesnadny. **QC: 81 86 68 S16**

Lafayette

The Carriage House of Lafayette
1735 Cumberland Rd (Rte 40)
(614)852-5297

Antiques, furniture, clocks & watches. **Hrs:** Tue-Fri 11-9, Sat 10-9, Sun 12-6 (closed Mon). **CC:** V/MC/DIS **QC: 35 48**

LaGrange

Shoppes of Union Station [G]
612 N Center St
(216)355-4343

Hrs: Mon-Sat 10-5, Sun 12-5. **Dir:** N of LaGrange on Rte 301.

Lakewood

Antiques at Hall House
16906 Detroit Rd
(216)228-4255

Local antiques & collectibles. **Hrs:** Wed-Sun 12-5 or by appt.

Bonnieview Antiques
1392 Bonnieview Ave
(216)221-1447

Mahogany furniture, antiques. **Hrs:** Tue-Sun 12-5, call ahead advised.

Forget-Me-Nots
15232 Madison Ave
(216)228-9595

Furniture, pottery, lamps, vintage clothing, glassware, jewelry & linens. **Hrs:** Mon-Tue

11-5:30, Thu-Sat 12-6, Sun 1-5. QC: 83 61
81

Madison Avenue Antique Center [G]
16426 Madison Ave
(216)221-7119
Hrs: Wed-Sun 12-5.

Relics
15502 Madison Ave
(216)221-0040

Furniture, collectibles, pottery & glassware.
Hrs: Mon-Sat 11-6 (Thu 1-6). QC: 48 61

Lancaster

Lancaster Antique Emporium
201 W Main St
(740)653-1973

Furniture & glassware. Hrs: Mon-Sat 10-5,
Sun 12-5. CC: V/MC/DIS QC: 48 61

Summer House Antiques
720 N Columbus St
(740)653-7883

Furniture & smalls. Hrs: Tue-Sat 11-5, Sun
1-5. QC: 48

Uniquely Yours Antiques
139 W Fifth Ave
(740)654-8444

Furniture & smalls. Hrs: Mon-Sat 10-5, Sun
12-5. CC: V/MC/DIS QC: 48

Lebanon

Broadway Antique Mall [G60]
15-19 S Broadway
(513)932-1410

Furniture, pottery, glassware, toys, primitives, clocks, advertising, dolls, china &
jewelry. No crafts. Hrs: Mon-Sat 10-5, Sun
12-5. Sz: L CC: V/MC/DIS.

Gene & Rosemary Chute

Paintings

19th & 20th Centuries
Lebanon, Ohio 45036
10 Sycamore Street
(513) 932-1141

Fri / Sat 10 - 5
Sun 1 - 5

Captain Jack's East India Co
35 E Mulberry St
(513)932-2500

Furniture & glassware. Hrs: Mon-Sat 10-5,
Sun 12-5. CC: V/MC/DIS QC: 48 61

Linda Castiglione & Rick Almanrode Antiques
15 E Main St
(513)933-8344

Hrs: Sat-Sun 1-5 or by appt.

Gene & Rosemary Chute — Paintings
10 Sycamore St
(513)932-1141 • (513)932-3482

Paintings from 1800 to 1940, primarily
American but also some European, very
nicely displayed in a restored home in the
village of Lebanon. Pr: $200-2,000 Est:1990
Hrs: Daily by chance/appt. Sz: M Assn:
LADA Dir: Main St W to downtown

Lebanon. Turn R on Sycamore (1 blk beyond The Golden Lamb), then 1-1/2 blks on R. Free parking across the street. **QC: 7 8 12**

Country Traditions
30 E Mulberry St
(513)933-0811

Primitives & country, custom reproductions. **Hrs:** Mon-Sat 11-5, Sun 12-5. **QC: 34 56 S17**

Fox Run Antiques [G12]
21 E Main St
(513)933-0224

Fine American antique furniture, in paint & refinished, samplers, lighting, textiles, baskets, pantry boxes, quilts, coverlets, rugs, paintings, watercolors & silhouettes. **Pr:** $25-6,000 **Est:** 1996 **Hrs:** Mon-Sat 10-5, Sun 12-5. **Sz:** M **Assn:** LADA **Dir:** I-71 Exit 32 to Lebanon. **QC: 51 65 82**

The Garden Gate
34 S Broadway
(513)932-8620

Antiques & gifts for the gardener. **Hrs:** Mon-Sat 10-5:30, Sun 12-5.

Gerhardt Tribal Art
33 N Broadway
(513)932-9946 • (513)932-9317 (fax)

Unusual & extensive selection of tribal art & Asian antiquities for the serious collector. **Hrs:** Daily 9:30-5:30 **Own:** Charles H Gerhardt.

Golden Carriage Antique Mall [G]
120 S Broadway
(513)932-5507

Furniture, collectibles & jewelry. **Hrs:** Mon-Sat 11-5, Sun 12-5. **QC: 32 63**

Hardy's Interiors & Antiques
208-1/2 Wright Ave
(513)932-2951

Furnishings, accessories, upholstery & refinish service. **Hrs:** Mon-Sat 9-5. **QC: 36 S22 S16**

Hunter's Horn Antiques Center [G]
35 E Main St
(513)932-5688

Quality antiques & collectibles including period American & country furniture, glass, porcelain. **Hrs:** Mon-Sat 10-5, Sun 12-5. **CC:** AX/V/MC/DIS **Own:** Sue Hall. **QC: 48**

Jeff Vice's Restoration & Vice's Antiques
519 Mound Ct
(513)932-7918

Furniture, architectural & advertising. **Hrs:** Mon-Fri 9-5, Sat 9-12. **QC: 48 3 39**

Knickerbocker Gallery
41 E Mulberry St
(513)933-9222

Antiques, reproductions, garden accessories & home furnishings. **Hrs:** Mon, Fri & Sat 11-5, Sun 12-5. **QC: 36**

Main Antiques
31 E Mulberry
(513)932-0387

Architectural. **Hrs:** Mon-Sat 10-5, Sun 12-5. **QC: 3**

Larry Melvin Antiques
223 E Main St
(513)932-8345

Early furniture & accessories. **Hrs:** By appt only. **Own:** Larry & Judy Melvin. **QC: 52 34**

Miller's Antique Market [G]
201 S Broadway
(513)932-8710

One of southwest Ohio's largest group

$\mathcal{P}$endragon
COLLECTION $\mathcal{E}$ INC.

Importers of 18th & 19th Century English and European Antique Furniture and Accessories

36 South Broadway
Lebanon
Ohio 45036

Phone: (513) 933-9191
Fax: (513) 933-9174

Opening hours:
Mon-Sat 10am-5pm
Closed Sunday

---

shops. Country, period & Victorian furniture, glass, china, linens, coverlets, quilts, brass, books & accessories. Primitives & a general line of antiques. **Hrs:** Mon-Sat 10-5, Sun 12-5. **Sz:** H **Dir:** Across from the Lebanon Train Station. **Own:** Gerald Miller.

Mulberry Street Antiques [G15]

31 E Mulberry
(513)932-8383

General line. **Hrs:** Mon-Sat 10-5, Sun 12-5. **CC:** V/MC/DIS.

Oh Suzanna

16 S Broadway
(513)932-8246

Quilts, linens & jewelry. **Hrs:** Mon-Sat 10:30-5, Sun 12-5. **Own:** Joan Townsend. **QC:** 84 81 63

Pendragon Collection Inc

36 S Broadway
(513)933-9191 • (513)933-9174 (fax)

Specializing in English & European 18th & 19th C Georgian mahogany & oak furniture, oil paintings, leather-bound books, tall-case clocks & all types of decorative boxes. **Pr:** $20-20,000 **Est:** 1993 **Hrs:** Mon-Sat 10-5. **Sz:** M **CC:** AX/V/MC **Dir:** 29 mi N of Cincinatti. I-71 N Exit 28 (Hwy 48).Go N 5 mi on Hwy 48. Shop is directly across from the historic Golden Lamb Inn. **Own:** Fred & Barbara Aberlin. **QC:** 54 7 36

Shoe Factory Antique Mall [G60]

120 E South St
(513)932-8300 • (513)932-4227

Collectibles & a general line. **Hrs:** Mon-Sat 10-6, Sun 12-5. **Own:** Penny Haas.

Signs of Our Times

2 S Broadway
(513)932-4435
longoria@one.net
www.signsofourtimes.com

Specializing in 20th C toys & collectibles.
Hrs: Mon-Sat 11-6, Sun 12-5. **QC:** 87

Treasure's Dust Antiques & Collectibles

135 N Broadway
(513)932-3877

Hrs: Daily 10-6.

Type-tiques

20 S Broadway
(513)932-5020 • (513)398-9226
www.lebanon-ohio.com/type-tiques.html

Printing memorabilia. Type drawers, wood
type, lead & copper type, engravings. **Est:**
1973 **Dir:** Across from the Golden Lamb.
Own: Russ & Claire Clements & Chris
Ashe.

Uniquities [G]

27 W Mulbery St
(513)934-5660

18th, 19th & 20th C antiques, china, glass,
silver, brass, fine arts, furniture, lighting,
architectural & garden accessories. **Est:**
1997 **Hrs:** Mon-Sat 10-5, Sun 12-5. **Sz:** L
Own: Gerald Miller.

Whimsey & Nostalgia

12 W South St
(513)932-0046

Smalls, pictures, collectibles & small furniture. **Hrs:** Tue-Fri 11-5, Sat 10-5, Sun 1-5.

Lewisburg

The National Trail Antique Market [G]

109 N Commerce St
(937)962-2114

Hrs: Tue-Sat 10-6, Sun 12-6. **Dir:** 1/2 mi off
I-70, exit 14: N on Rte 503 to Commerce St.

Necessaries

Close stool or necessary stool: A box-like stool containing a chamber pot originating
around 1500 and made for the next 300 years. The close stool is thus, predictably when we
think about it, one of the earliest forms of furniture. The term is also used to refer to an 18th
century chair, often of the highest quality, used for the same purpose.

Night table: A small stand, originating in about 1750, with a cupboard to hold a chamber pot.
The cupboard door may be hinged, or, on finer examples, tambour. Chippendale designed
elaborate versions, often disguised as small chests of drawers — polite society obviously liked
the furniture for its natural functions to be as discrete as its words for them.

Commode: This French word for "convenient" was originally applied to a small, highly decorated chest of drawers, but the Victorians used it to refer to a piece of furniture designed for
the "conveniences," that is, a chamber pot, wash basin, and pitcher.

Commode chair, or, in the vernacular, **potty chair:** A chair with a hole in the seat to accommodate a chamber pot, usually with deep seat rails to hide it.

Sideboard: Perhaps a surprising inclusion in this group of terms, but in the 18th century, one
of the cupboards at each end of a sideboard often contained a chamber pot, so that, when the
women had withdrawn after dinner, the men need not allow the calls of nature to interrupt
their man-talk and their drinking.

Plumbing: A 19th century invention which, thankfully, rendered all of the above obsolete.

Lithopolis

Lithopolis Antique Mart [G50]
9 E Columbus St
(614)837-9683
General line. **Hrs:** Mon-Sat 10-5, Sun 1-5.

Lockland

Lockland Antique Mall [G30+]
110 Mill St
(513)761-2228 • (513)777-7181
salden@mailexcite.com
Collectible glassware, pottery, general Americana & antiques. Also furniture from 1900-1950s. **Pr:** $2-2,500 **Est:** 1996 **Sz:** L **CC:** V/MC/DIS **Dir:** I-75N Exit 12: W (L) on Davis St, then R on Mill St. I-75S Exit 12: R on Cooper, R on Wyoming to R on Mill St. Near Cincinnati. **Own:** Steve & Kathy Alden. **QC:** 22 32 48 S8 S12

Logan

Artisan & Antique Mall [G]
703 W Hunter
(740)385-1118
General line. **Hrs:** Mon-Sat 10-8, Sun 10-6. **CC:** V/MC/DIS.

Logan Antique Mall [G85]
12795 Rte 664
(740)385-2061
General line. **Hrs:** Mon-Sat 10-8, Sun 11-6. **CC:** V/MC/DIS.

> Visiting one of our advertisers? Please remember to tell them that you "found them in the Green Guide."

The Peddlar's Barn
390 W Main St
(740)385-7652
Antique & reproduction furniture. **Hrs:** Mon-Sat 9-5, Sun 11-4. **QC:** 48 56

Spring Street Antique Mall [G60]
55 S Spring St
(740)385-1816
General line. **Hrs:** Mon-Sat 10-6, Sun 12-6. **CC:** V/MC/DIS.

Loveland

Branch Hill Antique Market
392 Bridge St
(513)683-8754
A two-story country house plus three bldgs filled with antiques. **Est:** 1983 **Hrs:** Fri, Sat, Mon 11-5, Sun 12-5. **Dir:** I-275 Exit 52 (Loveland/Indian Hill): L to Hopewell Rd, R 1 blk.

Loveland Antique Mall [G]
204 W Loveland Ave
(513)677-0328
Antique furniture & smalls. **Hrs:** Mon-Sat 11-6, Sun 12:30-6. **CC:** V/MC/DIS **QC:** 48

Mongenas Antiques
600 Hanna Ave
(513)683-8888
English, American & Continental furniture, early brass, copper, artwork, sporting antiques, garden, ceramics, leather-bound books, needlework, coat & hat racks & trees & leather goods. **Hrs:** By appt only. Exhibiting at Duck Creek Antique Mall. **Own:** Ray & Kathy Mongenas. **QC:** 20 23 48

Gary & Martha Ludlow Inc.

American Furniture & Accessories

Part of our everchanging stock of guaranteed 18th and early 19th century American furniture and complementing accessories. We also wish to purchase items of this quality. All inquiries will be handled promptly and confidentially. We hope you will call or visit us soon.

BY APPOINTMENT
5284 GOLFWAY LANE

(440) 449-3475
LYNDHURST, OHIO 44124

Lyndhurst

Gary & Martha Ludlow Inc
5284 Golfway Ln
(440)449-3475

Fine American furniture of the 18th & early 19th C plus complementing accessories from andirons to mirrors to theorems. **Pr:** $200-35,000 **Est:** 1978 **Hrs:** By appt only. **Sz:** M **Assn:** ADA **Dir:** East side of Cleveland, only seconds from I-271. Call for directions. **QC: 52 68 1 S1 S9 S16**

Madison

Colonel Lee's Antiques
120 N Lake Rd
(440)428-7933

Furniture & collectibles. Restoration & repair of furniture, trunks & frames. **Hrs:** Thu, Sat-Sun 11-4:30. **Dir:** Rte 528 1 mi N

of I-90. **Own:** Robert & Carol Fay Lee. **QC: S16**

Memory Shoppe
(440)298-3553

Antiques & collectibles. **Hrs:** By appt only. **Own:** Irma Krauss.

The Red Geranium
5662 N Ridge W (Rte 20)
(440)428-4777

General line of antiques. **Hrs:** Mon-Sat 10-5, Sun 11-5. **Dir:** 2 mi W of Rte 528. **Own:** Peter Gress

Maineville

Four Chimneys Antiques
172 E Rte 22-3
(513)683-6486

Early country & primitive furniture & accessories. **Hrs:** By chance/appt. **Dir:** I-71 Exit

28 to Rte 48 S 3 mi to Rte 22-3. Near Lebanon. **Own:** Jim & Pat Goodman.

Pinetop Collectibles
1897 US Rte 22-3
(513)683-9975

A unique backroads shop. One-of-a-kind primitives, garden ornaments & quilts. Special glassware, pottery & flags. **Pr:** $5-1,000 **Est:** 1994 **Hrs:** May-Dec Sat 9-4. **Sz: M Dir:** I-71 to Fields Ertel to Montgomery Rd. L on Montgomery 4 mi to sign (last driveway on R before bridge). **Own:** Janis Farrell. **QC: 48 60 78 S12 S4 S15**

Mansfield

The Antique Gallery
1700 S Main St
(419)756-6364

General line. **Hrs:** Tue-Sat 10-5, Sun 12-5. **CC:** V/MC.

Carrousel Antique Mall [G50]
118 N Main St
(419)522-0230
www.ohioantiques.com/carrousel

"A merry-go-round of quality antiques & collectibles." **Hrs:** Mon-Sat 10-5. **Sz:** L **Dir:** 1 mi S of US 30 Expressway, OH Rte 13 exit.

Cranberry Heart
1461 Ashland Rd
(419)589-0340

Antiques, primitives, collectibles. **Hrs:** Tue-Fri 10-5, Sat 10-4.

The Cricket House Antiques
825 Park Ave W
(419)524-7100

Victorian & period furniture, children's items, toys, dolls, primitives, glassware, porcelain. **Hrs:** Tue-Sat 11-5, Sun 1-5.

Mid-Ohio Antique Mall [G35]
155 Cline Ave
(419)756-5852

General line. **Hrs:** Daily 10-5.

Yester-Year Mart [G45]
1237 Park Ave W
(419)529-6212

Hrs: Mon-Sat 10-9, Sun 1-5. **Dir:** West Park Shopping Ctr.

Mantua

Mantua Manor [G4]
4624 W Prospect Ave
(330)274-8722

General line. **Hrs:** Tue-Sat 10-5, Sun 1-5.

Marblehead

Schoolhouse Gallery
111 W Main St
(419)798-8332

General line. **Hrs:** May-Sep daily 10-5; Oct-Dec Mon-Fri 10-5.

Marietta

Antiques & Needful Things
177 Front St
(740)374-6206

Early 1800s furniture, glassware, mirrors, pictures & decorative. **Hrs:** Mon-Sat 9-5, Sun 12-5.

Fort Harmar Antiques
154 Front St
(740)374-3538

Specializing in American furniture, glass-

Use the Service QuickCode indexes at the back of the book to find restorers, appraisers, refinishers, and other specialty service providers.

ware, dolls & toys. **Hrs:** Daily 11-5. **CC:** V/MC/DIS.

Riverview Antiques
102 Front St
(740)373-4068

American, English, European antiques. **Hrs:** Daily 9:30-5:30, Sun 10-5.

Stanley & Grass
166 Front St
(740)373-1556

Antiques, furniture, iron beds, quilts. **Hrs:** Mon-Sat 10-5, Sun 12-5. **CC:** V/MC.

Tin Rabbit Antiques [G15]
204 Front St
(740)373-1152

General line. **Hrs:** Mon-Sat 10-5, Sun 12-5.

John Walter — The Tool Merchant
The Old Tool Shop / 208 Front St
(740)373-9973 • (740)373-9059 (fax)
toolmerchant@sprynet.com

Buy/sell/trade vintage woodworking tools. Huge inventory of fine hand tools. Owner is author of "Antique & Collectible Stanley Tools Guide to Identity & Value." **Pr:** $5-15,000 **Est:** 1985 **Hrs:** Mon-Sat 10-5, Sun by appt. **Sz:** S **CC:** V/MC **Dir:** I-77 Exit 1. **QC:** 86 1 18 S1 S8 S12

Marysville

Marysville Antique Mall [G]
117 S Main St
(937)354-2020
(888)249-5274

Furniture, glassware, toys, coins & collectibles. **Hrs:** Mon-Sat 10-6, Sun 12-5 (closed Tue). **QC:** 48 61 87

Mason

DuPriest Antiques & the Unusual
207 W Main St (State Rte 42)
(513)459-8805

Hrs: Tue-Sat 12-5:30. **Dir:** 5 mi S of Lebanon. **Own:** Michael DuPriest.

Route 42 Antique Mall [G26]
1110 Reading Rd (Rte 42)
(513)398-4003

General line. **Hrs:** Tue-Sat 11-5, Sun 12-5 (closed Mon). **CC:** V/MC.

McComb

Bread & Butter Antiques & Collectibles [G3]
104 W Main St
(419)293-3715

Quality furniture & collectibles. **Hrs:** Mon-Sat 10-6, Sun 12-6. **CC:** V/MC/DIS.

Medina

Broadway Antiques
326 N Broadway St
(330)722-3536

Pattern glass, oil lamps, early furniture, porcelain, miniatures, linens, vintage jewelry. **Hrs:** By chance/appt.

Butlers Cove 1894 Antiques
1342 Medina Rd
(330)239-1311
(800)627-0601

Furniture, primitives, glassware, fishing & sporting items. **Hrs:** Tue-Sun 11-5.

Creations of the Past
44 Public Sq
(330)725-6979

Antiques, collectibles, smalls, jewelry. **Hrs:** Mon-Sat 10-5, Sun 12:30-4. **Dir:** Adjacent to Old Phoenix Bank.

Granny's Attic
4184 Pearl Rd
(330)725-2277 • (330)225-3300

Furniture, antiques, glassware, primitives, collectibles, household. **Hrs:** Wed & Sat 10-6, Thu-Fri 10-8, Sun 12-5. **QC: S8**

Heirloom Cupboard
239 S Court St
(330)723-1010

Hrs: Tue-Sat 11-5, Sun 12:30-4. **Own:** Jane Riegger.

Ruth Keneda Antiques
3186 Stony Hill Rd
(330)239-2571

Country furniture & accessories, in paint & refinished. **Hrs:** By appt/chance. **Dir:** At the NW corner of Stony Hill & Remsen Rds. **QC: 34 48**

Medina Antique Mall [G300+]
2797 Medina Rd
(330)722-0017
(800)766-0177

Antiques & collectibles. **Hrs:** Daily 10-6.

Medina Depot Antique Mall [G]
602 W Liberty St
(330)722-6666

General line. **Hrs:** Mon 11-3, Tue-Sat 11-5, Sun 12-5.

Ormandy's Trains & Toys
10 Public Sq
(330)722-1019 • (216)647-3903 (fax)

Authorized dealer of Marklin, Lionel & LGB model trains. Antique toys. Service

& repair. **Hrs:** Mon-Sat 10-5, Sun 12-5. **QC: 87**

Our Shop Antiques
6180 Lafayette Rd
(330)722-1963

Costume jewelry, handbags, vintage wear, collectibles. **Hrs:** Thu-Sun 11-4.

Marjorie Staufer
2244 Remsen Rd
(330)239-1443

Large stock of fine American country furniture & smalls, 1730-1850, in paint or old finish. Treenware, redware, stoneware, homespuns & more. **Pr:** $50-6,000 **Est:** 1968 **Hrs:** By chance/appt. Call ahead advised. **Sz:** M **Assn:** NHADA **Dir:** 1 mi from Medina off Rte 3 or Rte 18 exit, S of Cleveland. **QC: 34 51 88**

Stone Porch Antiques & Collectibles
677 W Liberty St
(330)722-7950

Antiques, collectibles & crafts. **Hrs:** Tue-Sun 11-4. **CC:** V/MC/DIS.

Brothers Antique Mall / Sunset Strip [G50+]
6132 Wooster Pike
(330)723-7580 • (330)725-5124 (fax)
(800)243-6362

Antique mall with complete furniture restoration/upholstery service. **Hrs:** Mon-Fri 10-5, Sat 9-5, Sun 12-5. **QC: S16**

Trade Winds Gallery [G]
2648 Medina Rd
(330)723-5700 • (330)725-5124 (fax)
(800)328-7453
peyote@aol.com

Fine antiques, furniture, lamps, art glass, Native American Indian artifacts, oriental rugs, jewelry, clocks, porcelain, china, pottery, general line. **Hrs:** Tue-Fri 1-6, Sat-Sun 12-5.

Mentor

Maggie McGiggles Antiques
8627 Mentor Ave (Rte 20)
(440)255-1623

Furniture, books, glass, toys & dolls. **Hrs:** Mon-Sat 11-5, Tue 11-6, Thu by chance/appt, Sun 12-5 (Oct-Apr). **Dir:** Between I-90 and Rte 2, 1/2 mi E of Rte 615. **Own:** Carol Illner. **QC: 48 61 87**

Mesopotamia

The Clock Works at Fannie Mae Emporium
8809 St Rte 534
(440)693-4482

General line. **Hrs:** By chance/appt. **Dir:** N of intersection of Rte 534 & Rte 87, on the commons of historic Mesopotamia. **Own:** Ken & Frances Gibney. **QC: S7**

Miamisburg

Charles Hodges
916 E Central Ave
(513)866-3439

Folk art, painted furniture & pottery. **Hrs:** By appt only. **QC: 41 51 22**

Miamitown

Antiques & Things
6755 St Rte 128
(513)353-1442

General line. Specializing in chairs & rockers. **Hrs:** Mon-Sat 11-5, Sun 12-5.

Cade's Crossing Antiques
6868 St Rte 128
(513)353-2232

General line. **Hrs:** Mon-Sat 10-5, Sun 11:30-5.

D & D Victorian & Country Specialties Antiques
8008 Main St
(513)353-3443

General line. **Hrs:** Tue-Sun 11-5.

Miamitown Antiques
6655 St Rte 128
(513)353-4598

Hrs: Mon-Sat 11-5, Sun 12-5.

Sweet Annie's Antiques
6849 St Rte 129
(513)353-3099

Victorian, oak & primitive antiques. **Hrs:** Mon-Sat 10-5, Sun 11:30-5.

Werts & Bledsoe Antique Mall [G20]
6818 St Rte 128
(513)353-2689

General line. **Hrs:** Daily 10-5. **Dir:** I-74 exit 7 R onto Hamilton-Cleves (St Rte 128).

Middlefield

Country Collections Antique Mall [G30]
15848 Nauvoo Rd
(440)632-1712

Victorian, country & primitive furniture, smalls & collectibles. **Hrs:** Mon-Sat 10-4. **Dir:** N of Rte 87, S of Rte 322. **Own:** Kathy Lewis, Mgr. **QC: 58 32**

Green Guides make great gifts for all occasions.
Call Toll Free(888)875-5999 or visit your
local bookstore or antiques dealer.

Middletown

Middletown Antique Mall [G]
1607 Central Ave
(513)422-9970

General line. **Hrs:** Mon-Sat 11-5, Sun 11-4.

Milan

Crosby's Antiques
4 N Milan St
(419)499-4001 • (419)499-2535 (fax)

Early country furniture in cherry, walnut & tiger maple. Early pattern glass, fairings, Staffordshire, dolls & children's items, oil paintings, American folk art & accessories (decorative antique). **Pr:** $15-5,000 **Est:** 1974 **Hrs:** Apr-Dec Tue-Sat 11-4, Sun 12-4; Jan-Mar Thu-Sat 11-4, Sun 12-4. **Sz:** M **CC:** V/MC **Dir:** OH Tpke Exit 7 S on Rte 250 1.5 mi to Rte 113 E. Turn L at light on square (Main St). **Own:** Pam Crosby. **QC:** 1 34 48 S1

Golden Acorn Books
32 Park St
(419)499-7010
(800)634-5090
www.milanohio.com/goldenacorn.htm

Wonderful open bookshop in a restored mercantile building on the village square specializing in books on antiques and collectibles. Always 2000+ books in stock. Special orders & shipping encouraged. **Pr:** $1-200 **Est:** 1989 **Hrs:** Tue-Sat 10-5. **Sz:** M **CC:** V/MC **Dir:** OH Tpke Exit 7: 2 mi S on Rte 250 to State Rte 113 E. Shop on village square. **Own:** Elizabeth Kile. **QC:** 19 S19

Leo & Sons Antique Furniture Showroom
1 N Main St
(419)499-4570

Hrs: By chance/appt. **QC:** 48

Milan Wholesale Antiques
29 Park St
(419)499-2306 • (419)663-3352

Specializing in early country paint, tiger maple furniture, decorated stoneware, folk art & appropriate country smalls. To the trade only. **Pr:** $2-10,000 **Est:** 1986 **Hrs:** Mon-Fri 12-4 or by appt anytime. **Sz:** L **Dir:** OH Tpke Exit 7: 2 mi S on Rte 250 to State Rte 113 E. **QC:** 1 51 52

G W Samaha Antiques
28 Park St
(419)499-4044

An old-fashioned antiques dealer in exceptionally fine period American furniture, art & appropriate accessories. **Est:** 1934 **Hrs:** Thu-Fri 11-4 or by chance/appt. **Dir:** OH Tpke Exit 7 S on Rte 250 1.5 mi to Rte 113 E. In the Kelley Bldg on the village green. **Own:** Bill Samaha. **QC:** 1 36 7

Sights & Sounds of Edison
21 S Main St
(419)499-3093

Specializing in anything Edison but also carry a general line of antiques & collectibles. Many repair parts available for Edison phonographs & other machines. Custom-made wood horns for most phonographs. **Est:** 1993 **Hrs:** Jun 15-Sep 1 Mon-Sat 10-5, Sun 12-5; Sep 2-Jun 14 Tue-Sat 10-5, Sun 12-5. **Sz:** L **Assn:** MI Ant Phon Soc, Buckeye Ant Radio & Phono Club **Dir:** OH Tpke Exit 7: Rte 250 S to Milan (follow signs). **Own:** Don & Roberta Gfell. **QC:** 2 31 68 S16

Milford

Early's Antique Shop
123 Main St
(513)831-4833

Furniture & glassware. **Hrs:** Mon-Fri 10-5, Sat 10-2. **CC:** V/MC.

Village Mouse Antiques
26-32 Main St
(513)831-0815

General line. **Hrs:** Mon-Sat 10-5, Sun 1-5 or by appt. **CC:** V/MC/DIS/AX.

Wits' End
841 Roundbottom Rd
(513)831-3300

Country antiques, custom lamps, Woodstock lampshades, Lt Moses Willard chandeliers. **Hrs:** By appt only. **Own:** Nan Gordon. **QC:** 34 65

Millersburg

Antique Emporium
113 W Jackson St
(330)674-0510

Victorian & country furniture, glassware, textiles, toys, primitives, vintage clothing & jewelry. **Hrs:** Mon-Sat 10-5, Sun 10-4. **QC:** 87 83 61

Holmes County Amish Flea Market Inc [G300]
3149 SR 39
(330)893-2836 • (330)893-3523 (fax)
(800)245-3258

Large selection of collectibles, antiques, crafts, woodcrafts, furniture, produce & practical buys. Home-cooked meals, fresh-squeezed lemonade, homemade ice cream & apple dumplings. No smoking. Handicap accessible. **Pr:** $20-30 **Est:** 1992 **Hrs:** Jun 4-Dec 19 Thu-Sat 9-5; Apr 3-May 30 Fri-Sat 9-5. **Sz:** H **CC:** AX/V/MC/DIS **Dir:** I-77 Exit 83: W on State Rd 39 14 mi E. **Own:** Ben & Laura Mast. **QC:** 16 36 85 S13 S15

Minster

Bit O'Country Antiques
278 S Main St
(419)628-2612

Country antiques. **Hrs:** Mon-Thu by chance/appt, Fri-Sat 11-5, Sun 1-5. **QC:** 34

Mogadore

Ivy's Attic Antiques & Uniques
37 S Cleveland Ave
(330)628-0650

Furniture, oil lamps, collectibles. **Hrs:** Tue-Thu 11-6, Fri 11-8, Sat 11-5, Sun 1-5.

Montpelier

Village Trading Post
123 Empire St
(419)485-4996

Antiques, crafts, collectibles. **Hrs:** Mon-Sat 10-5, Sun 1-5.

> Use the Specialty QuickCode indexes at the back of the book to find dealers who specialize in your area of interest.

Morrow

David T Smith & Co

3600 Shawhan Rd
(513)932-2472 • (513)932-3233 (fax)
dtsmith@davidtsmith.com
www.davidtsmith.com

Reproduction furniture & Redware pottery.
Hrs: Tue-Sat 10-5.

Mt Vernon

Colonial Antique Mall [G25]

9030 Columbus Rd
(740)392-7947 • (740)393-0244
beever@ecr.net

Country furniture, oak, quilts, primitives,
stoneware, Heisey, glass, trunks, tools, toys,
lots of variety, emphasis on quality (no
crafts). **Pr:** $5-5,000 **Est:** 1976 **Hrs:** Daily
11-5 exc major hols. **Sz:** L **CC:** V/MC/DIS
Dir: 40 min NE of Columbus, OH. I-71 N
to State Rd 36 E to Mt Vernon. **Own:**
Charles & Dolores Beever. **QC:** 48 84 34
S8 S12

Farley & Moore Antiques Ltd [G60]

104 S Main St
(740)392-4590

Glassware, furniture, jewelry, linens, books,
prints, pottery. **Hrs:** Daily 10-5.

Third Edition Antiques

14 S Main St
(740)393-2777

Art pottery, furniture, glassware, china &
collectibles. **Hrs:** Tue-Sat 11-5, Sun by
chance.

Visit our web site at
www.antiquesource.com for more
information about antiquing in the
Midwest and New England.

Mt Victory

House of Yesteryear Antique Mall [G20]

125 S Main St
(937)354-2020

General line. **Hrs:** Mon-Fri 10-4, Sat 10-5,
Sun 12-6. **CC:** V/MC/DIS.

Victory Corner Antiques

305 E Taylor St
(937)354-5475

Furniture, advertising & glassware. **Hrs:**
Sat-Sun 1-5, Mon-Fri by chance/appt. **QC:**
39 48

New Albany

Prairie House Antiques

6060 E Dublin Rd
(614)855-2442

General line. **Hrs:** Wed-Sat 10-5. **CC:**
V/MC.

New Baltimore

Mack's Barn Old-Tiques & Antiques [G]

14665 Ravenna Ave
(330)935-2746

Hrs: Mon & Wed-Sat 11-5, Sun 12-5
(closed Tue). **Dir:** South of Ravenna on Rte
44 between Rte 619 and Rte 224. **Own:**
Cheryl Mack.

New Carlisle

Midwest Memories [G]

123 S Main St
(937)846-1002

Hrs: Mon-Sat 10-6, Sun 12-6. **Dir:** State
Rte 235.

New Concord

Margaret Lane Antiques
2 E Main St
(740)826-7414

Cambridge glass matching service & general line. **Hrs:** Mon-Fri 10-12 & 1-5, or by appt. **Dir:** Located on State Rte 40 & Rte 22.

New Philadelphia

Riverfront Antique Mall [G]
1203 Front St SW
(330)339-4448
(800)926-9806
ramoh@tusco.net
www.riverfront-antique.com

Hrs: Jun-Aug Mon-Sat 9-8, Sun 9-6; Sep-May Mon-Sat 10-8, Sun 10-6. **CC:** AX/V/MC/DIS **Dir:** I-77 Exit 81. Rte 39 E to first traffic light, then R.

New Vienna

Village Antique Mall [G30]
191 Main St
(937)987-2932

General line. **Hrs:** Tue-Sat 10-6, Sun 11-5. **Own:** Steve Porter.

Newark

Park Place Antiques [G30]
14 N Park Place
(740)349-7424

General line. **Hrs:** Mon-Sat 10-5.

Newcomerstown

Decker's Antiques & Gifts
9006 Stonecreek Rd
(330)339-5709

Glassware, furniture & pottery. **Hrs:** By chance/appt. **QC: 61 48**

North Canton

Route 43 Antique Mall
8340 Kent Ave NW
(330)494-9268

Furniture, clocks, dolls, toys, jewelry, lamps & books. **Hrs:** Mon-Sat 10-5, Sun 12-5. **QC: 87 35 38**

North Ridgefield

R & R Antiques
32390 Lorain Rd
(440)327-0314

Furniture, glassware & lamps. **Hrs:** Mon-Sat 10-6, Sun 1-5:30. **QC: 48 61**

North Ridgeville

Blue Barn Interiors and Antiques [G]
33060 Center Ridge Rd
(440)327-4050

Antiques & collectibles. **Hrs:** Mon-Sat 10-5, Sun 12-5.

Candy's Weathervane Antiques & Collectibles [G]
35694 Center Ridge Rd
(440)327-6841

Furniture, primitives, pottery & glassware. **Hrs:** Mon-Sat 10-5, Sun 12-4. **QC: 48 61**

Hatchery Antique Mall [G35]
7474 Avon Belden Rd
(440)327-9808 • (440)243-6555

Hrs: Daily 12-6 (Fri til 8). **CC:** V/MC/DIS.

Northfield Center

Olde Brandywine Antiques
9320 Olde Eight Rd
(216)467-9262

Furniture, glassware, primitives & tools.

Hrs: Mon-Sat 10-5, Sun 12-5. Dir: At Rte 82 & Brandywine Rd. Own: Annella & Thaine Johnson.

Porch Door's Antiques
33 E Aurora Rd
(216)468-2187

General line. Hrs: Tue-Sat 10-6, Sun 12-5.

Norwich

Bogart's Antiques
7527 E Pike
(740)872-3514 • (740)826-7439

Country, primitives, glassware & furniture. Hrs: Mon-Sat 10-5:30, Sun 12-5:30. Dir: Off Rte 22 & Rte 40 E of Zanesville. QC: 48 61

Kemble's Antiques
55 N Sundale Rd
(740)872-3507

Exceptional period 18th & early 19th C American furniture, clocks, oriental rugs, Victorian student lamps, chandeliers, oil paintings, quilts, stoneware, baskets, porcelain & other decorative accessories.

Hrs: Mon-Sat 10-5 or by chance/appt. Sz: H Own: Roland, Marilyn, Brent & Valerie Kemble. QC: 52 65 7

Olde Trail Antiques
7650 E Pike
(740)872-4001

Hrs: Mon-Sat 10-5, Sun 12-5. Dir: E of Zanesville on Rte 22 & 40.

White Pillars Antique Mall [G]
7525 E Pike
(740)872-3720

Country, primitives, glassware, furniture & pottery. Hrs: Mon-Sat 10-5:30, Sun 12-5:30. Dir: Located E of Zanesville on Rte 22 & Rte 40. Own: Betty Ward. QC: 48 61

Oak Harbor

Country Collections
2139 S Portage Rd
(419)898-5800

Antiques & collectibles. Hrs: Daily 11-5 (closed Mon in Win). Dir: 2-1/2 mi S of Oak

Some Furniture Parts

Astragal: A plain, semi-circular molding often applied to cabinets but most commonly used to face the mullions on the glass doors of cabinets and bookcases.

Pilaster: A flat-faced column protruding from a wall or other surface. Placed for decorative effect rather than as a support.

Apron: The lower front edge of a piece of furniture, sometimes elaborately shaped.

Mullion: A thin strip of wood holding and separating the panes of glass in a glazed door or window. Sometimes confused with....

Muntin: A vertical piece of wood holding and separating panels, sometimes confused with....

Stile: A vertical member, often load-bearing, that frames a paneled door or chest, or a chair back. Stiles often extend downward to form legs, as on a paneled chest, or the back of a chair.

Rail: A horizontal member, often used with stiles to frame a panel. Also used for seat rails and crest rails on chairs.

Stretcher: Rail joining the legs of tables or chairs to strengthen them.

Harbor on Rte 19. Turn R at Vern Miller Chevy Olds onto Cullman Rd. At dead end, turn L onto S Portage Rd, 1st drive on L.

Oberlin

Main Street Antiques [G20]
335 S Main St
(440)775-4112

Furniture, books, glass, pottery, primitives & lamps. **Hrs:** Daily 11-5. **QC: 48 61 18**

Windmill Resale Shoppe
525 N Main St

Antiques, collectibles, books, jewelry, furniture & tools. **Hrs:** Tue-Sat 11-4. **QC: 48 86**

Olmstead Falls

Trackside Antique Mall [G15]
9545 Columbia Rd
(440)235-1166

Toys & advertising. **Hrs:** Daily 11-4. **QC: 87 39**

The Waring Homestead
8134 Columbia Rd
(440)235-6220

Collectibles, books & prints. **Hrs:** Mon-Sat 10-5, Sun 12-5. **QC: 32 74**

Orwell

Stone House Antiques
39 N Maple Ave
(440)437-5175

General line. **Hrs:** Thu-Sat 9-5, Sun 11-5, or by appt. **Own:** Jim & Rosemary Jones.

Ottawa

Stowe's Art & Antiques
934 N Defiance St
(419)523-5468

A studio-gallery (featuring Bruce Stowe's works) housing a unique collection of antiques in an 1880s brick Victorian house. **Pr:** $1-5,000 **Est:** 1989 **Hrs:** Mon-Sat 10-6, Sun 1-6. **Sz:** M **Dir:** Exit 159 from Findlay, OH, W 23 mi to N side of Ottawa on State Rd 15. 2-story brick house past McDonald's. **Own:** Bruce J Stowe. **QC: 61 7 S13 S16 S17**

Painesville

My Country Place
2200 Mentor Ave
(440)354-8811

Pottery, old world Santas, nutcrackers. **Hrs:** Tue-Sat 11-4 (til 5 in Sum), Sun 12-4. **Dir:** 1 mi E of Heisley Rd. **Own:** Arnold & Dorris Dutton.

Ye Olde Oaken Bucket
776 Mentor Ave
(440)354-0007 • (440)269-8830

General line. **Hrs:** Daily 11-5. **Own:** Linda Morse & Tom Jerpbak.

Parkman

Auntie's Antique Parlor Mall [G]
15567 Main Market
(440)548-5353

Antiques & collectibles. **Hrs:** Daily 10-5. **Sz:** H **Dir:** Located 1 mi W of Rte 528 on Rte 422.

Pataskala

H & R Antique Center
1063 Pike St
(740)927-4053

General line. **Hrs:** Wed-Sat 10-5, Sun 1-5.

Old Country Antiques
8932 Hazelton-Etna Rd
(740)927-4144

Furniture, primitives & country antiques. **Hrs:** Wed-Sun 10-6. **QC: 48 34**

TC Antiques & Toy Mall [G80]

I-70 & State Rte 310 S
(740)927-4665

Advertising, collectibles, elegant glass, furniture, pottery, toys. **Hrs:** Daily 10-6. **Sz:** H

Peninsula

The Antique Roost

1455 Hines Hill Rd
(330)657-2687

General line. **Hrs:** By chance/appt.

Downtown Emporium Antiques

1595 Main St
(330)657-2778

Collectibles, postcards, political, Disneyana. **Hrs:** Tue-Sat 11-5, Sun 1-5.

Innocent Age Antiques

6084 N Locust St
(330)657-2915

Advertising, Art Deco, Coca-Cola, art pottery, toys, Disneyana, jewelry, furniture, sterling, silverplate. **Hrs:** Wed-Sat 11-5, Sun 12-5. **Dir:** 1/2 blk N of Rte 303.

Olde Players Barn [G15]

1039 W Streetsboro (Rte 303)
(330)657-2886 • (330)657-2252

Large selection of furniture & accessories in room settings. **Pr:** $10-2,000 **Est:** 1989 **Hrs:** Fri-Mon 11-5. **Sz:** L **CC:** V/MC **Dir:** On State Rte 303 between US Rte 21 & State Rte 8. OH Tpke exit 11 or 12, I-271 exit 12 or 13. **Own:** James W & Nina L Alvis, Mgrs. **QC:** 1 34 48

Perry

Dad's Old Store

4184 Main St
(440)259-5547

Furniture & collectibles. **Hrs:** Apr-Dec Fri-

Sat 11-5 or by appt. **Dir:** Between Rte 84 & Rte 20. **Own:** Dave Shearer. **QC:** 48

Main Street Antiques

4179 Main St
(440)428-6016

General line. **Hrs:** Wed-Sat 11-5, Sun by chance. **Dir:** Between Rte 84 & Rte 20. **Own:** Linda & Jay Morris.

Jones & Jones Ltd

114 W Indiana Ave
(419)874-2867

Furniture, jewelry, books, maps, paintings. **Hrs:** Mon, Wed-Sat 11-5, Sun 1-5 (closed Tue).

Perrysburg Antiques Market

116 Louisiana Ave
(419)872-0231

Hrs: Mon-Sat 10:30-5:30, Sun 11-4. **Dir:** In the heart of historic downtown Perrysburg.

Pioneer

Pioneer Antique Mall [G52]

103 Baubice St
(419)737-2341

General line. **Hrs:** Mon-Sat 10-6, Sun 1-5, or by appt. **CC:** V/MC/DIS.

Margaret Throp Antiques & Collectibles

State St - State Rte 15
(419)737-2371

General line. **Hrs:** By chance/appt. **CC:** V/MC/DIS.

Poland

Stagecoach Inn Antiques & Collectibles

303 S Main St
(330)757-3103

General line. **Hrs:** Mon-Sat 11-5 or by appt. **Own:** Betty & Merle Madrid & Suzanne Homrighausen.

Pomeroy

Hartwell House
100 E Main
(740)992-7696

Primitive furniture. **Hrs:** Mon-Sat 10-4:30.

Portsmouth

Laura & Bill McKinney Antiques
604 2nd St
(740)353-2856

General line. **Hrs:** Tue-Sat 10:30-5.

Printer's Attic
438 2nd St
(740)354-4457

Rare, old & collectible newspapers & prints.
Hrs: Fri-Wed 9-6 (closed Thu).

Powell

Country Reflections
87 W Olentangy St
(614)848-3835

General line. **Hrs:** Tue-Sun 10-5. **CC:**
V/MC/DIS.

Depot Street Antiques Mall [G27]
41-47 Depot St
(614)885-6034

Hrs: Tue-Sat 10-5, Sun 12-5.

Early Days Antiques
71 W Olentangy St
(614)848-4747

Hrs: Tue-Sat 11-5, Sun 1-5. **CC:**
V/MC/DIS.

Liberty Antique Mall [G25]
18 N Liberty St
(614)885-5588

General line. **Hrs:** Tue-Sat 11-5, Sun 12-5
(closed Mon).

The Manor at Catalpa Grove
147 W Olentangy St
(614)798-1471

French, English & American furniture &
accessories. **Hrs:** Tue-Sat 11-5, Sun 12-5.
CC: V/MC **QC: 48**

Powell Antique Mart
26 W Olentangy St
(614)841-9808

Hrs: Tue-Sat 10-5, Sun 12-5.

Samplers I

Sampler: A piece of needlework in various patterns with examples of letters and figures for use as a "sample" in marking household linens and textiles. Many included lines of verse, figures and houses.

The earliest samplers from the 17th and early 18th centuries were references of stitches and patterns. They were ongoing projects, to which a woman would add a band as she learned another design or stitch. These long narrow samplers, without borders, were not for display, but were rolled up and put away when not in use.

In the 18th century, samplers became the learning and reference tools of girls aged eight to sixteen. Most girls produced two: the earlier was a simple one, in which she learned the letters and figures to mark initials on linen and clothing; the second was fancier and more decorative and prepared her to make needlework pictures. Most were signed and dated. Samplers grew squarer as the century passed until by its end some were wider than they were deep. Most had borders and were designed to be framed for display. The period from 1785 to 1810 saw the most intricate samplers which took even the most industrious girl many months to complete.

Powell Village Antiques [G19]
8 N Liberty St
(614)885-3094

General line. **Hrs:** Sun-Tue 12-5 (closed Mon), Sat 11-5. **CC:** V/MC/DIS.

Ravenna

AAA I-76 Antique Mall [G450+]
4284 Lynn Rd
(888)476-8976

Hrs: Daily 10-6 (closed Xmas, Thanks, Easter). **Dir:** I-76 Exit 38B, 14 min E of Akron, 88 min W of Pittsburgh.

Copper Kettle Antiques & Collectibles
115 E Main St
(330)296-8708

Furniture, glassware, primitives, books, tools, weapons. **Hrs:** Mon-Sat 10-5, Sun 12-5. **Own:** Nancy & Brian Shaffer.

Farnsworth Antiques Associates [G10]
126 E Main St
(330)296-8600

General line. **Hrs:** Mon-Sat 10-5 (Thu til 8), Sun 12-5. **CC:** V/MC/DIS.

The Hitching Post
7467 Rte 88
(330)296-3686

Glass, china, furniture & primitives. **Hrs:** By chance/appt. **Dir:** 2 mi N of Rte 14. **Own:** Doris McDaniel.

Ohio Trader's Market & Antiques Inc [G]
645 S Chester St
(330)296-7050

General line. **Hrs:** Daily exc Mon.

Timeless Treasures
129 E Main St
(330)296-7800

Antiques & collectibles. **Hrs:** Mon & Wed-Sat 11-5, Sun 12-5. **Own:** Linda & Jeff Nicolaus.

Remington

Remington House Antiques
9440 Main & Loveland-Madeira Rd
(513)984-6533

Hrs: Mon-Fri 11-5 (closed Wed), Sat 10-5, Sun 12-5.

Richfield

Bendict's Antiques
4138 W Streetsboro
(330)659-3427

General line. **Hrs:** Mon-Sat 12:30-5, Sun by chance/appt.

Geranium House
3930 Broadview Rd
(330)659-0760

Antiques & collectibles: Fenton, Westmoreland, furniture & accessories. **Hrs:** Mon-Sat 11-5. **Dir:** Corner Rte 303 & Broadview. **Own:** Ginny Bishop.

Parkside House Antiques
2595 Boston Mills Rd
(330)659-4461

Furniture & smalls. **Hrs:** By chance/appt. **QC:** 48

Ripley

Olde Piano Factory Antique Mall [G16]
307 N Second St
(937)392-9243

General line. **Hrs:** Mon-Sat 10-5, Sun 12-6.

Wag's River Village Antiques

14 Main St
(937)392-4754

Furniture & collectibles. **Hrs:** Mon-Sat 10-5, Sun 12:30-5:30. **QC: 48 32**

Ross

Venice Historical Antique Mall [G100+]

4299 Hamilton-Cleves Rd
(513)738-8180

General line. **Hrs:** Daily 11-7. **CC:** V/MC/DIS.

Rowsburg

Papa & Nana's Antiques & Collectibles

163 Rte 250 E
(419)869-7715

Glassware, china, Victorian, toys, Art Deco, Art Nouveau, furniture. Specializing in Limoges, R S Prussia & Royal Bayreuth. **Hrs:** Mon & Wed-Sat 10-5, Sun 12-5. **Dir:** 6 mi E of I-71 Exit 186.

Russell

Crossroad Antiques

14860 Chillicothe Rd
(440)338-8582

General line. **Hrs:** Tue-Sat 11-5, Sun 12-5. **Dir:** Rte 306, N of Rte 87. **Own:** Diane Gunther & Judy Weis.

Rocker Shop Antiques

14948 Chillicothe Rd
(440)338-5287

Furniture & accessories. **Hrs:** Thu-Sat 11-5, Sun 12-5. **QC: 48**

Sandusky

Bay Window Antiques

223 E Market St
(419)625-1825

Glass & china, jewelry, furniture. **Hrs:** Tue-Sat 11-5.

"Hobson's Choice" Tiques-M-Porium

135 Columbus Ave
(419)625-1825

Furniture, jewelry, collectibles. **Hrs:** Mon-Sat 11-5.

Now & Then Shoppe

333 W Market St
(419)625-1918

Furniture & collectibles. **Hrs:** Mon-Sat 10-5.

Steuk Antique Barn

1001 Fremont Ave
(419)625-0803

Furniture, glassware & collectibles. Ohio's oldest winery. **Hrs:** Apr-May & Sep-Dec Sat-Sun 12-5; Jun-Labor Day daily 10-6. **Dir:** Junction State Rd 2 & 6 W.

Shandon

Red Door Antiques

4843 Cincinnati-Brookville Rd
(513)738-0618 • (513)385-6218

Quality Victorian furniture & accessories as well as country pieces & accessories. **Pr:** $5-10,000 **Est:** 1976 **Hrs:** Tue-Sat 10-5, Sun 12-5. **Sz:** M **CC:** V/MC/DIS **Dir:** I-275 exit Rte 127 R 5 mi to Ross, then L onto Rte 128 to 2nd light. Turn R on Rte 126 3 mi. **Own:** William H Harris. **QC: 50 58 89**

Sharon Center

William Hromy Antiques
5958 Ridge Rd
(330)239-1409

Country antiques & accessories, early fabrics, Shaker, hand-dipped candles, handmade country furniture & garden benches. Split seat repair. **Hrs:** Thu-Sun 10:30-5. **QC: 34 80 57**

Marilee's
1331-1/2 Sharon Copley Rd
(330)239-1755

Vintage clothing, jewelry & accessories. **Hrs:** Tue-Thu & Sat 12-4:30. **QC: 83**

Smithville

Smithville Antique Mall [G20]
637 E Main St
(330)669-3332

Furniture, primitives, jewelry, advertising, glassware, china, clocks, linens. **Hrs:** Tue-Sat 10-5, Sun 12-5.

South Vienna

Johnson Lampshop
8518 Old National Rd
(937)568-4551

Antique & traditional lamps, shades & fixtures. **Hrs:** Mon 10-7, Tue-Fri 10-5, Sat 10-4 (closed Sun).

Spencerville

Ohio Antique Market [G100]
113 S Broadway St
(419)647-6237

General line. **Hrs:** Thu-Tue 12-5 (closed Wed).

Spencerville Antique Mall [G14]
127 N Broadway
(419)647-4050

Marbles, glassware, furniture. **Hrs:** Mon-Wed & Fri-Sat 11-5, Sun 1-5 (closed Thu). **CC:** V/MC/DIS.

Spring Valley

Gayle Almanrode Art & Antiques
1 Bellbrook Ave
(937)862-4115

Paintings, oriental rugs, early 1800 furniture, garden items, architectural, sterling & textiles. **Est:** 1967 **Hrs:** Sun 12-5 or by appt. **Sz:** L **QC: 7 80 3**

Springboro

Victoria's Antiques
505 S Main
(513)748-4914

General line. **Hrs:** Mon-Fri 11-5, Sat 10-5, Sun 12-5.

Springfield

AAA I-70 Antique Mall [G200+]
4700 S Charleston Pike
(937)324-8448

Jewelry, advertising tins, guns, clocks, postcards, primitives, figurines, dolls, toys, china, glassware, pottery, furniture, books, tools, lamps. **Hrs:** Daily 10-6 (closed Xmas, Thanks, Easter). **CC:** V/MC/DIS/AX **Dir:** I-70 Exit 59.

Jane Collins Antiques
(937)399-7166 • (937)399-8206 (fax)
simonkent@aol.com

A mix of English garden & architectural antiques with early furniture prior to 1850 with original or old finish, early ceramics & needlework & textiles. Blue & white is usually in abundance; stone carved troughs, urns, terra cotta garden pots. **Pr:** $25-5,000 **Hrs:** By appt only. **QC: 60 3 52**

Heart of Ohio Antique Center [G600+]

4785 E National Rd
(937)324-2188

Est: 1998 **Hrs:** Daily 9:30-6. **Sz:** H **Dir:** I-70 Exit 62. **Own:** Bruce Knight.

The John Foos Manor Antique Gallery & B&B

810 E High St
(937)323-3444 • (937)322-9224
(937)322-9224 (fax)

In an 1860s Italian Renaissance Manor, antiques, furnishings & appropriate smalls & accessories staged in period room settings. Also quality exact reproductions of 17th & 18th C formal & country furniture by area craftsman. **Pr:** $2-25,000 **Est:** 1995 **Hrs:** Daily 11-5. **Sz:** H **CC:** AX/V/MC/DIS **Dir:** I-70 Exit 59: Rte 41 to Springfield. **Own:** Dick & Patty Brown. **QC: 2 7 48 S12**

Knight's Antiques

4750 E National Rd
(937)325-1412

General line of American & English antiques from Chippendale to Depression glass. **Hrs:** Daily 9:30-5:30.

Old Canterbury Antiques

4655 E National Rd
(937)323-1418

Furniture. **Hrs:** Daily 10-3.

Spring Acres Antiques

4200 E National Rd
(937)322-3143

18th & 19th C furniture. **Hrs:** By appt only. **Own:** Michael Junk. **QC: 52**

Springfield Antique Center [G400]

1735 Titus Rd
(937)322-8868

Hrs: Daily 10-6. **CC:** V/MC/DIS **Dir:** I-70 exit 59, opposite Fairgrounds.

St Mary's

Stroh's Antiques

Rte 2 Box 55 (Old 33A)
(419)394-3089

Furniture. **Hrs:** By chance/appt.

Strasburg

Kandle's Antiques

1180 N Wooster Ave
(330)878-5775

Country furniture, accessories & primitives. **Hrs:** By chance/appt.

Suffield

Creative Cupboard

1433 State Rte 43
(330)628-8179

Hrs: Daily 10-5.

Ivory Manor

1496 State Rte 43
(330)628-3901

Antiques, art, collectibles, primitives, glassware, furniture. **Hrs:** Daily 10-5.

Sugarcreek

Dutch Valley Furniture & Antique Mall [G]

1373 Old State Rte 39
(330)852-4026

Victorian & period furniture, glassware, linens, quilts, books, toys & collectibles. **Hrs:** Apr-Dec Mon-Sat 9-8; Jan-Mar Mon-

Thu 9-6, Fri-Sat 9-8. **Dir:** 1 mi E of
Sugarcreek. **QC: 58 52 81**

Sunbury

Carriage House Antiques
49 W Cherry St
(740)965-5006

Victorian furniture & glassware. **Hrs:** Tue-
Sun 11-5.

Cherry Street Antiques
34 W Cherry St
(740)965-4101 • (614)888-6447

Single-owner shop with general line of mer-
chandise with emphasis on country. Also a
summer shop in the UP of Michigan, 45 mi
W of Mackinaw Bridge. **Pr:** $1-1,000 **Est:**
1988 **Hrs:** Aug 20-Jun 15 daily 9:30-5. **Sz:** M
CC: V/MC **Dir:** I-71 Exit 131: 4 mi E on
Rte 37 just N of Columbus. **Own:** Tom &
Judy Jones. **QC: 48 34 79**

Coffee Antiques
25 E Granville
(740)965-1113

Furniture, smalls & glassware. **Hrs:** Mon-
Wed, Thu & Sat 10:30-5 (closed Fri & Sun).
QC: 48 61

King's Antiques
29 W Cherry St
(740)965-2098

Furniture, primitives, crocks, china,
Depression glass & collectibles. **Hrs:** Mon-
Sat 8-dark, Sun 1-6. **Own:** Audrey King.
QC: 48 32 61

Pieces of the Past
4 E Cherry St
(740)965-1231

Vintage clothing, linens, quilts, flow blue.
Hrs: Mon-Fri 12-5, Sat 10-5, Sun 1-4.

Village Antiques
S Columbus St
(740)965-4343

General line. **Hrs:** Mon-Sat 9-6.

Weidner's Village Square Antique Mall [G25]
31 E Granville St
(740)965-4377 • (740)965-5913 (fax)

In an old drugstore, prehistoric artifacts,
estate jewelry & Americana. Art, books,
glass, pottery, furniture, toys & collectibles,
as well as books on antiques, wooden
display cases & stands. **Pr:** $1-5,000
Est: 1991 **Hrs:** Mon-Sat 10-6, Sun 11-6.
Sz: L **CC:** V/MC/DIS **Dir:** I-71 Exit 131:
E on St Rte 37 toward Sunbury 4 mi, then
turn R on Columbus St (light at the village
square) 1 blk, then L on Granville St.
Own: Janie Jinks-Weidner. **QC: 48 64 1
S10 S12**

Sylvania

King Street Antiques [G]
5633 N Main St
(419)882-4136

Hrs: Tue 10-4, Wed-Sat 10-6.

Wayne Siddens Antiques
5270 Alexis Rd
(419)882-1557

Oil paintings, art & cut glass, oriental rugs,
silver, china, period furniture & lamps.
Appraisals & estate liquidations. **Hrs:** Mon-
Thu 11-5.

Tipp City

Benkin Antique Gallery [G40]
14 E Main St
(937)890-3614 • (937)890-4487 (fax)

Located in historic canal town of Tipp City.
Three floors of 1880 furniture store &
funeral home. No crafts or reproductions.
Pr: $50-500 **Est:** 1990 **Hrs:** Mon-Sat 10-5,
Sun 1-5. **Sz:** H **CC:** V/MC **Dir:** I-75 Exit
68: W 1 mi to downtown. 15 mi N of
Dayton. **Own:** Ben Staub. **QC: 48 19
34 S12**

Toledo

Ancestor House Antiques & Appraiser

3148 Tremainsville Rd
(419)474-0735

Glass, fine American lamps (Tiffany, Handel & Pierpoint), silver & china cabinets. **Hrs:** Tue-Fri 12-5, Sat 12-4. **CC:** V/MC **Dir:** Near Alexis Rd.

Cobblestone Antique Mall [G40]

2635 W Central Ave
(419)475-4561

Glassware, vintage clothing & collectibles from the 1950s & 60s, furniture & lighting from 1890s on. **Est:** 1993 **Hrs:** Mon-Sat 10-5, Sun 12-5. **CC:** V/MC/DIS **Dir:** Rte 23N to Central Ave exit, then E 4 mi. Shop on S side. **Own:** Fred Smith.

Custer Antiques [G]

1020 Laskey Rd
(419)478-4221

European & American furniture, oriental rugs & paintings. **Hrs:** Tue-Fri 10-5, Sat 11-4 (closed Sun-Mon). **QC:** 48

Keta's Antiques/Oriental Rugs [G]

2640 W Central Ave
(419)474-1616 • (419)474-1616 (fax)
(800)888-KETA

Hrs: Mon-Sat 11-5, Sun by chance. **Sz:** L **CC:** AX/V/MC/DIS **Assn:** TAADA. **QC:** 49 76

Leffler's Antiques [G]

2646 W Central Ave
(419)473-3373

Perfumes & paintings a specialty. Also furniture, art, cut glass, jewelry, paintings, oriental rugs, stained glass & toys. **Hrs:** Mon-Sat 10-5.

Port Lawrence Antiques

912 Monroe
(419)255-1006

From art to architectural. **Hrs:** Wed-Sat 11-4. **Dir:** Monroe at 10th. In the historic Holland Building.

Warehouse Antiques

2611 W Central Ave
(419)475-3130

Hrs: Mon-Sat 11:30-7:30. **Dir:** At Douglas.

Samplers II

By the early 19th century, as women became busier with household management, visiting, and shopping, the time-consuming intricate needle work of the earlier generation gave way to simpler, quicker styles. The quality of samplers declined, and by the middle of the century they were no longer part of a genteel girl's education.

An unmarried girl worked hard with her needle, not just to fill her dowry chest, but also to present herself as an attractive young woman, particularly when a young man had come to visit. As she sewed she sat prettily, her hands were occupied, showing her industry, her eyes looked down, showing her demureness, yet her ears and mind were open to the young man paying court. In genteel families, needlework was as close as a girl could come to flirting.

Needlework was a two-edged sword in a woman's life. On the one hand it was an art form in which she could express her imagination and creativity, on the other it confined her to a narrow female propriety, in which her hands were active, but her mind and voice were not.

Uniontown

The Antique Shoppe
12930 Cleveland Ave NW
(440)699-8040

Glassware, jewelry, pottery, linen, collectibles, lamps, paintings, furniture & toys. **Hrs:** Mon-Sat 10-5. **CC:** V/MC **QC: 87 61 32**

Ashley's Antiques & Interiors
12980 Cleveland Ave
(440)699-5370

Featuring fine classic style furniture. **Hrs:** Mon-Sat 10-5.

Colonial House Antiques [G6]
13075 Cleveland Ave NW
(440)699-9878

Hrs: Mon-Sat 10-5, Sun 12-5. **CC:** V/MC.

J & K Antiques and Liquidations
13443 Cleveland Ave
(440)699-1088

Hrs: Mon-Sat 10-5 (closed Fri), Sun 12-5.

Uniontown Antique Mall [G]
13443 Cleveland Ave NW
(440)699-6235

Glassware, pottery, toys. **Est:** 1979 **Hrs:** Mon-Sat 10-5, Sun 12-5. **Own:** Barbara Weil & Dolores Morris. **QC: 61 87**

Wayside Antiques
12921 Cleveland Ave
(440)699-2992

Primitives, collectibles, furniture. **Hrs:** Mon

10-5, Thu & Sat 11-5 or by chance/appt. **Own:** Edna Barnes. **QC: 32 48**

Unionville

The Green Door & The Red Button
6891 S Ridge E
(440)428-5747

Victorian furniture, lamps, oriental rugs, flow blue, toys & advertising. **Hrs:** Tue-Fri 1-6, Sat-Sun 11-6 or by appt. **Own:** Donna & Tony Barski. **QC: 58 87 39**

Little Mountain Antiques
7757 S Ridge E (Rte 840)
(440)428-4264

General line. **Hrs:** Daily 11-6, By chance/appt. **Own:** Bob & Peg Shaw.

Unionville Antiques
7918 S Ridge E (Rte 84)
(440)428-4334

General line. **Hrs:** Tue-Fri 1-6, Sat-Sun 11-6. **Dir:** Between Rte 528 & Rte 534, across from Unionville Tavern. **Own:** Harry Carver.

Valley City

Days Gone By
6714 Center Rd (Rte 303)
(330)483-4661

General line. **Hrs:** Tue-Sat 10-4, Sun 12-4.

Wadsworth

Antique Design
112 Main St
(330)334-6530

Antiques & collectibles. **Hrs:** Mon-Tue 11-5, Wed-Thu & Sat 11-6, Sun 12-5.

Christmas Kittens
369 S Main St
(330)334-9051

Antiques, primitives, glassware, linens. Also

architectural pieces & turn-of-the-century collectibles. **Hrs:** Wed-Sat 11-5, Sun 1-4:30.

House of Wilhelm
235 High St
(330)335-5120

Crafts, linens, collectibles, furniture, Victorian items & decorative accessories. **Hrs:** Tue-Sat 10-5, Sun 12-5.

Lady Sodbuster Antiques
121 E Prospect St
(330)336-5239

In an original carriage house next to a c 1820 log cabin, primitives & a general line. **Hrs:** Wed-Sat 11-5, Sun 1-5.

Wadsworth Antique Mall [G]
941 Broad St
(330)336-8620

Furniture, pottery, glassware, linens. **Hrs:** Wed-Fri 10-5, Sat 10-4, Sun 1-5.

Wapakoneta

Alley Cat Antiques
117 W Auglaize St
(419)738-7193

Furniture, smalls, primitives & Victorian. **Hrs:** Tue-Sat 11-5, Sun 1-5. **QC: 48 89**

Auglaize Antique Mall [G80]
116 W Auglaize St
(419)738-8004

Primitives, collectibles & glassware. **Hrs:** Mon-Sat 10-5, Sun 12-5. **CC:** V/MC/DIS **QC: 61 32**

Washington Court House

Past & Present Memories
109 E Court St
(740)333-3222

Jewelry, Depression & fine glass & furniture.

Hrs: Mon-Sat 10:45-5, Sun 12-5. **CC:** V/MC/DIS **Dir:** Across from the Courthouse. **QC: 61 48**

The Storage House
153 S Hinde St
(740)335-9267

Primitives, cupboards, furniture for home & garden. **Hrs:** Mon-Sat 9:30-8, Sun 1-5. **CC:** V/MC/DIS **QC: 48**

Waterville

Civil War Antiques
17 N 3rd St
(419)878-8355

Civil war antiques. **Hrs:** Mon-Thu 10-5. **QC: 4**

Mill Race Antiques [G35]
217 Mechanic St
(419)878-8762

Hrs: Mon-Sat 10-5:30, Sun 12:30-4:30. **CC:** V/MC/DIS.

Wauseon

Big Bear Antiques [G15]
117 S Fulton St
(419)335-1447

Hrs: Mon-Sat 10-5 (closed Sun). **CC:** V/MC

Waynesville

American Spice Antiques
258 S Main St
(513)897-5100

Painted country furniture & accessories. **Hrs:** Mon 10-3, Tue-Sat 10-5, Sun 11-5. **Own:** Betty Maudlin. **QC: 51 34**

Back in the Barn Antiques
241 S Main St
(513)897-7999

Specializing in oak furniture. **Hrs:** Thu-Sat 11-5. **QC: 50**

Baker's Antiques

98 Main St
(513)897-0746

Country furniture including corner cupboards, step-back cupboards & pie safes;
woodenware, pewter, art, tools. **Hrs:** Tue &
Thu-Sun 10:30-5:30 by chance. **QC: 34 48**

Bittersweet Antique Mall [G]

57 S Main St
(513)897-4580

Hrs: Mon-Fri 10-5, Sun 12-5.

Brass Lantern Antiques

100 Main St
(513)897-9686

Refinished furniture & accessories. **Hrs:**
Daily 11-5. **Own:** John & Mary Purdum.
QC: 48

The Coker Collection

155 S Main St
(513)897-4666

Furniture restoration. **Hrs:** By chance/appt.
QC: S16

Cranberry Corners Antique Mall [G]

93 S Main St
(513)897-6919

Hrs: Tue-Sun 12-5.

Crazy Quilt Antiques

221 S Main St
(513)897-8181

Hrs: Sat-Sun 12-5.

Gilbert's Bottleworks

70 N Main St
(513)897-3861

Advertising, store tins, historical flasks, open
pontil medicines, bottles & jars from Shaker
communities. **Hrs:** Tue, Thu, Sat & Sun
11-5.

Golden Pomegranate Antique Mall [G]

140 S Main St
(513)897-7400

Hrs: Tue-Sat 11-5, Sun 12-5.

Hammel House Inn Antiques

121 S Main St
(513)897-3779 • (513)897-9686

Country antiques & accessories. **Hrs:** Daily.
QC: 34

The Highlander House

22 S Main St
(513)897-7900

Hrs: Wed-Sun 12-5 (til 6 in Sum).

Little Red Shed Antiques [G]

85 Main St
(513)897-6326

Hrs: Mon-Sat 11-5, Sun 1-5:30.

Miscellany Collection

49 S Main St
(513)897-1070

Hrs: Wed-Sun 12-5.

My Wife's Antiques

75 Main St
(513)897-7455 • (937)435-8287

Furniture, country antiques, Victoriana & a
general line. **Hrs:** Tue-Sun 10-5.

The Olde Curiosity Shop [G40]

88 S Main St
(513)897-1755

Est: Daily 12-5.

Remember When? Antiques
43 Main St
(513)897-2438 • (937)278-0410
Hrs: Wed-Sun 12-5.

The Singleton House
55 S Main St
(513)897-1331

Antiques, furniture & collectibles. **Hrs:** Tue-Sun 12-5.

Spencer's Antiques
278 S Main St
(513)897-7775

Hrs: Daily 11-6. **Sz:** H.

Tiffany's Treasures
273 S Main St
(513)897-0116 • (937)252-6869

Antiques, furniture, collectibles. **Hrs:** Mon-Sat 10-5, Sun 10:30-5.

Velvet Bear Antiques
61 S Main St
(513)897-0709

Haviland, furniture, primitives, linens, quilts, jewelry, china. **Hrs:** Daily 11-5.

Village Antiques
143 High St
(513)897-3048

Cherry & walnut furniture. **Hrs:** Wed-Sun 12-5.

The Village Clock Shop
N Main St
(513)897-0805

Antique clocks, clock parts & clock repair. **Hrs:** Wed-Sun 12-5. **QC: 35 S7**

> Visit our web site at www.antiquesource.com for more information about antiquing in the Midwest and New England.

Waynesville Antique Mall [G]
69 S Main St
(513)897-6937

Antiques & collectibles. Complete brass & copper refinishing service. **Hrs:** Daily 11-5. **Own:** Bob Kerr.

Wellington

The General Store
151 Depot St
(440)647-6621

General line. **Hrs:** Mon-Sat 10-6, Sun 12-5. **Own:** Rich & Judi Learmonth. **QC: S16**

Village Antiques
126 W Herrick Ave
(440)647-3623

Antiques & collectibles. **Hrs:** Mon-Sat 11-5, Sun 12-5.

The Wellington Livery Antiques
139 Herick Avenue W
(440)647-0077

Furniture & collectibles. **Hrs:** Thu-Sat 11-6, Sun 12-6 (closed holidays). **CC:** V/MC.

Wellsville

Seven Sisters Antiques & Christmas Shop [G]
965 Township Line Rd
(330)532-2466

Hrs: Mon-Sat 10-5, Sun 12-5. **Dir:** Rte 11 to Rte 45 S 6.3 mi, then L on Township Line Rd.

West Chester

Hidden Treasures Antiques [G]
8825 Cincinnati-Dayton Rd
(513)779-9908

Full line of antiques & collectibles. **Hrs:**

Tue-Fri 11-5, Sat 11-6, Sun 1-5. **Dir:** I-75 exit 21, S 1/2 mi on R.

Van Skaik's Antiques

9355 Cincinnati-Columbus Rd
(513)777-6481

Specializing in quality antique furniture — period, Victorian, oak & 1920s-40s — in a variety of sizes, time periods & prices. Also an extensive line of reproduction hardware for antiques. **Pr:** $25-3,500 **Est:** 1970 **Hrs:** Tue-Sat 9:30-6, Sun 12-5 (closed Mon). **Sz:** L **CC:** AX/V/MC/DIS **Dir:** I-275 Exit 46: N on Rte 42 2-1/4 mi. Shop on L. **Own:** Ken & Shalini Van Skaik. **QC: 48 58 50 S16 S17**

West Salem

Deb's Unique Antique Mall

Rte 42
(419)853-4288

Hrs: Thu 12-5, Fri 11-6, Sat 11-6, Sun 12-5.

Westerville

Heart's Content Antique Mall [G7]

9 N State St
(614)891-6050

Hrs: Mon-Sat 10-5, Sun 12-4. **CC:** V/MC.

Westlake

Red Barn Antiques

28275 Detroit Rd
(440)835-0567

Oak, primitive & country furniture. **Hrs:**

> Use the Service QuickCode indexes at the back of the book to find restorers, appraisers, refinishers, and other specialty service providers.

Thu-Sun 11-5. **Dir:** 5 mi E of Avon French Creek on Detroit Rd, I-90 exits 157 & 158. **QC: 50**

Willard

Margo's Antique Mall [G]

1320 S Conwell Ave (Rte 224 E)
(419)935-6255

Antiques & collectibles **Hrs:** Tue-Sat 10-6, Sun 12:30-6.

Time & Treasures

113 Myrtle Ave
(419)935-1756

Furniture, clocks & railroad memorabilia. **Hrs:** Wed-Sat 1-5. **Own:** Bob & Virginia Harlan. **QC: 48 35 67 S7**

Willoughby

Crooked Creek Antique Mall (I) [G27]

34000 Chardon Rd (Rte 6)
(440)994-6594

Vintage clothing, jewelry, country, primitives, dolls, glassware & furniture. **Hrs:** Mon-Sat 10-5, Sun 12-5. **Dir:** 1/4 mi W of Rte 91. **Own:** Deborah Simone. **QC: 83 48 61**

Crooked Creek Antique Mall (II) [G17]

4122 Erie St
(440)975-1606

Vintage clothing, collectibles, jewelry, country, primitives, dolls, furniture & glassware. **Hrs:** Mon-Sat 10-5. **Own:** Deborah Simone. **QC: 83 38 48**

Friends Antiques

4119 Erie St
(440)946-1595

Victoriana & Edwardian. **Hrs:** Tue-Sat 11-5, by appt. **Own:** Carol Baggott. **QC: 89**

Market Square Antiques

24 Public Sq
(440)975-1776

Furniture & accessories. **Hrs:** Tue-Sat 10-5, Sun 12-5, or by appt. **Dir:** Rte 20 & Rte 174, across from city hall. **Own:** Betty Seberino. **QC: 48**

Mr Willoughby's Antiques

14 Public Sq
(440)951-5464

Hrs: Mon-Fri 10-5, Sat 10-6, Sun by chance.

Rhay's Treasures

4128 Erie St (Rte 20)
(440)942-6878

Hrs: Tue-Sat 11-5 (Thu til 6).

Wilmot

1881 Antique Barn [G]

927 US Rte 62
(330)359-7957

Furniture, glassware & tools. **Hrs:** Mon-Sat 10-8. **QC: 48 61 86**

Wooster

Norton's Antiques Etc

9423 Ashland Rd
(330)262-6439

Glass, pottery & smalls. Roseville, Rookwood. **Hrs:** By chance/appt. **QC: 61**

Midwestern Glass

Carnival glass: An inexpensive iridescent glass often called "the poor man's Tiffany." It was invented by Frank Fenton of Newark, Ohio, in 1907, and was quickly taken up by other glassworks in Ohio and Pennsylvania. The earliest color was yellow, but chemists quickly learned how to make almost the whole color spectrum. Carnival glass was made in a huge variety of shapes and designs.

Heisey glass: Augustus Heisey and his three sons started making glass in Newark, Ohio in 1893. In 1900 they adopted their famous trademark of a diamond containing an "H." In the 1920s Heisey acquired the original Sandwich glass molds and produced pieces that are hard to distinguish from the original Sandwich. Between 1923 and 1930, the company specialized in colored glass, but they remain best known for their Verlys glass, which is frosted into various designs, but which is uncolored.

Greentown glass: Often called "chocolate glass" because of its color, this glass was made by by the Indiana Tumbler and Goblet Company, of Greentown, Indiana, from about 1900 until 1903, when the factory burned down. The colors ranged from dark brown to light tan, and the glass was produced in many patterns, of which the holly amber, and the robin with berry are perhaps the most popular today.

Cambridge glass: Factory founded in Ohio in 1901 and closed in 1958. The "Crown Tuscan" pattern is popular today, particularly its figural candlesticks, often in the form of nudes or dolphins.

The Imperial Glass Company of Bellaire, Ohio, operated from 1901 till 1984. It produced carnival glass in large quantities as well as other glassware from molds acquired from Heisey and Cambridge.

Zanesville glass: The Zanesville Glass Manufacturing Company was one of the earliest in Ohio and produced hollowware, bottles, and historical flasks by the blown three mold process from 1815 until 1851.

Uptown/Downtown [G30+]
215 W Liberty
(330)262-9735

Antiques, glass, furniture, collectibles. **Hrs:** Mon-Sat 10-6, Sun 12-5. **Sz:** L.

Xenia

Antiques Plus [G25]
30 S Detroit St
(513)376-0622

Furniture & glassware. **Hrs:** Mon-Fri 10-5, Sat 9-5, Sun 12-5. **CC:** V/MC **QC: 48 61**

Simply Antique
63 S Detroit St
(937)376-1245

Glassware & furniture. **Hrs:** Sun-Fri 11-5, Sat 9:30-5. **CC:** V/MC.

Youngstown

Antique Alley [G]
104 E Midlothian Blvd
(330)783-1140

Antiques & collectibles. **Hrs:** Mon-Sat 10-5, Sun 12-4.

Antiques on Market
6331 Market St
(330)726-4829

Dishes, furniture, glassware & costume jewelry. **Hrs:** Wed-Sat 11:30-4:30. **Dir:** N of Beakley Medical Ctr. **QC: 48 61 63**

I-680 Antique Mall
9026 South Ave
(330)726-9261

Furniture. **Hrs:** Mon-Sat 10-5, Sun 12-5. **QC: 48**

Thomas E Marsh Antiques Inc
(216)743-8600

Architectural antiques. **Hrs:** By appt only. **QC: 3**

Zanesville

A Le Clara Belle Antiques
4868 E Pike
(740)454-2884 • (740)452-0950

Furniture, glassware, clocks & primitives. **Hrs:** Daily 10-6. **Dir:** Rte 22 & Rte 40 E of Zanesville. **QC: 48 35 61**

Allie's Antiques
524 Main St
(740)452-2280 • (740)453-5336

Hrs: Daily 12-5.

AntiQs & Things
6595 Park Ln
(740)872-4002 • (740)872-3751

Pottery, primitives, furniture & glassware. **Hrs:** Mon-Sat 10-5:30, Sun & holidays 12-5:30. **Dir:** 10 mi E of Zanesville off State Rte 40. I-70 between exit 160 & 164. **Own:** Marlene & Alva Richardson. **QC: 48 61**

Christine's Unique Antique Mall [G]
28 N 7th St
(740)455-2393

Hrs: Mon-Sat 10-6, Sun 12-5.

Clossman Antiques Market [G]
621 Main St
(740)450-2567

Furniture including country, primitive, Shaker & Victorian; art glass, tools, vintage accessories, local pottery, porcelain, glassware, flow blue, Fiesta, Zane Grey books & collectibles & breweriana. **Hrs:** Mon-Sat 10-5, Sun 12-5. **Dir:** I-70 exit 7th St or Underwood, 3 blks S. **QC: 48**

Downtown Antiques & Collectibles
509 Main St
(740)450-7941

Hrs: Mon-Sat 10-4.

Elaine's Antique Mart [G]
531 Main St
(740)452-3627
General line. **Hrs:** Mon-Sat 10-6, Sun 12-5.

Fike's Antiques & Collectibles
530 Main St
(740)450-8525
Hrs: Mon-Sat 10-5, Sun 1-5.

Gee's Antiques & Collectibles
904 W Main St
(740)453-6609
Specializing in Hull pottery, glassware & collectibles. **Hrs:** Mon-Fri 9:30-5. **Dir:** Located on Rte 40 in Zanesville, W of the Y-bridge. **QC: 61 32**

Heritage Book Store
313 Woodlawn Ave
(740)452-6840
Hrs: Tue-Fri 12-6, Sat 12-5.

Lane's Antiques
5100 Bellview Dr
(740)453-7546
Hrs: By appt only.

Log Hollow
2825 Chandlersville Rd
(740)453-2318
Primitive & country furniture; cane, rush & splint seat repair; reproduction furniture hardware. **Hrs:** Mon-Sat 11-7, Sun by appt. **Dir:** E of Zanesville on State Rd 146. **QC: S6 S17**

Market Street Gallery
822 Market St
(740)455-2787
(800)338-7711
hawk@marketstreetgallery.com
www.marketstreetgallery.com/market1.htm
Hrs: Mon-Fri 9-5, by appt.

Olde Town Antique Mall [G80]
527 Main St
(740)452-1527
Furniture, glassware, primitives & collectibles. **Hrs:** Mon-Fri 10-5, Sat 11-5, Sun 12-5. **QC: 48 61 S1**

Old Toll House
3485 Moxahala Park Rd
(740)452-4420
Furniture & quilts. **Hrs:** By appt only. **Dir:** Located in S Zanesville off Rte 22 & Rte 93. **QC: 48 84**

Seven Gables Antiques
1570 S River Rd
(740)454-1596
Furniture, glassware, pottery & collectibles. **Hrs:** Mon-Sat 9-6, Sun 11-5. **Dir:** Located S of Zanesville on Rte 60. **QC: 48 61 32**

Seventh Street Antiques
142 N Seventh St
(740)454-8755
Pottery, glassware, & collectibles. **Hrs:** Daily 8-10. **QC: 61 32**

Side Door Antiques
303 W Monroe St
(740)452-5572
Primitives, furniture, stoneware, flow blue & quilts. **Hrs:** Wed-Fri 11-5, Sat 11-3 or by appt. **Dir:** Located 2-1/2 blocks N of I-70. **QC: 48 84**

Snooper's Antiques & Collectibles
613 Main St
(740)452-3627
Hrs: Daily 10-5.

Thee Antique & Angel Emporium
17 N Seventh St
(740)455-3364
Hrs: Sun 11-5.

West Pike Antiques
3508 W Pike
(740)453-8791

Pottery, glassware, china, furniture. **Hrs:**
Tue-Sun 10-5. **QC: 48 61**

Zoar

Jack Adamson Antiques
245 E Third St
(330)874-3918

Folk art, furniture & accessories. **Hrs:** Thu-
Sat 11-5. **QC: 41**

Cobbler Shop Antiques
121 E 2nd St
(330)874-2600

Country furniture & accessories, children's
ABC plates. **Hrs:** Daily, call ahead advised.

Wisconsin

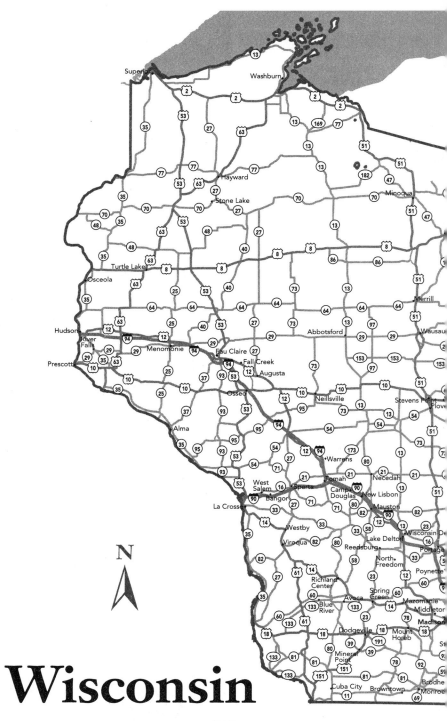

N

Wisconsin

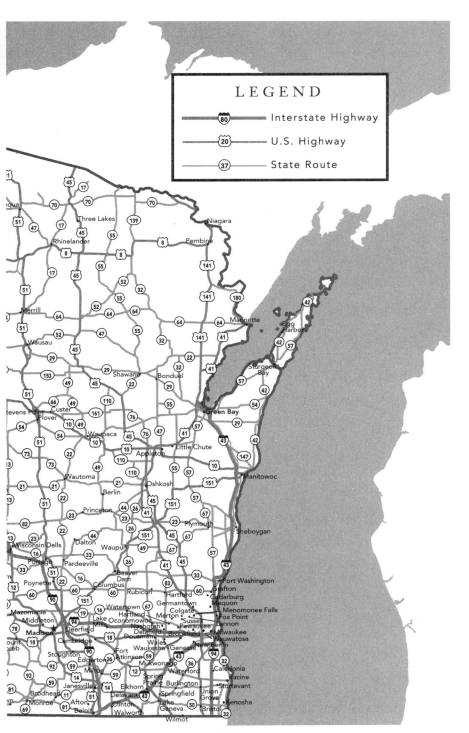

LEGEND

—⟨80⟩— Interstate Highway

—⟨20⟩— U.S. Highway

—⟨37⟩— State Route

219

Abbotsford

Abbotsford Antique Mall [G5]
101 N 1st St
(715)223-6479
Hrs: Mon-Sat 10-5, Sun 11-4. **CC:** V/MC/DIS/AX.

Dorothy Mazza Antiques
123 S 4th St
(715)223-4925
Hrs: Fri-Mon 10-5:30 (closed Tue-Thu).

Afton

Country Lady Antiques
5316 Afton Rd
(608)752-8066
Hrs: Thu-Sat 10-5, Sun 10-4.

Alma

Lone Pine Antiques
S1401 Spring Creek Rd
(608)685-4839
Old rough furniture & glassware. **Hrs:** By chance/appt. **QC: 48 61**

Appleton

The Harp Gallery
2495 Northern Rd
(920)733-7115 • (920)733-1736 (fax)
Specializing in better antique furniture as well as home furnishings including lighting, clocks, china & silver, pictures & mirrors. Upholstery & decorating fabrics also available. Regular deliveries to Milwaukee, Chicago, Madison & St Louis. **Pr:** $2-20,000 **Est:** 1985 **Hrs:** Mon-Fri 10-5:30, Sat 10-5, Sun 12-5. **Sz:** H **CC:** AX/V/MC/DIS **Dir:** Hwy 41 exit Prospect "BB" E to frontage Northern Rd. **Own:** Rebecca & Ken Melchert. **QC: 35 48 58 S15 S22**

Miller Antiques
1425 S Outagamie
(920)734-2130
18th & 19th C New England furniture & accessories. Tall-case American clocks a specialty. **Hrs:** By appt only. Pls call ahead. **Assn:** WADA **Own:** Jim & Bernice Miller. **QC: 35 52**

On the Avenue Antique & Art Mall [G65+]
513 W College Ave
(920)954-9404
Hrs: Sun-Thu 10-6, Fri-Sat 10-8. **CC:** V/MC.

Sherman's Military Antiques
1042 E Lindbergh St
(920)739-4588
Hrs: By appt only. **QC: 4**

Augusta

Stone Street Collectibles
131 S Stone St
(715)286-5283
In a restored 1870 building, furniture & decorative smalls, quilts, stained glass, original fine art. **Hrs:** Mon-Sat 10-5.

Thode's Mercantile
104 W Lincoln St
(715)286-5364
Antique toys, glassware & linens, fishing lures, furniture. Country to classic, primitive to Victorian. **Hrs:** Mon-Sat 10-5:30.

Avoca

Yankee Pedlar
Hwy 133
(608)532-6597
General line concentrating on country, Norwegian & American Indian. **Hrs:** By chance/appt. Call ahead advised. **Assn:** WADA **Dir:** 3/4 mi E of Avoca. **Own:** Terry Ziebarth. **QC: 34**

Bangor

Jan's Antiques & Collectibles
1902 Ruedy St
(608)486-2648

Furniture, graniteware, Depression glass.
Hrs: Daily by chance/appt. **Dir:** Between
Tomah & La Crosse. I-90 exit 15, N to IGA
store, left on 18th Ave, then left to Ruedy St.
Own: Jan & Vilas Lash. **QC: 48 61**

Beaver Dam

General Store Antique Mall
150 Front St
(920)887-1116

Country, Victorian furniture, advertising
items, quilts, toys, jewelry, elegant glassware,
linens, dolls, trunks, graniteware, stoneware,
wicker, books, dolls & paintings. **Hrs:** Daily
10-5. **CC:** V/MC.

Tree City Antiques
114 Front St
(920)885-5593

Victoriana & smalls. **Hrs:** Daily 10-5. **CC:**
V/MC/DIS/AX. **QC: 89**

Beloit

Brasstown Antiques
810 E Grand Ave
(608)362-6409

Hrs: Fri-Sat 12-4.

Caple Country Antiques
309 State St
(608)362-5688

Antique furniture & glass. Specializing in
large oak pieces as well as many Victorian
accessories, nicely displayed. **Pr:** $5-5,000
Est: 1991 **Hrs:** Mon-Fri 10-5, Sat 9-4. **Sz:**
M **CC:** V/MC/DIS **Dir:** I-90 exit Hwy 75 to
Holiday. N toward Beloit to State St. **Own:**
Richard & Vickie Caple. **QC: 50 48 61 S16
S6 S22**

Gaslight Antiques
626 Miller Rd
(608)362-1110
Hrs: Mon-Fri 8:30-5, Sat-Sun 10-2.

Nest Egg Ltd
816 E Grand Ave
(608)365-0700
Jewelry, glass, china, furniture. **Hrs:** Tue-Fri
10-5:30, Sat 10-4. **QC: 68 41**

Rindfleisch Antiques
520 E Grande Ave
(608)365-1638
Hrs: By chance/appt.

Riverfront Antique Mall [G20]
306 State St
(608)362-7368
Hrs: Mon-Fri 9-5, Sat 9-4, Sun 12-4.

Berlin

Elaine's European & American Antiques
118 W Huron St
(920)361-2334

Furniture imported from around the world.
Hrs: Mon-Sat 10-6, Sun 11-5. **Sz:** H **CC:**
V/MC.

Picture That
102 E Huron St
(920)361-0255

General line. **Hrs:** Mon-Sat 9:30-5, Sun 11-
4. **CC:** V/MC.

Blue River

Riverwood Terrace Antiques
(608)537-2024

Period American and country furniture and
appropriate accessories. **Hrs:** By appt only.
Own: Bill Chitwood. **QC: 34 52**

Bonduel

Hearthside Antique Mall [G35+]
129 N Cecil
(715)758-6200
Hrs: Daily 10-5.

Bristol

Benson Corners Antique Mall [G90+]
20000 75th St
(414)857-9456

Antiques, collectibles, furniture, jewelry, decorative items. **Hrs:** Daily 10-5. **CC:** V/MC **Dir:** 5 min W of factory outlet at I-94 & Hwy 50.

Hawthorn Antiques Galleries [G]
Hwy 50
(414)857-2226

In a 75-year-old historic schoolhouse. **Hrs:** Daily 10-5. **Sz:** H **Dir:** Corner Hwy 50 & County Rd MB N, 2 mi W of I-94. **QC:** S8

Remember That Antique Mall [G]
Hwy 50
(414)537-2888

Hrs: Wed-Mon 10-5. **Sz:** L **Dir:** 19 min W of Factory Outlet Mall, 15 min E of Lake Geneva. **Own:** Jim & Judy Kutzler.

Victorian House Antiques
(414)857-2681

Victorian accessories, sewing tools, silver hollowware & figural napkin rings. **Hrs:** At

shows & by mail order. **Assn:** WADA **Own:** Ruth & Joe Chatilovicz. **QC:** 89 78

Brodhead

Center Avenue Antiques
1027 Center Ave
(608)897-2696
Hrs: Mon-Tue 10-5, Wed-Sat 9-5, Sun 12-5.

Brookfield

Stonewood Village Antiques
17700 W Capitol Dr
(414)781-7195

Antiques & collectibles in an 1865 farmhouse. **Hrs:** Mon-Sat 10-5, Sun 11-4:30.

Browntown

The Mill Street Antique General Store
102 S Mill St (Hwy 11)
(608)966-3250

Hrs: Apr-Oct Mon-Sat 10-9, Sun by chance/appt.

Burlington

Gingham Dog Antiques
109 E Chestnut St
(414)763-4759
Hrs: Mon-Sat 10-5, by chance/appt.

Caledonia

Valenti Antiques Inc [G30]
441 28th St (Hwy 41)
(414)835-7711

Glassware, advertising, primitives, jewelry, Victorian & early country furniture, dolls. **Hrs:** Daily 10-5. **Dir:** I-94 20 mi N of IL line. **QC:** S7

Cambridge

Cambridge Antique Mall [G25]
109 N Spring St
(608)423-9952

Hrs: Daily 10-5:30 (Fri til 8).

Camp Douglas

Mill Bluff Antiques
15987 Hudson Rd
(608)427-6728

General line. **Hrs:** May-Nov by chance/appt. **Dir:** 1 mi W of Mill Bluff Park, Hwy 12-16 between Oakdale & Camp Douglas. **Own:** Gladys Bergs.

Cedarburg

American Country Antiques
W61 N506 Washington Ave
(414)375-4140 • (414)242-0194
(414)242-9842 (fax)

Featuring 18th & 19th C furniture, period & American country painted & primitive, with appropriate accessories (brass, silver, treen, pewter, stoneware, quilts, rugs, china, folk art, paintings & English smalls). **Pr:** $20-2,000 **Est:** 1980 **Hrs:** Tue-Sat 11-5, Sun-Mon by chance/appt. **Sz:** M **CC:** V/MC **Assn:** WADA **Dir:** I-43 N to Hwy C, then 5 min W to Washington Ave. 20 min N of Milwaukee. **Own:** Peter & Donna Steffen. **QC:** 1 34 52 S15

Cedarburg Antiques
W61 N512 Washington Ave
(414)375-0276

Wide selection of antiques & finished & rough furniture from Country to Victorian. **Hrs:** Wed-Sat 11-5, Sun 12-5, Mon-Tue by chance/appt.

Cedar Creek Antiques [G8]
N70 W6340 Bridge Rd
(414)377-2204

Antiques & collectibles. **Hrs:** Mon-Sat 10-5, Sun 11-5.

Cedar Tree - Raven Nest
W62 N580 Washington Ave
(414)375-1776

Accessories for every room in the house from the past to the present. **Hrs:** Mon-Sat 10-5, Sun 12-5.

Alcoholic Antiques III

Wine funnel: A small funnel made from silver or plate used for decanting wine. It had a filter at the top to catch any lees, and its spout was angled at the bottom to send the wine down the glass side of the decanter so that its color could be checked.

Taster: A small bowl, with one or two handles, made of silver or pewter, and used for tasting wine, beer, or other whiskey. They were sometimes hung on a cord round the neck of the cellar master as he moved round the cellar sampling his maturing stock. What a job!

Wine labels or **spirit labels:** Small shield-shaped labels hung on fine silver chains around the necks of decanters to identify their contents. Common from about 1775 until the end of the Victorian period and still reproduced, the labels most frequently found are Port, Madeira, Sherry, Whiskey, Gin, and Rum.

Corkscrew: The earliest ones, usually of steel, were made around 1600, and are now very rare. Much more common are silver handled ones, produced in Birmingham, England, from about 1775, and imported in large quantities for the rapidly growing American middle class. The 19th century saw a huge proliferation of corkscrews whose handles were made in almost every metal in forms that ranged from the beautiful through the curious to the obscene.

The Collectors Gallery

W63 N706 Washington Ave
(414)375-3340

A varied gathering of fine antiques, collectibles & antique & estate jewelry. **Hrs:** Mon-Sat 10-5, Sun 11-5. **Dir:** 1st fl of West Bldg at Cedar Creek Settlement.

Creekside Antiques [G]

N69 W6335 Bridge Rd
(414)377-6131

A varied selection of quality antiques & collectibles. Furniture, glassware, china, linens, sports memorabilia, books, tools, toys, advertising, kitchen & 1950s. **Pr:** $1-5,000 **Est:** 1991 **Hrs:** Mon-Sat 10-5, Sun 11-4 (closed Xmas, New Years, Easter & Thanks). **Sz:** M **CC:** V/MC **Dir:** On scenic Cedar Creek "at the bridge on Bridge Road." **Own:** Leo & Carol Neis. **QC: 67 32 48**

Crow's Nest

N66 W6404 Cleveland St
(414)377-3039

Fine china, glassware, tin, pewter & brass with an English country flair. **Hrs:** By chance/appt. **Own:** Betty Woest.

Dime a Dance

N70 W6340 Bridge Rd
(414)377-5054

Vintage clothing, laces, jewelry & antique furniture. **Hrs:** Mon-Sat 10-5, Sun 12-5. **Own:** Mary Petrey.

Don's Resale & Antiques

N57 W6170 Portland Rd
(414)377-6868

Hrs: Mon & Wed-Sat 10-5 (closed Tue & Sun).

Patricia Frances Interiors

W62 N634 Washington Ave
(414)377-7710

Antiques, collectibles, fine household furnishings. **Hrs:** Mon-Sat 11-5. **Own:** Pat Boeck.

From the Heart

W63 N 635 Washington Ave
(414)376-1016

Hrs: Tue 12-5, Wed-Sat 10-5, Sun 12-5. **CC:** V/MC/DIS.

Heritage Lighting

W62 N572 Washington Ave
(414)377-9033 • (920)683-8827
(414)377-9197 (fax)
heritage@lsol.net
www.antiquelights.com

A complete antique lighting showroom including kerosene, gas & electric fixtures & lamps. Restoration, glassware & parts. **Pr:** $1-27,000 **Est:** 1952 **Hrs:** Mon-Sat 10-5, Sun by chance. **Sz:** M **CC:** AX/V/MC/DIS **Dir:** I-43 exit C W to downtown Cedarburg. 20 min N of Milwaukee. **Own:** David Skarda. **QC: 65 S1 S16**

The Irish Trader Ltd

N70 W6340 Bridge Rd
(414)375-7474
(888)474-7474

Direct importer of 19th C Irish waxed pine in restored condition. **Hrs:** Mon-Sat 10-5, Sun 11-5.

Nouveau Antique & Jewelry Parlor

W62 N594 Washington Ave
(414)375-4568

Specializing in antique glassware, jewelry & Victorian furniture. **Hrs:** Mon-Sat 10-5, Sun 1-4. **QC: 61 58**

Robin's Nest Antiques & Gifts

N70 W6340 Bridge Rd
(414)377-3444

Victorian & country antiques, European fine

rt cards, antique jewelry, buttons, lace & linens. **Hrs:** Mon-Sat 10-5, Sun 11-5.

Santa Fe Shop
N70 W6340 Bridge Rd
(414)376-1497

A large selection of antique and turn-of-the-century furniture as well as foods, cookware, cookbooks & silver jewelry from the Southwest. **Hrs:** Mon-Sat 10-5, Sun 11-5.

Spool 'n Spindle Antiques
N70 W6340 Bridge Rd
(414)377-4200

Diverse & ever-changing inventory of antique furniture & accessories from the 1850s through the Depression. **Hrs:** Mon-Sat 10-5, Sun 11-5.

Stone House Antiques
2088 Washington Ave (Hwy NN)
(414)675-2931

A blend of country & Victorian. Ironstone, flow blue, primitives & linens. **Hrs:** Tue-Sat 10-5, Sun 12-5.

Clinton

Nana's House of Antiques
244 Allen St
(608)676-5535

Hrs: Mon-Sat 10-4, Sun 11-4.

Smoke House Antiques [G20]
402 Front St
(608)676-2251

Hrs: Mon-Sat 10-4, Sun 12-4.

Order an additional copy of the Green Guide for yourself or a friend by calling Toll Free (888)875-5999 or visit your local antiques bookstore or nearest antiques dealer.

Studio B
223 Allen St
(608)676-5392
Hrs: Thu-Sun 12-5.

Colgate

Monches Country Store
4990 Monches Rd
(414)628-1680

Specializing in fine prints, Staffordshire china & brass. Dealers always welcome. **Hrs:** By chance/appt. **Assn:** WADA **Own:** Nancy Woll. **QC: 74 30 20**

Columbus

Antique Shoppes of Columbus Mall [G]
141 W James St
(920)623-2669
Hrs: Mon-Sat 10-4:30, Sun 12-5.

Charisma Antiques
118 S Ludington
(920)623-0317
Hrs: Mon-Sat 10-4, Sun 12-4.

Columbus Antique Mall [G]
239 Whitney St
(920)623-1992
Own: Dan & Rose Amato.

Kurth Mansion Antiques
902 Park Ave
(920)623-3930
Hrs: Mon-Sat 10-4 (closed Tue), Sun 12-4.

Cuba City

Tin Lantern Antiques Mall [G]
118 S Main St
(608)744-3634

Furniture, dishes, glassware, stoneware, jewelry, dolls, trunks, antique dishes, paintings

& lots more. **Pr:** $10-150 **Est:** 1994 **Hrs:** May-Oct Mon-Sat 10-5, Sun 12-5; Nov-Apr Mon & Wed-Sat 10-4:30, Sun 12-4:30 (closed Tue). **Sz:** M **CC:** AX/V/MC/DIS **Dir:** Hwy 80 - Main St across from the hardware store. 15 min N of Galena. **Own:** Lucille Thiltgen. **QC: 31 48**

Custer

North Star Antiques & Country Store

3000 County Rd J
(715)592-5070

Antiques, collectibles, gifts, lace curtains, candles. **Hrs:** May-Dec Thu-Sat 11-5, Sun 12-4. **Dir:** 12 mi NE of Stevens Point off Hwy 66 on J N 3 mi.

Oldies But Goodies Antiques

7345 Deer Rd
(715)592-4661 • (715)445-3116

Hrs: Apr-Oct Mon-Sat 10-5, Sun 12-5; Nov-Mar Mon, Fri & Sat 10-5, Sun 12-5.

Dir: 6 mi E of Stevens Point. **Own:** David & Georgine Demling.

Dalton

Pine Plantation Antiques

W2110 Cty Rd B
(414)394-3284

Early American pattern glass, Depression glass, china, pottery, lamps, silverplate flatware, furniture & a general line. **Hrs:** May-Oct Wed-Sat or by chance/appt. **Dir:** 2-1/2 mi E of State Hwy 22 on County Rd B. 7 mi SE of Montello, 7 mi W of Kingston. **Own:** Harriette Glover. **QC: 61**

Deerfield

Dovetail Antiques

119 S Main St
(608)764-1454
dovetail@bmark.com
www.dovetailantiques.com

Specializing in quality antique Victorian,

Candles I

In the 17th and 18th centuries candles were costly, either in cash, on the rare occasions when they were bought, or in labor, where candlemaking was yet one more slow and repetitive task for the colonial woman. Common candles were made of tallow, finer ones of wax.

Tallow was made by boiling animal fat in water until it rose to the top where it was skimmed off, only to be boiled up again and again until all impurities were gone. Then a large kettle of pure tallow was hung over the fire.

Candles were made from this tallow either by dipping or molding. For dipping, long poles with short, removable cross pieces were laid across two chair backs in front of the fire. A wick of flax or cotton was hung from each cross piece and dipped in the hot tallow. By the time the last crosspiece had been dipped, the first would have hardened enough to be dipped again, and this process was repeated until the candles were thick enough to use. Great skill was needed to keep the tallow at the right temperature: too hot and it would melt the tallow off the wick, too cold and it congealed unevenly and lumpily. Not surprisingly colonial housewives took great pride in well-made, even-burning candles.

Making candles in molds was quicker, but the molds had to be bought, whereas the equipment for dipping was all home-made. Tin or, more rarely, pewter candle molds for making between two and twenty-four candles at a time were common domestic utensils.

Bees wax and bayberry wax were prepared in much the same way as tallow. Spermiceti, a fatty substance from the head of the sperm whale, was popular from the 1730s onward because its candles were about twice as bright as tallow ones.

American, European & primitive furniture, original oil and watercolor paintings and antique Burmese imports, of the late 18th, 19th & early 20th C. **Est:**1997 **Hrs:** Thu-Sat 10-5, Sun 11-4 (closed Mon-Wed). **Sz:** M **CC:** V/MC **Own:** John Matthews.

Old Deerfield Antiques [G40]
37 N Main St
(608)764-5743

Hrs: Mon-Sat 10-5, Sun 11-4.

Delafield

Celtic Antiques & Gifts
810 N Genesee St
(414)646-3000

18th & 19th C Irish country pine, mahogany, brass & lamps. **Hrs:** By appt only.

The China Cupboard
700 N Genesee St
(414)646-7350

Hrs: Sum Tue-Sat 11-4, Sun 11-4; Win Wed-Sat 11-4, Sun 12-4.

Delafield Antiques Center [G75]
803 Genesee St
(414)646-2746

Reference books, 18th, 19th & early 20th C furniture, accessories & art. **Hrs:** Mon-Sat 10-5 (Fri til 8), Sun 12-5. **Dir:** I-94 exit 285 (Delafield/Hwy C). **Own:** Ron & Debbie Christman, Mgrs. **QC: 52 19 23**

Rickety Robin Antiques
703 Milwaukee St
(414)646-8870

General line of antiques, glassware, furniture, silver, paper, jewelry & collectibles. **Pr:** $1-1,000 **Est:** 1977 **Hrs:** Mon-Sat 11-5, occasional Sun. **Sz:** M **Dir:** I-94 exit 285. 20 mi W of Milwaukee, 50 mi E of Madison. **Own:** John & Julie Platz.

Delavan

Antiques of Delavan
299 E Walworth Ave
(414)728-9977

Hrs: Mon-Sat 10-5, Sun 12-4.

Beall Jewelers
305 E Walworth Ave
(414)728-8577

Jewelry. **Hrs:** Mon-Sat 9-5:30 (Thu & Fri til 8).

Buttons & Bows
312 E Walworth Ave
(414)728-6813

Hrs: Daily 11-5.

Delavan Antique & Art Center Inc [G85]
230 E Walworth Ave (Hwy 11)
(414)740-1400

Hrs: Mon-Thu 11-6, Fri-Sat 11-8, Sun 12-5. **CC:** AX/V/MC/DIS **Dir:** W of Lake Geneva in historic downtown Delavan.

Remember When Antiques & Collectibles
313 E Walworth Ave
(414)728-8670

Hrs: Mon-Sat 9:30-5:30 (Fri til 8), Sun 12-5.

Dodgeville

Carousel Collectibles & Antiques
121 N Iowa St
(608)935-5196 • (608)935-5025 (fax)
carousel@mhtc.net

Handpainted carousel horses, furniture,

Use the Specialty QuickCode indexes at the back of the book to find dealers who specialize in your area of interest.

primitives, glassware, paper collectibles. **Hrs:** Mon-Sat 9-5:30, Sun 11-4. **CC:** V/MC **Own:** Jack Reynolds & Cherie Greek. **QC: 46**

Woodshed Antiques

4574 Hwy 23 N
(608)935-3896

Rural Wisconsin antiques; pine, walnut & cherry furniture, ironstone, china, glassware & whatever found in local attics & basements. **Pr:** $25-1,000 **Est:** 1959 **Hrs:** Daily 10-6 by chance/appt. **Sz:** L **Dir:** 5 mi N of Dodgeville, WI. Near Gov Dodge State Park, House on the Rock & Taliesin. **Own:** William Treweek. **QC: 1 34 55 S9 S11 S16**

Eau Claire

Antique Emporium

306 Main St
(715)832-2494

Huge inventory of Victorian furniture, china & glassware, jewelry, books, postcards, linens, collectibles, military antiques. In an 1898 Masonic Temple with many natural history exhibits throughout the 3-story building. **Est:** 1981 **Hrs:** Mon-Sat 10-5:30. **Dir:** I-94 to Rte 53N to Main St.

Antique Partners

2124 Birch St
(715)834-1001

Glass, pictures, frames, lamps, plates, books, collectibles, furniture, figurines, old things, prints, cards, records. **Hrs:** Mon-Sat 10:30-5. **Dir:** I-94 to Rte 53N. On the corner of Birch St & Starr Ave.

Main Street Galleries

306 Main St
(715)832-2494

Specializing in ephemera, books, magazines, post & trade cards, Victorian scraps, antique

frames, prints. Custom framing by appt. **Hrs:** Mon-Sat 10-5:30. **Dir:** I-94 to Rte 53N to Main St. **QC: 39 18 S13**

Piney Hills Antiques

5260 Deerfield Rd
(715)832-8766

Furniture, stoneware, primitives, glassware, lighting, advertising, jewelry, linens. **Hrs:** Mon-Sat 10-5, Sun 11-5 (closed Jan & Feb). **Dir:** From Eau Claire, Hwy 93 S to Deerfield Rd, E 1 mi.

Rice's Antiques

202 S Barstow
(715)835-5351

Depression glass, furniture, toys, other glass & china, collectibles, stoneware, advertising, beer items, Fenton, kitchenware. **Hrs:** Mon-Sat 10-5:30.

Edgerton

Antique & Art Gallery

104 W Fulton St
(608)884-6787

Antiques, art & paintings. **Hrs:** Daily 10-5 (closed Tue).

Moseley-Paul Co

9854 N Kidder Rd
(608)868-6860

Stoves. **Hrs:** By appt only.

Nine R's Antiques

202 S Main St
(608)884-4710

Hrs: Fri-Sun 10-5.

Pete's Ghost Antiques

11947 Dallman Rd
(608)884-9508

Hrs: Tue-Sat 9-5.

Sisters Act

114 W Fulton St
(608)884-6092

Hrs: Tue-Sat 10-5.

Use the Service QuickCode indexes at the back of the book to find restorers, appraisers, refinishers, and other specialty service providers.

Thymes Past Antique Mall [G]
14 W Fulton
(608)884-2094
Hrs: Mon-Sat 10-5, Sun 11-4.

Egg Harbor
Olde Orchard Antique Mall [G100+]
7381 Hwy 42
(920)868-3685
Hrs: May-Oct Mon-Sat 9-5, Sun 10-5. **CC:** V/MC/DIS.

Elkhorn
Bits of Past & Present
W5691 State Rd 11
(414)723-4763
Hrs: Tue-Sat 10-5.

Heirlooms
12 S Wisconsin St
(414)723-4070
Hrs: Mon-Sat 10:30-5.

Powell's Antique Shop
14 W Geneva St
(414)723-2952
Hrs: Wed-Sun 10-4:30.

Twin Pines Antique Mall
5438 State Rd 11
(414)723-4492
Hrs: Tue-Sun 10-5. **Dir:** 1/2 mi W of Elkhorn.

Van Dyke's Antiques
20 S Wisconsin St
(414)723-4909
Hrs: Mon-Tue & Thu-Sat 10-5.

Fall Creek
Cheshire Farm Antiques
E10415 Cty Rd D
(715)877-2228
Granary & building full of furniture, jewelry, primitives, garden accents, frames & prints in a country setting. **Hrs:** Most days 9-6. **Dir:** 1 mi E of Hwy 53 on County Rd D.

Engelwood Antiques
Township Rd
(715)877-3468
Victorian & turn-of-the-century refinished furniture, lamps, lighting, porcelain, glass, Art Deco, linens, jewelry, tools, fishing lures. **Hrs:** Tue-Sat 10-5, Mon by chance (closed Sun). **Dir:** From Fall Creek go N on County Rd D to County Rd N to County Rd NL to Township Rd. Between August & Cadott, 27 to NL. Look for signs.

Fort Atkinson
The Antiques Exchange Mall [G15]
232 S Main St
(920)563-8500
Hrs: Daily 10-5.

Fox Point
Scott Lace & Dennis Buettner
(414)351-7080
Early to mid-19th C American primitive & formal country furniture, painted immigrant pieces, 19th C decorative arts, garden accessories & architectural artifacts. **Hrs:** By appt only. **Assn:** WADA. **QC:** 52 60 3

Genesee

Brookdale Village [G]
W305 S4095 Brookhill Rd
(414)548-0056 • (414)968-4621

Hrs: Apr-Nov Wed-Sun 10-4. **Dir:** Hwy 59
W of Waukesha to Brookhill Rd (just before
Hwy 83). Turn N on Brookhill Rd to
Brookdale Village.

Germantown

Pilgrim Antique Mall [G]
W156 N11500 Pilgrim Rd
(414)250-0260

Hrs: Mon-Sat 10-5, Sun 12-4.

Grafton

Gordon's Antiques
2275 N Port Washington Rd
(414)377-4313

Victorian to country, emphasizing lighting,
art glass, postcards & American Indian. **Hrs:**
Wed-Mon 10-5 (closed Tue). Call ahead in
Win. **Sz:** L **Assn:** WADA **Dir:** Hwy 32 1-
1/2 mi S of Port Washington. **Own:** Gordon
Kirsten. **QC: 65 61**

Grafton Antique Mall [G]
994 Ulao Rd
(414)376-0036

Clocks, art, Depression glass, vintage jewelry, paintings, linens, books, furniture, toys &
decoys. **Hrs:** Daily 10-5. **QC: 7 48 35**

Seth's Antiques
1233 Twelfth Ave
(414)376-1862

Quality antiques in a spacious setting.
Featuring Victorian furnishings, glassware,

> Use the Specialty QuickCode
> indexes at the back of the book to
> find dealers who specialize in your
> area of interest.

art pottery & lighting. **Hrs:** Mon-Sat 10-5,
Sun 12-5.

Green Bay

Antique Collector's Corner
898 Elmore St
(920)497-7141

Buy/sell/trade toys, circus, men's collectibles, armor, swords, war relics, side
show, antique guns. Divorced men's
appraisals. **Pr:** $10-1,000 **Est:** 1950 **Hrs:**
May-Dec Mon-Sat 10-5; Jan-Apr Mon-Fri
12-5. **Dir:** Hwy 41 W: Ashland Ave to
Elmore St. **Own:** Jim Palmer. **QC: 4 39
87 S1**

Ginny's Antiques & Collectibles
3808 Riverside Dr
(920)336-3666

Hrs: Tue-Fri 11:30-3:30.

Packer City Antiques
712 Redwood Dr
(920)490-1095

Hrs: Mon-Sat 9-5. **Dir:** Corner of Mason &
Oneida.

Red's Antiques
1344 Main St
(902)437-3596

Hrs: Daily 10-2.

Yesteryears Antiques
611 9th St
(920)435-4900

Furniture, glass & pictures. **Hrs:** Mon-Sat
10-4. **CC:** V/MC **Dir:** Corner of 9th &
Ashland. **QC: 48 61**

Hartford

Erin Antiques
1691 Hwy 83 S
(414)673-4680

General line. **Pr:** $5-2,500 **Est:** 1970 **Hrs:**
Daily from 10. **Sz:** S **Assn:** WADA **Dir:** 1/2

blk S of Hwy 167 on Hwy 83. **Own:** Audrey Marty. **QC: 22 23 5**

Hartford Antique Mall [G]
147 N Rural St
(414)673-2311
Hrs: Daily 10-5.

Sharron's Antiques
135 N Main St
(414)673-2751 • (414)673-5456

Case piece furniture, specializing in ethnic Wisconsin pieces (1840-1880s) of cherry, walnut, butternut & birch. A line of smalls including Bakelite kitchen utensils & Mexican silver jewelry & tin. Also a large selection of pressed glass kerosene lamps. **Pr:** $9-5,600 **Est:** 1973 **Hrs:** Mon-Fri 10-5, Sat 10-4, Sun 12-4. **CC:** V/MC/DIS **Assn:** WADA **Dir:** I-94 exit Rte 41 N. Turn W on Hwy 60 6 mi to Hwy 93 (Main St). 2 blks N on Main. 45 min N of Milwaukee. **Own:** Sharron & Steven Cypher. **QC: 1 32 34 S1 S12 S16**

Hartland

Hartland Antiques [G28]
418 Merton Ave - #3B
(414)367-9828 • (414)367-0998 (fax)
Charming multi-dealer mall with Victorian & Arts & Crafts furniture, paintings, prints, textiles, china & numerous smalls. Hot coffee, fresh cookies & sentimental music. **Pr:** $1-1,200 **Est:** 1996 **Hrs:** Mon-Sat 10-5, Sun 11-4. **Sz:** L **CC:** V/MC **Dir:** Hwy 16 to Merton Ave or Hwy 94 to 83 N to Hwy 16 to Merton Ave. **Own:** Gwyneth Wilson & Meredith Button. **QC: 50 36 61 S10 S4 S8**

Hayward

Nelson Bay Antiques
Nelson Lake Rd
(715)634-2177

Glass, pottery, furniture, stoneware, primitives. Oldest shop in northern Wisconsin. **Hrs:** Good Friday to Oct 15 daily 9:30-4. **Dir:** Hwy 63 N from Hayward 4-1/4 mi to Nelson Lake Rd. Turn L & follow signs. **Own:** Jean Nelson. **QC: 48 61 22**

Red Shed Antiques [G8]
County Rd B
(715)634-8458
redshed@win.bright.net
www.win.bright.net/~redshed

The area's largest display of horsedrawn wagons & buggies. Country wagon wheels, farm accessories, lodge furnishings, fishing lures, pottery, glassware, quilts, rugs &

Blue and White Porcelain II

Flow blue, originally called "flowing blue": Transferware produced in numerous patterns in which the cobalt blue ink flowed, or smeared, during firing. The resulting out-of-focus look was colorful and popular, and flow blue was widely produced in England and the Netherlands from 1830 to 1900. Its popularity was welcomed by the manufacturers, because the flowing disguised the smudges that were made if the transfer was moved slightly as it was laid on the item: this enabled them to deskill the decorating process even more, and thus to pay even lower wages to the women and girls who did the job.

Historical blue: A blue-and-white china made in Staffordshire for the American market from about 1820 to 1840. The pattern shows American scenes or historical events surrounded by a flowered border. Each factory had its own border, but the same scenes were copied by many factories. English scenes were also produced, but it is the American ones that are most eagerly collected. "Second period" historical blue was popular from about 1850 to 1920. It showed a greater number of scenes, many of which were specially printed as souvenirs for the growing tourist trade. It is often printed in a lighter blue than the deep cobalt blue of the first period, is easier to find, cheaper, and widely collected.

more. **Est:** 1991 **Hrs:** Daily 10-5. **Sz:** L **Dir:** 1.5 mi E of Hwy 27 on County Rd B. **Own:** Don & Chris Mrotek. **QC:** 34 79 60 S12 S2

Hudson

Abigail Page Antiques [G20]
503 Second St
(715)381-1505
Hrs: Mon-Sat 10-6 (Fri til 7). **CC:** V/MC.

Janesville

Lee Foster's
City Hall Antiques
218 W Milwaukee St
(608)752-5188

19th C American furniture in walnut, cherry, original finish & original paint, always a surprise or two. **Pr:** $50-6,000 **Hrs:** Wed only 11-7. **Sz:** M **CC:** V/MC **Assn:** WADA **Dir:** Central downtown Janesville. **QC:** 51 52 34 S12

Franklin Stove Antiques
301 W Milwaukee St
(608)756-5792

Franklin stoves, furniture & collectibles. **Hrs:** Mon-Sat 10-5.

General Antique Store
8301 US Hwy 14
(608)756-1812

Advertising, glass. **Hrs:** Daily 1-5.

Pipsqueak & Me
220 W Milwaukee St
(608)756-1752
(800)964-6488

Refinished & original surface walnut, cherry, pine & figured maple furniture, American c 1800-1860; quilts, artwork, some original paint, no collectible junk. An eye for the unusual in any category. We stand behind what we sell. Will ship anywhere. **Pr:** $20-5,000 **Est:** 1979 **Hrs:** Mon-Sat 11-5

(closed Sun & hols). Call ahead recommended. **Sz:** L **CC:** V/MC **Assn:** WADA **Dir:** I-90 exit Hwy 26 S 4 mi. Cross river 3 blks on R or follow directions to historic downtown. **Own:** Phillip Schauer. **QC:** 48 1 84 S9 S12 S16

Yesterday's Memories
4904 S Hwy 51 S
(608)754-2906
Hrs: Mon-Sat 10-5, Sun 12-5.

Kenosha

Apple Lane Antiques
9730 Burlington Rd (Hwy S)
(414)859-2017

18th & 19th C furniture & accessories. Civil war items. No crafts or reproductions. **Est.** 1976 **Hrs:** Apr-Dec Wed-Sat 10-5, Sun 12-5. **Dir:** On Hwy S 1-1/2 mi E of I-94 exit 142 **Own:** Harold & Gerrie Thurber. **QC:** 52 4

The Cypress Tree
722 50th St
(414)652-6999
Hrs: Sun-Fri 10:30-5.

Dairyland Antique Mall [G90+]
5220 120th Ave
(414)857-6802
Hrs: Daily 9-5. **Dir:** I-94 & Hwy 158.

Greta's
4906 7th Ave
(414)658-1077

Antiques & furniture, 1800s to Art Deco **Hrs:** Fri-Sat 10-5.

Helen's Remember When Antiques [G27]
5730 6th Ave
(414)652-2280
Hrs: Mon-Sat 11-5, Sun 12-5.

Hyde N Seec Antiques
5623 6th Ave
(414)654-8111

Christmas collectibles, European fine glass & art pottery. **Hrs:** By appt only.

Memory Lane Antiques
1942 22nd Ave
(414)551-8452

Porcelain, glassware, lamps, clocks, silver, jewelry & fine collectibles. **Est:** 1972 **Hrs:** Tue-Sat 1-5. **CC:** V/MC **Dir:** I-94 exit 158 or 142: E to 22nd Ave, then N to 19th St.

Monnes Gallery / Miracle Antiques
5813 Sixth Ave
(414)605-9044

Hrs: Wed-Sun 12-5.

Racine Antique Mall II [G]
611 58th St
(414)605-9818

Hrs: Sat-Sun 11-5.

Red Barn Antiques
12000 Sheridan Rd
(414)694-0424

Hrs: Wed-Sun 10-6.

Sara Jane's Antique Centre [G]
716-720 58th St
(414)657-5588

Pattern & Depression glass, art glass, Bakelite, estate & signed costume jewelry, vintage textiles & linens, millinery, old books, collectibles. **Hrs:** Wed-Mon 11-5. **CC:** V/MC/DIS **Dir:** I-94 to Hwy 158 (52nd St) to Sheridan Rd. R 6 blks to 58th S. L 1 blk. **QC: 61 63 64**

Tutbury Antiques
724 58th St
(414)652-5910

Victorian to Mission to Contemporary. American, English & French furnishings.

Pottery, glassware, vintage clothing, jewelry, Victorian & deco-style lighting. **Pr:** $5-1,500 **Est:** 1993 **Hrs:** Jun-Aug daily 11-5; Sep-May Sat-Mon 11-5. **Sz:** L **CC:** V/MC/DIS **Dir:** Hwy 158 E exit Hwy 32. R 6 blks to 58th St, L 2 blks. **Own:** John Fox. **QC: 49 58 36 S8 S18 S22**

La Crosse

4th Street Antique Gallery [G20]
119 4th St S
(608)782-7278

Hrs: Mon-Sat 10-5, Sun 11-4:30. **CC:** V/MC.

Antique Center of La Crosse Ltd [G50]
110 S 3rd St
(608)782-6533 • (608)781-4948

Charming, century-old building downtown with three floors of fine antiques & collectibles. **Pr:** $1-3,000+ **Est:** 1986 **Hrs:** Mon-Sat 9-5:30, Sun 11-4. **Sz:** H **Dir:** I-90 to Rte 53 to downtown. **QC: 20 58 61 S1**

Caledonia Street Antique Mall [G40+]
1213 Caledonia St
(608)782-8443

Hrs: Mon-Sat 10-5, Sun 11-4:30. **Sz:** L.

Renaissance Emporium
211 Historic Pearl St
(608) 796-0211 • (608)796-0212 (fax)
info@renaissanceemporium.com
www.renaissanceemporium.com

Victorian furnishings & art glass. **Hrs:** By appt only. **QC: 61 89**

Vintage Vogue
115 5th Ave S
(608)782-3722

Vintage clothing. **Hrs:** Mon-Sat 10-5. **CC:** V/MC/DIS.

Wild Rose & Hornets' Nest Antiques
1225 Caledonia St
(608)785-2998

A general line of quality antiques, collectibles, books, advertising, linens, furniture & decorative accessories at affordable prices. Inventory changes weekly. **Est:** 1993 **Sz:** L **CC:** V/MC/DIS **Dir:** I-90 exit 3: S on Hwy 53 (4th light), L at Clinton 1 blk — Old Towne N Caledonia St. **Own:** Patricia Ellenz.

Lake Delton
Old Academy Antiques Mall [G20]
Hwy 12
(608)254-4948

Hrs: Apr-Sep daily 10-5:30.

Our Gang Antique Mall [G20+]
Hwy 23
(608)254-4401

Hrs: Apr-Oct Mon-Sat 10-5.

Lake Geneva
Lake Geneva Antique Mall [G]
829 Williams St
(414)248-6345

Hrs: Daily 10-5 (Fri til 8).

Sign of the Unicorn Ltd
233 Center St
(414)248-1141

Specializing in 18th & 19th C prints including botanicals, natural history, architectural & views. Conservation framing, French matting & hand-finished frames. Frame restoration. Lathe copying services also available. **Pr:** $25-1,000 **Est:** 1986 **Hrs:** Mon-Sat 10-5, Sun 12-5. **Sz:** M **CC:** AX/V/MC/DIS **Assn:** WADA **Dir:** Rte 12 to Lake Geneva.

N on Center St, 1/2 blk on E side. **Own:** Frank & Judy Scott. **QC: 74 66 18 S13 S16 S18**

The Steffen Collection
611 Main St (Hwy 50)
(414)248-1800

Hrs: Mon-Sat 10-5, Sun 12-5.

Lake Mills
Gwenn's Antiques
121 W Lake
(920)648-6183

19th & 20th C furniture, toys, linens, glassware, gold & sterling jewelry. **Hrs:** Sun-Wed 12-5, Thu-Sat 10-5. **Dir:** Corner Lake & Church. **Own:** Gwen Waldo.

Lake Street Emporium
121 W Lake St
(920)648-5511

Hrs: Sun-Wed 12-5, Thu-Sat 10-5. **Dir:** Corner Lake & Church.

Old Mills Market
109 N Main St
(920)648-3030

Hrs: Daily 10-5.

Opera Hall Antique Center [G]
211 N Main St
(920)648-5026

Hrs: Daily 10-5.

Lannon
Betti Anne's Antiques
7291 N Lannon Rd
(414)255-6750

Hrs: Wed-Mon 11-5.

HOPKINS & CROCKER INC.

807 E. Johnson St.
Madison, WI 53703
608-255-6222

Open Tuesday-Saturday
12:00-5:00

Little Chute

Grand Avenue Antiques
(920)788-5004
Hrs: Call for hours.

Memories Antique Mall [G100+]
400 Randolph Dr
(920)788-5553

Hrs: Daily 10-6 (Fri til 8). **CC:** V/MC **Dir:** Hwy 41N & County N junction. L off ramp.

Madison

Antiques Mall of Madison [G]
4748 Cottage Grove Rd
(608)222-2049

A wide variety of antiques & collectibles, including furniture, lighting, pottery, glassware & china. **Est:** 1982 **Hrs:** Mon-Fri 10-6 (Thu til 9), Sat 10-5, Sun 12-5. **Sz:** H **CC:** V/MC/DIS **Dir:** Hwy 51 E 1/4 mi on Cottage Grove Rd behind Pizza Hut. **Own:** Tom Metcalfe.

Atomic Interiors
561 S Park St
(608)251-5255

Specializing in mid-century modern furniture & objects (1930s to 1960s). Furniture: Knoll (Bertoia, Saarinen), Heywood-Wakefield, vintage Herman Miller (Eames, Nelson, Noguchi, Panton). Nelson clocks,

Russel Wright & Eva Zeisel dishware. **Pr:** $10-1,500 **Est:** 1990 **Hrs:** Wed-Fri 12-3, Sat 11-5. **Sz:** M **Dir:** I-90 exit Hwy 12-18 W approx 5.5 mi to exit 261 AB. Right onto Park St. Shop is at corner of Park & Fish Hatchery Rd. Parking in rear. **Own:** David Vogel & Rebecca Rodriguez. **QC: 59 32 36**

Broadway Antiques Mall [G70]
115 E Broadway
(608)222-2241

Quality furniture, antiques & collectibles. **Pr:** $1-10,000 **Hrs:** Mon-Sat 10-5 (Thu til 9), Sun 11-5. **Sz:** H **Dir:** I-90 to Madison, Rte 12/18 (Beltline) to Monona Dr exit. **Own:** Wes Crawford. **QC: 48 32 S8**

Coffee Mill Antique Mall [G4]
3472 Hoepker Rd
(608)837-7099

Large inventory of smalls, furniture, replacement hardware in stock. Specializing in oil lamps & clocks. **Pr:** $1-2,000 **Est:** 1972 **Hrs:** Mon-Sat 1-5, Sun 12-5. **Sz:** L **Dir:** Corner Hwy 151 & Hwy C between Madison & Sun Prairie, 2 mi E of I-90-94. **Own:** Mike Kesselhon. **QC: 35 48 65 S17**

Florilegium Antiques
836 E Johnson St
(608)256-7310

Floral decorative items, old fabrics, rugs, lace, beaded bags, needlework & gardening.

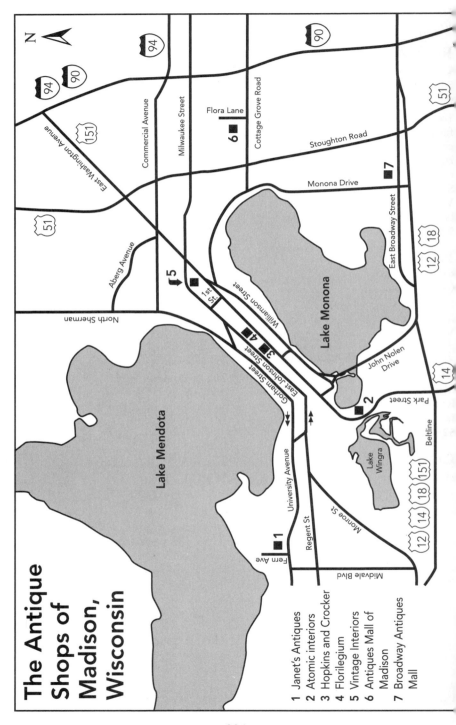

The Antique Shops of Madison, Wisconsin

Madison, WI

1 Janet's Antiques
2 Atomic Interiors
3 Hopkins and Crocker
4 Florilegium
5 Vintage Interiors
6 Antiques Mall of Madison
7 Broadway Antiques Mall

Hrs: Tue-Sat 12-5 (Thu til 7), Sat 10-5. **CC:** V/MC **Own:** Gretchen Nutt.

Randall Hopkins & Patricia Crocker Arts & Antiques

807 E Johnson St
(608)255-6222

18th & early 19th C English & American furniture. Pre-20th C oil paintings, watercolors & prints. Brass & silver, oriental rugs, plus an eclectic variety of decorative accessories. **Est:** 1994 **Hrs:** Tue-Sat 12-5. **Sz:** M **CC:** V/MC **Dir:** I-90/94 exit Rte 151 W 4.5 mi to Livingston St. Turn R for 3 blks to Johnson St. 1st business on R. **QC:** 7 52 54

Janet's Antiques

315 Fern Dr
(608)238-4474

Fine 18th & 19th C furniture & decorative items. Specializing in Federal, Empire, Victorian & Mission; lamps, cut glass, art glass, fine porcelain & silver. **Est:** 1973 **Hrs:** Mon-Sat 10-6. **Sz:** L **CC:** AX/V/MC/DIS **Assn:** NADA ACGA **Dir:** Hwy 12/18 W to Midvale Blvd. Cross University Ave to Kohl's parking lot, then R to sign. **Own:** Janet H Hoopes & Elizabeth J Barber. **QC:** 2 61 23 S1 S8 S9

Chris Kerwin Antiques & Interiors

839 Monroe St
(608)256-7363 • (608)256-2088 (fax)

A design-oriented business with antique & contemporary furniture & accessories. English & American antiques — brass, pewter, oriental ceramics, lamps & jewelry. **Pr:** $50-10,000 **Est:** 1968 **Hrs:** Mon-Sat 10-

5:30. **Sz:** L **CC:** V/MC **Dir:** 3 blks W of UW field house/football stadium. **Own:** Chris & Dan Kerwin. **QC:** 7 20 36 S15 S18 S22

Mapletree Antique Mall [G]

1293 Sherman Ave
(608)241-2599

Hrs: Mon-Fri 10-6 (Thu til 9), Sat 10-5, Sun 11-5.

Stony Hill Antiques

2140 Regent St
(608)231-1247

Madison's most eclectic gallery: Oriental rugs, African masks & statues, ethnographic textiles, fine art, antique furniture & decorative accessories, tribal jewelry, old books & more. **Pr:** $10-3,000 **Est:** 1977 **Hrs:** Tue-Sat 10-5. **Sz:** M **CC:** AX/V/MC/DIS **Dir:** 5 blks W of UW football stadium. **Own:** David H Ward. **QC:** 76 80 7 S12 S19

Treasure-Trove

2134 Regent St
(608)238-7116

A wide variety of antiques & collectibles, something for everyone. **Pr:** $1-1,200 **Est:** 1996 **Hrs:** Tue-Sat 10-6, Sun 10-4. **Sz:** M **Dir:** I-90-94: Beltline exit (Rtes 12-18) to Madison. Exit Park St to Regent St, L on Regent 4 blks W of UW Field House/Randall Stadium. **Own:** Marge Sparacino. **QC: 32 48 87 S12**

Vintage Interiors

2615 E Johnson St
(608)244-3000

20th C modern (1900-1980) furniture, lighting, decorative arts, industrial design, Art Deco & 1950s. **Hrs:** Tue-Sat 12-6 (Sun-Mon by chance). **Dir:** At North St. **Own:** Michael Port. **QC: 59 5**

Manitowoc

Antique Mall of Manitowoc [G20]

301 N 8th St
(920)682-8680

Hrs: Mon-Sat 10-5, Sun 11-5.

Pine River Antique Shop

7430 Cty Hwy Cr
(920)726-4440
mcnamara@lakefield.net

General line. Architectural antiques. **Est:** 1997 **Hrs:** Daily 11-5. **Dir:** On I-43 exit 144. **QC: 3**

Timeless Treasures

112 N 8th St
(920)682-6566

Women's, men's & children's vintage cloth-

ing & accessories. We helped costume "Titanic." Jewelry, linens, laces as well as candles, florals, cards, teddy bears & decorative accessories. **Pr:** $1-300 **Est:** 1993 **Hrs:** Tue-Sat 10-5, Sun 12-4 by chance. **Sz:** S **CC:** V/MC **Dir:** I-43 to Hwy 151E. At S 26th St turn L 1 blk to Washington St, then R at S 8th S, then L 2nd blk after bridge on L. **Own:** Dawn & Jim Steckmesser. **QC: 63 81 83**

Washington Street Antiques [G30]

910 Washington St
(920)684-2954

Hrs: Daily 10-5. **CC:** V/MC.

Marinette

Midcountry Antiques

W2575 County Rd B
(715)582-3538

A general line of antiques with emphasis on the country style of old paint, folk art, quilts, garden stuff, primitives & metalware. All housed in a quaint log home in a country setting. **Pr:** $6-6,000 **Est:** 1991 **Hrs:** Mon-Sat 10-6 (closed Sun). Call ahead advised. **Sz:** M **CC:** V/MC **Dir:** N of Green Bay, WI, off Hwy 41. Watch for billboard on Hwy 41 at Schacht Rd between Peshtigo & Marinette. **Own:** James Austin. **QC: 34 41 80 S12**

Weathervane Antiques

1059 Marinette Ave (Hwy 41)
(715)735-5077

A general line including china, glass, crocks, stoneware & graniteware, books, milk bottles. **Hrs:** Daily 10-4:30. **QC: 22**

Mauston

Antique Mall of Mauston [G]

101 N Union St
(608)847-7559 • (608)847-3061 (fax)

Twenty antique-filled rooms in two buildings. Also old-fashioned candy & ice cream

Use the Specialty QuickCode indexes at the back of the book to find dealers who specialize in your area of interest.

shoppe. Conveniently located off I-90-94. **Pr:** $5-5000 **Est:** 1985 **Hrs:** Daily 9:30-6 or by appt. **Sz:** L **Assn:** WCWADA **Dir:** I90-94 exit 69: Follow Hwy 82 W 2 blks to light. **Own:** G Frank. **QC: 34 61 32 S1 S12 S18**

Country School Antiques
N5506 Sumiec Rd
(608)562-3726

Hrs: By chance/appt. **Dir:** Off Hwy 12-16, 4 mi W of Mauston. **Own:** Ed & Betty Sumiec.

Mazomanie

A American Antiques
US Hwy 14
(608)767-2608

Furniture, toys, art, dolls, clocks, postcards, quilts, crocks, lamps, dishes, Indian, Norwegian; fine jewelry (estate & costume); sterling & silver plate. **Est:** 1962 **Hrs:** Mon-Sat 9-5, Sun 12-5. **Dir:** W of Black Earth, WI, on Hwy 14. **Own:** Karen & Richard Rahn. **QC: 48 64 78**

Menomonee Falls

Attic Memories
N89 W16683 Appleton Ave
(414)251-4040

Hrs: Tue-Sun 10-4:30.

Menomonee Falls Antiques
N88 W16683 Appleton Ave
(414)250-0816

Hrs: Daily 10-6.

Needful Things
N88 W16733 Appleton Ave
(414)250-1050

Hrs: Tue-Sat 10-5, Sun-Mon 11-4.

Menomonie

Apple Basket Antiques
E5480 708th Ave
(715)235-4650

Hrs: Tue-Sun 12-5, Sat 10-5.

Candleholders II

Chandelier: Candelabra hung from the ceiling.

Candle slide: A small pull-out slide, usually in a secretary or gaming table, designed to hold a candlestick.

Candle stand: A small, easily portable table, typically on a tripod base, for a candlestick or lamp. Forms range from primitive through country to formal. Some have built in candleholders whose height is adjustable by means of a central post threaded like a screw.

Torchere: A tall candlestand, always formal, often very sophisticated, and usually in pairs.

Floor candleholder: A tall iron candleholder on a tripod base, usually for two or more candles whose height could be adjusted by a spring or screw devise.

Sticking Tommy: A simple iron candleholder mounted on a horizontal spike that could be stuck into a beam or wall crevice. Used in mines as well as in houses.

Loom light: An iron candleholder shaped like an elongated "S" that could be hung on the top bar of a loom.

Rushlight holder: A hinged iron device for holding a rushlight at about a forty-five degree angle, at which it burnt most cleanly and efficiently.

Mequon

Elizabeth Ford Antiques
11412 N Port Washington Rd
(414)241-1070 • (414)242-4364
Hrs: By appt only.

L & L Antiques
10620 W Freistadt Rd
(414)242-5226

Pre-1920s furniture refinished & unfinished.
Hrs: Sat 10-5 or by chance.

Merrill

Aunt Lu's Antiques
923 E Main St
(715)539-3337 • (715)536-3785
auntlus923@aol.com

A complete line of quality antiques.
Depression glass, furniture, glassware & all
types of collectibles for the discriminating
antique shopper. **Pr:** $1-2,000 **Hrs:** May 2-
Sep 27 Fri-Sat 9-4, Sun 10-4. **Sz:** M **Own:**
Dennis & LuAnn Grefe. **QC:** 48 32 1 S12

Merton

The Golden Swan / Mother Hubbard's Cupboard
7148 Main St
(414)538-1550 • (414)538-2650 (fax)

150-year-old general store building with a
great selection of antique furniture, garden
antiques & store fixtures. **Pr:** $5-5,000 **Est:**
1978 **Hrs:** Mon-Fri 10-5:30 (Thu til 8), Sat
10-5, Sun 11-4. **Sz:** L **CC:** AX/V/MC/DIS
Dir: I-94 exit Rte 83 N to VV (E) to Merton.
Own: Don & Joan Boche. **QC:** 58 55 60

Middleton

Middleton Antique Mall [G75]
1819 Parmenter St
(608)831-5515

Located in Middleton's first commercial
building (c 1856) & filled with the area's top
antique dealers. Shop with confidence where
everything is pre-1950. No reproductions,
no crafts. **Pr:** $5-5,000 **Est:** 1998 **Hrs:** Mon-
Fri 10-7, Sat 10-5, Sun 12-5. **Sz:** L **CC:**
V/MC/DIS **Dir:** On Madison's W side, 2
blks off University Ave on Parmenter St in
Middleton. **Own:** Jane & Jim Geving. **QC:**
34 48 1 S8 S12 S19

Milton

Campus Antiques Mall [G]
609 Campus St
(608)868-3324

Hrs: Mon-Sat 10-5, Sun 12-5.

Goodrich Hall Antiques
501 College St
(608)868-2470

Hrs: Tue-Sat 10-5, Sun 12-5.

Milton Collectibles Mall [G]
209 Parkview Dr
(608)868-7595

Hrs: Mon-Sat 10-5, Wed 1-5, Sun 12-5.

Whitford Hall Antiques
525 College St
(608)868-4939

Hrs: Mon-Sat 10-5, Sun 12-5.

Milwaukee

American Estates
2131 S Kinnickinnic Ave
(414)483-2110

Paper, sheet music, old catalogs. **Hrs:** Daily
9-5.

Ameri-Victorian Lights of Olde
203 N Water St
(414)223-1130

Large inventory of quality Victorian lighting
& fixtures, painted & stained glass lamps,
including Tiffany, Handel, bedroom sets,

armoires, desks. Residential & commercial dealers welcome. **Hrs:** Mon-Sat 11-5. **QC: 65**

Antique Center Walker's Point [G48]

1134 S 1st St
(414)383-0655

Antiques & collectibles as well as vintage clothing. In the heart of the historic Walker's Point area. **Hrs:** Mon & Wed-Sat 10-5, Sun 12-5.

Antiques by Loraine

4520 W Burleigh St
(414)445-7080

Hrs: Mon-Fri 1-6.

Peter Bentz Antiques & Appraisers

771 N Jefferson St
(414)271-8866

Silver, jewelry & fine art. **Hrs:** By chance/appt. **QC: S1**

Calico Cat Antiques

3056 S Delaware Ave
(414)481-1522

American furniture, turn of the century: oak, walnut, Victorian & fine country investment pieces: cherry, butternut, walnut, pine & maple. Professional restoration available. **Hrs:** Mon-Sat 9-5, call ahead advised. **Assn:** WADA. **QC: 50 58 34 S16**

Centuries Antiques

326 N Water St
(414)278-1111

Fine antiques, furniture, paintings, glass, china, pottery, silver, books, rugs & more. **Hrs:** Fri-Mon 11-5.

Clinton Street Antiques

1110 S 1st St
(414)647-1773

Furniture, primitives, advertising, collectibles & curiosities. **Hrs:** Wed-Mon 11-5 (Mon by appt only).

D & R International Antiques Ltd

137 E Wells St
(414)276-9395 • (414)276-9755 (fax)
drintlantiques@execpc.com
www.antiqnet.com/drintl

An exceptional selection of 18th & 19th C European & American furniture, clocks & fine art. Also porcelain, lighting & unique decorative accessories. Expert in French antiques with 25 years experience in Paris. No reproductions. **Est:** 1966 **Hrs:** Wed-Sat 11-5. **Sz:** L **Assn:** WADA NAWCC **Dir:** I-94 to I-794E to Plankinton Ave. Turn L (N) 3 blks to Wells St, then R (E) over the Milwaukee River. Shop at E end of 1st bldg on R across from Pabst Theater. **Own:** Darlene & Ratko Pavlovic. **QC: 47 35 7 S12**

Echol's Antiques & Gifts

6230 W North Ave
(414)774-5556

Glassware, porcelain, metalware & furniture. **Hrs:** Tue-Fri 10-5, Sat 9-3. **CC:** V/MC/DIS. **QC: 48 61**

Eileen's Warehouse Antiques

325 N Plankinton Ave
(414)276-0114

Furniture, antiques, collectibles & curios. **Hrs:** Wed-Mon 11-5 (closed Tue).

Fifth Avenue Antiques

422 N 5th St
(414)271-3355

Quality furniture & collectibles. Refinishing & delivery. **Hrs:** Mon-Tue & Fri-Sat 10-5, Wed 10-9, Sun 12-5. **Dir:** Across from Amtrak.

Gallery of Antiques

1005 S 60th St
(414)771-9166
(800)522-9166

Victorian & oak furniture, period furnishings, lamps & pottery. **Hrs:** Mon-Fri 8-5, Sat 10-4 or by appt. **Dir:** Corner of 60th & Mineral St. **QC: 58 50**

Grace Graves' Haviland Matching Service Ltd

219 N Milwaukee St
(414)291-9111 • (414)291-9018 (fax)
hmsgraves@aol.com

Specialists in identifying & seeking replacement pieces for Haviland china (French & American). Complete sets, single pieces, collector items available. Mail order. **Pr:** $12-2,000 **Est:** 1980 **Hrs:** By chance/appt. **Sz:** S **CC:** V/MC **Assn:** WADA **Dir:** Just off Rte 43 N & I-794 E. **QC: 23 23 S9 S18**

Susan Kruger Antiques

401 Madison St
(414)542-7722
Hrs: Tue-Fri 12-5, Sat 10-5.

Lights of Olde

203 N Water St
(414)223-1130

Victorian furniture. **Hrs:** Mon-Sat 11-5.

Milwaukee Antique Center [G75+]

341 N Milwaukee St
(414)276-0605

Wisconsin's oldest antique mall. Everything from quality to knick-knacks. **Est:** 1974 **Hrs:** Mon-Fri 11-5, Sat 10-5, Sun 12-5; Jul-Aug Mon-Fri 10-5.

Usual & Unusual Antiques

1134 S 1st St
(414)383-3559

General line & architectural antiques. **Hrs:** Mon & Wed-Sat 10-5, Sun 11-5.

Water Street Antique Market Inc [G]

318 N Water St
(414)278-7008

Fine furniture & showcased smalls. Art Deco, country jewelry, dolls, books, Victoriana. **Hrs:** Mon-Sat 11-5, Sun 12-5. **Assn:** WADA **Own:** Kevin Travis.

Wishful Things

207 E Buffalo St
(414)765-1117 • 765-0785 (fax)
luvglass@mail.execpc.com
www.bmark.com/wishfulthings.antiques/

Specializing in art glass, from antique to contemporary. American glass, featuring Tiffany, Steuben, Hawkes, Quezal, Durand, Mt. Washington, New England, Hobbs, Consolidated, and Phoenix. **Hrs:** Mon-Fri 9-5, Sat-Sun by chance/appt. **Own:** Fred & Jo Wishnie. **QC: 61**

Mineral Point

The Foundry Books

105 Commerce St
(608)987-4363 • (608)987-3627 (fax)
connors@foundrybooks.com
www.foundrybooks.com

General antiquarian & out-of-print bookstore emphasizing Wisconsin history, maps, documents & literature. **Pr:** $5-3,000 **Est:**

1995 **Hrs:** Apr-Oct daily 12-6; Nov-Mar Fri-Sun 12-6 or by chance/appt. **Sz:** S **CC:** V/MC/DIS **Dir:** 40 mi SW of Madison on Hwy 151. **Own:** Dean Connors. **QC: 1 66 74**

Green Lantern Antiques
261 High Street
(608)987-2312
glantiques@aol.com

Private shop in historic building with large selection of English pottery, oil lamps, Doulton, Victorian glassware, parlor furniture, paintings & quality smalls. Handicap accessible. **Pr:** $5-3,000 **Hrs:** Apr-Nov Wed-Sun; Dec-Mar Fri-Sat only. Call for off-hour shopping year-round. **Sz:** M **CC:** AX/V/MC/DIS **Assn:** WADA **Dir:** Rte 151 between Madison, WI & Dubuque, IA, in downtown historic district. **Own:** Frank H Jett & Eric Bailey. **QC: 23 89 65 S1 S12**

Jail Alley House Antiques
111 Jail Alley
(608)987-2029

Art pottery, furniture, glassware & tramp art. **Hrs:** Daily 10-5.

Livery Antiques [G15]
303 Commerce St
(608)987-3833

Antiques from the ages to the 1950s, in the rough or ready to use. **Pr:** $10-2,000 **Est:** 1990 **Hrs:** Apr-Oct daily 10-5. **Sz:** L **CC:** V/MC **Dir:** 15 mi S of House on the Rock & Governor Dodge State Park. **Own:** Dan Darrow. **QC: 34 55 1**

Paper Mountain Books
114 High St
(608)987-2320

Ridnour's Antiques
14 Fountain St
(608)987-3317 • (608)987-2999
ridnour@mhtc.net

American & English country furniture & related accessories. Garden & architectural items. Textiles, sewing, buttons, bottles, paper ephemera. Wholesale warehouse by appt only. **Est:** 1974 **Hrs:** May-Oct Mon-Sat 10-5, Sun 12-4; Nov-Apr by appt only. Call ahead strongly advised. **Sz:** M **CC:** V/MC/DIS **Assn:** WADA **Dir:** Midway between Madison & Dubuque, IA, on Hwy 151. Located in downtown historic district. **Own:** Glen & Harriet Ridnour. **QC: 55 34 60**

Minocqua

Attic Antiques [G]
415 Oneida St
(715)358-5022
(800)639-9928

Antiques & collectibles. **Hrs:** Daily exc Xmas. **Dir:** Downtown.

Finders Keepers
Hwy 70 W
(715)356-7208

Hrs: Mon-Sat 10-4:30, Sun by chance.

Island City Antique Market [G]
8661 Hwy 51 N
(715)356-7003

Northern Wisconsin's largest display of authentic antiques & collectibles. **Pr:** $1-3,000 **Est:** 1990 **Hrs:** Mon-Sat 10-5, Sun 11-3. **Sz:** L **CC:** V/MC **Dir:** On Hwy 51 in Minocqua, between Paul Bunyan's & McDonald's.

Stoney Creek Gardens & Antiques
Hwy 51
(715)358-7090 • (715)356-7311
(715)356-4216 (fax)
ptsinc@newnorth.net

Area's largest garden center with antique room & a special selection of antiques planted with flowers. **Pr:** $1-1,200 **Hrs:** May-Oct 15 Mon-Sat 8-6, Sun 9-4. **Sz:** S **CC:** V/MC **Dir:** 2 mi S of the Minocqua Bridge on Hwy 51.

Monroe

Bev's Attic Treasures
1018 17th Ave
(608)325-6200
Hrs: Fri 10-5.

Garden Gate Floral & Antiques
1717 11th St
(608)329-4900
(800)701-4985
Hrs: Mon-Sat 8:30-5:30.

It's a "Bunch of Crock" Antiques & Collectibles
1027 16th Ave
(608)328-1444

General line of antiques, furniture, Carnival glass & Depression glass in two large rooms. **Pr:** $5-1,000 **Est:** 1989 **Hrs:** Tue-Sat 10-4, Sun 12-4. **Sz:** M **CC:** V/MC/DIS **Dir:** 40 mi SW of Madison, WI; 1 hr NW of Rockford, IL; 2 hrs from Chicago. On Monroe's Historic Square. **Own:** Larry Cerutti & Charles Angotti. **QC: 34 32**

Monroe Antiques Mall [G30+]
1003 16th Ave
(608)328-8000

General line of antiques & collectibles with a wide range of merchandise on two floors. Roseville, Carnival glass, Depression glass. Two floors. **Pr:** $1-1,000 **Est:** 1996 **Hrs:** Tue-Fri 10-5, Sat 10-4, Sun 12-4. **Sz:** L **CC:** V/MC/DIS **Dir:** On Monroe's historic square. 40 mi SW of Madison, WI; 1 hr NW of Rockford, IL; 2 hr from Chicago & Milwaukee. **Own:** Larry Cerutti & Charles Angotti. **QC: 2 52 32**

New Moon Antiques
1606 11th St
(608)325-9100 • (608)325-9700
newmoon@inwave.com
www.inwave.com/~newmoon

Come see what a real antique shop looks like. A family-owned business in business for 25 years. Two large floors full of quality antiques as well as a warehouse full of treasures 1 blk away. **Pr:** $1-5,000 **Est:** 1985 **Hrs:** Mon-Fri 9-5, Sat 10-4. **Sz:** L **Assn:** ANA **Dir:** On Monroe's historic Courthouse Square. **Own:** David Letta & Steve Moon. **QC: 33 50 58 S1 S9 S12**

Mt Horeb

First Street Antiques [G25+]
111 S First St
(608)437-6767 • (608)437-5850

Best prices in town & a friendly atmosphere, with a "rough room" for do-it-yourself projects. **Pr:** $1-3,000 **Est:** 1995 **Hrs:** Mon-Sat 10-5, Sun 11-5. **Sz:** L **CC:** V/MC **Dir:** Main St to First St. Across from the Post Office. **Own:** Fred & Mary Smith. **QC: 32 48 S10 S4 S1**

Hoff Mall Antique Center [G30]
101 E Main St
(608)437-4580

A show & sale everyday in the restored A Hoff Building. Quality in quantity. **Pr:** $5-15,000 **Est:** 1987 **Hrs:** Mon-Sat 10-5:30, Sun 11-5. **CC:** V/MC/DIS **Dir:** 20 mi W of Madison, WI. **Own:** Barbara & Bill Crawford.

Isaac's Antiques [G30]
132 E Main St
(608)437-6151

Three floors with a general line in the historic theater building. **Est:** 1995 **Hrs:** Mon-Sat 10-5, Sun 11-5. **Sz:** L **CC:** V/DIS **QC:** 34 31 24 S12

Lucy's Attic [G]
528 Springdale St
(608)437-6140 • (608)437-6140 (fax)

At the gateway to the troll capital. A variety of antiques & collectibles. **Hrs:** Daily.

Main Street Antiques [G20]
126 E Main St
(608)437-3233 • (608)223-0782
jplambeck@aol.com

Quality range of furniture and smalls from 19th C furniture, china, glass & silver to early 1900s vintage clothes & jewelry. Our dealers find wonderful things of many different persuasions & change their inventory frequently. **Pr:** $1-2,000 **Est:** 1988 **Hrs:** Mon-Sat 10-5, Sun 11-5. **Sz:** L **CC:** AX/V/MC **Dir:** 20 min W of Madison, WI, on Rtes 18-151. **Own:** Judy Plambeck. **QC:** 34 22 64

Yapp's Antique Corner
504 E Main St
(608)437-8100
Hrs: Daily 10-5.

Mukwonago
Country Junction
101 N Rochester
(414)363-9474
Hrs: Tue-Sat 10-5, Sun 12-4.

Root Cellar Antiques
103-B N Rochester St
(414)363-4230
Hrs: Tue-Sat 10-5, Sun 12-4.

Wagner's Antiques
213 Jefferson St
(414)363-3924

Oak & country furniture & appropriate accessories. Restoration. **Hrs:** By chance/appt. **Assn:** WADA. **QC:** 50 S16

Nashotah
Pam Ewig Antiques
(414)367-8027

19th C American furniture & accessories. **Hrs:** By appt only. **Assn:** WADA **Own:** Pam & Bob Ewig. **QC:** 52

Necedah
Northland Collectors Mart
211 Main St
(608)565-3730

Glassware, primitives, furniture & collectibles. **Hrs:** Apr-Sep Mon-Sat 10-5,

Sun 11-4; Oct-Dec Mon-Sat 10-4, Sun 11-4; Jan-Mar Thu-Sat 10-4, Sun 11-4. **QC: 61 48 32**

Neillsville

Olde Hotel Antique Shoppe & Mall [G15]
105 W 7th St
(715)743-6757 • (715)743-3001
elmhorst@badger.tds.net

Wide selection of antiques, collectibles & gifts including linens, lace, buttons, Depression glass & furniture. **Pr:** $5-500 **Est:** 1991 **Hrs:** Mon-Fri 10-5, Sat 10-4. **Sz:** M **CC:** V/MC/DIS **Dir:** I-94 to Rte 10 to Neillsville. L at light onto Hwy 73 downtown. **Own:** Virginia Elmhorst. **QC: 87 63 81 S1 S8 S12**

New Berlin

Early Times Antiques
6280 S Racine Pl
(414)679-0046

Refinished furniture & country accessories. **Hrs:** By appt only. **Assn:** WADA **Own:** Paul & Kathleen Martin. **QC: 34**

New Lisbon

Red Oaks Antiques
N5710 Hwy 12-16
(608)562-3420

Hrs: By chance/appt. **Dir:** 3-1/2 mi E of New Libson on Hwy 12-16 between Oakdale & Camp Douglas. **Own:** Anita Lowe.

Niagara

Niagara Emporium
1049 Main St
(715)251-4190

Antiques from Wisconsin's Northwoods. Primitives & lodge décor at reasonable prices. **Pr:** $2-2,000 **Est:** 1988 **Hrs:** Daily 10-9. **Sz:** M **CC:** V/MC/DIS **Dir:** 100 mi N of Green Bay, WI, on Hwy 141. **Own:** Ray & Diane Soderberg. **QC: 34 79 86**

North Freedom

A to Z Antiques
E9243 State Hwy 136
(608)522-4945

General line & furniture on 2 levels in a 100-

Drinking Glasses II

Dram glass: A short drinking glass for strong drink, whose conical bowl often had a solid lower part.

Sham dram: A dram glass with a bowl that looks as though it holds more than it does. Often used by innkeepers who had to drink with each customer but also remain competent through a long evening.

Toastmaster glass: A finer version of the sham dram designed to ensure that the final toast was (almost) as clearly articulated as the first.

Rummer: A general name for a large, stemmed glass, usually with the rim narrower than the bowl. Used mainly in taverns.

Toddy rummer: The largest of all 18th century glasses, often with a finely engraved bowl, used for drinking hot toddy.

Toddy: A drink made with liquor and hot water, often sweetened and spiced with cloves. Well suited to a New England winter.

year-old barn. **Hrs:** Daily early spring to late fall. **Dir:** 5 mi W of Baraboo, 1-1/2 mi N of N Freedom Railroad Museum. **Own:** Allegra & Albert Zick.

Oconomowoc

Country Echoes Antiques
7706 Brown St
(414)474-7555

Hrs: Wed-Sat 10:30-4:30. **Dir:** 4 mi N of Hwy 16 on Hwy P or 1 mi S of Mapleton.

Curious Antiquities
169 E Wisconsin Ave
(414)567-8280 • (414)567-4320 (fax)
(888)567-8281

Art & artifacts: original Audubon prints, 19th C Japanese woodblocks, Egyptian jewelry & artifacts, Roman coins & artifacts, shipwreck coins, pre-Columbian artifacts, 19th C Congolese weaponry, armor & swords, Civil War prints, maps. **Hrs:** Mon-Wed 10-5:30, Thu-Fri 10-7, Sat 10-5, Sun 11-3. **Dir:** Hwy 16 to Wisconsin Ave. In the Old Theatre Mall. **QC:** 2 74 33

Killer Antiques
173 E Wisconsin Ave
(414)567-8280

Large furniture from castles & manor houses from Europe. **Hrs:** Mon-Wed 10-5:30, Thu-Fri 10-7, Sat 10-5, Sun 11-3. **Dir:** Downtown, just E of the Old Theatre Mall. **QC:** 48

Mapleton Antiques
8755 Brown St
(414)474-4514

Hrs: Daily 10-5. **Dir:** E of Oconomowoc on Hwy P (Brown St) 5 mi N of Mapleton.

Marsh Hill Ltd
456 N Waterville Rd
(414)646-2560

Flow blue, Staffordshire, candlesticks. **Hrs:** Thu-Sun 12-5 (May to Xmas) by appt.

Parasol Antiques
1014 Lake Country Ct
(414)569-2910

Victorian figural silverplate hollowware & napkin rings. **Hrs:** By appt only. **Assn:** WADA **Own:** Carmen Slater. **QC:** 78

Osceola

Osceola Antiques [G20]
117 Cascade St
(715)294-2886
(888)294-2889
oscantiq@centuryinter.net
www.vistawave.com/antiques/

NW Wisconsin's largest antique shop & exclusive gift shop. General line of antiques plus furniture & home hardware, custom framing, light fixtures, over 1000 books on antiques & an ice cream, candy & cappuccino parlor. **Pr:** $1-5,000 **Est:** 1992 **Hrs:** Mon-Sat 10-5, Sun 11-5. **Sz:** H **CC:** V/MC/DIS **Dir:** 19 mi N of Stillwater, MN, on WI Hwy 35. **Own:** Jeff Reardon. **QC:** 3 19 32 S13 S10 S12

Oshkosh

Originals Antique Mall [G100]
1475 S Washburn
(920)235-0495

Hrs: Daily 10-6. **Sz:** H **CC:** V/MC/DIS/AX.

Wagon Wheel Antiques
2326 Oregon St
(414)233-8518

Antiques & collectibles. **Hrs:** Mon-Fri 8-5.

Osseo

Gilbertson & Gilbertson
W11822 Hawkweed Ln
(715)597-2269 • (715)597-3398 (fax)
gilberts@win.bright.net

Specialists in early American country antiques, especially items in as-found condition & items with untampered surfaces. Specialties include folk art, furniture & small utilitarian objects. **Pr:** $10-3,000 **Est:** 1987 **Hrs:** By appt only. **Sz:** M **Assn:** WADA **Dir:** 5 mi SE of Osseo. **Own:** Donald & Eric Gilbertson. **QC: 1 41 51 S1**

Many Little Things Mall
216 W 7th St
(715)597-2879

Glass, toys, primitives, books, china, furniture, kitchenware, crafts, stained glass. **Hrs:** Mon-Sat 10-5, Sun 11-4.

Pardeeville

The Mansion
106 N Main St
(608)429-3441

Antiques & collectibles in a restored Victorian house. Quality furniture, glassware, silver, linens, jewelry, baskets, pictures, mirrors. **Hrs:** Thu-Sat 9-4 (closed Jan). **Own:** Lucille Wopat.

Pembine

Woodsong Gallery [G70]
N18360 Hwy 141
(715)324-6482

The area's best selection of northwoods fine art, locally made handcrafts, antiques of all kinds, gifts & collectibles. **Pr:** $1-2,500 **Est:** 1994 **Hrs:** Daily 9-6. **Sz:** L **CC:** AX/V/MC/DIS **Dir:** At Hwy 141 & Hwy 8. **Own:** Steve & Bobbi Felder. **QC: 59 32 S19**

Pewaukee

Old Lynndale Farm
N47 W28270 Lynndale Rd
(414)369-0350

Folk art & antiques. **Hrs:** Mon-Fri 10-5:30, Sat 10-4, Sun 12-4. **Dir:** Hwy 16 exit 184 (Jungbluth Rd): N on KE 1 blk, then JK (Lynndale Rd) E to barns 1/2 mi.

Plover

Mall Antiques & Collectibles [G]
Hwy 51 & County Rd B
(715)341-7980

Hrs: Daily. **Sz:** H **Dir:** In Plover Mall at corner Hwys 51 & County Rd B (exit 153 off Hwy 51).

Village Vendor
3010 Wilson Ave
(715)341-8822

Antiques, collectibles, vintage things & gifts. **Hrs:** Tue-Sat 10-5.

Plymouth

Back from the Past Antiques
107 E Mill St
(920)893-5658

Hrs: Mon-Sat 10-4.

Hub City Antique Mall [G47]
127 E Mill St
(920)893-9719

Hrs: Mon-Sat 9-5, Sun 12-5. **CC:** V/MC.

Jewels by Jeanne
N7448 County Rd J
(920)876-2643

Specializing in antique jewelry, glass & china. **Hrs:** By appt only. **Assn:** WADA **Own:** Jeanne Petermann. **QC: 64 61**

Timekeepers Clocks & Antiques
11 Stafford St
(920)892-TIME

Specializing in clocks & watches with a large selection of furniture, art pottery, fountain pens, coins & currency & vintage jewelry as well as a general line. In-house clock & watch repair. **Hrs:** Daily 10-5. **Sz:** L **CC:** V/MC/DIS **Own:** Bob & Barbara Lardon. **QC: 35 48 22 S7**

Port Washington

Port Antiques
314 N Franklin
(414)284-5520
Hrs: Daily 10-5. **Own:** Mike & Joan Stiever.

Portage

Antique Mall & Strip-It Shoppe [G]
114 W Cook St
(608)742-1640
www.portageantiques.com
Full-service mall featuring furniture stripping, refinishing, repairs, upholstery & replacement hardware. **Hrs:** Mon-Fri 9-5:30, Sat 9-5, Sun 11-4. **Dir:** 35 min from Madison, 10 min from I-90/94 at intersection of Hwys 33, 51 & 16. **QC: S16**

Duck Creek Antiques
N6510 Hwy 51 S
(608)742-8885
Hrs: Mon-Wed, Fri & Sat 9-5:30, Thu 9-8, Sun 11-4. **Dir:** 3 mi S of downtown on Hwy 51.

Maloney's Antique Shop
127-1/2 W Cook
(608)742-3133
Hrs: Mon-Sat 10-4 (call ahead advised). **Dir:** Upstairs.

Poynette

Seward's Folly
Seward & Main Sts
(608)635-4785
A quaint 19th C barn featuring quality country antiques, toys & holiday items. **Hrs:** Mon-Fri 11-5, Sat 9-5. **Own:** Jerry & Lois Brockel.

Prescott

Boardwalk Antiques
202 Broad St N
(715)262-0019
Hrs: Call for hours.

Cellar Antiques
215 Broad St
(715)262-3559
Specializing in furniture & pottery but have a good selection of antiques including lighting & primitives. **Pr:** $1-1,200 **Est:** 1989 **Hrs:** Sat 11-5, Sun 12-5. **Sz:** M **Dir:** Located in Western WI, 30 min from Mpls/St Paul. In the "cellar" of Cobblestone Gifts. **Own:** Mia Monteith & Diane Hoyse. **QC: 50 60 65 S4 S6 S16**

Prescott Antique Mall [G22]
213 N Broad St
(715)262-3426
Antiques, collectibles, furniture, primitives. **Hrs:** Daily from 10:00.

River Bank Antiques [G10]
220 Broad St N
(715)262-4279
Hrs: Mon-Sat 10-5, Sun 11-5.

Princeton

Melchert's Antiques
605 S Fulton St
(920)295-4243
Hrs: Daily 10-5.

River City Antique Mall [G54]
328 S Fulton St
(920)295-3475
Hrs: Mon-Sat 10-5, Sun 12-5. **CC:** V/MC/AX.

Victorian House Antiques
330 W Water St
(920)295-4700
Specialize in furniture & refinishing. **Hrs:** Mon, Wed-Sat 10-4:30, Sun 11-4:30 (closed Tue). **CC:** V/MC.

Racine

Ace & Bubba Treasure Hunters
218 6th St
(414)633-3308
Hrs: Mon-Sat 10-5.

Avenue Antiques
1436 Washington Ave (Rte 20)
(414)637-6613
Hrs: Mon-Sat 10-4:30.

Koenig's Corner Gallery
300 Main St
(414)638-1238
Hrs: Tue-Sun 10-6.

The Manor on Taylor Antique Mall [G]
1913 Taylor Ave
(414)634-0483
Hrs: Tue-Sat 10-5, Sun 11-4. **CC:** V/MC **Own:** Tom & Joan Trimberger.

Racine Antique Mall [G]
310 S Main St
(414)633-9229
boheme48@rocketmail.com
Austrian, German & Czechoslovakian furniture from Biedermeir to Art Deco, Czech art glass, pottery, perfume bottles & jewelry. **Hrs:** Mon-Sat 11-5. **QC: 53**

Red Lighthouse Antiques
1402 Washington Ave (Rte 20)
(414)637-6091
Hrs: Mon-Sat 12-5.

Travel through Time Antiques
1859 Taylor Ave
(414)637-7721
Furniture & primitives. **Est:** 1986 **Hrs:** By chance. **Own:** Jeff Orwell.

Reedsburg

Big Store Plaza Antique Malls I-II-III [G80]
195 E Main St / 121 S Webb St
(608)524-4141 • (608)524-4141 (fax)
Three antique malls in downtown Reedsburg. Clean & well-arranged. **Pr:** $1-1,500 **Est:** 1987 **Hrs:** Mon-Sat 10-5, Sun 12-4. **Sz:** L **CC:** V/MC/DIS **Dir:** I-94 N exit Hwy 12: L on Rte 12 to Rte 33 W to Reedsburg, 10 min from I-94. **Own:** Merv & Jeanie Jaech. **QC: 48 19 S19**

Rhinelander

Second Hand Rose Antiques
1309 Lincoln St
(715)369-2626
Buying & selling a complete line of antiques & collectibles including furniture, glassware, china, pottery, silver, kitchen items, tools, toys, paper, linens, jewelry & vintage clothing. Items from 1870-1970. **Pr:** $1-2,000 **Est:** 1976 **Hrs:** May-Oct Mon-Sat 10-5, Sun 11-4; Nov-Apr Mon-Sat 10-5 by chance/appt (closed Sun). **Sz:** M **Dir:** On Bus Hwy 8 just past K-Mart. **Own:** Rosemary Shalbreek. **QC: 32 48 83 S1 S12 S8**

Richland Center

Ray's Trading Post
17251 Hwy 14
(608)536-3803

Antiques & collectibles. **Hrs:** By chance/appt. **Sz:** M **Dir:** 8 mi W of Richland Ctr. **Own:** Ray Sharp.

Valley Antiques [G30]
186 S Central Ave
(608)647-3793

Hrs: Mon-Sat 9:30-5, Sun 10-5. **CC:** V/MC.

River Falls

County Line Antiques
19 County Rd F
(715)425-9118

Hrs: Sat-Sun 9-6 or by chance.

Homestead Antiques
208 N Main St
(715)425-9522

Pictures, jewelry, linen & furniture. **Hrs:** Mon-Sat 9:30-5:30. **CC:** V/MC **QC: 48 81**

Rubicon

Nancy Andrich Antiques
N1455 Hwy P
(920)474-4593

American country furniture & accessories. **Hrs:** By chance/appt. **Assn:** WADA **Dir:** 4 mi N of Mapleton on Dodge County Hwy P. Watch for log house just N of Washington Rd.

Sheboygan

Sheboygan Antiques
336 Superior Ave
(414)452-6757

Hrs: Daily 10-5 (closed Sun & Thu).

Three Barns Full #2 [G6]
N7377 Hwy 42
(920)565-3050 • (920)758-2462

Large selection of formal & primitive furniture as well as a general line of antiques & collectibles. **Pr:** $2-1,500 **Est:** 1992 **Hrs:** Daily 10-5. **Sz:** H **CC:** AX/V/MC/DIS **Dir:** I-43 exit 128: 1 mi N on Hwy 42. **Own:** Al Miller. **QC: 32 34 48 S8 S12**

Candles II

Taper: A thin candle, sometimes rigid, and sometimes a thinly waxed multi-thread wick that could be coiled up. Tapers were rarely used as lighting, but rather to light candles or to melt sealing wax.

Candlebox: A long, narrow, lidded box used for storing candles horizontally. Most were made of wood or tin, but brass, pewter, and even silver ones may be found. They may be wall-hung or free-standing. Lids may be sliding or hinged. Wooden ones are usually square in section, but those made out of metal are often cylindrical.

Rushlights were the cheapest "candles" of all. They were made by soaking the pith of the cat o' nine tails reed in tallow. If short, they were burned directly in a rushlight holder, but longer ones were loosely coiled and moved up in the holder as they burned down.

Grisset: An iron implement for soaking reeds in hot tallow to make rushlights. It resembled a ladle with a long, narrow, shallow bowl.

Candlewood: A resinous pitch pine common along the New England coast. When cut and split into pieces about the size of a candle it gave a good light, but smoked and dropped a pitchy substance. For poorer households its cheapness and easy availability overcame these drawbacks, and it was widely used.

Sparta

Mill House Antiques
715 S Court St
(608)269-6493

Furniture, pictures, linens & mirrors. **Hrs:** Daily 9-5 (call advised). **QC: 48 81**

The Old Frontier Antiques
Hwy 21
(608)269-4189

Furniture, glassware & primitives. **Hrs:** Apr-Nov Tue-Sun 9-5. **Dir:** 3 mi E of Sparta or 12 mi W of Tomah, Hwy 21 between Sparta & Fort McCoy. **QC: 48 61**

Sparta Antique Mall [G25]
100 S Water St
(608)269-0789

Hrs: Mon-Sat 10-5, Sun 11-4:30.

Spring Green

Love House Antiques
316 S Winsted St
(608)588-7335

Specialize in Depression glass & a general line. **Hrs:** Daily 10-5 (closed Tue).

The Rock Step Antiques
192 S Lexington St
(608)588-2701

18th & 19th C American furniture & accessories. **Hrs:** 10-5 by chance/appt. **Assn:** WADA **Own:** Ken Weitzel. **QC: 52**

Spring Prairie

Hemenway House Antiques
State Rd 120
(414)723-2249

Furniture & glass. **Hrs:** Sat-Sun 12-5.

Springfield

Springfield Architectural Antiques
7242 Spring St
(414)248-4076

Hrs: Sat-Sun 12-5.

Stevens Point

Buckaloo's Antiques
(715)345-1846

Flow blue, fine china, cut glass, art glass, jewelry & furniture. **Hrs:** By appt only. **Assn:** WADA **Own:** Virginia Buckaloo.

The Memory Market
2224 Patch St
(715)344-2026

Antiques & collectibles. **Hrs:** Wed 5-8, Thu 12-4 & Sat 10-4. **Own:** Judy Bablitch.

Second Street Antiques
900 Second St
(715)341-8611 • (715)341-2589

General line of furniture, antiques & collectibles. **Hrs:** Fri & Sun 12-4, Sat 10-4. **Own:** Pete Kelley.

Sweet Briar
1157 Main St
(715)341-8869

Antiques, country & folk art accessories, gifts & collectibles in an early 1900s brick corner building. **Hrs:** Mon-Fri 10-8, Sat 10-4:30, Sun 12-4.

Today's Treasures & Tomorrow's Antiques
741 Second St N
(715)344-8870 • (715)341-1541

Hrs: Thu only. **Own:** Bonnie & Persy Ross.

Stone Lake

Reflections of the Past
100 Main St
(715)865-5505
rfltopast@aol.com

Eclectic selection of pottery, glassware, jewelry, miscellany & a variety of collectibles. Fair prices & friendly service with new items added every week. **Pr:** $1-500 **Est:** 1994 **Hrs:** May-Oct 11 Sun-Mon 9-3, Thu-Sat 9-5 (closed Tue-Wed). **Sz:** M **CC:** V/MC **Dir:** Hwy 70 between Spooner & Hayward. **Own:** Lorraine & Frank Benson. **QC: 22 34 32**

Stoughton

Ice House Antiques [G15]
195 E Main St
(608)873-1778

Hrs: Daily 10-5:30 (Thu til 8). **CC:** V/MC.

Stoughton Antique Mall [G60]
524 E Main St
(608)877-1330

Hrs: Daily 10-5 (Thu til 8). **CC:** V/MC.

Sturgeon Bay

Westside Antiques
22 S Madison Ave
(920)746-9038 • (920)743-8297

Real old-time storefront antique shop. China, glass, toys (esp soldiers & trains), jewelry, books, furniture, cameras, pewter, sterling, crocks, fishing, nautical, primitives, old prints, frames, postcards, license plates & tools. **Pr:** $0.25-500 **Est:** 1995 **Hrs:** May-Oct Mon-Sat 10-5; Nov-Apr Thu-Sat 10-5. **Sz:** S **Dir:** Hwy 42/57 exit Bus 42/67 into Sturgeon Bay. **Own:** Jack & Jessie Burkhardt. **QC: 34 36 87 S1 S8 S12**

Sturtevant

Antique Castle Mall [G36]
1701 SE Frontage Rd
(414)886-6001

Hrs: Daily 10-5 (closed Tue Jan-May). **Dir:** I-94 & Hwy 20.

Carridge House Antiques
9525 Durand Ave
(414)886-6678

Turn-of-the-century & oak furniture, bottles & cookie jars. **Hrs:** Tue-Sat 10-5, Sun 11-5 (closed Mon).

The Revival Antique Shop
9410 Durand Ave
(414)886-3666

An old church basement filled with treasures from the past. Furniture, glassware & a general line of collectibles. **Pr:** $2-2,000 **Est:** 1978 **Hrs:** Tue-Fri 10-2:30, Sat 11-5. **Sz:** M **Dir:** I-94 exit Hwy 11: 2 bldgs E of School Days Antique Mall **Own:** John & Chris Poorman. **QC: 48 23 34**

School Days Mall [G]
9500 Durand Ave
(414)886-1069

Hrs: Tue-Sat 10-5, Sun 12-5.

Superior

Doherty's Antiques
207 39th Ave E
(715)398-7661

Primitives, lamps & crocks. **Hrs:** Mon-Fri 8-4:30, Sat 9-1.

Superior Antique & Art Depot [G29]
933 Oakes Ave
(715)394-4611

Hrs: Daily 10-5. **Sz:** L **CC:** V/MC/DIS.

Sussex

Mindy's Antiques

N56 W22053 Silver Spring Dr
(414)246-3183 • (414)246-4128

18th & very early 19th C furniture & accessories of the period. New England & Pennsylvanian early American antiques in gallery off home. Two levels in room settings. **Pr:** $50-20,000 **Est:** 1960 **Hrs:** Thu-Sat 10-4. **Sz:** M **CC:** V/MC **Dir:** I-94 W to Rte 164 N to Silver Spring Dr E. **Own:** Betty L Mindemann. **QC: 1 41 52 S1 S9 S18**

Steeple House Antiques

N63 W23811 Main
(414)820-0487

Hrs: Mon-Sat 11-5.

Three Lakes

Dobbs House Antiques

(715)546-8141

Antiques & collectibles in a restored 125-year-old home of one of Three Lakes' most prominent former citizens. **Pr:** $9.95-995

Est: 1994 **Hrs:** May-Oct daily 10-4. **Sz:** S **CC:** V/MC **Own:** Kay Luczak. **QC: 32 48 S9 S12**

The Hodge Podge Lodge [G200]

1760 Superior St
(715)546-8141

Art, antiques & crafts. **Pr:** $0.99-999 **Est:** 1993 **Hrs:** Jun-Aug Mon-Sat 9-5, Sun 9-4; Sep-Apr Mon-Sat 10-4. **Sz:** M **CC:** V/MC **Own:** Kay Luczak. **QC: 36**

Tomah

Antique Mall of Tomah [G65]

I-94 & Hwy 21 E
(608)372-7853 • (608)372-6552 (fax)

A diversified selection of quality antiques at affordable prices for the beginner or advanced collector. Furniture, primitives, jewelry, glassware, china, crocks, toys, coins, paper, tools, books & the unusual. **Hrs:** Apr-Dec Mon-Sat 8-8, Sun 9-5; Jan-Mar daily 9-5. **Sz:** H **CC:** V/MC/DIS **Dir:** I-94 exit 143. **Own:** Carolyn Habelman. **QC: 32 48 67 S13 S19**

Oil Lamps

Betty lamps, unlike the women who used them, were cheap, smelly, and comparatively inefficient. When whale or sperm oil became available in the middle of the 18th century, the oil lamp quickly evolved. It consisted of a domed foot supporting a covered font that held one or two wicks vertically. The earliest oil lamps were made of pewter or tin, and in the 19th century glass and brass became popular. The oil lamp underwent three major improvements: the wide flat wick adjusted by a spiked wheel appeared toward the end of the 18th century. In 1783 the Argand round burner and wick was invented. It gave the brightest and steadiest light yet seen but was itself improved even further by the invention of the glass chimney. "Invention" may not be quite the right word here, for the chimney appears to have resulted from a happy accident in which one of Argand's workmen broke the bottom of a glass font he was heating, and noticed how well the flame was drawn up through hollow cylinder. History does not tell us if he got promoted or fired.

Font: The part of a lamp that holds the oil or grease.

Wick: A piece of cotton, flax, rag, or rush used to soak the oil out of the font where it can be lit.

Klock Corner
Rte 1 Box 397
(608)372-9026

Antique clock sales & repairs. **Hrs:** Sun-Fri 9-5:30, Sat 9-12 or by appt. **Dir:** 2 mi W on Hwy 21 from Hwy 12 to M North & E South. **QC: 35 S7**

Oakdale Antique Mall [G45]
151 W Woody Dr
(608)374-4700

Hrs: Daily 9-5. **Dir:** I-90-94 exit 48 (Oakdale).

Turtle Lake

Countryside Antiques
12 Hwy 8 & 63
(715)986-2737

Old stoves, Depression glass, primitives, collectibles & furniture. **Pr:** $1-2,500 **Est:** 1975 **Hrs:** Mon-Sat 9-5. **Sz:** L **CC:** V/MC **Dir:** Hwy 8 & 63, 1/4 mi W of Turtle Lake. **Own:** Ruth & Dan Michaelson. **QC: 61 34 S12 S19**

Union Grove

Storm Hall Antique Mall [G]
835 15th Ave (Hwy 11/45)
(414)878-1644

Hrs: Tue-Sat 11-5, Sun 12-5. **Sz:** L.

Viroqua

Small Ventures Antiques [G30+]
518 Walnut St
(608)637-8880

Wide selection of antiques & collectibles, Native American artifacts, hunting & fishing collectibles & primitives. **Pr:** $1-6,000 **Est:** 1997 **Hrs:** Mon-Wed & Fri-Sun 10-6, Thu 12-8. **Sz:** L **Dir:** Hwy 14/61 N from Madison, WI, to Viroqua. At 2nd light take Hwy 56 E on Decker St, then 4 blks to East Ave. Follow signs. **Own:** Robin Elkington. **QC: 48 32 79**

Wales

Christman Antiques
323 E Summit Ave
(414)968-4913

18th & 19th C furniture, accessories & art. **Hrs:** By appt only. **Assn:** WADA **Own:** Ron & Debbie Christman. **QC: 52 7 36**

Walworth

American Pioneer Antiques
108 Madison St
(414)275-9696

Hrs: Thu-Sat 10:30-5, Sun 12-5.

Bittersweet Farm
114 Madison St
(414)275-3062

Hrs: Mon-Sat 10-5, Sun 12-5.

On the Square Antique Mall [G]
109 Madison
(414)275-9858

Hrs: Mon-Sat 10-5, Sun 11-5. **Sz:** H **Dir:** Jct of Hwy 67 & 14.

Parlor & Pantry Antiques
400 Kenosha St
(414)275-6016

Hrs: Mon-Sat 10-4 (closed Tue), Sun 12-4.

Raggedy An-tiques
216 S Main St
(414)275-5866

Hrs: May-Dec Mon-Sat 10:30-5 (closed Tue & Wed), Sun 12-5; Jan-Apr Fri, Sun, Mon 10:30-4:30, Sun 12-4:30.

Van's Antiques
Hwy 14 W
(414)275-2773

Hrs: Tue-Fri 1-5, Sat & Sun 10-5.

Warrens

Gray House Treasures
403 Main St
(608)378-4516 • (608)372-5239
General line. **Hrs:** Daily 10-4. **Dir:** I-94
Warrens exit.

Washburn

The Wooden Sailor Antiques [G5]
18 W Bayfield St
(715)373-2680 • (715)373-2758
sockness@ncis.net

General line of antiques & collectibles from
furniture to glassware to advertising and
then some. We pride ourselves on reasonable prices, friendly, relaxed atmosphere &
great music. **Pr:** $1-1,000 **Est:** 1994 **Hrs:**
May 15-Oct Tue-Sat 10-5, Sun 11-6; Nov-
Dec & Mar-Apr Thu-Sat 10-5, Sun-Wed by
chance. Closed Jan-Feb. **Sz:** M **CC:** V/MC
Dir: Downtown Washburn on Hwy 13 in
the beautiful Lake Superior region of northern Wisconsin. **Own:** Peter Sockness. **QC:**
32 48 74

Waterford

Dover Pond Antiques
28016 Washington Ave
(414)534-6543

Ever-changing selection of 19th C antiques:
furniture, folk art, quilts & one-of-a-kind
things, in an 1887 timbered-ceiling barn.
Est: 1979 **Hrs:** Mar-Dec Wed-Sat, Sun by

chance; closed Jan-Feb. **Sz:** L **Dir:** On State
Hwy 20, 1-1/2 mi E of Waterford. **Own:**
Sally & Jeff Johnson. **QC:** 34 48 36

Freddy Bear's Antique Mall
2819 Beck Dr
(414)534-2327
Hrs: Daily 9:30-5.

Heavenly Haven Antique Mall [G]
318 W Main St
(414)534-4400

Glassware, furniture, primitives &
Victoriana. **Hrs:** Daily 9:30-5. **QC:** 48
61 89

Watertown

Red Apple Antiques
401 E Main St
(920)261-2326 • (920)925-3876

Fine country furniture in oak, walnut, cherry, pine & mahogany. Large diningroom
sets. **Hrs:** By appt only. **Own:** Alice & Don
Strube. **QC:** 50 48

Watertown Antiques Market [G55]
210 S Water St
(920)206-0097 • (414)544-4947
(920)262-2382 (fax)

Ever-changing assortment of fine antiques
& select collectibles attractively displayed in
a unique Old World atmosphere. Furniture,
primitives, fine art, quilts & textiles, china,
pottery, porcelain, silver, jewelry, books,
toys, advertising. **Est:** 1977 **Hrs:** Mon, Wed,
Thu 10-6, Tue & Fri 10-8, Sat 10-5, Sun 12-
5. Extended holiday hrs. **Sz:** L **CC:**
V/MC/DIS **Dir:** I-94 exit 267 (Hwy 26): 7
mi N, then R on Milwaukee St, then L on S
Water St. Between Madison & Milwaukee.
Own: Keith & Sue Johnson & Vicki Welsh.
QC: 48 22 36 S8 S10

Waukesha

Arcadian Collectibles
900 Arcadian Ave
(414)574-1201
Hrs: Wed & Fri 12-5:30, Thu 12-7, Sat 11-4.

A Dickens of a Place Antique Center [G30]
521 Wisconsin Ave
(414)542-0702

Quality furniture, primitives, china, glassware, jewelry & collectibles. Hrs: Mon-Sat 10-5, Sun 12-5. Dir: I-94 W to Waukesha (exit 295): S 6 lights, bldg straight ahead. Entrance in rear. Own: Wallace C Anderson.

The Heirloom Doll Shop
416 E Broadway
(414)544-4739
Hrs: Mon-Fri 10-6, Sat 10-5.

Just a Little Bit of Country
N4 W22496 Blue Mound Rd
(414)542-8050

Pine cupboards & tables. Hrs: Mon-Sat 10-5:30, Sun 12-5. QC: 48

Waupaca

Danes Home Antiques [G40]
301 N Main St
(715)256-0693

Opulent historic setting — three floors full. Emphasis on quality furniture & lighting. Pr: $20-10,000 Est: 1993 Hrs: Mon-Tue & Thu-Sat 10-5, Sun 10-4 (closed Wed). Sz: H CC: V/MC/DIS Dir: Midway between Stevens Point & Appleton. Hwy 10 Waupaca exit. Own: R Morin & T Hoffman. QC: 65 50 58

Grey Dove Antiques
118 S Main St
(715)258-0777
Hrs: Mon-Sat 10-5, Sun 11-5.

Halfway House Antiques
1426 Rural Rd
(715)258-4234

Furniture & primitives. Hrs: Daily 10-5. Dir: Hwy 22 R onto Rural Rd in the historic village. QC: 58

Walker's Barn
E 1268 Cleghorn Rd
(715)258-5235
walkers@pitnet.net

A wonderful mixture of antiques, oak reproduction tables, chairs, curios & hutches, Amish furniture & crafts, German clocks & beer steins, collectibles & consignment & handcrafted pieces. Pr: $1-3,000 Est: 1975 Hrs: Jun-Sep 15 Mon-Sat 10-5, Sun 12-5; Sep 16-May Tue-Sat 10-5, Sun 12-5. Sz: L CC: V/MC/DIS Dir: Hwy 10 to Waupaca exit (Hwy 22S & K). S on Hwy 22 4 mi to Cleghorn Rd, then W 1/2 blk. Own: Linda & Bob Yerkes. QC: 34 56 S8 S16

Waupun

Blue Heron Antiques
425 E Main St
(920)324-9880

Furniture, glassware, jewelry. Hrs: Mon-Sat 10-5, Sun 12-5. CC: V/MC.

Little Bit of Everything Antique Mall [G20]
24 E Main St
(920)324-5502
Hrs: Daily 10-5.

Wausau

Ginny's Antiques
416 3rd St
(715)848-1912

Pr: $5-3,800 Est: 1990 Hrs: Mon-Fri 11-5, Sat 11-4. Sz: L CC: V/MC Assn: WADA Dir: Hwy 51N exit 193: R on Bridge St, R on 5th St, R on Jefferson St, R on 3rd St

1/2 blk. **Own:** Virginia Romanski. **QC: 1 7 36 S1 S7 S8**

Rib Mountain Antique Mall [G68]
3300 Eagle Ave
(715)848-5564
Hrs: Mon-Sat 10-5, Sun 12-5.

Wautoma

Silver Lake Antique Mall
Hwy 21/73 E
(920)787-1325
Furniture. **Hrs:** Daily. **QC: 48**

West Salem

Historic Salem
99 E Jefferson
(608)786-1675 • (608)786-1666

A general offering of antiques & collectibles as well as used books (hardcover & paperback). **Pr:** $1-850 **Est:** 1986 **Hrs:** Mon-Fri 8-6, Sat 9-5, Sun 9-5. **Dir:** I-90 to County Trunk B. L 3 blks, shop on L. **Own:** Errol R Kindschy. **QC: 18 48 32 S1 S8**

Westby

Country Collectables [G4]
105 S Main St
(608)634-3955

Furniture, glassware, pottery, dolls, toys, primitives, textiles, clocks, baskets, tools, Indian & Norwegian antiques. **Est:** 1986 **Hrs:** Mon-Sat 9-5, Sun 10-4. **Sz:** L **CC:** V/MC/DIS **Assn:** WCWADA **Dir:** I-90

exit 25: Turn R off exit onto Sparta Hwy (Rte 27S) 24 mi. From La Crosse, 29 mi SE on Hwy 14/61/27 S. **Own:** Alden & Ellin Solberg. **QC: 31 38 42**

Wilmot

The Country Cottage
30714 112th St
(414)862-9833 • (414)862-2234
Hrs: May-Nov: Fri 1-5, Sat-Sun 11-4:30.

Mary's on Main Antiques
Main St
(414)862-9694 • (414)862-2234
Hrs: Apr-Dec: Fri 1-5, Sat 10-5, Sun 11-5; Dec-Mar: Sat 10-4, Sun 11-4, or by chance/appt.

Wilmot Heritage Antiques
11340 Fox River Rd
(414)862-9290

Glassware (Depression, Heisey, Fostoria & Fenton), furniture, books & kitchenware. **Hrs:** Fri 1-5, Sat-Sun 10-5. **QC: 61 48 18**

Ye Possibility Shoppe Inc
11215 Fox River Rd
(414)862-6535
Hrs: Wed-Sun 10-5.

Wisconsin Dells

Antique Mall of Wisconsin Dells [G65+]
1730 Oak St
(608)254-2422
Hrs: Daily 10-5.

Use the Specialty QuickCode indexes at the back of the book to find dealers who specialize in your area of interest.

Antique Mall of Wisconsin Dells II [G250+]

Hwy 12
(608)254-2422

Hrs: Daily 10-8. **Dir:** I-94 exit 82.

Days Gone By Antique Mall [G65+]

729 Oak St
(608)254-6788

Hrs: Daily 10-5 (til 9 in Sum). **CC:** V/MC/DIS.

Old Settlers Antique Shop

W12778 Hwy 16
(608)742-6416

Advertising, gas pumps, toys, lamps & furniture. **Hrs:** May-Sep Sat-Sun 12-6 or by appt. **Dir:** Between Wisconsin Dells & Portage on Hwy 16. **Own:** Karl & Linda Heckel. **QC:** **48 39 87**

Part II

Services and Related Information

Service Providers

Appraisers

Frederick Dosé Appraisals Ltd
778 Pleasant Ave
Highland Park, IL
(847)433-1090

Insurance, estate, divorce, donation appraisals of fine art, antiques, furniture & decorative arts. Expert witness testimony. Former art history faculty at Colgate University. Call for consultation. References. Published author. **Hrs:** By appt only. **Assn:** ISA, CAA, FHSL, AIA **Own:** Frederick P Dosé Jr. **QC: 7 48 78 S1 S9**

Galerie St James
1037 South Boulevard
Oak Park, IL
(708)386-5319 • (708)386-1566 (fax)
Est: 1961 **Hrs:** Daily 9-5. **CC:** AX/V/MC/DIS **Assn:** NAA **Dir:** A short distance off the Eisenhower Expressway at the Harlem Ave exit. **Own:** Jim Bohenstengel. **QC: S1 S2 S12**

Hefner Antiques
Evanston, IL
(847)328-2522
plehef@aol.com

Insurance, estate & divorce appraisals; consulting, research & speaker. **Hrs:** By appt. **Own:** Patricia Hefner. **QC: S1**

Alice Kaide Appraisal Service
Mt Prospect, IL
(847)392-7307

Residential contents appraisals including antiques. **Hrs:** By appt only. **Assn:** ASA Sr member. **QC: S1**

Appraisals by Betty Kolpas
Mt Prospect, IL
(847)392-4144

Antiques, decorative arts & residential contents appraisals for estate, insurance & liquidation purposes. Also conduct estate & liquidation sales. **Hrs:** ASA Sr member. **QC: S1**

Karen S Rabe
Lake Forest, IL
(847)604-8770 • (847)356-2124 (fax)

Estate, divorce & insurance appraisals of residential contents, antiques & collectibles. Broker, consultant, claims specialist. **Hrs:** By appt only. **Assn:** ISA CAPP. **QC: S1**

Coreys Yesteryears
1250 E Wayzata Blvd
Wayzata, MN
(612)476-0009

Insurance, estate & probate appraisals. Estate sales: licensed, bonded & insured. **Hrs:** By appt. **Dir:** In the Wayzata Home Center. **QC: S1 S12**

Marrinan Appraisal Service
2176 Fairmount Ave
St Paul, MN
(612)699-4721

Appraisals of personal property. Specializing in furniture, ceramics, glass, coins, silver Orientalia & collectibles. **Assn:** AAA **Own:** James H Marrinan. **QC: S1**

North Coast Antiques & Liquidations
Strongsville, OH
(440)768-7371

Appraisals, sales & consignments. **Own:** Mary Foster Wainio. **QC: S1**

Sorting-It-Out Estate Sales
4140 Floral Ave
Cincinnati, OH
(513)932-3488 • (513)531-6712

Estate sales & personal property liquidations. **Hrs:** By appt only. **Own:** Jacquie Denny & Teresa Newberry. **QC: S12**

William Wartmann Appraisal Associates

Madison, WI
(608)255-0138 • (608)884-8414

Appraising antiques, silver, artwork & ethnographic art. **Hrs:** By appt only. **Assn:** WADA **QC: S1**

Art Restorers

Deller Conservation Services

Geneva, IL
(630)232-1708

Conservation services for the decorative arts. Surface preservation, structural stabilization, loss compensation, collection evaluation. **Hrs:** By appt only. **Own:** Craig Deller. **QC: S16**

Great Lakes Art Studio

320 N Damen
Chicago, IL
(312)226-6166

Fine art restoration: repair, fabrication, casting, patinas & fine finishes. Period hardware & lighting fixtures. Work on bronze, aluminum, steel, iron, copper, brass, pewter, silver; ceramics, plaster wood & other media. **Hrs:** By appt. **QC: S16**

Melnick Art Restoration Inc

588A Roger Williams Rd
Highland Park, IL
(847)266-9444

Oil paintings & ceramics restoration. **Hrs:** By appt only. **Own:** Bob Melnick. **QC: S16**

Old World Restorations Inc

5729 Dragon Way
Cincinnati, OH
(513)271-5459

Paintings, porcelain, pottery, frames & metals. Free estimates. **Hrs:** Mon-Fri 9-5:30, Sat 9-12. **QC: S16**

Studios of Jack Richard

2250 Front St Mall
Cuyahoga Falls, OH
(330)929-1575

Hrs: Tue-Fri 11:30-5. **QC: S16**

Steven L Rulka, Conservator

28 Cincinnati Ave
Lebanon, OH
(513)933-0541

Specializing in the restoration of porcelain, pottery, bisque, ivory; oil paintings, frames, watercolors; metal & sculpture; Russian icons; lacquerware; cloisonné. **QC: S16**

Weibold Studio Inc

413 Terrace Pl
Terrace Park, OH
(800)321-2541
www.wiebold.com

Restoration of oil paintings, frames, gold leaf, papier-mache, murals, frescoes, miniatures, silver, bronze, brass, copper, gold, ormolu, chandeliers, beveled mirrors, clocks, porcelain, art pottery, ceramics, terra cotta, cloisonné, ivory, jade & more. **QC: S16**

Yoder Conservation Inc

12702 Larchmere Blvd
Cleveland, OH
(216)231-7880

Painting conservation. **Hrs:** By appt. **Own:** Allyn Rosser. **QC: S16**

Sugarloaf Studios

W174 Lang Rd
Oconomowoc, WI
(920)474-4157 • (920)474-4135 (fax)
winkley@execpc.com

Museum-quality reproductions, antique restoration, repairs. Ceramics, wood, plaster, metals, artifacts, sculpture. **Own:** Robert C Winkley . **QC: S17 S16**

Auctioneers

Butterfield, Butterfield & Dunning
755 Church Rd
Elgin, IL
(847)741-3483

Monthly auctions. Call for schedule. **Est:** 1896 **Hrs:** By appt. **QC: S2**

Christie's Fine Art Auctioneers
200 W Superior St, Ste 406
Chicago, IL
(312)787-2765 • (312)951-7449 (fax)

Midwest office of the international auction house. **Hrs:** Mon-Fri 9:30-5:30. **QC: S2**

Direct Auction Galleries
7232 N Western Ave
Chicago, IL
(773)465-3300

Antiques & collectibles: furniture, figurines, art, silver, pottery & porcelain, glass, toys, dolls, lighting fixtures, Victorian, Deco, 50s. **CC:** AX/V/MC/DIS **QC: S2 S8**

Larry Lorenz Auction
11753 N 8000 East Rd
Grant Park, IL
(708)258-9276 • (708)258-0901 (fax)

QC: S2 S12

Gale Magnuson Auction & Appraisals
3770 Serenity Pkwy
Kankakee, IL
(815)932-0182

Hrs: By appt only. **QC: S1 S2**

New Era Auction Co
Grayslake, IL
(847)548-5922

QC: S2

John Toomey Gallery
818 North Blvd
Oak Park, IL
(708)383-5234 • (708)383-4828 (fax)

Oil paintings, prints, watercolors & pottery. Six sales annually. **QC: 7 22 S2**

American Antiques
Whiting, IN
(219)659-2617

Estate sales, appraisals & auctions. **QC: S1 S2**

Davies Auctions
Lafayette, IN
(765)449-4515

Own: Doug Davies. **QC: S2**

Golden Gavel Auctions
1905 Goodson Ct
South Bend, IN
(219)233-5229

QC: S2

Tracy Luther Auctions & Antiques
2556 E 7th St
North St Paul, MN
(612)770-6175

Auctions & estate sales. **QC: S2**

Rose Galleries Inc
2717 Lincoln Dr
Roseville, MN
(612)484-1415

Auction gallery specializing in estate & personal property including antiques, jewelry, fine home furnishings & art. **Est:** 1978 **Hrs:** Auctions every Wednesday. **QC: S2**

Blair Auctions Inc
25 Center St
Seville, OH
(330)769-3263 • (330)769-3263 (fax)

Estate sales & collections. Call for schedule. **QC: S2**

DeFina Auctions

591 St Rte 45
Austinburg, OH
(440)275-6674 • (440)275-2028 (fax)
definaauction@ncweb.com
www.definaauctions.com

Americana & fine art sale twice yearly. **Own:**
Mike DeFina. **QC: S2**

Garth's Auctions

690 Stratford Rd
Delaware, OH
(740)362-4771 • (740)548-6778
(740)363-0164 (fax)

The Midwest's leading independent auction
house. **CC:** V/MC **Dir:** Rte 23 N from
Columbus 8-9 mi to Stratford Rd. Turn R,
then L at first drive. **Own:** Auctioneers
Tom Porter, Tom King & Steve Bemiller.
See back cover of Guide. **QC: S2**

Old Barn Auction

10040 SR 224 W
Findlay, OH
(419)422-8531

Specializing in estates, households, antiques,
Indian relics, toys, guns, military, Civil War
items. **Hrs:** Mon-Fri 9-5. **QC: S2**

Clock Repair

Kerry's Clock Shop

71 N Milwaukee Ave
Wheeling, IL
(847)520-0335

Specializing in sales & repair of antique wall,
shelf & floor clocks. Located in an 1835

farmhouse at the Sale Barn Square Antique
Center. Free estimates, all work guaranteed.
Est: 1992 **Hrs:** Tue-Sat 10-5. **Sz:** S **CC:**
V/MC **Assn:** NAWCC BHI **Dir:** I-294 to
Lake Cook Rd W to Milwaukee Ave N 1/4
mi. **Own:** Kerry L Rasmussen. **QC: 35 S7**

Paul T Kwiatkowski

Grant Park, IL
(815)258-6274

Restoration of antique clocks & watches.
Hrs: By appt only. **QC: S7**

Tick-Tock

Palatine, IL
(847)991-4230
www.ticktockclock.com

Clock repairs & sales. Grandfather clocks a
specialty. **Hrs:** By appt. **Own:** Jim & Vicky
Denno. **QC: 35 S7**

Bill's Clockworks

8 W Columbia St
Flora, IN
(219)967-3056 • (219)967-4709 (fax)
(888)742-5625

Specializing in the repair & sale of antique
clocks, including cuckoo, 400 day & grandfather clocks. Owner has lifelong interest in
horology. We care for your heirloom as if it
were our own. **Pr:** $200-1895 **Est:** 1995
Hrs: Mon-Fri 9-6, Sat 9-5. **Sz:** S **CC:**
AX/V/MC/DIS **Assn:** AWI NAWCC **Dir:**
I-65 Brookston exit: 25 mi E on State Rd 18.
25 mi NE from Lafayette, IN, via State Rd
26 & State Rd 27. **Own:** William S
Stoddard. **QC: 35 S7**

Hickory Dickory Clock Gallery

132 E Main St
Madison, IN
(812)265-6113

Custom clocks & clock repair. **Own:**
Michael C LeSaux. **QC: S7**

Furniture Restorers

Alfredo Cisneros & Sons
295 E Illinois Rd
Lake Forest, IL
(847)234-7252

Upholstery, furniture, wood finishing, cane & rush, antique repair, restoration & slipcovers. **Dir:** Also at 28 Green Bay Rd, Winnetka, and 4833 W Armitage Ave, Chicago. **Own:** Carlos Cisneros. **QC: S6 S16 S22**

Elgin Refinishing
313 W Highland Ave
Elgin, IL
(847)695-1858

Furniture refinishing. **Hrs:** By appt only. **QC: S16**

Evanston Restoration
2205 Ashland Ave
Evanston, IL
(847)328-4720

Hrs: Mon-Fri 9-5. **QC: S16**

Genson's Then & Again
881 S Washington
Kankakee, IL
(815)939-9663

Furniture clinic: stripping, repair, refinishing. Mirror resilvering. **Hrs:** Mon-Fri 10-4, Sat by appt. **QC: S16**

Lloyd & Leota's Antiques & Restoration
10103 Main St
Hebron, IL
(815)648-2202

Handstripping & finishes, rushing, caning, spindles. **Hrs:** Daily 9-4:30. **QC: S16**

Wayne Co Stripping & Refinishing
10 S Main St
Greens Fork, IN
(765)886-6111
(800)298-2476

Flow-over stripping, antique furniture repair, complete restoration, custom woodworking. Antique furniture for sale. **Pr:** $5-5,000 **Hrs:** Mon-Fri 8-5, Sat 9-1. **Dir:** I-70 Exit 145 N to State Rd 38, then W 2 mi to shop. **Own:** Delayne & Shawne Land. **QC: 50 48 56 S5 S16 S17**

Hensler Furniture Restoration Inc
3100 Christy Way
Saginaw, MI
(517)792-1311 • (517)249-5291 (fax)
(888)HEN-SLER

Quality & complete furniture restoration. Carving duplication, veneer, reupholstering, bevel & bent glass duplication. Fire & water damage restoration & marble repair/replacement. **Est:** 1934 **Hrs:** Mon-Fri 10-5 (Mon til 6), Sat-Sun by appt. **Sz:** H **Assn:** SVAS AARC **Dir:** Just off M-84 in Saginaw Township. **Own:** Jerry, Brian & Scott Hensler. **QC: 48 58 59 S16 S17 S18**

Randy Bohn & Associates
Hastings, MN
(612)437-1785

Museum-quality restoration & conservation of fine antique furniture (wooden artifacts). Specializing in Old World finish & techniques. Complete conservation services to dealers, museums & private collectors nationwide. **Est:** 1979 **Hrs:** By appt only. **Assn:** AIC **QC: 52 54 56 S5 S16 S17**

Fielder Refinishing
Monroe, OH
(513)539-8595

Hand stripping, finishing & minor restoration. **Hrs:** By appt only. **Own:** Ken Fielder **QC: S16**

The Finishing Gallery
4720 N High St
Columbus, OH
(614)267-3527

Furniture restoration. **Hrs:** Tue-Fri 10-6, Sat 10-3. **QC: S16**

The Furniture Doctor
314 W Main Rd
Conneaut, OH
(440)593-4121

Victorian, oak & Depression furniture. **Hrs:** Mon-Fri 9-5, Sat 10-4 or by appt. **CC:** V/MC **QC: S16**

Old Time Treasures
141 Main St
Benton Ridge, OH
(419)859-2338

Furniture repair, refinishing, upholstery. **Hrs:** Tue, Wed, Fri 2-6; Thu 2-8; or by appt. **Own:** Nancy Diller. **QC: S22 S16**

Old Westend Antiques
518 S St Clair
Toledo, OH
(419)255-2620

Stripping & refinishing. **Hrs:** By appt only. **QC: S16**

Refinishing & Supply Co
350 Crocker Ln
Fostoria, OH
(419)435-8909

Furniture refinishing. Veneering, inlay & French polishing. **Hrs:** Mon, Tue, Thu & Fri 9-5, Wed 9-1, Sat by appt. **Own:** Jim Essman. **QC: S16**

Heide Rivchun Furniture Conservation
12702 Larchmere Blvd
Cleveland, OH
(216)231-1003

Restoration, carving & gilding, marquetry &

metal work, French polishing & cabinet work, objets d'art. **Hrs:** Tue-Fri 9-5, Sat 10-5. **QC: S16**

Swigart Refinishing Co Inc
2021 E Third St
Dayton, OH
(937)254-1141

Fine furniture restoration. Wood furniture, pianos, museum quality restorations. **Hrs:** Mon-Fri 7:30-12 & 1-4:30. **QC: S16**

Dennis Dittman / Golden Eagle Furniture Restoration
105 N Main St
Dousman, WI
(414)965-3115

Dennis Dittman provides full restoration services, stripping & mirror resilvering for museums, churches & private homes. **Est:** 1974 **Hrs:** By appt only. **QC: S16**

Metal Restorers

Al Bar-Wilmette Platers
127 Green Bay Rd
Wilmette, IL
(847)251-0187 • (847)251-0281 (fax)

Specializing in the preservation of old door & window hardware. Repair, cleaning, polishing, plating in all finishes — brass, bronze, copper, nickel & chrome. Work directly with homeowners & with architects & interior designers. **Est:** 1937 **Hrs:** Mon-Fri 8-5, Sat 8-3. **Sz:** L **CC:** V/MC **Dir:** Edens Expressway: Go E on Lake St to Green Bay Rd, then S. **Own:** Lee Bettenhausen. **QC: 3 65 78 S16 S17**

Baroque Silversmith Inc
5 N Wabash #400
Chicago, IL
(312)357-2813 • (847)677-7638

Sterling, copper, brass, pewter & silverplate repair, polish, expert gold plating; lamp repair; costume & antique jewelry repair, free estimates, free pick-up & delivery. **Est:** 1965 **Hrs:** By appt. **QC: S16**

The Bellows Shoppe Inc
1060 Gage St
Winnetka, IL
(847)446-5533

Antique light fixtures, polishing, silverplating, lamp repairs. **Hrs:** Mon-Fri 9-5, Sat 9-4. **QC: 65 S16**

Creative Brass & Metalworks
34691 Wilson Rd
Ingleside, IL
(847)740-7934

Brass & copper repair & polishing. **Hrs:** Mon-Fri 8-4. **QC: S16**

International Silver Plating
364 Park Ave
Glencoe, IL
(847)835-0705

Metal restoration including plating, repairing, refinishing, fabrication, restoration, polishing & lacquering on silver, brass, bronze, pewter, copper, gold & aluminum. **Est:** 1926 **CC:** V/MC **QC: S16**

Carr's Metal Polishing
16751 TR 173
Findlay, OH
(419)423-5779

Quality restoration of fine antique brass & copper. Also buy & sell. **Hrs:** By appt only. **Dir:** Second drive past TR 240. **QC: S16**

All-Bright Gallery
W53 N550 Highland Dr
Cedarburg, WI
(414)377-1500

Full line of metal and wood restorations. **Hrs:** Mon-Sat 10-5. **QC: S16**

Porcelain Restorers

B & B Restoration
24 W Mulberry St
Lebanon, OH
(513)934-3344
(888)716-6798

Restoration & repair of porcelain, pottery, bisque & ivory. Electric lamp repair. **Hrs:** By appt. **Own:** Bob Burk. **QC: S16**

Dunhill Antiques & Restoration
2309 Lee Rd
Cleveland Heights, OH
(216)291-1771

Porcelain restoration. **Hrs:** Mon-Sat 9-5. **S16**

Reproductions

Galleria 733
733 W Lake St
Chicago, IL
(312)382-0546 • (312)382-0548 (fax)

Specializing in high-quality handcrafted & carved pieces made to specification. Complete repair, restoration, refinishing & upholstery. Also showroom of country French, period & art deco to the trade only. **Hrs:** Mon-Fri 9-5, Sat 10-3 or by appt. **QC: S16 S17**

Doug Poe Antiques
4213W 500N
Huntington, IN
(800)348-5004

Antique reproduction hardware. **QC: S17**

Heirloom Brass Co
Dundas, MN • (507)645-4445 (fax)
(800)533-8055

Victorian, Eastlake & turn-of-the-century reproductions. Catalog. **QC: S17**

A Brass Bed Shoppe
12421 Cedar Rd
Cleveland Heights, OH
(216)371-0400 • (216)292-0026 (fax)

Reproduction solid brass & iron beds. Factory direct. Layaway & payment plans. Color catalog $2.00. **Pr:** $99-3,500 **Est:** 1977 **Hrs:** Tue-Sat 1-6. **Sz:** M **CC:** V/MC **Dir:** I-271 Exit Lyndhurst-Pepper Pike. Cedar Rd W 6 mi, on R across from Firestone Tire. **Own:** Dale J Shubert. **QC: 56 S17**

Matthew House
40 E Mulberry St
Lebanon, OH
(513)932-1956 • (513)932-1881

Period reproduction furniture & furnishings. **Hrs:** Mon-Sat 11-5:30, Sun 1-5. **QC: 56 S17**

Antiquity
715 Genesee St
Delafield, WI
(414)646-4911

Quality reproduction furniture. **Hrs:** Wed-Sat 10-5, Sun 12-5. **CC:** V/MC/DIS **Own:** Dennis & CeCe Bork. **QC: 56 S17**

Brass Light Gallery
131 S 1st St
Milwaukee, WI
(414)271-8300

Original restored antique & quality reproduction lighting for restoring a home, redecorating or building. Chandeliers, wall sconces, lamps. Traditional, Mission/Prairie, Victorian, European country. Lighting restoration. **Hrs:** Mon-Fri 10-5, Sat 10-3. **QC: 65 S16 S17**

Restorations (Other)

Player Piano Clinic & Emporium
6810 W 26th St
Berwyn, IL
(708)484-1020

Restoration & sales/service of antique player pianos, reed organs, melodeons, antique roller organs, organettes & other self-playing musical instruments. Restoration/sales of antique photographs. Fine reproduction Tiffany-style lighting. **Pr:** $3,500-20,000 **Est:** 1985 **Hrs:** Mon-Tue & Fri 11-5, Thu 11-8, Sat 10-5 (by appt only Sat Jun 1-Sep 8). **Sz:** M **CC:** AX/V/MC/DIS **Dir:** I-290 W of Chicago to Harlem Ave. Exit S on Harlem to 26th St, E 4 blks to store. I-55 S of Chicago to Harlem Ave. Exit N to 26th St, E 4 blks to store. **Own:** James K Jelinek. **QC: 69 32 36 S16 S1**

Bohnet Electric Company
2918 N Grand River Ave
Lansing, MI
(517)327-9999 • (517)327-9995 (fax)

Lamp repair & parts. Stained glass, lamp shades, lamps, ceiling fans, lighting glassware. **Est:** 1908 **Hrs:** Mon-Fri 8-5, Sat by appt. **CC:** AX/V/MC **Dir:** 3 blks W of Martin Luther King/Logan St. **QC: 65 S16**

Frances K Faile
928 W Lewiston
Ferndale, MI
(810)545-4699

Textile conservation. **QC: S16**

> Use the Service QuickCode indexes at the back of the book to find restorers, appraisers, refinishers, and other specialty service providers.

Sandor's

6689 Center Rd (Rte 303)
Valley City, OH
(330)483-4040 • (330)483-4040 (fax)

Hardware & supplies for restoration as well
as materials for caning, rush wicker & refinishing. **Hrs:** Tue-Sat 11-4, Sun 12-4. **QC:
S16**

The Stained Pane

15726 W High St (Rte 87)
Middlefield, OH
(440)632-0928

Stained glass restoration & repair. **QC: S16**

Antiquing Periodicals

The Midwestern antiques collector has plenty to read. Brief descriptions and contact information for some of the more widely circulated national magazines and newspapers, as well regional publications, follow. A number of these publications are available free of charge at auctions, antiques shows, and group shops.

The American Antiquities Journal

A quarterly tabloid covering the southern Midwest and featuring articles, ads, shop reports, and trade news. Editors: Nancy Wilson and Sharon Leach. 126 East High Street, Springfield, OH 45502. (937)322-6281, (800)557-6281, (937)322-0294 (fax).

Antique and Collectible News

A regional monthly for Illinois, Indiana, and states to the south with articles, club news, and advertisements. PO Box 529, Anna, IL 62906. (618)833-2158, (800)833-2699, (618)833-5813 (fax), reppert@midwest.net.

The Antique Collector and Auction Guide

A weekly insert in *Farm and Dairy* containing auction ads and news, shows, and articles. Editor: Susan Hogan. PO Box 38, Salem, OH 44460. (216)337-3419, (216)337-3164, (216)337-9550 (fax).

Antique Review

The Midwest's major newspaper for the serious antiques collector. Monthly. Show and auction reviews and calendar, authoritative articles, book reviews and many ads. The single best source for information about Midwest shows and auctions. Editor: Charles Muller. PO Box 538, Worthington, OH 43085. (614)885-9757, (800)992-9757, (614)885-9762(fax), www.antiquereviewohio.com.

Antiquing Periodicals

The Antique Trader Weekly

A widely circulated publication with thousands of ads per issue, national show and auction calendars, and articles. Editor: Linda Keilbach. PO Box 1050, Dubuque, IA 52004. (800)334-7165, (800)482-4155, (800)531-0880 (fax), 76143.72@compuserve.com, www.csmonline.com

Art & Antiques

Art & Antiques, a monthly color magazine, emphasizes the fine & decorative arts but includes occasional articles on other aspects of antiquing. Editor in Chief: Paula Rackow. PO Box 11697, Des Moines, IA 50340-1697. (212)752-5557, (212)752-7147 (fax), artantqmag@aol.com.

Auction Action News

Weekly reports of auctions, prices, and photos in Wisconsin, Michigan, Illinois, Minnesota, and Iowa. Editors: Bob and Jeni Olsze. 131 East James Street, Columbus, WI 53925. (414)623-3767, (800)580-4568 (fax).

The Buckeye Marketeer

A monthly paper covering shows, flea markets, and auctions. PO Box 958, Westerville, OH 43086. (614)895-1663.

Collector Magazine & Price Guide

Monthly magazine on collectibles and the current market. Features a 25-page price guide. Editor: Linda Kunkel. Antique Trader Publications Inc, PO Box 1050, Dubuque, IA 52004. (800)334-7165, (800)482-4155, (800)531-0880, 76143.72@compuserve.com, www.csmonline.com

The Collector

An Illinois monthly newspaper of collectibles and antiques, shows, flea markets, event reviews, want and for sale section. Editor: Lois Bowman. PO Box 148, Heyworth, IL 61745. (309)473-2466, (309)473-2940, (309)473-3610 (fax).

Collectors Journal

Weekly auction paper for collectibles and antiques, auction results, auction and flea market calendar, articles. Editor: Kathy Root. PO Box 601, Vinton, IA 52349. (319)472-4763, (319)472-4764, (319)472-3117 (fax).

Early American Homes

A bimonthly color magazine with substantive articles on antiques, the construction and decoration of early houses, social history and other related subjects. Senior Editor: Mimi Handler. 6405 Flank Drive, Harrisburg, PA 17112. (717)657-9555.

The Great Lakes Trader

Michigan's leading trade paper. Monthly. Many ads, show calendar and reports, articles and advice. Editor: Greg Wilcox. 132 South Putnam, Williamston, MI 48895. (517)655-5621, (800)785-3637, (517)655-5380 (fax).

The Magazine ANTIQUES

The Magazine ANTIQUES covers the full range of the decorative and fine arts and is the most scholarly of the publications described here. Individual articles cover historic houses, ceramics, glass, silver, furniture, textiles, folk art, painting, sculpture, gardens, and architecture. Since 1922 *the* antiques publication in the United States and very much collected itself. Full color illustrations and advertisements add to its appeal and usefulness. Editor: Allison Eckardt Ledes. PO Box 10547, Des Moines, IA 50347. (800)925-9271.

Maine Antique Digest

Despite its name, a monthly paper in six to eight sections covering the whole of the American antiques market. MAD keeps its finger on the pulse of the antiques trade and attracts over 25,000 subscribers in 50 states and foreign countries. Detailed show and auction reviews, book reviews, specialty columns, and extensive advertising make this the primary information source for antiques dealers and serious collectors alike. MAD also features a large and rapidly evolving web site. Editor: Samuel C Pennington. Box 1429, Waldoboro, ME 04572. (207)832-7534, mad@maine.com, www.maineantiquedigest.com.

Ohio Collectors' Magazine

Covers the Ohio collectibles and flea market scene. Five issues per year. Editor: Don Baker. PO Box 1522, Piqua, OH 45356.

The Old Times

The main monthly newspaper for Minnesota, northern Wisconsin, and Iowa. Articles, antique tours, news, and ads. Editor: Tom Ratzloff. PO Box 340, Maple Lake, MN 55350. (800)539-1810, (320)963-6010 (fax), oldtimes@lkdllink.net.

NewsWarman's Today's Collector

Monthly magazine for collectibles, ads, auction results, calendar of auctions, shows, flea markets. Editor: Julie Ulrich. 700 East State Street, Iola, WI 54990. (715)445-2214, (715)445-4087 (fax), info@krause.com, www.krause.com.

Yesteryear

Monthly newspaper for the north central states featuring articles, shop directory, flea markets, shows, and ads. Editor: Michael Jacobi. PO Box 2, Princeton, WI 54968. (920)787-4808, (920)787-7381 (fax).

Museums & Historic Homes

ILLINOIS
Alton

Koenig House
849 E 4th St
(618)462-2763

Historic home with authentic period furnishings.

Belvidere

Boone County Historical Museum
311 Whitney Blvd
(815)544-8391

Hours: Tue & Thu 8-12 & 1-3:30.
Admission: Adults $2, seniors $1.50.
Directions: Corner of Whitney Blvd and S State St.
Wheelchair accessible: Yes.

Collections of historic tools, dolls, clothes, transportation, Civil War artifacts, and local memorabilia.

Bloomington

David Davis Mansion
1000 E Monroe St
(309)828-1084

Hours: Thu-Mon 9-5.
Admission: Free.

Suggested donations: Adult $2, children $1.
Directions: I-55 exit Veterans Pkwy (in Normal) S 3.7 mi, W on Empire 1.6 mi, S on Linden to Monroe. I-39 exit US 51 S 4 mi, E on Washington, N on Davis.
Wheelchair accessible: First floor only.

Authentically restored and furnished house built in 1872. Italianate and Second Empire architecture, Eastlake and Renaissance revival furnishings, original gasoliers, marble fireplaces.

Cairo

Magnolia Manor
2700 Washington Ave
(618)734-0201

Hours: Mon-Sat 9-5, Sun 1-5. Closed Christmas and New Year's Day.
Admission: Adults $5.
Directions: 2 blks W of Sycamore St, between 27th and 28th.
Wheelchair accessible: No.

A 14-room Italianate house furnished and decorated in period and containing a bed slept in by General Grant.

Chicago

Art Institute of Chicago
111 S Michigan Ave
(312)443-3600

Hours: Mon- Fri 10:30-4:30 (Tue til 8), Sat

10-5, Sun & holidays 12-5.
Admission: Donations suggested: Adults $7, seniors and students $3.50.
Directions: I-90 exit Monroe St E to Columbus Dr. Park in Monroe garage.
Wheelchair accessible: Yes.

An internationally renowned museum and gallery, with a major collection of Impressionist paintings. Of special interest are the Thorne miniature rooms, built to 1/12 scale, which illustrate the history of antiques and interior design from the 16th C. A good collection of American folk art.

Frederick C. Robie House

5757 Woodlawn Ave
(708)848-1976
Hours: Tours Mon-Fri at 11, 1 & 3; Sat-Sun at 11 & 3:30. Closed major holidays.
Admission: Adults $8, seniors and children 7-18 $6.
Directions: Lake Shore Dr exit 53rd St, then L on Woodlawn.
Wheelchair accessible: No.

One of Frank Lloyd Wright's most important houses.

Cobden

Cobden Museum

206 Front St
(618)893-2067
Hours: Sat-Sun 12:30-4:30.
Admission: Free.
Directions: In downtown.
Wheelchair accessible: Partial.

Antiques, glassware, Civil War and other militaria, and American Indian artifacts.

Danville

Vermilion County Museum

116 N Gilbert
(217)442-2922
Hours: Tue-Sat 10-5, Sun 1-5. Closed major holidays.
Admission: Adults $1, children 6-14 $0.50,

children under 5 free.
Directions: On IL Rte 1, 3 mi N of I-75, exit 215.
Wheelchair accessible: No.

Good 19th C furnishings, a bed Lincoln slept in, doll collection, Civil War memorabilia, and other historical artifacts.

DeKalb

Elwood House Museum

509 N First St
(815)716-4609
Hours: Tours Tue-Fri 1 & 3, Sat-Sun 1, 2 & 3.
Admission: Adults $4, children $1, children under 6 free.
Directions: Rte 38 (Lincoln Hwy) to N First St. Turn W onto Augusta and R into driveway.
Wheelchair accessible: First floor only.

The opulent home of Colonel Isaac Elwood, the "barbed wire baron," filled with its original Victorian and Colonial Revival furnishings and artwork, large collection of figural Staffordshire, a Victorian playhouse, carriage house, and gardens. Extensive collection of barbed wire history.

Edwardsville

Madison County Historical Museum

715 N Main St
(618)656-7562
Hours: Wed-Fri 9-4, Sun 1-4. Closed Jan, major holidays.
Admission: Free.
Directions: IL Hwys 159 and 143, 5 blks N of the County Administration Building and Courthouse.
Wheelchair accessible: Partially.

A Federal style mansion built in 1836 with period furnished rooms and displays of antiques, quilts, and historic costumes. Also exhibits of American Indian and pioneer artifacts.

Galena

The Belvidere Mansion

1008 Park Ave
(815)777-0747

Hours: Daily 11-4, Memorial Day - Oct.
Admission: $5 ($6 combined with Dowling House).
Directions: 1st R after bridge.
Wheelchair accessible: No.

Italianate 22-room mansion built in 1857 for J Russel Jones, a steamboat magnate. Furnished in high Victorian style and including pieces from Liberace's estate and the infamous green drapes from *Gone with the Wind*.

Dowling House

220 Diagonal St
(815)777-1250

Hours: Fri-Sun 10-3.
Admission: See Belvidere Mansion (above).
Directions: From Main St take L on Diagonal.
Wheelchair accessible: No.

Built of native limestone in 1826 as a general store and residence, Galena's oldest house is furnished with primitives and contains an extensive collection of Galena pottery.

Ulysses S Grant Historic Home

500 Bouthillier St
(815)777-0248 or 777-3310

Hours: Daily 9-5.
Admission: Donations.
Directions: Cross bridge to Main St, turn L on Park, R on Bouthillier.
Wheelchair accessible: First floor only.

This 1860s brick house in the Italianate-bracketed style contains its original furnishings.

Glenview

The Grove

1421 Milwaukee Ave
(847)299-6096

Hours: Mon-Sat 8-4:30, Sat-Sun 9-5.
Admission: Free.
Directions: I-94 exit Lake Ave W to Milwaukee Ave S.
Wheelchair accessible: No.

123 wooded acres contain a 1-room schoolhouse, a log cabin, and Redfield House, a prime example of the Louis Sullivan School of Chicago architecture. Everything, from the furniture to the fruit trees, is accurate to the period.

Jacksonville

David Strawn Art Gallery

331 W College
(217)243-9390

Hours: Sep-May Tue-Thu 4-6, Fri-Sun 1-3.
Admission: Free.
Directions: Downtown.
Wheelchair accessible: First floor only.

An elegant historic home that contains an antique doll collection, antiques from the 1880s, Southwestern and pre-Columbian pottery, and rotating exhibits. The permanent collections are on the second floor.

Kanakee

Kanakee County Historical Society Museum

8th and Water Sts
(815)932-5279

Hours: Mon-Fri 10-3, Sat-Sun 1-4. Closed major holidays.

Admission: Donations.
Directions: In Small Memorial Park. Take Wall St (IL 113) S from Court St.
Wheelchair accessible: No.

An 1860s home furnished in period, containing collections of early housewares, period costumes, period furniture, and early firearms.

Lombard

Lombard Historical Society Museum
23 W Maple St
(630)629-1885

Hours: Wed, Sat, Sun 1-4.
Admission: Donations.
Directions: I-355 exit North Ave E, S on Main St, W on Maple St.
Wheelchair accessible: No.

An 1870s house furnished and decorated in period.

McLeansboro

McCoy Memorial Library
118 S Washington Ave
(618)643-2125

Hours: Mon, Wed, Fri 1-4. Closed major holidays.
Admission: Free.
Directions: SW corner of McLeansboro Sq, 2nd floor of library.
Wheelchair accessible: No.

Original furnishings of the 1880 home, including a Wooten desk. Also collections of antique fans, militaria, and arrowheads.

Oakland

Dr Hiram Rutherford's Home
4 Pike St
(217)346-2031

Hours: Jun-Aug daily 1-3.
Admission: $2.
Directions: Just off Rte 133 in Oakland.

Wheelchair accessible: No.

The house offers an interesting look into mid-Victorian lifestyle.

Oak Park

Frank Lloyd Wright Home and Studio
951 Chicago Ave
(708)848-1976

Hours: Tours Mon-Fri at 11, 1 & 3; Sat-Sun at 11 & 3:30. Closed major holidays.
Admission: Adults $8, seniors and children 7-18 $6.
Directions: I-290 exit Harlem Ave, N to Chicago Ave, E 3 blks.
Wheelchair accessible: No.

The furniture, architecture, and community designs of his prairie school period. Oak Park has 30 Wright-designed buildings. An audio-cassette guided tour is available.

Historic Pleasant Home
217 Home Ave
(708)383-2654

Hours: Tours Thu-Sun at 1, 2 & 3.
Admission: Adults $4, students $3. Tours free on Thu.
Directions: I-290 exit Austin N to Madison, W to Home Ave, N to Pleasant St.
Wheelchair accessible: No.

An opulent Prairie-style mansion of 33 rooms designed in 1897 by George Maher.

Paris

Edgar County Historical Museum
408 N Main St
(217)463-5305

Hours: Wed-Fri 9-4, Sat 9-12, Sun 1:30-3:30.
Admission: Free.
Directions: Downtown.
Wheelchair accessible: Yes.

A Victorian home furnished and decorated in turn-of-the-century style.

Peoria

Lakeview Museum of Arts and Sciences

1125 W Lake Ave
(309)686-7000
www.lakeview-museum.org
Hours: Tue-Sat 10-5, Sun 1-5. Closed major holidays.
Admission: Adults $3, seniors $2, students $1.50.
Directions: I-74 exit University N, R on Lake Ave.
Wheelchair accessible: Yes.

Specialist collection of Illinois River decoys, Illinois jacquard coverlets, and other folk art. Rotating exhibits of antiques and folk art.

Quincy

Governor John Wood Mansion

425 S 12th St
(217)222-1835
Hours: Jun-Aug daily 1-4; Apr-May & Sep-Oct Sat-Sun 1-4.
Admission: Adults $2, students $1.
Directions: 5 blks S of Maine St, at intersection of State and 12th Sts.
Wheelchair accessible: No.

A Greek revival house built in 1835 and furnished in period. Regularly rotating exhibits include dolls, 19th C clothing & Civil War artifacts.

The Lincoln Douglas Valentine Museum

101 N 4th St
(217)224-3355
Hours: Mon-Sat 10-4.
Admission: Free.

Directions: 4th and Maine Sts.
Wheelchair accessible: Yes.

A heartwarming collection of old and unusual valentines from all over the world.

The Quincy Museum

1601 Maine St
(217)224-7669
Hours: Tue-Sun 1-5.
Admission: Donations.
Directions: I-36 exit Broadway, L on 18th St, R on Maine St.
Wheelchair accessible: Yes.

The first floor is furnished and decorated in 1890s fashion, the other two floors house rotating exhibits.

Rockford

Midway Village and Museum Center

6799 Guilford Rd
(815)397-9112
Hours: Thu-Sun 12-4. Closed major holidays.
Admission: Adults $5, children $3.
Directions: I-90 exit Bus 20 (State St) W, N on Bell School Rd, W on Guilford Rd.
Wheelchair accessible: No.

The village contains 24 authentically restored and furnished homes, shops, and businesses from the turn of the century.

Time Museum

7801 E State St
(815)398-6000
Hours: Tue-Sun 10-5.
Admission: Adults $3, seniors $2, children $1, groups of 15+ $2.
Directions: I-90 at exit Bus 20.
Wheelchair accessible: Yes.

One of the world's finest collections of time-measuring devices from the earliest sundials to atomic clocks containing antique clocks and watches from around the world. Important collection of American clocks and watches from the 18th to 20th C.

Springfield

The Executive Mansion
Fifth and Jackson Sts
(217) 782-6450

Hours: Tue, Thu, Sat 9:30-11 & 2-3:30.
Admission: Free.
Directions: Downtown, two blks from Capitol, enter by gate on 4th St.
Wheelchair accessible: Yes.

The Governor's mansion is filled with antiques and historic artifacts. Sixteen state rooms are open for viewing, including the state dining room, the library, and the Lincoln bedroom.

Old State Capitol
Fifth and Adams Sts
(217)785-7961

Hours: Daily 9-5.
Admission: Donations.
Directions: Downtown.
Wheelchair accessible: Yes.

Magnificently restored with period furnishings, this is where Lincoln delivered his "House Divided" speech and lay in state before his burial.

St Charles

St Charles Heritage Center
Main Museum
2 E Main St
(630) 584-6967

Hours: Mar-Dec Sun-Fri 12-4 .
Admission: Donations.
Directions: In the St Charles Municipal Building.
Wheelchair accessible: Yes.

Extensive collections of 19th C household wares, Civil War memorabilia, and American Indian artifacts.

> Use the Specialty QuickCode indexes at the back of the book to find dealers who specialize in your area of interest.

Vernon Hills

Cuneo Museum and Gardens
1350 N Milwaukee Ave
(847)362-3042

Hours: Mar-Dec Tue-Sat 10-5, tours of Mansion at 11 & 2.
Admission: Adults $10, seniors $9, students $5.
Directions: I-94 exit Hwy 60 (Townline Rd) W, then N on Milwaukee Ave.
Wheelchair accessible: Yes.

A 1914 mansion designed by Benjamin Marshall and featuring Old Master paintings, 17th C tapestries, oriental rugs, sculpture, and formal gardens.

INDIANA
Aurora

Hillforest Mansion
213 Fifth St
(812)926-0087
dearborncounty@org/hillforest

Hours: Apr-Dec Tue-Sun 1-5. Closed major holidays.
Admission: Adults $3.50, students $1.50, children under 7 free.
Directions: I-275, exit 16, 6 mi W on US Rte 50 to Aurora. Take IN 56 to Main St and go up the hill to Fifth St.
Wheelchair accessible: First floor only.

An 1855 Italianate mansion with steamboat-inspired architectural features. Twelve rooms furnished and decorated in period including "trompe l'oeil" wall paintings.

Bloomington

Wylie House Museum
307 E 2nd St
(812)855-6224
bvwillia@indiana.edu
www.indiana.edu/~libwylie

Hours: Mar-Nov Tue-Sat 1-4.

Admission: Free.
Directions: From Court House Square, S on College Ave, W on 2nd St.
Wheelchair accessible: Yes

Recreation of the home of Indiana University's first president as it was in the 1840s. Also historic flower, herb, and vegetable gardens.

Carmel

Museum of Miniature Houses

111 E Main St
(317)575-9466

Hours: Wed-Sat 11-4, Sun 1-4. Closed major holidays and first two school weeks of Jan.
Admission: Adults $2, children $1.
Directions: I-465 exit US Rte 31 N, R on Old Meridian St, R on Main St.
Wheelchair accessible: Yes.

Collection of antique and contemporary dollhouses, miniature rooms, vignettes, and accessories. Rotating exhibits of porcelain, jewelry, silhouettes, and other antiques.

Corydon

Corydon Capitol State Historic Site

202 E Walnut St
(812)738-4890

Hours: Mid-Mar to mid-Dec Tue-Sat 9-5, Sun 1-5.
Admission: Donations.
Directions: I-64 exit 105, S on Hwy 135 to Hwy 337 S to downtown.
Wheelchair accessible: Yes.

The Governor's mansion recreates the first

year of Indiana's statehood and is furnished in three periods: 1820s, 1840s, and 1870s.

Evansville

Evansville Museum of Art and Science

411 SE Riverside Dr
(812)425-2406

Hours: Tue-Sat 10-5, Sun 12-5.
Admission: Donations.
Directions: I-164 to Rte 41 N, W on Lloyd Expressway, S on Riverside Dr.
Wheelchair accessible: Yes.

A general museum with large collection of fine art. Also furniture, ceramics, and domestic goods.

Reitz Home Museum

224 SE First St
(812)426-2179

Hours: Tue-Sat 11-3:30, Sun 1-3:30.
Admission: Adults $5, students $2.50, children 12 and under $1.50.
Directions: From Lloyd Expressway exit on Third St S, R on Walnut, L on First St.
Wheelchair accessible: Carriage House only.

French Second Empire mansion built, furnished, and decorated from 1871 to 1890s. Period furniture, much of which is original to the house, and exceptional decorations including damask-covered walls, hand-painted ceilings, Moorish design wainscotting, parquet floors, marble fireplaces, and stained glass windows.

Greentown

Greentown Glass Museum

112 N Meridian St
(765)628-6206

Hours: May 15-Oct 31 Tue-Fri 10-12 & 1-4; Mar 1-Dec 31 Sat & Sun 1-4.
Admission: Donations.
Directions: On US Rte 31 N at stoplight in Greentown.
Wheelchair accessible: Yes

Large collection of Greentown glass produced by the Indiana Tumbler and Goblet Co between 1894 and 1903. Includes exhibition of the subtle difference between the originals and imitations.

Lafayette

Greater Lafayette Museum of Art

101 South 9th St
(765)742-1128
glma@pop.nlci.com

Hours: Tue-Sun 11-4. Closed major holidays.
Admission: Free.
Wheelchair accessible: Yes.

Excellent collections of Rookwood pottery and of Indiana artists.

Indianapolis

Indiana State Museum

202 N Alabama St
(317)232-1637
(317)232-7090 (fax)
crawfdjr@indy.net

Hours: Mon-Sat 9-4:45, Sun 12-4:45. Closed major holidays.
Admission: Free.
Directions: In downtown, 1 blk N of the Market Square Arena.
Wheelchair accessible: Yes.

A general museum with rotating exhibits, many of which focus on Indiana life and antiques.

Morris-Butler House Museum

1204 N Park Ave
(317)636-5409
mbhouse@indy.net
www.historiclandmarks.com

Hours: Tue-Sat 10-4, Sun 1-4, tours every 30 mins, last tour 3:30. Closed major holidays and from Christmas Eve to mid-Jan.
Admission: Adults $5, children 6-16 $2,

children under 6 free.
Directions: 6 blks E of Meridian St (US 31) and 16th St: R on Park Ave to 12th St. Museum on R, free parking on L.
Wheelchair accessible: Yes.

Collections of mid-Victorian decorative arts including a Meeks and Belter rococo revival parlor, other period rooms, a Wooton secretary, and a large collection of Indiana art and sculpture. Superb stenciled ceilings, elaborate wallpaper, and plasterwork.

Michigan City

Barker Mansion

631 Washington St
(219)873-1520
(219)873-1520 (fax)

Hours: Tours Mon-Fri at 10:00, 11:30 & 1:00 all year. Tours Sat & Sun at 12:00 & 2:00 Jun- Oct only.
Admission: Adults $3, children 12 and under $0.50.
Directions: I-80/90 or I-94 exit on US 421. N to downtown, W on 7th St. Mansion is on corner of 7th and Washington.
Wheelchair accessible: No.

A large English manor-type mansion completed in 1905 retaining its turn-of-the-century opulence. It contains antiques and objets d'art from many periods and countries, as well as fine period carvings in wood and marble. Historic gardens.

New Albany

Culbertson Mansion State Historic Site

914 E Main St
(812)944-9600
(812)949-6134 (fax)

Hours: Tue-Sat 9-5; Sun 1-5 Mar 15-Dec 15 only.
Admission: Free. Suggested donation: Adults $2, children $1.
Directions: I-84 exit 123 S to Main St. Mansion on corner of E Main and 10th Sts.
Wheelchair accessible: No.

Victorian house furnished and decorated in period. Good collection of furniture dating 1840-1895.

Ligonier

Indiana Historic Radio Museum

800 Lincolnway S (SR 5)
(219)894-9000

Hours: May-Nov Tue, Wed & Sat 10-3; Dec-Apr Sat 10-2.
Admission: Donation.
Directions: On SR 5, 1/2 mi N of junction with US 6.
Wheelchair accessible: Yes.

Over 400 antique and classic radios, also advertising, telegraphy, and other related equipment.

South Bend

Northern Indiana Center for History

808 W Washington
(219)235-9664
(219)235-9059 (fax)

Hours: Tue-Sat 10-5, Sun 12-5.
Admission: Whole site: Adults $8, seniors $6.50, students $4. History center only: Adults $3, seniors $2.50, students $2. Historic houses only: Adults $6, seniors $5, students $3.
Directions: I-80/90 exit 77 S on Rtes 31-33 to downtown. W on Washington St, S on Chapin St, W on Thomas St.
Wheelchair accessible: History center: Yes. Historic houses: No.

A ten-acre museum complex containing a history center and two historic houses and gardens. Copshaholm, the Oliver Mansion, is a 38-room mansion built in 1896 by Joseph Oliver. It retains the family's original furnishings, some dating to the mid-17th C. There is also an 1870s workers' home, furnished to reflect the life of a 1930s Polish working-class family.

Vevay

UP Schenck House

W Market St
(800)435-5688

Hours: Daily 9-5.
Admission: Adults $2, tours conducted by owner.
Directions: I-75 Warsaw exit E to Hwy 42 W to Hwys 56/156 W 7 mi to Vevay, then L on Market St.
Wheelchair accessible: No.

Fine Mississippi river plantation house built in 1844 containing collections of furniture, historic artifacts, woodenware, and tools.

Vincennes

Old French House and Indian Museum

First and Seminary Sts
(812)882-7886
(800)886-6443

Hours: Tue-Sat 9-12 & 1-5, Sun 1-5 Memorial Day to Labor Day.
Admission: Adult $1, students $0.50.
Directions: Downtown.

French Creole house built in 1806 by the fur trader and Indian interpreter Michel Brouillet. Furnished in period, exhibit on the fur trade, Indian and Indiana pre-history museum.

Grouseland

3 W Scott St
(812)882-2096

Hours: Mar-Dec daily 9-5; Jan & Feb daily 11-4. Closed major holidays.
Admission: Adults $3, students $2, children under 12 $1.
Directions: Cross Lincoln Bridge S, then E on N 2nd St, N on Scott.
Wheelchair accessible: No.

A brick mansion built in 1804 furnished and decorated in period.

MICHIGAN
Acme

The Music House

7377 US Rte 31 N
(616)938-9300
Hours: May-Oct Mon-Sat 10-4, Sun 12-4;
Nov-Dec Fri-Sat 10-4, Sun 12-4.
Admission: Adults $6.50, children under 16
$2, children under 6 free.
Directions: 8 mi N of Traverse City on US
Rte 31.
Wheelchair accessible: Yes.

Guided tours feature performances of a large
collection of automated instruments from
music boxes to pipe organs in turn-of-the-
century settings such as a saloon, a store,
and a theatre. Also displays of antique
phonographs, radios, and juke boxes. Allow
2 hours for full tour.

Concord

Mann House

Hanover St
(517)524-8943
Hours: Wed-Sun 12-4:30, Memorial Day to
Labor Day.
Admission: Free.
Directions: M60, downtown, turn E at
blinker light.
Wheelchair accessible: No.

An 1883 house with its original furnishings
and decorations.

Copper Harbor

Astor House Museum
Minnetonka Resort

560 Gratiot St
(904)672-1887
Hours: May 15-Oct 15 daily 9-6..
Admission: Adults $2.
Directions: Corner of US 41 and M26.
Wheelchair accessible: Yes.

Antique doll collection, tools, Indian
artifacts, nautical antiques, and antiquarian
books.

Dearborn

Henry Ford Museum and Greenfield Village

20900 Oakwood Blvd
(313)271-2455
(800)TELL-A-FRiend
www.hfmgv.org
Hours: Daily 9-5. Closed Thanksgiving &
Christmas. Village buildings closed Jan 5-
Mar 31.
Admission: One-day admission to either the
Museum or the Village: Adults $12.50,
seniors $11.50, children 5-12 $7.50, children
4 and under free. Two-day admission to
both the Museum and the Village: Adults
$22, children 5-12 $12.50, children 4 and
under free. Group rates and annual rates
available.
Directions: Follow signs.
Wheelchair accessible: Museum: Yes.
Village: Some buildings inaccessible.

The Henry Ford Museum and Greenfield
Village is the largest indoor-outdoor museum in North America with over 1 million
artifacts.

The Museum has a major collection of
almost every type of antique. Furniture:
17th-20th C, particularly strong in Federal,
Empire, and Modernism, and with
important Pilgrim Century pieces.
Ceramics: Stoneware, Redware, Chinese
Export, and English Export. Glass: Huge
collection of all forms of American glass, as
well as imported. Large collections of
American pewter and silver. A major
collection of early lighting. Domestic artifacts and tools.

The Village is a collection of shops,
workshops, and houses. All houses are
furnished and decorated authentically in
their period. They include a 17th C English
house, an early 18th C house from
Connecticut, a New England house c 1790,

Noah Webster's house c 1835, a plantation house, c 1860, an early farmstead redecorated in 1885, and the Wright Brothers' house of 1903.

Flint

Sloan Museum
1221 E Kearsley St
(810)760-1169
Hours: Tue-Fri 10-5, Sat-Sun 12-5; Jul-Aug open Mon 10-5.
Admission: Adults $4, seniors $3.50, children 5-12 $3, children under 5 free.
Directions: I-475 exit 8A: 1 blk E on RT Longway Blvd.
Wheelchair accessible: Yes.

The Museum specializes in cars and automobiliana, but also includes period furnishings, household wares, and commercial goods from the early to mid-20th C.

Grosse Pointe Shores

Edsel & Eleanor Ford House
1100 Lake Shore Rd
(313)884-4222
dpierce@fordhouse.org
www.fordhouse.org
Hours: Apr-Dec Tue-Sat 10-4, Sun 12-4; Jan-Mar Tue-Sat 1-4.
Admission: Adults $5, seniors $4, children $3.
Directions: From I-94 take Eight Mile Rd exit. E on Vernier, N on Lake Shore Rd.
Wheelchair accessible: No.

A stately home of 60 rooms built in the 1920s on 87 landscaped acres furnished with American, English, and French antiques. Important paintings, sculpture, oriental porcelain, and other objets d'art are also displayed.

Jackson

Ella Sharp Museum
3225 Fourth St
(517)787-2320
Hours: Tue-Fri 10-4, Sat-Sun 11-4. Closed major holidays.
Admission: Adults $2.50, seniors $2, children 5-15 $1, children under 5 free, family $5.
Directions: From I-94 go E on Michigan, the S on West St, the R on Fourth.

This elegantly furnished Victorian home stands on 530 acres which contain a school, woodworking shop, print shop, doctor's office, and tower barn.

Lansing

Michigan Historical Museum
717 W Allegan St
(517)373-0510
Hours: Mon-Fri 9-4:30, Sat 10-4, Sun 1-5.
Admission: Free.
Directions: 2 blks W of the State Capitol. From I-496, follow Capitol Loop signs.
Wheelchair accessible: Yes.

Many exhibits of Michigan's industrial history, also a lumber baron's mansion and a 1930s bungalow furnished in period.

Manistee

Manistee County Historical Museum
425 River St
(616)723-5531
Hours: Tue-Sat 10-5.
Admission: Adults $1.50, family $4.
Directions: US 31 to downtown, L on River St.
Wheelchair accessible: Yes.

Use the Service QuickCode indexes at the back of the book to find restorers, appraisers, refinishers, and other specialty service providers.

Housed in a country store built in 1871 with original fixtures and fittings, the museum contains antique clocks, housewares, and pioneer and civil war exhibits.

Montrose

Montrose Historical and Telephone Museum
144 E Hickory
(810)639-6644

Hours: Sat-Sun 1-5 and by appt. Closed major holidays.
Admission: Free.
Directions: I-75 exit M 57 (Vienna Rd) W to Montrose. N at light on Nichols, E on E Hickory.
Wheelchair accessible: No.

A telephone museum including hands-on working exhibits of antique equipment.

MINNESOTA
Le Sueur

W W Mayo House
118 N Main St
(507)665-3250

Hours: Memorial Day-Labor Day Tue-Sun and holidays 1-4:30; May 15-Memorial Day & Labor Day-Oct 15 Sat, Sun and holidays 1-4:30.
Admission: Adults $2, seniors $1.50, children $1.
Directions: Downtown.
Wheelchair accessible: No.

House furnished and decorated as in the 1850s.

Little Falls

Charles A Lindberg House
1200 Lindberg Dr S
(320)632-3154

Hours: May-Labor Day Mon-Sat 10-5, Sun 12-5; Labor Day-late Oct Sat 10-4, Sun 12-4.
Admission: Adults $5, seniors $4, children $3.
Directions: Two miles S of Little Falls.
Wheelchair accessible: Yes.

1906 house with original furnishings, a history center about Lindberg's aviation exploits, and nature trails.

Minneapolis

Minneapolis Institute of Arts
2400 3rd Ave S
(612)870-3131

Hours: Tue-Sat 10-5 (Thu til 9), Sun 12-5.
Admission: Free. Charge for special exhibits except Thu 5-9.
Directions: I-94 exit 11th St S. At 2nd light turn L on 3rd St S.
Wheelchair accessible: Yes.

Major collections of furniture, ceramics, and other decorative arts. In the Christmas season shows decorated rooms from many periods.

Ord Godfrey House
Richard Hughes Sq
University Ave
(612)870 8001

Hours: Jun-Sep Fri-Sun 12-3:30.
Admission: Adults $1, seniors $0.50, children $0.25.
Directions: From downtown cross Hennepin Bridge, then R on University Ave 1 blk, Richard Hughes Sq on R.
Wheelchair accessible: No.

Costumed interpreters guide visitors through Minneapolis's oldest house, furnished and decorated in period.

Moorhead

Comstock House
506 Eighth St
(218)291-4211

Hours: Late May-Sep Sat & Sun 1-4:15.
Admission: Adults $3, seniors $2, children $1.50.
Directions: Downtown.
Wheelchair accessible: No.

1882 house with original Eastlake furnishings, china, crystal, and tapestries.

New Ulm

Harkin Store
(507)354-2016

Hours: May Sat-Sun 10-5; Jun-Aug Tue-Sun 10-5; Sept to mid-Oct Fri-Sun 10-5.
Admission: Adults $1, children free.
Directions: On County Hwy 21, 8 mi NW of New Ulm.
Wheelchair accessible: Yes.

When the railroad passed Harkin by, the store was forced to close in 1873. Most of the original inventory remains on the shelves.

St Paul

Alexander Ramsey House
265 S Exchange St
(612)296-8760

Hours: Tours May 5-Nov 27 Tue-Sat 10-3. Extended hours Nov 27-Dec 31.
Admission: Adults $5, seniors $4, children $3.
Directions: From W 7th St go 1 blk S on Walnut St.
Wheelchair accessible: No.

James J Hill House
240 Summit Ave
(612)297-2555

Hours: Tours Wed-Sat 10-3:30 (reservations recommended).
Admission: Adults $5, seniors $4, children $3.

Directions: 1 blk NE of Cathedral of St Paul.
Wheelchair accessible: Yes.

Shakopee

Murphy's Landing
2187 E Hwy 101
(612) 445-6900

Hours: Memorial Day-Labor Day Tue-Sun 10-5 and select weekends in May and Sep.
Admission: Adults $8, seniors & students $6.
Directions: Follow signs on Hwy 101.
Wheelchair accessible: Partially.

A fur trading village of the 1800s with authentically furnished buildings and costumed interpreters and craftspeople, all on a wooded river valley site 1.5 miles long.

Taylors Falls

Folsom House
272 Government St
(612)465-5535

Hours: Memorial Day weekend-Oct 15 daily 1-4:30.
Admission: Adults $1.50, students $0.50.
Directions: North of US Rte 8 on the St Croix River.
Wheelchair accessible: No.

1854 house built and furnished in the Federal and Greek Revival style popular with New Englanders who settled in this area.

OHIO

Akron

Stan Hywet Hall and Gardens
714 N Portage Path
(330)836-5533
(330)836-2680 (fax)
lbass@stanhywet.org
www.stanhywet.org

Hours: Apr-Dec daily 9-6; Jan-Mar Tue-

Sat 10-4, Sun 1-4.
Admission: Adults $8, seniors $7, children 6-12 $4.
Directions: I-77 exit Rte 18 E, N on N Portage Path.
Wheelchair accessible: Partially.

The hall is a 65-room Tudor revival mansion built in 1915 that was the home of F.S. Sieberling, the co-founder of Goodyear. It contains the original furnishings, art, and objets d'art, and is set in 70 acres of historically significant gardens and grounds.

Barnesville

Barbara Barbe Doll /Museum
211 North Chestnut St
(614)425-2301

Hours: May-Sept Wed-Sun 1-4.
Admission: $2.
Directions: On Rte 800 in downtown.
Wheelchair accessible: Yes.

The Museum contains over 3,500 dolls, including many bisque and wax examples, and is housed in the "Female Seminary," an 1838 girls' school.

Cambridge

Degenhart Paperweight and Glass Museum
65323 Highland Hills Rd
(614)432-2626

Hours: Mon-Sat 9-5, Sun 1-5. Closed major holidays.
Admission: $1.50.
Directions: Corner of State Rds 77 and 22.
Wheelchair accessible: Yes.

The museum tells the history of glassware produced in Ohio, Pennsylvania, and Northern West Virginia including Midwestern pattern glass, paperweights, Cambridge glass, and Degenhart Crystal Art Glass.

National Cambridge Collectors Museum
9931 East Pike
(740)432-4245

Hours: Apr-Oct Wed-Sat 9-4, Sun 12-4; Mar Fri-Sat 9-4, Sun 12-4. Closed major holidays.
Admission: Adults $1.50, seniors $1, children 5-12 $0.75.
Directions: I-77 exit E on US 40, 1/8 mile on L.
Wheelchair accessible: Yes.

Over 5000 pieces of Cambridge glass, tools, moulds, etching plates, and video of glass making. Factory records available for research.

Canal Winchester

Mid-Ohio Historical Museum
700 Winchester Pike
(614)837-5573

Hours: Apr-Dec Wed-Sat 11-5. Closed holiday weeks.
Admission: $3, children under 5 free.
Directions: Off Rte 33 and Gender Rd.
Wheelchair accessible: Yes.

An outstanding collection of thousands of rare dolls and toys, a working Lionel train display, a miniature circus collection. The dolls date from the 17th C to Barbie.

Cincinnati

Cincinnati Art Museum
953 Eden Park Dr
(513)721-5204

Hours: Tue-Sat 10-5, Sun 12-6.
Admission: Adults $5, seniors and students $4.
Directions: I-71 downtown exit, follow signs.
Wheelchair accessible: Yes.

Nationally acclaimed art museum with a strong decorative arts collection including many examples of Rookwood Pottery.

Cincinnati Fire Museum

315 West Court St
(513)621-5553

Hours: Tue-Fri 10-4, Sat-Sun 12-4. Closed major holidays.
Admission: Adults $3, seniors $2.50, children $2.
Directions: 3 blks N of Convention Center in downtown.
Wheelchair accessible: Yes.

Firefighting items and equipment from 1788 to the present.

Taft Museum

316 Pike St
(513)241-0343

Hours: Mon-Sat 10-5, Sun & holidays 12-5.
Admission: Adults $4, seniors and students $3.
Directions: I-75 exit 5th St E, S on Pike St.
Wheelchair accessible: Yes.

Masterpieces of European and American painting, Chinese porcelain, and European decorative arts housed in restored federal style rooms.

William Howard Taft National Historic Site

2038 Auburn Ave
(513)684-3262
www.nps.gov/ohio

Hours: Daily 10-4. Closed major holidays
Admission: Free.
Directions: I-71 N, exit 2, L at light onto Dorchester, R on Auburn. I-71 S exit 3, L on Auburn.
Wheelchair accessible: Yes.

The birthplace of the 27th President reflects the life of the Taft family from 1857 to 1877.

Cleveland

Dittick Museum of Medical History

11000 Euclid Ave
(216)368-3648
(216)368-0165 (fax)

Hours: Mon-Fri 10-5, Sat 12-5.
Admission: Free.
Directions: I-90 exit Martin Luther King Blvd S, then E on Euclid.
Wheelchair accessible: Yes.

One of the major collections of medical history artifacts in the United States.

Dunham Tavern Museum

6709 Euclid Ave
(216)431-1060

Hours: Wed & Sun 1-4.
Admission: $2.
Directions: I-90 exit Carnegie St E to E 55th St, S to Euclid, then E.
Wheelchair accessible: 1st floor and gardens.

Cleveland's oldest building on its original site houses collections from its tavern days, 1824-1857. Historic gardens.

Western Reserve Historical Society Museum

10825 East Blvd
(216)721-5722

Hours: Mon-Sat 10-5, Sun 12-5.
Admission: Adults $6.50, seniors $5.50, children $4.50.
Directions: I-90 exit Martin Luther King Blvd S to East Blvd.
Wheelchair accessible: Yes.

General historical collection including antiques and decorative arts.

Columbus

Kelton House Museum and Garden

586 E Town St
(614) 464-2022
(614) 464-3346 (fax)

Hours: Mon-Fri 10-5, Sun 1-4.
Admission: Adult $1.50, seniors and students $1.
Directions: I-71 exit Broad St to downtown, L on Washington, L on Town St.
Wheelchair accessible: Yes.

Housed in a restored Greek Revival home built in 1852, the museum exhibits furniture, textiles, and ceramics. Large collection of music boxes. Victorian gardens.

Ohio Historical Center and Ohio Village

I-71 and 17th Ave
(614)297-2300
(800)-OLD-OHIO
www.ohiohistory.org

Hours: Historical Center: Jan-Nov Mon-Sat 9-5, Sun & holidays 10-5; Dec Mon & Tues 9-5, Wed-Sat 9-8:30, Sun 10-8:30. Closed Thanksgiving, Christmas, New Year's Day. Ohio Village: Jan-Mar Sat 9-5, Sun 10-5; Apr-Nov Wed-Sat 9-5, Sun 10-5; Dec Wed-Sun 11:30-8:30. Closed Thanksgiving, Christmas, and Wed after Mon holidays.
Admission: Village and Center: Adults $5, children $1.25. Center only: Adults $2.50, children $0.50.
Directions: 17th Avenue, off I-71.
Wheelchair accessible: Partial.

The Historical Center houses the Christopher collection of 18th and 19th C furniture, a large collection of spatter and Gaudy Dutch ceramics, and Currier and Ives lithographs; also Ohio ceramics, glass, and decorative arts. The Village recreates the daily life of a Civil War era town.

Crooksville

Ohio Ceramic Center

State Rd 93
(614) 697-7021

Hours: May-Oct Wed-Sat 10-5, Sun 12-5.
Admission: $1.
Directions: On SR 93 between Crooksville and Roseville.
Wheelchair accessible: Yes.

A large collection of ceramics produced in east central Ohio from 1800-1920, including Hull, McCoy, Roseville, Weller, Ransbottom, Watt Gonder, Shawnee, Ungemach, and Brush.

East Liverpool

Museum of Ceramics

400 E 5th St
(330)386-6001
www.ohiohistory.org

Hours: Mar-Nov Wed-Sat 9:30-5, Sun & holidays 12-5. Closed Thanksgiving. Dec-Feb: Groups by appointment.
Admission: Adults $5, seniors $4.50, children 6-12 $1.25.
Directions: On US Rte 30, about 30 mi W of Pittsburgh.
Wheelchair accessible: Yes.

East Liverpool was a major center of ceramics manufacturing. This museum, housed in a historic building, features extensive collections of ceramics produced in the region in the 19th C. Specialties include yellowware, Rockingham, and Lotus Ware.

Freemont

Rutherford B Hayes Presidential Center

1337 Hayes Ave
(419)332-2081

Hours: Mon-Sat 9-5, Sun & holidays 12-5. Closed major holidays.
Admission: Home and museum: Adults $8.50, seniors $7.50, children $5. Home or museum (one only): Adults $5, seniors $4, children $1.25.
Directions: I-80/90 exit 6 Rte 53 S, follow signs.
Wheelchair accessible: Museum only.

The Hayes's 33-room Victorian mansion contains original furnishings, paintings, and photographs and gives a glimpse of life in the "Gilded Age" from 1877-1900. The 25-acre estate also features the first presidential library and tomb of the 19th President.

Georgetown

The Ulysses S Grant Home

219 E Grant Ave
(937)378-4222
Hours: Mon-Sat 9-5.
Admission: Donations.
Directions: From US Rte 32 take Rte 125 exit to Georgetown, R onto Main St, R onto E Grant.
Wheelchair accessible: No.

Grant's boyhood home including family heirlooms, furnishings from the 1820s to 1860s, and Civil War memorabilia.

Kent

Kent State University Museum

Rockwell Hall
(330)672-3450
(330)672-3218 (fax)
jdruessed@kent.edu
www.kent.edu/museum
Hours: Wed-Sat 10-4:45 (Thu til 8:45), Sun 12-4:45.
Admission: $3 suggested donation.
Directions: Corner of Rte 59 and Lincoln St.
Wheelchair accessible: Yes.

Collections of costume, design, interior furnishings, and style reflecting social life from the 17th C to the present.

Lebanon

Glendower State Memorial

105 S Cincinnati Ave
(513) 932-1817
Hours: Jun-Aug Wed-Sat 12-4, Sun 1-4. Closed July 4th, Labor Day. Labor Day to Nov Sat 12-4, Sun 1-4. Dec: call for hours.
Admission: Adults $3, children $1.
Directions: I-75 exit Rte 63 E, S on Rte 48. I-71 exit Rte 123 W, S on Rte 48.
Wheelchair accessible: No.

One of Ohio's finest Greek Revival Homes,

Glendower features Empire and early Victorian furnishings.

Warren County Historical Society Museum

105 S Broadway
(513)932-1817
wchs@compuserve.com
Hours: Tue-Sat 9-4, Sun 12-4. Closed major holidays.
Admission: Adults $3, children (K-12) $1.
Directions: I-75 exit Rte 63 E. I-71 exit Rte 123 W.
Wheelchair accessible: Yes.

Extensive Shaker collection, early Americana, toys, clocks, guns and clothing, farming, furniture, and folk art.

Martins Ferry

Sedgewick House Museum

627 Hanover St
(304) 281-8329
www.ohighway.com
Hours: May-Sep Tue-Sat 12-4.
Admission: $1.
Directions: SR 7 exit Hanover St W.
Wheelchair accessible: No.

A collection of Northwood glass, Imperial glass, textiles, quilts, linens, and vintage clothes.

Massillon

Massilon Museum

121 Lincoln Way E
(330)833-4061
(330) 833-2925 (fax)
Hours: Tue-Sat 9:30-5, Sun 2-5.
Admission: Free.
Directions: I-77 from N exit OH Rte 21, S to Lilian Gish Blvd, R onto Lincoln Way. From S exit US 30 W to OH Rte 21 N to Lilian Gish Blvd, R onto Lincoln Way.
Wheelchair accessible: Yes.

A broad collection featuring American folk art, Massillon glass, ceramics, metal, fine and decorative arts, textiles, quilts and coverlets, costumes, tools and utensils. Also local history and circus exhibits.

Heisey Co since 1897. Also tools, molds, etching plates, and factory designs. Extensive archives for research.

Milan

Milan Historical Museum

10 Edison Dr
(419)499-2968

Hours: Apr-May & Sep-Oct daily 1-5; Jun-Aug Mon-Sat 10-5, Sun 1-5. Closed major holidays.
Admission: Donation.
Directions: I-80/90 exit 7, S on Rte 250 to Rte 113. Follow signs to Historic District.
Wheelchair accessible: Partially.

A 7-building complex including two homes, a blacksmith's shop, a store, and a carriage shop. Exhibits include the Mowry glass collection and the Coulton doll collection. Costumes, decorative arts, mechanical banks, porcelain, netsuke, guns, and other collections. Lovely gardens.

Newark

National Heisey Glass Museum

169 W Church St
(740)345-2932
(740) 345-9638 (fax)
heisey@infinet.com

Hours: Tue-Sat 10-4, Sun 1-4. Closed major holidays.
Admission: $2.
Directions: In Veterans Park, corner of 6th and Church St.
Wheelchair accessible: Yes.

A collection of more than 4,500 pieces of hand-made glass produced in Newark by the

Norwich

National Road/Zane Grey Museum

8850 East Pike
(740)872-3143
(800)752-2602
www.ohiohistory.org

Hours: May-Sep Mon-Sat 9:30-5, Sun 12-5; Mar-Apr & Oct-Nov Wed-Sat 9:30-5, Sun 12-5. Closed Dec-Feb.
Admission: Adults $5, children $1.25.
Directions: At exit 164 of I-70, 10 mi E of Zanesville at Norwich.
Wheelchair accessible: Yes.

Besides memorabilia of novelist Zane Grey and of the first federal highway, this museum contains a large collection of Zanesville art pottery and decorative tile.

Sandusky

Eleutheros Cooke House

1415 Columbus Ave
(419)625-9331

Hours: Apr-Dec Tue-Sat 10-3, Sun 12-3. Closed major holidays.
Admission: $4.
Wheelchair accessible: No.

This 1840s stone and brick house is a notable example of Greek Revival architecture and is furnished and decorated with period antiques.

Shaker Heights

Shaker Historical Museum

1640 S Park Blvd
(216)921-1201

Hours: Tue-Fri & Sun 2-5. Closed holidays.
Admission: Free.
Directions: I-271 exit Chagrin Rd W, then S on Lee Rd, W on S. Park.

Wheelchair accessible: No.

An extensive collection of Shaker furniture and artifacts, together with other antiques and local memorabilia.

Sharon Woods Park

Sharon Woods Village

Rte 42
(513)563-9484

Hours: May-Oct Wed-Fri 10-4, Sat-Sun 1-5. Closed major holidays.
Admission: Adults $3, seniors $2, children 6-12 $1, children under 6 free.
Directions: I-275 exit 46, go 1 mile S on Rte 42.
Wheelchair accessible: No.

A collection of period buildings moved to the site and furnished in period giving a full picture of nineteenth-century rural life.

Toledo

The Toledo Museum of Art

2445 Monroe St
(419) 255-8000

Hours: Tue-Sat 10-4.
Admission: Free.
Directions: One blk off I-75, follow signs.
Wheelchair accessible: Yes.

Major collections of art and artifacts including one of the largest collections of glass in the world.

Westerville

The Ross C. Purdy Museum of Ceramics

735 Ceramic Pl
(614)890-4700
(614)899-6109 (fax)
ymanring@acers.org
www.acers.org

Hours: Mon-Fri 8-5.
Admission: Free.
Directions: I-270, exit Cleveland Ave N, R on Schrock Rd, R on Ceramic Place.

Wheelchair accessible: Yes.

The museum of the American Ceramic Society houses a collection of over 2,000 ceramic pieces ranging from the 18th C to space shuttle tiles.

WISCONSIN

Appleton

Amelia Bubolz Doll Collection

c/o Secura Insurance Co
2401 S Memorial Drive
(920)739-3161

Hours: Mon-Thu 8-3:30, Fri 8-12:30.
Admission: Free.
Directions: Hwy 41 to Hwy 441, exit L on Appleton Rd, 1/2 mi to Secura.
Wheelchair accessible: Yes.

1,000 dolls from 1850 to the present including china, bisque, papier-mache and composition. Also teddy bears, Indian dolls, and antique toys.

Hearthstone Historic House Museum

625 W Prospect Ave
(920)730-8204
fr.hearthstone@.com

Hours: Tue-Fri 10-4, Sun 1-4.
Admission: Adults $4, children $2.
Directions: From Hwy 41, go E on Prospect Ave.
Wheelchair accessible: No.

An 1880s mansion furnished and decorated in Eastlake style. It was the first house in the world to be lighted by a central hydroelectric station using the Edison system, and retains its original "electroliers." Also rotating exhibits of Haviland china and tablescapes.

Blue Mound

Little Norway
3537 Highway JG
(608)437-8211
Hours: May-Jun & Sep-Oct daily 9-5; Jul-Aug daily 9-7.
Admission: Adults $7, seniors $6, children $2.50.
Directions: Hwy 18/151 exit Cave of the Mounds Rd.
Wheelchair accessible: No.

Guided tours through an 1850s Norwegian pioneer farmstead, including many original cabins and a Stavkirke, built in Norway for Chicago's 1893 World's Fair, which contains a large collection of Norwegian and Norwegian-American folk art.

Cassville

Stonefield
(608)725 5210
Hours: May-Jun & Sep-Oct daily 10-4; Jul-Aug daily 10-5.
Admission: Adults $6, seniors $5, children $3.
Directions: On the Mississippi River, on County Rd VV, off Hwy 133, 1 mi N of Cassville.
Wheelchair accessible: Museum building only.

Stonefield is a museum of agricultural history and village life built on the estate of Wisconsin's first governor. It houses an extensive collection of agricultural machinery and implements.

Eagle

Old World Wisconsin
S103 W37890 Hwy 67
(414)594-6300
Hours: May 1-Oct 31 Mon-Fri 10-4, Sat-Sun 10-5.

Admission: Adults $9.50, children $4.50.
Directions: 1-1/2 miles S of Eagle on Hwy 67.

An outdoor museum of immigrant farm and village life, with 65 buildings staffed by costumed workers engaged in traditional crafts. Farmsteads of Germans, Poles, Scandinavians, and Yankees, historic breeds of oxen and horses.

Fond du Lac

Historic Galloway House and Village
336 Old Pioneer Rd
Hours: Memorial Day to Labor Day daily 10-5 (gate closed at 4 pm).
Admission: Adults $4, students $1.
Directions: From I-41 take Main Street N, then take 1st R onto County Rd VV, then L onto Old Pioneer Rd.

A 30-room lumber baron's mansion built in 1847 and furnished with antiques, the house is surrounded by 23 historic buildings including a country store, a photographer's shop, a church, and a newspaper office depicting life at the turn of the century.

The house is also part of Fond du Lac's innovative "Talking Houses Tour" on which 14 privately owned historic houses tell their history and describe their architecture on AM radio to visitors parked within 200 feet. For details of the tour contact Fond du Lac's Convention and Visitor's Bureau, 19 W Scott St, Fond du Lac, WI 54935 (920)923-3010.

Green Bay

Heritage Hill State Historical Museum
2640 S Webster Ave
(800)721-5150
www.netnet.net/heritagehill
Hours: May & Sep & Nov 26-Dec 11 Sat-Sun 10-5; Jun-Aug Tue-Sun 10-5.
Admission: Adults $6, seniors $5, children

5-12 $3, children under 5 free.
Directions: From I-43 go W on Rte 172, from Hwy 41 go E on Rte 172. Go N on Webster.
Wheelchair accessible: Yes.

20 buildings on 44 acres arranged in four periods: La Baye depicts the fur trading and missionary period of 1672-1825; Fort Howard reproduces a military frontier settlement c 1836; Small Town 1871 includes the oldest wooden house in the state (c 1800), and an 1870 Greek revival house, both furnished in period, as well as a range of commercial, public, and religious buildings; Belgian Farm 1905 reflects the Belgian immigrant life of the area. The buildings contain collections of furniture, ceramics, glass, and early household wares.

Neville Public Museum

210 Museum Place
(920)448-4460
Hours: Tue 9-4, Wed 9-9, Thu-Sat 9-4, Sun 12-4.
Admission: Donations.
Directions: From Hwy 41 take Dousman exit. Go 3 mi E on Dousman, then R on Museum Place.
Wheelchair accessible: Yes.

A museum of art, history, and science that includes collections of ceramics, glass, furniture, and household wares.

Hudson

The Octagon House

1004 Third St
(715)386-2654
Hours: May-Oct & 3 weeks after Thanksgiving Tue-Sat 10-12 & 2-4:30, Sun 2-4:30.
Admission: Adults $3, seniors $2.
Directions: Follow signs from downtown.
Wheelchair accessible: No.

An 1854 house furnished and decorated in period with a special collection of dolls, toys, and children's clothing.

Madison

The Elvejhem Museum of Art

800 University Ave
(608)263-2246
Hours: Tue-Fri 9-5, Sat-Sun 11-5.
Admission: Free.
Directions: Follow signs to the University of Wisconsin Campus.
Wheelchair accessible: Yes

Major collections in both the fine and decorative arts, including European and Chinese export porcelain, early glass, silver, and furniture from William and Mary to Modernist.

Helen Louise Allen Textile Collection

1300 Linden Drive
(608)262-1162

A collection of over 10,000 textiles, particularly strong in American needlework, lace, quilts, and coverlets. A research collection not on permanent display but available to the serious collector on request.

The State Historical Society Museum

N Carroll St
(608)264-6555
Hours: Tue-Sat 10-5, Sun 12-5.
Admission: Free to Wisconsin residents, other adults $2, children under 18 $1.
Directions: On the Capitol Square.
Wheelchair accessible: Yes.

Permanent exhibition of Wisconsin furniture, ceramics, and household wares, and of American Indian artifacts. Also rotating exhibitions.

Menomonie

Wilson Place Museum

101 Wilson Circle
(715)235-2283
(715)235-5411
(800)826-6970

Hours: Memorial Day-Labor Day daily 1-5; Spr & Fall Sat-Sun 1-5.
Admission: Adults $4.50, students $3, children 12 and under $1.
Directions: I-94 exit 41 S, 2 mi S on Broadway, beside the Lake Menomin bridge.
Wheelchair accessible: No.

The original Wilson place was built in 1856 as a colonial mansion. In 1892 it was remodeled into the Queen Anne style, and in the 1920s it was changed yet again into a Mediterranean-style villa. It is magnificently decorated and furnished in high 19th C and turn-of-the-century styles and has beautiful formal gardens. Collections include furniture, silver, porcelain, clothing, and Christmas ornaments.

Milwaukee

The Captain Frederick Pabst Museum

2000 W Wisconsin Ave
(414)931-0808

Hours: Mon-Sat 10-3:30. Closed Good Friday, Easter, July 4, Thanksgiving, Christmas Eve, Christmas Day, New Year's Eve, New Year's Day.
Admission: Adults, $7, seniors, $6, children ages 6-17 $3, children under 6 free.
Directions: I-94 exit 26th St N, then W on Wisconsin Ave to 20th St.
Wheelchair accessible: Yes.

Completed in 1893, this brewery baron's mansion with 37 rooms, 12 baths, and 14 fireplaces was built in the Flemish Renaissance style. It is noted for its architectural detailing, particularly its unique wood carving, plaster work, and wrought iron work. Regular guided tours show the house

and its furnishings and tell visitors some of the history of German immigrants and the brewing industry.

Milwaukee Art Museum

750 N Lincoln Memorial D
(414)224-3200
www.mam.org

Hours: Tue-Sat 10-5, Thu til 9, Sun 12-5. Closed New Year's Day, Thanksgiving, Christmas Day.
Admission: Adults $5, students & seniors $3, children under 12 free.
Directions: 1/8 mi N of I-794 (exit 1F) on Lincoln Memorial Dr.
Wheelchair accessible: Yes

The museum houses the Frank Lloyd Wright and Prairie School Collection of art and design, as well as important collections of impressionist, modern, and contemporary art.

Milwaukee Public Museum

800 W Wells St
(414)278-2700
smedley@mpm1.edu
www.mpm.edu

Hours: Daily 9-5. Closed major holidays
Admission: Adults $5.50, seniors $4.50, students $3.50.
Directions: I-94 exit 43 E.
Wheelchair accessible: Yes.

A large general museum that includes recreations of early Milwaukee life, decorative arts, decoys, and rotating exhibits.

Mineral Point

Pendarvis

114 Shake Rag Street. 53565
(608) 987 2122

Hours: May 1 to Oct 31 daily 9-5 (last tour 4 pm).
Admission: Adults $6.50, seniors $5.85, children 5-12 $2.70.
Directions: Go S on Shake Rag St, off Hwy 151.
Wheelchair accessible: Assistance avail-

able, please call ahead.

A Cornish miners' colony of stone-and-log houses built in the 1830s and 1840s. The houses are nestled into a hillside and connected by paths winding through gardens of native flora.

Mount Horeb

Mount Horeb Historical Museum

100 S Second St
(608)437 3645
Hours: Fri-Sat 10-5:30, Sun 12:30-5.
Admission: Donation.
Directions: Downtown, go S on Second St off Hwy 151 at the lights.
Wheelchair accessible: Yes.

Exhibits include an 1870 Norwegian American farm home, a 1918 home, a 1920s hospital, and a 1930 store, all appropriately furnished and decorated. Ethnic and folk materials of the upper Midwest.

Neenah

The Bergstrom-Mahler Museum

165 North Park Ave
(920)751-4658
Hours: Tue-Fri 10-4:30, Sat-Sun 1-4:30. Closed Dec 24-26, Jan 1, Good Friday, Memorial Day, July 4, Labor Day, Thanksgiving.
Admission: Free, donations accepted.
Directions: From Hwy 41, take Main St E exit. Main Street becomes Wisconsin Ave. Turn L on North Park Ave.
Wheelchair accessible: Yes

The museum houses the world's foremost paperweight collection of over 1900 pieces. It also contains a large Germanic glass collection with examples from the 16th to the 19th C. Besides being a museum, it is a community arts center offering a wide range of programs and events.

Oconto

Beyer Home Museum

917 Park Ave
(920)834-6206
Hours: Jun-Labor Day Mon-Sat 10-4, Sun 12-4.
Admission: Adults $3, students 6-18 $1, children under 6 free, family $7.50.
Directions: In downtown on Main St. Watch for "Museum" signs.
Wheelchair accessible: No.

Restored Victorian northern mansion furnished and decorated in period. Annex contains logging implements, old Oconto storefronts, American Indian artifacts.

Prairie du Chien

Villa Louis

(608)326 2721
Hours: Jul 1-Oct 31 daily 9-5 (last tour 4 pm).
Directions: On St. Feriole Island, Prairie du Chien.
Wheelchair accessible: No.

The home of the Dousmans, a pioneer family who made good in the fur trade, railroads, river boats, and land speculation, the villa is an opulent Victorian country estate standing on the Mississippi River plain. It is furnished with elegant family antiques, art, and heirlooms.

Spring Green

Taliesin

Hwy 23 at County Hwy C
(608)588-7900
www.taliesinpreservation.com
Hours: Daily May 1-Nov 1; by appt Apr, Nov, Dec.
Admission: $8 to $60. Call for reservations.
Wheelchair accessible: No.

Built in the early years of this century by Frank Lloyd Wright, to house a creative community that is still active, Taliesin is a large home, studio, and theater. A wide range of tours is offered.

Sturgeon Bay

Collector Showcase

3910 Hwy 42-57
(920)743-1515
(920)743-6788

Hours: Mid-May to mid-Oct daily 9-5.
Admission: $2.50.
Directions: 3 mi N of Sturgeon Bay bridge on Bypass 42-57.
Wheelchair accessible: Yes.

1000 antique dolls, 1000 Barbie dolls, 500 mechanical store window displays, 45 antique cars.

Door County Museum

18 N 4th Ave
(920)743-5809

Hours: May-Oct daily 10-4:30.
Admission: Donations.
Directions: Hwy 42/57 exit Business 42/57 to corner of Michigan St and 4th Ave.
Wheelchair accessible: Yes.

Fine glassware collection and many domestic artifacts.

Superior

Fairlawn Mansion Museum

906 E 2nd St
(715)394-5712

Hours: Daily 9-5. Closed major holidays.
Admission: Adults $5, seniors, students $4, children 6-2 $3, children under 6 free.
Directions: On the lake front, on Hwys 2 and 53.
Wheelchair accessible: First floor only.

This 42-room mansion was built in 1890, and its first floor rooms are furnished and decorated in period. The second and third floors house collections reflecting American Indian, pioneer and immigrant life, and the industries of logging, shipping, railroading, farming, and mining.

Antiques Show Promoters

Antique Network
20 Village Lane
Grosse Point, MI 48230
(313)886-8286 • (313)886-1254
Show(s): Columbus Academy Antiques Show, Christ Church Antiques Show (Grosse Point, MI), Liggett University School Show. **Promoters:** Wendy Jennings & Susie McMillan.

C & C Promotions
323 Summit Ave
Wales, WI 53183
(414)646-5555
Show(s): Delafield Antique Show. **Promoters:** Ron & Debbie Christman & Steve & Sharron Cypher.

Ronald Cox
1830 S Muessing Rd
Indianapolis, IN 46239
(317)862-3865
Show(s): Hoosier Antiques Exposition.

Creative Management Productions Inc
PO Box 343
Holt, MI 48842
(517)676-2079
(517)676-6615 (fax)
Show(s): Superfest (ten shows in one: antiques & collectibles, arts & crafts, toy & doll, gem & mineral, coin & stamp, sports cards & car shows). Three times a year. **Est:**

1987 **Dir:** Ingham County Fairground (700 Ash St, Mason, MI). **Promoter:** Jeff Taylor.

Dolphin Promotions
PO Box 7320
Fort Lauderdale, FL 33338
(954)563-6747
(954)566-1982 (fax)
dolphinpromotions@worldnet.att.net
www.antiqnet.com/dolphin
Show(s): Spring, Summer & Fall O'Hare Antiques Shows offer a wide range of quality antiques, furniture & art. 250-400 select dealers from across the United States, Canada & Europe bring to Chicago the finest in antiques for over 23 years. **CC:** V/MC **Assn:** PSMA **Dir:** Kennedy Expressway (I-190) to River Rd or I-294 to O'Hare. **Promoter:** Robert H Smith, Pres.

Sue Hall
35 E Main St
Lebanon, OH 45036
(513)933-0111
Show(s): Hudson Antiques Celebration, Lebanon Historical Society Antiques Show.

Steve & Barbara Jenkins
Box 580
Fishers, IN 46038
(317)598-0012
(317)598-9007 (fax)
Show(s): Crutcher Antique Show (Indianapolis).

Phil & Jeanne Jessee

811 W Spring Valley Rd
Centerville, OH 45458
(937)434-1364
(937)434-1364 (fax)
Show(s): Hospice of Dayton Antiques Show.

Kennedy Productions Inc

1208 Lisle Pl
Lisle, IL 60532
(630)515-1160
(630)515-1165 (fax)
Show(s): Pheasant Run Antique Show (St Charles, IL). **Est:** 1987 **Dir:** 4051 E Main St, 2 mi W of Rte 59. **Promoter:** Joanne Kennedy.

Lake County Promotions

PO Box 461
Grayslake, IL 60030
(847)223-1433
(847)356-1362 (fax)
Show(s): Grayslake Antiques & Collectibles. **Hrs:** Mon-Fri 10-3.

Robert C Lawler

1510 N Hoyne Ave
Chicago, IL 60622
(773)227-4464
(773)227-6322 (fax)
www.antiquemarkets.com

Show(s): Goodwill Antiques Show, Centreville Antiques Market, Sandwich Antique Market, Grand Rapids Rotary Antique Fair & Sale, Greenfield Village Antique Show & Sale, Minneapolis Institute of the Arts.

Luck Promotions Inc

PO Box 5473
Akron, OH 44334
(330)867-6724
Show(s): Akron Antique Market.

M & M Enterprises

19946 Great Oaks Circle S
Clinton Township, MI 48036
(810)465-9441
(810)469-1706 (fax)
mandminfo@aol.com
www.antiqnet/M&M
Show(s): Michigan's Home & Garden Antiques Market, Southfield Pavilion Antiques Exposition, Michigan Modernism Exposition, Southfield Americana Antiques Show & Sale, Petosky Antiques Festival, Grand Traverse Antiques Festival, Greater Columbus Antiques Show. **Promoter:** Michael Butler.

Michigan Antique Festival

2156 Rudy Ct
Midland, MI 48642
(517)687-9001

Bunny Nolt

7644 Exploration Dr
Worthington, OH 43785
(614)885-1673
Show(s): Worthington Historical Society Antique Show.

Prime Promotions

2097 Hawthorne Ave
St Paul, MN 55119
(612)771-3476
(612)776-3066
Show(s): Minnesota Antique Spectacular.

Ridnour's Antiques

PO Box 309
Mineral Point, WI 53565
(608)987-3317
ridnour@mhtc.net
Show(s): Mineral Point Real Antiques Show.

Jennifer A Sabin

2978 Asbury Ct
Miamisburg, OH 45342
(937)291-2711
Show(s): Heartland Antiques Show (Richmond, IN) & Quaker Antiques Market (Wilmington, OH).

Springfield Antique Show & Flea Market
PO Box 2429
Springfield, OH 45501
(937)325-0053
(937)399-3201 (fax)

Promoters: Bruce & Vivalyn Knight.

Roma & Dick Taylor / Jean & Ted Taylor
PO Box 370
Burton, OH 44021
(440)834-0264
(440)636-5405

Show(s): Great Geauga Antiques Market (Burton, OH).

Zurko's Midwest Promotions
211 W Green Bay
Shawano, WI 54166
(715)526-9769
(715)524-5675 (fax)

Part III

Indexes

Index I:
Alphabetical Index to Dealers

Index II:
QuickCode Index to Specialties

8 Art (Landscapes/Townscapes)

9 Art (Marine/Nautical)

10 Art (Miniatures)

11 Art (Objets d'Art)

12 Art (Portraits/Figures)

15 Art (Still Life)

16 Baseball Cards

17 Baskets

18 Books/Manuscripts

33 Coins/Medals
Illinois

49 Furniture (Arts & Crafts/Mission)

Index III:
QuickCode Index to Services

S8 Consignment

About the Editors

Lisa Freeman and John Fiske are co-owners of Fiske & Freeman: Fine and Early Antiques, specializing in period formal and high country furniture and appropriate accessories. They exhibit at shows throughout New England and the Midwest. They are also the owners of AntiqueSource, Inc., a publishing company specializing in print and electronic directories for antiques collectors and dealers. They have previously coedited *Sloan's Green Guide to Antiquing in New England*.

Lisa Freeman was a scholarly publisher for 17 years, most recently as director of the University of Minnesota Press. John Fiske is professor of communication arts at the University of Wisconsin, Madison, where he has taught since 1987. An Englishman by birth, he has authored or coauthored 8 books on television, mass media, and contemporary popular culture.